EDUCATIONALIZATION AND ITS COMPLEXITIES

Religion, Politics, and Technology

Educationalization and Its Complexities

Religion, Politics, and Technology

Edited by
ROSA BRUNO-JOFRÉ

UNIVERSITY OF TORONTO PRESS
Toronto Buffalo London

© University of Toronto Press 2019
Toronto Buffalo London
utorontopress.com
Printed in the U.S.A.

ISBN 978-1-4875-0534-9

∞ Printed on acid-free, 100% post-consumer recycled paper.

Library and Archives Canada Cataloguing in Publication

Title: Educationalization and its complexities: religion, politics, and technology / edited by Rosa Bruno-Jofré.
Names: Bruno-Jofré, Rosa del Carmen, 1946– editor.
Description: This collection introduces the reader to the results of the symposium Educationalization of Social and Moral Problems in the Western World and the "Educationalization of the World": Historical Dimensions through Time and Space, held at the Faculty of History, Pontificia Universidad Católica de Chile in Santiago, in 2017. | Includes bibliographical references and index.
Identifiers: Canadiana 20190087528 | ISBN 9781487505349 (hardcover)
Subjects: LCSH: Social problems – Study and teaching.
Classification: LCC LC192.2.E38 2019 | DDC 370.11/5—dc23

This book has been published with the help of a grant from the Federation for the Humanities and Social Sciences, through the Awards to Scholarly Publications Program, using funds provided by the Social Sciences and Humanities Research Council of Canada.

University of Toronto Press acknowledges the financial assistance to its publishing programme of the Canada Council for the Arts and the Ontario Arts Council, an agency of the Government of Ontario.

 Canada Council for the Arts   Conseil des Arts du Canada

 ONTARIO ARTS COUNCIL
CONSEIL DES ARTS DE L'ONTARIO
an Ontario government agency
un organisme du gouvernement de l'Ontario

Funded by the Government of Canada   Financé par le gouvernement du Canada

Contents

Artist's Statement   ix

Introduction: Problematizing "Educationalization"   3
ROSA BRUNO-JOFRÉ

Part I: Contesting Views of Processes of Educationalization at the Intersection with Christianity

1 The Dignity of Protestant Souls: Protestant Trajectories in the Educationalization of the World   27
DANIEL TRÖHLER

2 Multiple Early Modernities and "Educationalization": Reframing the Confessional Debate on Education, Politics, and Religion in Early Modern Europe   50
CARLOS MARTÍNEZ VALLE

3 Catholicism and Educationalization   67
ROSA BRUNO-JOFRÉ

4 Antigonish, or an "Education That Is Not Educationalization"   92
JOSH COLE

Part II: Catholicism, Spirituality, and Educationalization

5 Educationalization of the Modern World: The Case of the Loretto Sisters in British North America   113
ELIZABETH M. SMYTH

6 New Educational Approaches of Women Religious in the Global South, 1968–1980   129
HEIDI MacDONALD

7 The Educationalization Process and the Roman Catholic Church in North America during the Long Nineteenth Century   154
JOSEPH STAFFORD

8 Educationalization in the Spanish Second Republic and the Expulsion of the Jesuits from Spain   177
JON IGELMO ZALDÍVAR

9 Waldorf Education and the Educationalization of Spirituality in the Plural Context in Late Twentieth-Century Spain   195
PATRICIA QUIROGA UCEDA

Part III: Educationalization and the Right to Education/Schooling

10 Educationalization, Schooling, and the Right to Education   215
FELICITAS ACOSTA

Part IV: Educationalization and Democratic Spaces in the Digital Era

11 Educationalization as Technologization   239
WILLIAM F. PINAR

12 Countering Patterns of Educationalization: Creating Digital Tools for Critical Evidence-Based Thinking   254
ANA JOFRE

Part V: Educationalization as a Tool of Colonization and Its Counter-Dimension in Indigenous Educational Agendas: Limits and Possibilities

13 Educationalization in Canada: The Use of Native Teacher Education as a Tool of Decoloniality   277
BONITA UZORUO

14 Indigeneity and Educationalization   293
CHRIS BEEMAN

15 Capuchin Missions in Mapuche Territory: The Education of an
    Original People in Chile from 1880 to 1930   312
    SOL SERRANO AND MACARENA PONCE DE LEÓN

Concluding Analysis: Turning the Problem on Its Head – Looking
to New Critical Directions   335
JOSH COLE AND IAN McKAY

List of Contributors   353

Index   359

Artist's Statement

The arch motif explored the series of images that appear throughout this book is intended to establish a visual metaphor for an entrance into areas of academic inquiry imbued with the complexity found in educationalization. While this metaphor remains constant throughout all the images, the specific architectural context of the arch motif in each image has the capacity to set forth iterations unique to the individual elements present. The religious, secular, public, private, and academic sites found in these images provide contextual layers for reflection, but, for many viewers, it may be the juxtaposition of elements in the compositions that provide the most informative platforms for creating meaning in relation to the topics explored in these writings.

The interaction between lintels and arches may prompt the viewer to consider the extent to which the relationship between these differing methods of spanning structural fenestrations was a purposeful synectic contrast or an intended synthetic confluence. Similarly, the interaction between intersecting arches that result in ambiguous shapes caused by low illumination levels raises observational questions relating to the role of alignment in perception as well as reconstructive questions concerning the amount of data required to articulate with accuracy the features of existing forms with reduced visual input. The root metaphor of the arch is thus offered not as an illustration of content but as a prompt for active consideration of the directions in which educationalization is currently being explored. Indeed, it is the active engagement with individually identified visual elements that is the intended focus of each image as well as the overall heuristic goal of the choices made in selecting the photographs. The wide range of juxtapositions resulting in apparent contrasts and others that result in ambiguity are focused on providing flexible visual cues for the reader to reflect on the topics explored by the authors of the chapters in this volume.

Artist's Statement

The image entitled *arched inclinations above* is a photograph taken at the Episcopal Cathedral Church of Saint John the Divine in New York City. The images *intersecting portals observed* and *leaving aligned vaults* are depictions of religious and secular spaces at Mont-Saint-Michel in Normandy, France. The photograph *time records movement* is part of an in-progress series of images depicting the preservation of architectural artefacts at Guildwood Park in Toronto, Ontario. The photograph *brackets create space* was created at University College, University of Toronto.

Alan R. Wilkinson
Kingston, ON
December 2018

EDUCATIONALIZATION AND ITS COMPLEXITIES

Religion, Politics, and Technology

aligning keystone masks © Alan R. Wilkinson

Introduction
Problematizing "Educationalization"

ROSA BRUNO-JOFRÉ

This collection introduces the reader to the results of the symposium Educationalization of Social and Moral Problems in the Western World and the "Educationalization of the World": Historical Dimensions through Time and Space, held at the Faculty of History, Pontificia Universidad Católica de Chile in Santiago, in 2017. The symposium was funded by a Connection Grant from the Social Sciences and Humanities Research Council of Canada[1] and received extensive financial support from the Pontificia Universidad Católica de Chile, the Faculty of History, Geography, and Political Science at that university, and the Universidad de Deusto (Spain). The symposium involved the Theory and History of Education International Research Group (THEIRG), located within the Faculty of Education at Queen's University in Kington, Ontario, and the History of Education Group of the Faculty of History at the Pontificia Católica in Santiago. Senior and junior historians, educational theorists, and curricular theorists exchanged ideas and provided input on the papers presented. While discussions on educationalization have taken place in European educational circles in the past two decades and, to some extent, in the United States, this symposium brought a new dimension to the subject by including in the conversation Catholicism, rights to education, historical studies grounded in Canada and Chile, Indigenous issues, and the concept of educationalization in relation to our digital age.

The term "educationalization" – initially *pedagogisierun* (pedagogization) – has been in use in Europe for some time, as Depaepe and Smeyers (2008), Depaepe et al. (2008), Depaepe (2012), and Tröhler (2016) have indicated. "Pedagogization" was replaced with "educationalization" to capture the trend in modernizing societies of transferring social responsibilities onto schools – with the function of schools thus evolving from the need to enforce moral behaviour, to solving social inequalities and to building a citizenry and improving productivity

(Depaepe and Smeyers 2008, 379; Depaepe 2012). In other words, "educationalization" has been used as a general concept for identifying the orientation of putting schooling in the service of solving social problems of various kinds that were not originally perceived as necessarily educational. Some authors have established a relationship between the process of educationalization and the process of the institutionalization of "childhood" and the growth of expertise in this field. "Educationalization" as a historiological conceptual tool has been further developed to encompass discussions of the expansion of schooling within the modern state and in processes of modernization. The process of educationalization has been deemed an essential characteristic of Western modernity (particularly late modernity). The term has also been utilized for making sense of the modern world and the modern self, as defined in educational terms (see chapter 1 by Tröhler in this volume), to pinpoint cultural or mental patterns as well as the educationalization of behaviour per se. In this respect, and combined with the position that education is connected to the process of modernization itself, it is possible to advance the notion of the "educationalization of the world," as Tröhler does in this volume.

By and large, "educationalization" carries a negative connotation. It has been argued that the trend to educationalize social problems has moved attention away from underlying structures of injustices (Labaree 2008). In this way, Labaree contends, the process of educationalization both provides stability and legitimates a social structure of inequality.

The use of "educationalization" within the discipline of history developed out of the initiative taken by distinguished historians of education to construe specific historiological tools emerging from their field. As a scholar of history and a member of a faculty of education, I understand the historicity of education as a complex subject and I acknowledge the utility of developing concepts that will help to build explanations as well as uncover trends in *longue durée* analysis. However, I concur with Martin Schiralli, who writes that "the study of education is a congeries of coherent applications of the social and behavioural sciences, curriculum-based subject matters, philosophy and common sense."[2] I also think, as does Schiralli, that "what counts as a coherent set of such applications over time will vary significantly with changes in the fabric of social life, the economy, and the prevailing modes of meaning and communication." These variations will resonate also in any historical analysis of education, which further increases the complexity of the field of study. Therefore, I am in agreement with Depaepe's and other authors' preferred focus of working out specific concepts that allow for some level of abstraction without denying the unique and intertwined historical reality of educational phenomena. "Educationalization" is a promising concept, although I have reservations about the way it has been applied and how its meaning has been construed.

On another note, if we are to apply the concept to a specific analysis – and by this I mean if we are to speak of the educationalization of social problems – I would prefer to construe that process as an extension of various pedagogical knowledges through schooling to cover all dimensions of life, in particular, the needs that would fit with a particular religious, social, political, and/or economic, or even cultural, project. A case in point is that current uses of technology, as William Pinar writes in chapter 11, "Educationalization as Technologization," could be construed as creating a STEM (science, technology, engineering, and mathematics) state of mind and thus as acquiring a central place in processes of educationalization.

I would also problematize the use of "educationalization" as a heuristic concept, and the construction of its historical meaning. Education has an inherent socializing component. I agree with Bridges (2008) that education cannot be freed from the educationalization of social issues. The historical shape that the pattern of educationalization took over time – if we want to use the explanatory power of the concept – deserves explanations that go into analysis of the contexts of structures and discourses in a *longue durée* frame, considering *conjonctures*, intersections of gender, sexuality, class, domination, and so on. In all this, there should be an implicit understanding that there is content, direction, and purpose, and, furthermore, that there is a link between conceptions of education and the intentionality behind the process of educationalization.

If we were to approach education as schooling or as educational interventions guided by institutions or organizations, it would become important, following Basil Bernstein (1990), to pay attention to "the relation among discourses, social relations, division of labour, and transmission systems which create the relation between ideology and consciousness [and to how] [s]ymbolic control translates power relations into discourse and discourse into power relations" (134). However, it is here where I encounter the limits of educationalization as a concept construed with strong negative connotations. Power relations can, of course, be interrupted, and educational intervention can certainly be pursued as a counter-discursive and even political practice. The case of the Movement of Grassroots Education (Movimiento de Educacion de Base), sponsored by Catholic bishops in Brazil in the early 1960s in the midst of the educational projects of the US Alliance for Progress, is a good example of such an interruption. Thus, although it is useful to examine the intentionality behind policies and practices that we are conceptualizing as "educationalization," we need to be cautious about its all-embracing character. In this volume, Ana Jofre discusses the creation of digital tools for critical evidence-based thinking (chapter 12), and Josh Cole explores a historical case in Canada of "education that is not educationalization" (chapter 4).

I also agree with Bridges's (2008) view that the educationalization of social problems in a broad sense can be seen as a characteristic of a normally functioning government, and that there are cases when state intervention may be seen as appropriate. Bridges makes a powerful point when he writes that "the strong complaint (that it is always inappropriate to look for educational solutions to economic and social problems) seems difficult to maintain without emptying education of rationale and content" (470). The author refers here to the capacity of educational programs and institutions to contribute to social, economic, and political change. In more or less open societies, the state needs to negotiate claims, even insofar as transformative language may be diluted, produce eclectic recommendations, and re-address human rights–related wrongdoing, often through educational policies and curricula. To cite a recent example, Indigenous peoples in Ontario, Canada, have been bringing to the official school curricula their dramatic experience in residential schools and their cultural values in order to generate awareness in new generations. In the schools they run, there are serious efforts made to work out alternative educational aims, even as they work with the official curricula. The Ministry of Education has responded to recommendations and reports, in particular those from the Truth and Reconciliation Commission, to foster greater understanding of the historical and contemporary experience of Indigenous people in Canada. Education through schooling, in other words, has become the means through which to generate awareness of one of the most painful issues in Canada's history of colonization and to further Indigenous people's goals. Overall, educational policies – and this is important when analysing educationalization, particularly in contemporary times – are indeed constrained by transnational capital and by responses to supranational organizations and non-governmental organizations, domestic pressures and demands (for example, the government's need to maintain political legitimacy), and the system's own internal needs and self-interests (Burbules and Torres 2000).

As hinted at above, I deem it imperative that the examination of conceptions of education – and not just references to the learning of something – be integrated into the conversation under view. Mentioning environmental education as part of the processes of educationalization is not the same as referring to learning driving skills. Concepts such as training and indoctrination seem to be conflated with the concept of education within the notion of "educationalization." A grounded analysis would be expected to unpack those concepts. There is also the danger of conflating education with schooling or with a particular understanding of education.

Attention to conceptions of education and clarification of those concepts will not only highlight the potential oppressive side of, or the nuances sustaining, the intentionality to generate a self-governing citizenry, for example, but also help us understand other dimensions of educational practices. These dimensions may include critical reflective practices implemented by specific groups of teachers, counter-discursive practices as in the case of the Indigenous peoples in Canada, or openly political practices such as the popular education movement in Latin America in the 1970s. To rephrase my point here, while it is important to recognize that subjects are conditioned by social, cultural, linguistic, political, and ideological forces, there is danger in embracing the idea of an individual or collective self as exhausted by those external forces. Such a subject becomes dehistoricized. From a pedagogical perspective, when using "educationalization," it would be best to avoid the possibility of bestowing upon educational/pedagogical interventions tremendous power (and even displaying a nihilist shade) without hope and space for the exercise of agency. We also ought not to renounce the seeking of practical critiques and "transgressions," nor should we leave aside an ethically defensible conception of education and educational aims.

Where do we place in our analysis educational aims such as awareness of the interconnectedness of life and of shared human dignity? What about "the level of the individual person endeavoring to cultivate ('culturate') her or his life as meaningfully and seriously as circumstances permit" (Hansen 2010, 43)? It can be argued that most definitions of "educationalization" as an analytical tool exclude these considerations.

Another concern I have regarding "educationalization" takes me back some time ago, when I wrote, with an idealistic bent: "Education, it has been said again and again, has a concern with the good life, notions of justice, relationships between self and others, and between humans and the natural world; it should be desirable and transformative. Educational theories of necessity became, in the latter part of the twentieth century, sensitive to claims of social and political movements and started to engage with notions of diversity, and de-centered power" (Bruno-Jofré 2012, 1). Education has a normative character; it has to do with dispositions and habits of mind, and it is commonplace to say that, particularly in formal education, it is linked to social and economic policies of one sort or another. So, despite the passage of time, and a re-assessment of some views I held at the time of my writing the above, I don't want to neglect the idealist component of education and its potential to engender desired social transformation and/or personal or social improvement in line with the pedagogical tenets of Paulo Freire.

In this as well I find echoes in Bridges. He writes: "We cannot really conceive of education without reference to some selection of the human qualities we want to cultivate and of the kind of social world we expect or perhaps want our pupils to occupy – and that selection requires an inescapable responsibility to invoke some normative conception of the human qualities and the social world we see as desirable" (2008, 466). An example of educationalization that is often used is the educationalization of our behaviour toward nature. Courses for future teachers normally include environmental education. I agree with this inclusion. The cosmology sustaining our conception of education has changed, and we have strongly questioned Western dominant cosmology and placed humans in a different relationship with God (Christian theologians were active in developing eco-spirituality), the earth, and the universe. Concerning the expansion of educational content and new curricula, as in the example indicated above, it would be prudent to utilize Bernstein's (1990) conception of "recontextualization." So, to follow Bernstein's lead, the inclusion in state schooling of pedagogized forms of knowledge, identities, and social structures from other societal fields would represent a case of the social transformation of categories of knowledge.

It would be key when discussing the understanding of current patterns of educationalization and their evolution to also consider the understandings of education and "excellence" within a dominant knowledge-based economy as an integral part of neoliberal globalization and of the changing nature of the relationship between capitalism and Western modernity (Dale 2014, 34; Bruno-Jofré and Hills 2011). In faculties of education, the observable crucial issue is the replacement of a language of education and educational aims with a language of learning, leaving aside the considerations that, as Biesta (2013; 2014) writes, students learn something and from someone, and that what they learn is for particular reasons. Biesta (2014) makes clear that learning is a process – individualistic and individualizing – while education is interested in content and purpose and in relationships.

Portelli (2012) poses a question to educators regarding their future work: How can we critically – even subversively – approach neoliberal practices in educational institutions and question the myth that the achievement gap can be reduced by improving test scores? How important is it to read the world as Freire asked us to? I would add: What kind of polity would we like to embrace? In some places in the world, European universals such as citizenship and understandings of Western freedom that are moved through processes of educationalization are denaturalized concepts.

How people are enacting values is also part of this picture. For example: How are educators combating discursive forms of racism in the curriculum? In 2015, Joyce E. King, in her presidential address to the American Educational Research Association, called for the dismantling of "epistemological nihilation" (embodied not only in physical and psychic violence against black people, but in curriculum "that does violence to Black students' spirit and thirst for knowledge") (King 2017, 211). She argued for solidarity and a moral instance to combat discursive forms of racism in praxis, policy, and research, and claimed "group belonging" to be a human right. She called for epistemological emancipation. Fleshing out the specificity of educationalization in relation to the schooling of African-American students and agency may provide an understanding of the characteristics of that particular pattern of educationalization in a broader context, and of the counter-discourse that has emerged.

Keeping the foregoing qualifications in mind, educationalization can be a powerful explanatory tool; the concept gains heuristic strength when used in relation to other concepts, and as long as agency is not left outside of the picture. Educationalization has explanatory and heuristic power within the context under analysis and within the historicity of the case, which involves local conditions including forms of political action in time and place – conditions not only crowded and disjointed, but also animated by dynamic and contesting socio-political forces. In such a context, the concept would have to take a "vernacular" character.

This collection makes a contribution to the historiographical debate on educationalization, by grounding its use in actual historical research and including curricular and philosophical reflection. In these contributions, the concept is re-signified, in that its heuristic power is expanded or problematized. The reader will find the chapters are organized in five parts: Part I offers contesting views of processes of educationalization at its intersection with Christianity and discusses historical causation in relation to the historical trend in modernity conceptualized as educationalization; Part II concentrates on Catholicism, spirituality, and educationalization; Part III is devoted to educationalization and the right to education/schooling; Part IV examines educationalization and democratic spaces in the digital era; and Part V deals with educationalization as a tool of colonization and its counter-dimension in Indigenous educational agendas. The collection closes with a concluding analysis.

Part I, "Contesting Views of Processes of Educationalization at the Intersection with Christianity," opens with Daniel Tröhler's chapter entitled "The Dignity of Protestant Souls: Protestant Trajectories in the Educationalization of the World." Tröhler, a historian of education, tries to explain how a particular mental pattern or reflex labelled "educationalization" became a dominant and fundamental way to understand the world and the self and a way to educationalize behaviours toward, for example, the environment. The contentious point in his argument is the historical causal link he establishes with Protestantism, more precisely in terms of Zwinglianism reaching this point after following the trajectories of Calvinism and Zwinglianism (Swiss Protestantism) and German Lutheranism. Apart from the transformations that he places around 1700, he identifies "Protestant psychology (*avant la letter*), or the Protestant conception of the soul, as the crucial principle allowing the educationalization of the challenges or problems that were detected with regard to these transformations." Tröhler then discusses the two paradigmatic educational ideologies that would culminate with the vision of *Bildung* on one side and the virtuous citizen on the other. He places particular emphasis on the idea of the soul (and its disposition to perfectability) as the exclusive place of salvation without institutional mediation – unlike the Catholic Church. By the end of the nineteenth century, school and curricula were major means of making citizens, even if they were not citizens, as in democratic republics. Catholic countries, in Tröhler's view, were behind educational expansion, and when Catholicism contributed to educationalization, it did so by using ideas and strategies that came from Protestantism.

The chapter that follows, "Multiple Early Modernities and Educationalization: Reframing the Confessional Debate on Education, Politics, and Religion in Early Modern Europe," was written by Carlos Martínez Valle. Martínez, a political scientist with a background in early European modernity, invites the reader to think beyond the parameters set by Tröhler and introduces a theological political discussion that challenges Tröhler's thesis. Martínez examines the theology of John Calvin and Martin Luther – their rejection of free will and millenarianism and anti-modernist positioning – as contested within Protestantism. He analyses the theories and ideas of John Milton, comparing them with those of the Jesuits Molina and Suárez – they, like Milton, were advocates of free will and charity/probabilism – and of a sensual epistemology. Martínez aims at pointing in his argument to the intra-confessional differences and inter-confessional similarities that, in his words, "turn 'Protestantism' and 'Catholicism' into terms of little use for historical analysis because they lead to overgeneralizations."

His analysis calls our attention to an important point – that the concept of "educationalization" could be used to analyse the requirements and objectives of society, and of the educational subsystem, which has "increasingly become functionally differentiated and self-referential." Furthermore, he points out that education has been a socially dependent subsystem even more than in early modernity, a time when both Catholics and Protestants adopted literacy methods to increase school attendance and secure religious indoctrination (confessionalization). Martínez focuses on Tröhler's thesis on the Protestant origins of educationalization and modern education. Various points made by Martínez are of relevance here, such as the difficulty of establishing a causal relation between orthodox Protestant psychagogies and schooling/literacy, since the latter was determined more by socio-economic and political than religious factors. In fact, it was enlightened absolutism that created schools in the process of state building. Certainly, schooling predated the Reformation and was rooted in humanism and scholasticism. Martínez's analysis of the Jesuits Molina and Suárez and the comparison with Milton leads him to conclude that, for example, there was nothing new or even Protestant in Zwingli's defence of tyrannicide, a point that Tröhler considers central for a form of republicanism and citizenship that led to educationalization. In fact, the Jesuits educated political cadres with the goal of education being the ability to lead an active and virtuous life. Readers can make up their own mind. Daniel Tröhler's chapter opens an interesting debate, although one can ponder the historical significance of the question of the origins of educationalization as coming from a particular branch of Protestantism, given the ubiquity of the uses of education, internal differences, uniqueness of Catholic social education, and the fluidity of educational ideas in term of theories and methods across confessions from the time of early modernity.

Historian Rosa Bruno-Jofré's chapter, "Catholicism and Educationalization," provides a long-term analysis, starting from early modernity, of Catholic involvement with education and forms of schooling. She builds on her extensive research on all things Catholic and the history of Catholic congregations from a social history, secular perspective. Complex intentionalities intersected confessionalization with the social teaching of the church and the concern with social illnesses generated by poverty, and with the political and theological dimension of a Catholic ordered society. Protestants and Catholics alike were involved in educational practices, and they generated pedagogies from early modernity. The point here is that, from very early on, Catholics, in their encounters with modernity and in response to Protestantism, played a significant role in schooling through their teaching congregations, as conveyed in Part III of this book; Catholics did not take their approach to education/educationalization from Protestantism, although it can be argued that there were mutual influences. Catholic interaction with the state, along with processes of social and functional differentiation, took various forms, from the church's carving its space in the educational system through its own schools to its being in open conflict with the state, in particular with liberal republican ones. The social teachings of the church led to various practices countering the described dominance of educationalization, in particular in the twentieth century. (One such practice is analysed in detail in the context of adult education in Nova Scotia, Canada, by Josh Cole in this volume.)

Bruno-Jofré makes the point that educational processes – forms of educationalization or proto-educationalization (using the concept to refer to the use of education/schooling to deal with challenges encountered by the church as well as societal problems) – were mediated not only by the official doctrine of the church, but also by contextual, theological, and social configurations and, often, by the enactment of intentionalities and individual agency rooted in the tradition of free will. The author reviews historical turning points to unsettle notions of "sameness" and uniformity in the church, a multifarious institution, accentuating its internal differences, the uniqueness of the congregations, dissensions with the magisterium, censorship from the magisterium, and even the consolidation of dissenting visions. Bruno-Jofré works out her points – which separate her interpretation from Tröhler's – by discussing historical moments in the intersection of the church and its plurality of cultural formations with modernity, having education/schooling as a point of reference. The chapter goes from early modernity – the sixteenth to eighteenth centuries – through the long nineteenth century, which O'Malley places from the French Revolution to 1958, when Pius XII died. The chapter concludes with a discussion of the long 1960s – a period designated by Marwick as the time between 1958 and 1974 – years of paradigmatic shift within the church and of dramatic changes in education, including an epistemic break in educational theory as a result of grassroots experiences and the systematization of the ideas of Catholic philosopher of education Paulo Freire.

Part I closes with a chapter by historian and Canadianist Josh Cole, entitled "Antigonish, or an 'Education That Is Not Educationalization,'" that expands the parameters of the concept and moves the discussion to a form of education that was counter-educationalization, protagonized by the Catholic Antigonish movement in the 1920s and 1930s, in eastern Nova Scotia, Canada. This movement, which was grounded in andragogy (adult education), was infused by rural ideologies and Catholic principles, utilized the mass media of the time, and broke the separation between school and society and between the teacher and the student. The leaders placed their faith front and centre, with all forms of cultural life tying faith to cooperative economics and utopian andragogy. This grassroots project was a Nova Scotian interpretation of the social teaching of the church, even as the magisterium was as doctrinal as it could be at the time. Thus, this critique of modern capitalism in the form of an enactment of a civic project had its unique bent. And, as Cole writes, "democracy was the beginning and the end point of Antigonish ... and its drive for 'an education that is not educationalization,'" within the context of a "counterpublic sphere" (a concept he borrows from Nancy Fraser) aiming at "intelligent political action." The Antigonish movement was a response to the consequences of liberal-democratic capitalism, and to modernity, in a particular part of Canada.

The details of the Antigonish project, which, incidentally, had a long-lasting influence on the missionary work of various congregations, remind us of the educational theories of another Catholic, Paulo Freire. Cole's chapter offers a historical example that illustrates the need to use the historiographical concept of educationalization in articulation with other concepts and theories. It also points to the variations and spaces inside the Catholic Church.

Part II, "Catholicism, Spirituality, and Educationalization," is developed by members of the group who have been conducting research on the history of Catholic education for many years. It opens with historian Elizabeth M. Smyth's "Educationalization of the Modern World: The Case of the Loretto Sisters in British North America," a chapter that challenges Tröhler's notion of educationalization of the modern world and, in particular, the links he established with Protestantism as a source of the process. Smyth skilfully narrates, through the use of multiple archival sources, the insertion of women's teaching congregations in the building of the state and its educational system in Canada, and its intersection with confessionalizing agendas, whether Catholic or Protestant. The congregations adopted the official curricula in their schools and pursued teaching certifications, engaging with modernity in a variety of ways, as the church itself did in spite of its anti-modernist discourse. The alignment of the curriculum with external agencies, writes Smyth, gave the sisters' students access to teacher education as well as music and business certification, and provided them with the credentials to enter professions, within the gender limitations of the time. Two congregations in Toronto, St Joseph and Loretto, established women's colleges affiliated with the University of Toronto through St Michael's College. This chapter introduces questions about the applicability of the concept of educationalization and the need to expand its heuristic capacity if we want to capture complex articulations of the trend described by the concept.

Historian Heidi MacDonald contributed "New Educational Approaches of Women Religious in the Global South, 1968–1980." The chapter refers to the work of the Sisters of Charity–Halifax in Peru and the Dominican Republic between 1968 and 1980. This congregation was devoted to elementary and secondary school teaching, and particularly to the education of the poor as inspired by St Vincent de Paul and Elizabeth Seton. From early modernity, the Catholic Church had seen schooling as a way to pursue confessionalization as well as to deal with social, economic, and political problems. In that sense, we can use the concept of educationalization beyond its relation to late modernity and even contemporary processes. MacDonald narrates that, in 1849, the archbishop of Halifax invited the Sisters of Charity–New York to provide Catholic students with an education that would allow them to have roles in politics, the professions, and business. Catholics held minority status in the United States and were the targets of anti-Catholic feelings. A century later, when Vatican II (1962–5) moved social justice to the forefront, the sisters turned their efforts to the southern hemisphere, specifically Peru and the Dominican Republic, and, in particular, to adult education. As with other congregations nourished by liberation theology and inspired by the approach to community work of the Coady Institute, the sisters' educational intervention can be construed as a counter-discourse and practice. The sisters used educational intervention to challenge the educationalization process (in its negative connotation), which pursued a particular economic and political agenda, in most cases with American support or alongside agendas that were not rooted in participatory democratic practices.

Joseph Stafford, a former history teacher with a thirty-year career in a Catholic school who completed his PhD with a thesis on the history of secondary Catholic religious education in Ontario and the impact of Vatican II, contributed a chapter entitled "The Educationalization Process and the Roman Catholic Church in North America during the Long Nineteenth Century." This chapter examines how the Catholic Church articulated an educationalization process in North America aimed at securing a place for the Catholic faith in the new order, beginning in the nineteenth century when the Holy See adopted neo-scholasticism – a form of strict neo-Thomism – to counter the "errors" of modernity. This process was linked to confessionalization, which did not share the intentionality of the larger educationalization process linked to the state. Yet it often converged with the state, although, at other moments, it competed for spaces in the overall system. Stafford identifies two stages: one, the imposition of neo-scholasticism; the other, the social work of Catholic Action. The educationalization process, he argues, was facilitated by the classicist culture dominant in North American Catholic circles. This was a culture aimed at integral wholeness, something to which every Catholic should aspire under the leadership of the church, rather than individually working out their own set of values. The result was the "Catholic mind," a particular mindset, even a collective world view, moulded by neo-scholasticism, while theologians in Europe pluralized neo-Thomism and embarked on what is known as "nouvelle theologie." This state of affairs lasted until Vatican II. However, the official implementation of policies did not imply that Catholic students embraced the vision of the magisterium, or even that they understood neo-scholasticism/neo-Thomism. In the long 1960s, the certainty that many Catholics had about their religion disintegrated and was replaced largely by an empiricist culture; at the same time, a search started for a process of educationalization suitable to contemporary Catholic life. The history of congregations and their teaching would eventually help in providing a more nuanced picture of what happened in schools.

Jon Igelmo Zaldívar, in his chapter "Educationalization in the Spanish Second Republic and the Expulsion of the Jesuits from Spain," explores educationalization, having as reference David Labaree's (2008) understanding of educationalization as aiming to stabilize and legitimize a social structure of inequality that could lead to conflict, thus making everything into a school subject. Igelmo uses rich archival sources to narrate the place the Jesuits had in the Spanish educational setting with their colleges and schools, and their expulsion from Spain in 1932, during the Second Republic. Jesuit faculties of theology and Jesuit schools were then occupied to serve republican educational goals and inculcate republican principles. Igelmo finds a discursive continuity in this dramatic process of change, in which republican leaders – many of them with ties to the Institucion Libre de Enseñanza – tried to replace the Society of Jesus in its leading historical role of educationalizing Spanish society from a Catholic perspective. In light of Bourdieu's theory of habitus, capital, and field, Igelmo establishes a continuity in the process of change. This continuity, he argues, is grounded in the disposition toward education being understood as a habitus, and is conveyed in the understanding of the uses of educationalization to cope with social and political problems or to transform society. The research Igelmo is further undertaking will help to historize the change he examines in this chapter and will allow for future discussions of points of contact and differences in the understanding of education and educational aims within substantively different political and philosophical foundations.

Part II closes with a chapter by Patricia Quiroga Uceda, entitled "Waldorf Education and the Educationalization of Spirituality in the Plural Context in Late Twentieth-Century Spain." Quiroga Uceda argues that the reception of Waldorf education in Spain during the last decade of Francoism, and the subsequent creation of educational centres during the democratic transition, was part of an educationalized spirituality. Waldorf schools, created by Rudolf Steiner in 1913, were grounded on anthroposophy, an esoteric spirituality that synthetized various religious creeds, including Christianity. The Waldorf schools arrived in Spain, a country where the Catholic Church had a dominant role in education and where other religious and spiritual conceptions had little presence, during a time of religious crisis and increasing pluralism. The author uses Charles Taylor's paradigm of secularization and Peter Berger's paradigm of pluralism to argue that Waldorf education in Spain fit with the spiritual and educational aspirations of a minority group of Spaniards at the end of the Franco regime and in the transition to a pluralistic society. This esoteric pedagogical model, in Quiroga Uceda's view, was a manner of educationalizing spirituality. It appealed to a population weary of Catholicism with an ethos that aimed at improving society and engaged children and families in an alternative pedagogy. There are currently thirty Waldorf schools in Spain.

Part III, "Educationalization and the Right to Education/Schooling," moves to institutional issues and policies and to the educatee as political subject. Argentinian educationalist Felicitas Acosta addresses the issues of rights to education within the framework of scholarization and the expansion of schooling in "Educationalization, Schooling, and the Right to Education." She uses Latin America as a point of reference in relation to the expansion of schooling within the framework of the right to education and makes the point that the framework of rights is related to educationalization. She places her argument in line with Tröhler's thesis on educationalization and sees the deployment of mass schooling as a means to address social problems and consolidate capitalism and the nation state. On the origins of the process, the Enlightenment idea of the social contract can be placed at the centre, since the social contract, in Acosta's view, positioned the state in the role of educator. The individual future (male) citizen became the new educational actor and object. In her view, from the perspective of the expansion of schooling, education and schooling became equivalent while an intensive process of educationalization was taking place. She discusses the configuration and various landmarks of the expansion of the educational system in Latin America, which occurred within a process of homogenization that aimed at national integration, although regional disparities were exhibited. Next, she examines developmentalist economic policies in the 1950s that generated expansion and then looks at the further expansion in the late 1980s. From this examination, she concludes that, when the right to education is understood as the right to schooling, it implies a broad scale "but it also implies that any educational supply is constructed *on the basis of* or *in tension with* the forms of schooling." Policies should be re-examined from this perspective.

Part IV, "Educationalization and Democratic Spaces in the Digital Era," deals with the impact of new information and communication technologies and social media. The chapter of curricular educationalist theorist William Pinar, entitled "Educationalization as Technologization," conceives "technologization" as a form of educationalization. Technology is expressed, he writes, as instrumental rationality, in the form of computers or other devices, reflecting a conviction that the salvation of humanity resides in the control of nature – even human nature. He uses as reference Tröhler's notion of the educationalization of the world, which is not limited to solving social problems but is connected to the process of modernization itself. Ideas of freedom, science, and modernization have converged in technologization, and in "the 'creative destruction' of culture it encourages, including shifts in subjectivity, politics, and schooling." Pinar juxtaposes George Grant's critique of technology with trends today, including the quantification of educational outcomes, the technologizing of teaching, and the moving of curriculum online. A main point Pinar makes is that "curriculum is no longer an ongoing ethical question – what knowledge is of most worth? – but whatever software designers deem saleable, 'learning activities' now redesigned as 'consumer goods.'" He goes back to Grant for how to respond, and uncovers Grant's idea that only in attuning ourselves to "deprival" can we "live critically" in the "dynamo" and provide a passage to the past "becoming historical."

Ana Jofre, a physicist, artist, and professor of creative arts and technology, takes a different stand in her contribution entitled "Countering Patterns of Educationalization: Creating Digital Tools for Critical Evidence-Based Thinking." In her view, digital communications should play a central role in educational processes. She converges in her interest with Josh Cole, who wrote about education that was not educationalization, with respect to schools with no walls and blurring the distinction between school and society. There are, however, questions regarding how people are dealing with digital information. Relying on Habermas's notion of the public sphere and the idea that not learning is unnatural, Jofre explores how to use digital technology in the public sphere, with a foundational interest in education for citizenship, and presents original projects within her own art and design practice that intersect with public humanities and public pedagogy. Jofres's tools are aimed at supporting and stimulating critical evidence-based thinking, with a focus on data.

Part V, "Educationalization as a Tool of Colonization and Its Counter-Dimension in Indigenous Educational Agendas: Limits and Possibilities," concentrates on various dimensions of educationalization as a pattern of educational intervention serving the ends of colonization while also acquiring unexpected significations. The issue goes back to the link to religion.[3]

Bonita Uzoruo, a teacher of Aboriginal ancestry and a graduate student in the Master of Education in World Indigenous Studies in Education program at Queen's University, contributed "Educationalization in Canada: The Use of Native Teacher Education as a Tool of Decoloniality." Uzoruo first discusses the Canadian government's use of education in the form of segregated industrial and residential schools run by religious of various Christian denominations, both Catholic and Protestant, as a tool for assimilation and cultural annihilation, and later as a project of integration with non-Natives, starting in the 1960s. She marks the difference between the characteristics of the work of Catholic missionaries in Chile, examined by Serrano and Ponce de León in this volume, and the way missionaries conducted their work in Canada in conjunction with the federal government. She then delves into the socio-political conditions of the 1960s and early 1970s that provided the contextual framework for how the First Nations regained control of their children's education and articulated a vision for an education oriented toward Indigenous values. Uzoruo then moves to the central piece in this decolonizing view of education, Native teacher education programs, and pays attention to a specific program, the Brandon University Northern Teacher Education Program, in the province of Manitoba. Her reflections centre, with an optimistic tone, on Native teacher education programs as educational tools of decoloniality, leading to a recovery of Aboriginal culture, language, and identity. In the end, the programs aim at overcoming social conditions and try to solve the consequences of (mis)education through (re)education.

Philosopher Chris Beeman contributed "Indigeneity and Educationalization." He refers to David Labaree's analysis of contemporary educationalization as a formalist process, in which public schools are a vehicle for societal aspirations to be expressed, with the non-stated expectation that education will not solve problems. Beeman examines the work of pioneers in educationalization, such as Marc Depaepe and Paul Smeyers, and applies Labaree's analysis to First Nation, Metis, and Inuit youth. He illuminates how the endeavour to educate these youth is understood as a convenient separation of a "problem" into a sphere in which it is unable to be solved, while keeping the appearance of an attempt to do so. Educationalization is thus seen as an aspect of colonization that can be applied to all students (not just Aboriginal students) who are part of a school that curtails their interaction with the more-than-human world – with mother earth. The point that Beeman also makes is that schooling has moved to serve the neoliberal interests of the state, which accentuate individual freedom and interest over public good. He argues that we need to understand residential schools as places in which culture was unlearned and where everything was different from the Indigenous children's lived experience: the children had to relinquish their identity and learn a new identity of "being a student." Beeman, who uses stories in his teaching, examines the report of the Truth and Reconciliation Commission from the perspective of educationalization, with particular references to the clauses regarding education and negotiations with the state, and notes that the structures around education are being manipulated by the state. His argument takes an even less hopeful turn when he points out that, from the perspective of educationalization – in line with Labaree's concept – the new approach may actually succeed in implicating Indigenous parents and culture in a more subtle form of colonization. Further, Beeman is concerned that goals like the closing of achievement gaps "might be an exact fit for the loss of an ontologically interconnected way of being with the world" as they could weaken even further the little that remains of the ontos of Indigeneity. This reflection is based on his observation that the Truth and Reconciliation Commission report does not convey an understanding of how different the ontos of Indigeneity is from that of "homo mobilis." Beeman introduces the reader to a discussion of Indigeneity, Autochthony, and ontological incommensurability, and also brings in the voices of Elders. He leaves the reader with questions that will motivate new ways of thinking on Indigeneity.

Part V closes with "Capuchin Missions in Mapuche Territory: The Education of an Original People in Chile from 1880 to 1930," written by Chilean historians Sol Serrano and Macarena Ponce de León. The chapter examines the missionary work of the Capuchin order of brothers from Bavaria, who constructed, in the authors' words, a narrative centred in the understanding that the Mapuche people possessed a genuine culture and essential values that would enable their culture to become a "civilized" one. The Bavarian Capuchins defended the organic character of the Mapuche culture and repudiated any form of racism. The mission consisted of stations that included a large field for vegetable gardens and grazing, a school, a house, and a church. Indigenous schools were installed in these rural areas, some with boarding schools. Mission stations aimed also at defending the Indigenous community and provided health care and material assistance in addition to religion and schooling. However, for political reasons, the local population, the Mapuche people, wanted Spanish, not Mapudungun, spoken in the schools. Consequently, the original conception of the early work of the Capuchin mission took a different direction.

Public schools followed, mostly in areas that were close to train stations, but the state left the Andean fringe to missionaries. The mission schools of the Bavarian Capuchins were used by the national state for its own strategy in the Araucanía, at a time when Chileans and immigrants were moving there and taking land, and when the schools had a mixed population. Here is where the authors situate educationalization. Yet the Mapuche people used education to defend their land and culture, in particular during the final stage of occupation, between 1910 and 1930. The Mapuche people perceived the skills provided by the public and missionary schools as important for the preservation of Mapuche culture. The "Chilenization" process had profoundly affected their way of life, but the Mapuche leaders used formal education to empower themselves and resist by defending their interests; this was clearly expressed in legal litigation and in the creation of societies such as the Sociedad Caupolicán Defensora de la Araucanía (1910), which was organized by primary school teachers, some of whom had attended mission schools, and the Sociedad Mapuche de Protección Mutua de Loncoche (1916), a precursor of the Gran Federación Araucana (1922), which sought territorial autonomy. This detailed chapter, grounded in many years of research in national and regional archives, provides a historical case that shows the complex facets of processes of educationalization and the need to expand the use of the concept, in line with other concepts that help in delving into reception, resistance, and agency, and in capturing the dynamics of educational interaction.

The book closes with a concluding chapter by Josh Cole and Ian McKay that anticipates new critical directions for scholarship in education.

This collection represents an attempt to deepen the discussion on educationalization, its construction as a concept, and its use; to explore educationalization in relation to Catholicism (a topic of research among many members of the Theory and History of Education International Research Group); to read the right to education in light of the concept of educationalization; to discuss "technologization" as a form of educationalization, and, as an alternative, the creation of digital tools for critical evidence-based thinking; and to look at the process of educationalization in reference to Indigenous experiences of education in Canada and Chile, including ontological questions regarding the basic stances of human beings toward the world around them, themselves, and each other.

This book acknowledges the pioneering work on educationalization as an explanatory and heuristic concept, as reflected in the seminars of the research group Philosophy and History of the Discipline of Education: Evaluation and Evolution of the Criteria for Educational Research (established in 1999 by the Research Foundation, Flanders, Belgium), subsequent publications, and a special issue of *Educational Theory*.[4]

The following chapters, which are, by and large, based on original research conducted over a long period of time, open up questions, grounded in meaning coming from the specificity of historical situations, about the uses of educationalization as a heuristic concept, and they invite further theorization. Is it historically sensible to extend the application of "educationalization" to early modernity, and in particular to Catholic schooling efforts after the Protestant reformations? Is "educationalization" a concept that allows for an understanding of counter-discursive or counter-hegemonic uses of education, or that explains the reception and appropriation of schooling by, for example, the Mapuche people in Chile? How do we capture the nuances of (educational) systems that are highly differentiated and self-referential, but also of counter-practices as well as the agency of subjects? As well, in light of the digitalization of our lives, the concept of educationalization of the world will need other conceptual tools. These probing questions investigated in this volume invite further exploration.

NOTES

1 Connection Grant of the Social Science and Humanities Research Council, file no 611-2016-0247. Award holder: Professor Rosa Bruno-Jofré (Queen's University). Co-applicants: Professor Sol Serrano (the host in Chile), Pontificia Universidad Católica de Chile, and Dr Jon Igelmo Zaldívar. Collaborators: Professor Daniel Tröhler (University of Vienna), Elizabeth M. Smyth (vice-dean, Graduate School, University of Toronto), and Carlos Martínez Valle (Universidad Complutense de Madrid).

2 Email from Martin Schiralli to the author, 27 August 2000.
3 It is worth noting here that the terminology used to refer to Indigenous peoples in Canada has changed over time, and the reader will notice that the authors tend to use the terms that appear in the documents they analyse. Thus, the authors use "Native" (dominant until the late 1980s), "First Nations" (which replaced "Indian"), "Aboriginal" people, and the more recent term "Indigenous" peoples.
4 Special issue of *Educational Theory* 58 (4) (November 2008).

REFERENCES

Bernstein, Basil. 1990. *Class, Codes, and Control: The Structuring of Pedagogic Discourse*. London: Routledge.
– 2000. *Pedagogy, Symbolic Control, and Identity: Theory, Research, Critique*. Lanham, MD: Rowman and Littlefield.
Biesta, Gert. 2013. "Interrupting the Politics of Learning." *Power and Education* 5 (1): 4–15. https://doi.org/10.2304/power.2013.5.1.4. www.wwwords.co.uk/POWER.
– 2014. "Good Education: What It Is and Why We Need It." *Queen's Education Letter* (Spring/Summer), 8–10.
Bridges, David. 2008. "Educationalization: On the Appropriateness of Asking Educational Institutions to Solve Social and Economic Problems." *Educational Theory* 58 (4): 461–74. https://doi.org/10.1111/j.1741-5446.2008.00300.x.
Bruno-Jofré, Rosa. 2012. "Should Developments in Information Technology Be Informed by Educational Aims?" Presentation at Global Forum, 2002, Shaping the Future: A World in Transition: The Promise of Broadband Services, Towards the Multimedia and Knowledge Society. George Washington University, 18 October. www.items-int.com.
Bruno-Jofré, Rosa, and George (Skip) Hills. 2011. "Changing Visions of Excellence in Ontario School Policy: The Cases of Living and Learning and for the Love of Learning." *Educational Theory* 61 (3): 336–50. https://doi.org/10.1111/j.1741-5446.2011.00407.x.
Burbules, Nicholas C., and Carlos Alberto Torres. 2000. "Globalization and Education: An Introduction." In *Globalization and Education: Critical Perspectives*, edited by Nicholas C. Burbules and Carlos Alberto Torres, 1–27. New York: Routledge.
Dale, Roger. 2014. "Globalization, Higher Education, and Teacher Education: A Sociological Approach." In *Teacher Education in a Transnational World*, edited by Rosa Bruno-Jofré and James Scott Johnston, 33–53. Toronto: University of Toronto Press.

Depaepe, Marc. 2012. *Between Educationalization and Appropriation: Selected Writings on the History of Modern Educational Systems*. Leuven, BE: Leuven University Press.

Depaepe, Marc, Frederik Herman, Melanie Surmont, Angelo van Gorp, and Frank Simon. 2008. "About Pedagogization: From the Perspective of the History of Education." In *Educational Research: The Educationalization of Social Problems*, edited by Paul Smeyers and Marc Depaepe, 13–30. Dordrecht, NL: Springer.

Depaepe, Marc, and Paul Smeyers. 2008. "Educationalization as an Ongoing Modernization Process." *Educational Theory* 58 (4): 379–89. https://doi.org/10.1111/j.1741-5446.2008.00295.x.

Hansen, David. 2010. "Cosmopolitanism and Our Descriptions of Ethics and Ontology: A Response to Dale Snauwaert's 'The Ethics and Ontology of Cosmopolitanism.'" *Current Issues in Comparative Education* 12 (2) (Spring): 41–4.

– 2012. "Discovering Cosmopolitanism as a Philosophy of Education for Our Era." *Queen's Education Letter* (Fall/Winter), 7–9.

King, Joyce E. 2017. "2015 AERA Presidential Address – Morally Engaged Research/ers: Dismantling Epistemological Nihilation in the Age of Impunity." *Educational Researcher* 46 (5): 211–22. https://doi.org/10.3102/0013189x17719291.

Labaree, David. 2008. "The Winning Ways of a Losing Strategy: Educationalizing Social Problems in the United States." *Educational Theory* 58 (4): 447–60. https://doi.org/10.1111/j.1741-5446.2008.00299.x.

Portelli, John. 2012. "The Challenges of Democratic Education and Cosmopolitanism in Neo-liberal Times." *Queen's Education Letter* (Fall/Winter), 9–11.

Tröhler, Daniel. 2016. "Educationalization of Social Problems and the Educationalization of the Modern World." In *Encyclopedia of Educational Philosophy and Theory*, edited by Michael A. Peters, 1–10. Singapore: Springer. https://doi.org/10.1007/978-981-287-532-7_8-1.

PART I

Contesting Views of Processes of Educationalization at the Intersection with Christianity

arched inclinations above © Alan R. Wilkinson

1 The Dignity of Protestant Souls: Protestant Trajectories in the Educationalization of the World

DANIEL TRÖHLER[1]

On 4 October 1957, the Soviet Union shocked the Western world with the launch of Sputnik, the first satellite ever in the orbit. The United States, as leader of the Western bloc in the Cold War, reacted with a double strategy. First, it founded the National Aeronautics and Space Administration (NASA) in 1958 to enhance aerospace. Second, in the same year, it passed its first national education law, the National Defense Education Act, expressing the view that "education is our first line of defense" (Rickover 1959, 15). This *educational* response to the Soviet lead in *astronautics*, understood as a *military* threat, may be somewhat surprising at first glance, but it points in fact to a particular cultural or mental pattern or reflex that today is discussed under the catchword "educationalization."

This observed pattern or reflex refers to the cultural phenomenon that we today very likely assign all different kinds of perceived social, economic, or military problems almost immediately to education, often without realizing why and how we are educationalizing these perceived problems. Yet, as anthropologist Margaret Mead is said to have once noted, "If a fish were to become an anthropologist, the last thing it would discover would be water" (quoted in Spindler 1982, 24). The general thesis of this chapter is about the water of this fish-anthropologist, about a particular culture that applies this educationalization of all kinds of perceived problems. The focus is neither on education (theories, institutions, practices) as such nor on the mere observation that (and how) the perceived social, economic, or military problems are almost immediately assigned to education. Rather, the thesis is an attempt to explain *how* this particular cultural or mental pattern or reflex labelled "educationalization" became possible in the course of history and how it developed from rather modest beginnings into a currently dominant way to understand the world and the self. The thesis thus deals with a historically grown (but also particular) way of making sense of the (modern) world and the (modern) self, which, strikingly, are often defined in educational ways – a fact that has led to the rise of the modern educational sciences with their theories and modern educational institutions with particular practices. In another context, I described this particular style of making sense of the world and the self linguistically as *langue*, as distinct from *parole* (Tröhler 2011; 2013a [Spanish translation]).

In what follows, I will substantiate and also differentiate this general thesis about our educationalized world as a particular pattern, or even as our fundamental pattern, of making sense of the world, as a particular *langue*, but beforehand I would like to give a few more illustrative examples of the educational(ized) culture in which we are embedded. For instance, when American marine biologist Rachel Carson published *Silent Spring* (1962) some five years after Sputnik, warning of the devastating effects of indiscriminate use of pesticides in agriculture, this triggered a movement called Environmental education.[2] It educationalized our behaviour toward nature, and this educationalization was expressed in many initiatives and activities, such as the erection of educational hiking trails teaching walkers about nature. Or, when, a few years later, the national crises during and after the Vietnam War, the oil crises in the 1970s, and the near collapse of the automobile industry in the early 1980s led in the United States to the perception of "a nation at risk" – an idea reflected in the title of a report of the National Commission on Excellence in Education (1983) – the conclusion was that there was an official need for a thorough reform of the American school – an "imperative for educational reform," as the subtitle of the same report put it. Similarly, in the Western World in gernal and in the United States in particular, rising teenage pregnancy rates in the 1960s led to an educationalization of sex through the introduction of sex education in schools, which gained new urgency with the linking of HIV/AIDS to sexual behaviour in the 1980s. And when immigrant adolescents in the suburbs of Paris and Lyon protested violently in 2005, their behaviour was not seen primarily as a reaction to their poor living conditions or poor life chances but as an expression of the wrong education, as France's prime minister Dominique de Villepin stated in 2005.[3]

These examples are all from the last six decades, and they are all from the West. However, it would be wrong to conclude that they are restricted to the last sixty years in the West, even though – and here is the *substantiation* of the thesis – educationalization of the world can in fact be interpreted as a Western, and more precisely as a Protestant, way to interpret and to interact with the world and its (perceived) challenges and problems.[4] Thereby – and here is the *differentiation* of the thesis – distinct Protestant trajectories in the educationalization of the world can be identified, and these distinct trajectories derive from competing dominant Protestant religions, most of all between the two Swiss Protestantisms on the one side – Calvinism and Zwinglianism (together often labelled as Reformed Protestantism) – and German Lutheranism (evangelical Protestantism) on the other. And here it seems that it is not so much the differences in theology in the narrower sense that played a crucial role between the Swiss and Luther[5] but more the political dimensions of these two Protestantisms.[6]

In the balance of this chapter, in five steps I will present some evidence for the substantiated and differentiated thesis about the Protestant roots of our educationalized (Western) world and the cultural construction of the modern self and its distinct trajectories. First, I will identify specific transformations around 1700 that were almost predestined to trigger educational reactions in the Protestant regions. Second, I identify Protestant psychology (*avant la lettre*), or the Protestant conception of the soul, as the crucial principle allowing the educationalization of the challenges or problems that were detected with regard to these transformations. In a third step, I focus on the two different Protestantisms (reformed and evangelical), in particular with regard to their respective political theologies in order to (in step 4) identify the two paradigmatic educational ideologies that were becoming dominant towards 1800, culminating in the vision of *Bildung* on one side and the virtuous citizen on the other. Finally, I present my conclusions, also with regard to the fact that (of course) educationalization of the world is not restricted to Protestantism – not *any more*.

Transformations around 1700 as Fundamental Challenges in Interpreting the World

It is not unlikely that all historical periods could be honoured by being deemed crucial for development, all depending on what Jürgen Habermas called *Erkenntnisinteresse* (Habermas 1965). *Erkenntnisinteresse* can be translated as "knowledge interests" (or "recognitional interests") that emerge within particular discourses and that structure history accordingly. In this context, the rise of education as a particular way to think about individuals or people, or even about humankind, and as a more and more institutionalized practice serving to implement these ideas and ideals, is often related to what historiography has honoured as the Age of Enlightenment. It is said that the Enlightenment resulted, among other things, in the creation of the modern sciences, in the emergence of modern education in the second half of the eighteenth century, and also in the American Declaration of Independence in 1776 and the French Revolution in 1789. Interestingly enough, it is often claimed that the Age of Enlightenment ended with the French Revolution, after which the Enlightenment's offspring, modern education and the republican form of government, seemed to prevail over the course of the next two centuries.

In my analysis of the educationalization of the world I wish to draw attention first to a time period *before* the second half of the eighteenth century, that is, to the fifty to one hundred years before and after 1700, when the conditions seem to have emerged in which the cultural shift toward the educationalization of the world became possible – in particular in Protestant circles. It is during this period that important – but not educational! – transformations occurred that were seen, at least in particular contexts, as challenges or problems for which education seemed to be more and more the proper answer. The theories expressing this educationalized culture or attitude became popular a good century later, at the end of the eighteenth century, and focused either on the education of the true human, as in the German (or Lutheran) case, expressing the idea of *Bildung*, or on the education of the virtuous citizen, as in the American or French, or the Swiss (or reformed Calvinist), way.[7]

The two transformations around 1700 that I want to highlight still affect us today, I believe. The first transformation concerned the way that people imagined history and past development and the future. The second concerned how people viewed the relation between money and politics. These two transformations replaced older perceptions and core notions that went back to the ancient world. The first (history and development/future) was initiated in France and the second (money and politics) in England. Together they created changes that were also perceived as challenges or "problems," which were addressed in many ways, and the educational way advocated in particular contexts seems eventually to have been deemed the most promising, with effects up to today.

The transformation in perceptions of history and development was initiated in France at the court of King Louis XIV at Versailles, when the ancients' way of looking at things came under attack in the famous "quarrel of the Ancients and the Moderns." Whereas up to the end of the seventeenth century, time, and thus history, had been seen, in analogy to the seasons, as an eternal cycle of events, around 1700 a linear way of thinking ("progress") came to prevail that was oriented toward the future and in which outcomes were open. At first, around 1680, this optimism applied only to progress in the sciences, but, some decades later, progress was seen also as a social and political program: Humanity would develop progressively toward peace, justice, and bliss, and political conditions that impeded this progress had to be destroyed. This view – legitimized by the theories of modern natural law, to which I return later – was the justification for the French Revolution of 1789.

The second transformation has to do with the relation of money to politics, which changed toward the end of the seventeenth century, at first in England. The change was symbolized by the foundation of the Bank of England, which allowed rich people to invest in government. Up to that time, an ideal had prevailed in Europe according to which dispassionate reason was supposed to guide politics. At the same time, the commercial economy had been considered something lower or baser, because it was accused of diverting attention and interest away from the common good and of exposing people to the passionate pursuit of profit. In this system of thought, calm and rational governing was seen as good, and passion-driven money making as bad (Raab 1964; Hirschman 1977). But around 1700 and up to the present day, this system of thought became lost, not least because the commercial economy had become a social fact and actually very important for politics. This ideological bias – the preference for dispassionate reason as a condition of good politics and the actual importance of the discredited commerce, connected to passions – had to be solved in order to legitimate the systems of political power, which depended more and more on money.

Like any other fundamental transformations, these two not only found enthusiastic supporters but also gave rise to existential uncertainty, critique, and debates; that is, these transformations were *perceived as problems* against the background of particular visions about the ideal social order. Several intellectual reactions can be detected, and the most sustainable among them seems to be the above-mentioned cultural shift toward educationalizing perceived problems in connection with this uncertain future that endangered the moral guidelines in interpreting the world and the self. The pivotal point of this cultural shift was the Protestant interpretation of the human soul and the dignity assigned to it.[8]

The Dignity of the Protestant Soul and Salvation

This chapter is not the place to make a detailed, systematic analysis of Protestantism and Catholicism. The major differences between them with regard to the topic at hand is the fundamental Protestant principle of *Sola scriptura* (by scripture alone), stating that God's message of salvation is mediated through the Bible and is, most importantly, in no need of completion by any institutionalized tradition represented in Catholicism by the Holy Mother Church, the pope, and the ordained personnel of the church – indeed, radically not.[9] This principle of "by scripture alone" is complemented by a second, "by faith alone," which is the idea that the sinfulness of human nature can be cured only by God's will and not by confession, good works, veneration of relicts and saints, or the Mass. Faith in God is fundamental, and faithful reading of the Bible and praying means that the Holy Spirit will "talk" to the believer's heart as the noblest part of the soul, with the individual's soul being the place of salvation. This idea of the soul as the exclusive "place" or "space" of salvation – that is, as the only possible way of saving the individual from sin and its consequences, a way that is in no need of any institutionalized mediation or institutionalized rituals such as confessions or indulgences as practices that are grounded in interactions between a lay person and an ordained dignitary – has proven to be an engine in the educationalization of the world.[10] Based on this *direct connection to God*, people can develop the other part of the soul, which is human reason.[11] In the course of, foremost, seventeenth-century theology, the pessimistic anthropology of the three founding "fathers" of Reformations was gradually replaced by a more optimistic interpretation that went along with the rising consciousness of progress, borne, if not exclusively, to the greatest extent by Protestant thinkers. Their visions of progress affected the sciences, socially useful knowledge, and the individual's soul (Tröhler 2017). Hence, the (Protestant interpretation of the) soul became the object of educational desire and intervention, for it was here – and only from here – that salvation could be expected at all.

With regard to the progress of the soul, the Lutheran theologian, philosopher, and lawyer Samuel von Pufendorf explained in his seminal work on natural law the connection between the human soul, human reason, and human dignity: "Man is of the highest dignity, because he has a soul, which is distinguished by the light of reason, by the ability to judge things and to decide freely, and that is familiar with many arts" (Pufendorf 1672, book II, ch. 1, p. 145).[12] In this Protestant way of defining the dignity of humankind, the pivotal point is precisely the individual's soul, and not institutionally the Holy Mother Church, as it would have been in Catholicism with its hierarchical construction of the world.

This idiosyncratic Protestant idea was further developed by later scholars of the natural law theory – for example, by the Lutheran theologian, philosopher, and lawyer Christian Wolff. In his fundamental work, *Jus naturae methodo scientifica per tractatum* (Natural Law, Treated According to the Scientific Method), Wolff confirmed human equality and dignity based on the fact that all "men" were created by (of course, the same) God and thus have a natural disposition of perfectibility – distinguishing them from all other beings on earth (Wolff 1746, § 759, p. 592).[13] The French ideal behind the quarrel of the Ancients and the Moderns, progression and perfection in the sciences, received here its inward – Protestant – counterpart. According to Wolff, inward perfectibility is an anthropological potential, as we might say today, and in principle independent of the degree to which particular individuals actually realize it in their life. Wolff therefore distinguishes an *essential* or natural perfectibility (*perfectio essentialis*) from an *accidental* state of the actual realization of perfectibility (*perfectio accidentalis*) that individuals may realize in their particular conditions of life (Wolff, 1739, Pars Prior, Part I, ch. 3, § 579, p. 530). *Essential* is the natural disposition, *accidental* the actual realization of this disposition in the life of the individual.

Against this background, it becomes evident what – in this Protestant context – education could mean in its overall aspiration – namely, a contribution to the perfection of the soul, understood as redemption of the duty arising from the dignity of every Christian and as an individual act of salvation, an advancing to the image of God, uninfluenceable by any "external" conditions of change and seductive powers. The *Imago Dei* concept, therefore, had a strong influence not only on the Protestant idea of natural law (and subsequently on human rights), as elaborated by Pufendorf and Wolff, but also on the idea of individual perfection and morally right behaviour as a crucial part in conducting the right kind of life. Here it is not so much, as in the French context, the sciences, or learning and knowledge, that are deemed to be important but rather the virtue of the soul, the heart, and, connected with it, human reason, together forming the essence of true humanity, the mind (*Geist*). This almost inherent scepticism toward knowledge (called, disparagingly, *Vielwisserei*) was not only a shared conviction in the sixteenth and seventeenth centuries but was also a part of the Protestant discourse of those considered to be "enlightened," such as the Lutheran theologian and philanthropist Carl Friedrich Bahrdt, who claimed that "masses of knowledge not only help nothing but are harmful" (1782, 627) – that is, they seduce the heart to "immorality," as the son of a Lutheran pastor, Johann Melchior Gottlieb Beseke, feared in his reflection upon self-learning (1786, 364). It is no coincidence that Zwingli had already reminded educators of a passage from the Bible, Matthew 5:8: "Blessed are the pure in heart, for they will see God" ([1523] 1995b, 226).

This principally inward conception of the Protestant soul, its dignity, and disposition to perfectibility, along with the two fundamental transitions discussed in the preceding section, already point to an explanation of why an educationalized culture could emerge during the long eighteenth century.[14] However, the existence of two distinct, and quite opposite, theories of education around 1900 suggests that the story is a bit more complex. The difficulty arises from the two competing Protestantisms of the sixteenth century, and these two competing theories become even more complex by the fact that the Lutheran natural rights theories – written in awkward Latin – had been translated into French by two Protestant French-Swiss philosophers and lawyers, Jean Barbeyrac (1674–1744) and Jean-Jacques Burlamaqui (1694–1748) (Zurbuchen 1991, 88ff). Based on these translations and, in fact, interpretations, the French discussion became more acquainted especially with the idea of gradual progression toward an expectable state of perfectibility. This idea served Rousseau[15] and the French *lumières* as the basis for the idea of progress as human perfectibility based on science and knowledge, formulated explicitly first by Turgot in the middle of the eighteenth century and then, more systematically, by his "disciple" Condorcet (Tröhler 2017). In the following discussion, however, I will focus only the two Protestant trajectories, ignoring the French development.

Evangelical and Reformed Protestantism

All the Protestant Reformers of the sixteenth century shared the fundamental principle of *Sola scriptura* and the idea that the process of salvation occurs in the heart of the faithful reader of the Bible. Yet what this salvation meant with regard to secular life was interpreted differently, and, accordingly, the educational ideologies that eventually emerged in the course of the seventeenth century – sharing the idea of perfecting the soul – were very different, too.

The most famous difference between Luther and Zwingli was the question of the Lord's Supper (Holy Communion, the Eucharist). Whereas Luther (and later the Lutherans) believed that the Eucharist allows the most profound experience of God's manifested grace, for it is Christ's actual Body and actual Blood that is being shared by the faithful during Holy Communion (Luther [1528] 1986, 190ff), Zwingli's (and later the Zwinglians) differing view was that the Eucharist did not change the substance of the bread and wine but rather that it had symbolic, memorial power, reminding the faithful of the resurrected Christ. According to Zwingli, only faithful commemoration of Christ would make the resurrected Christ present; he talks about the

Vergegenwärtigung, or spiritual presence, not the Real Presence, of Christ in the Lord's Supper (Zwingli [1523] 1995a, 171). Luther (like Catholics) seems to interpret the Eucharist in a *metonymic* way, in which Christ and the faithful are somehow unified, whereas Zwingli interprets it in a *metaphoric* way, in which the faithful, as individuals, are only reminded of communion with Christ, which strengthened their faith.

These differences may point to other differences that are more important to this context – namely, the political dimension, the political counterpart, of these two Protestantisms: Luther's evangelical and Zwingli's Reformed Protestantism. Luther's political theology was fundamentally dualistic and represents what later would be called the two kingdoms doctrine, which makes a sharp distinction between the kingdom of Christ and the secular kingdom. In Christ's kingdom, which is governed by the spiritual authority of the Word and the Sacraments, there is grace and forgiveness of sins, and there are no differences among humankind. The secular kingdom is governed by the temporal authority of the ruler, the sword, and the law; there is neither grace nor equality. Lutherans view the two kingdoms, both instituted by God, as mutually beneficial. The realm of Christ benefits from the temporal realm, because secular authority enforces peace in the world, and the temporal realm is served by the realm of Christ in its proclaiming of the Gospel through the Word. This evangelical Protestantism holds further that it is of prime importance not to confuse the two kingdoms: God rules the spiritual kingdom through the Gospel. The Gospel is not meant to rule the secular kingdom, which is ruled by its own power, laws, and force. Any attempt to use the Gospel to rule the secular world is therefore an error. Politically, this doctrine – particularly since it was accompanied by a state church – was tantamount to total deprivation of people's right of decision making. Freedom, in this tradition, is purely inward freedom, with no counterpart in the social-political realm of life.[16]

Here the difference between Luther and Zwingli becomes apparent. Influenced by emerging humanism, Zwingli's political theory was what later was called a form of "civic humanism" (Baron 1955) or (classical) republicanism (Pocock 1975).[17] According to this political ideology, citizens are free in principle and, by virtue of their freedom, they can act as law givers – and even as voters choosing their superiors. Zwingli questions the idea of hereditary monarchy and of a monarchy that has no consent of the people ([1523] 1995a, 393). Like Luther, Zwingli condemns revolts against those in power but *not* if – and this is in contrast to Luther – the whole community wants to remove them, because in this case the "removal conforms to God's will" (394). According to Zwingli, monarchy and, of course, tyranny are God's punishments of people who do not live according to natural law. If they did so, says Zwingli, "We would be in no need of any superiors, for we would all be brothers ... Then we would all agree that Tyrants are to be removed" (394). (Morally) good people need a form of government but no tyrants. Hence, this form of government is participatory; it is self-government.

Zwingli's classical-republican legitimation of tyrannicide[18] was sharply attacked by Luther, who did not hide his low esteem of Zwingli's political idea of self-government and, with it, the justification for tyrannicide (which became famous worldwide with Friedrich Schiller's drama *William Tell* and was further popularized by the opera of the same title by Gioachino Rossini). Luther unconditionally defended the right of monarchs, even if they were unjust in ruling over their subjects. Zwingli's intention to work toward worldly – that is, political and social – reform led Luther to make the accusation that Zwingli's republicanism presumed to "scorn everyone, including the princes and potentates." Luther defended the system of state sovereigns and gave civic humanism or classical republicanism no chances: "It is ... said that the Swiss have in the past killed their lords and in this way won their freedom ... Up to now the Swiss have paid in blood for this dearly and are still paying dearly; how this will end is easy to imagine ... I do not see any type of government to be as enduring as the one in which authorities are esteemed and venerated" (cited in Farner 1931, 18–20). To Luther it was evident that Zwingli would either cause or suffer damage (21).

It is foremost these political differences that led to different trajectories in formulating educational theories. While both theories focused equally on the individual's soul, one centred on fostering an inward free, true human, culminating in the ideal of *Bildung*, and the other a self-governed virtuous citizen.

Bildung and the Education of the Virtuous Citizen

Both Protestantisms relied on the principle of *Sola scriptura* and the idea that the salvation process would occur in the faithful soul of the individual while praying and reading the Bible, and both would agree that challenges in the world should be responded to by education, understood primarily as perfecting the soul. Where they differed was regarding the social and political dimension of the individual and, accordingly, the idea of how education should be theoretically legitimized.

Within the somewhat apolitical realm of Lutheranism, the doctrine of human perfectibility became translated, toward the end of the eighteenth century, into the theory of *Bildung* as total *inward* perfection of humankind, to which, as Humboldt said, every single individual is called upon to strive. *Bildung* meant inward perfection, understood as aesthetic harmonization of the soul. The "outer" counterpart was not the state or the idea of the republic but either the cosmopolitan vision of humanity in general (*Menschheit*) or, in the case of Fichte and others, the German nation and its mission for humankind. The Germans deliberately leveraged the concept of *Bildung* as a means of distancing themselves from the French idea of civilization – an idea the Germans criticized as centralist, courtly, alienated, and morally suspect – claiming, in contrast, that "culture" (*Kultur*) and *Bildung* were uniquely German and, in truth, superior to French ideas (Horlacher 2016). The curriculum at school therefore focused not so much on the empirical world and the sciences or mathematics but more on the ancient world of the Greeks and Romans, and the "methods" to convert or perfect the souls of the young individuals resided in the school subjects of Latin and Greek and, in higher education, hermeneutics. Hence, antiquity was much more than a mere object of study; it was the embodiment of an ideal.

One of the first proponents of this enthusiasm was Johann Joachim Winckelmann, a German art historian and archaeologist who, in *Reflections on the Painting and Sculpture of the Greeks* ([1755] 1765) emphasized the value of Greek aesthetics for the human mind (Horlacher 2016). Wilhelm von Humboldt, one of the founders of the German *Bildungstheorie*, confirmed that the Greeks were "a model, and its unattainability may encourage" us to follow them ([1807] 1961, 70). This aesthetic harmony was defined as a means for true education of the human being: "The true purpose of man – not the one that changing inclinations prescribe but the eternally unchanging reason – is the highest and harmonious *Bildung* of his potentials/powers to one whole" (Humboldt [1792] 1960, 64). "Perfection is not limited" (Humboldt [1797] 1960, 512) and represents the "inward spiritual vitality" (513). *Bildung*, Humboldt says, is to be found only "in oneself" (507, freely translated).

Expressed in the school curriculum, this idea sharply separates education (*Bildung*) from any kind of vocational training (*Ausbildung*). "All schools" of the state may "only focus on general *Bildung* of the human character," and any educational concern connected to the needs of living must be separated from it (Humboldt [1809] 1964, 188). Any kind of useful training has to be postponed to the stage when every human being has been educated first as a human character. General *Bildung* has to empower, purify, and compose human forces in order to perfect the human mind/mental disposition (*Gemüt*) (188). Again, the Greeks seem to be the model that was to be learned by every individual: "In this way, having learned Greek would be just as useful for the carpenter as would carpentry for the scholar" (189). Education in the sense of *Bildung* was designed to compensate for Germany's self-perceived political and scientific backwardness as compared to France or England (Horlacher 2016) and to bring an idea into play that claimed the highest dignity and expressed Germany's global mission.

Bildung became the epitome of the defiant self-confidence with which German intellectuals reacted to the scientific and political – that is, in their eyes, "only" outer – progress in France and in England. It held that, in contrast, *true* progress is inward and is not directly related to knowledge and politics. This idea differed essentially from the Swiss Protestant idea of education as "making" the classical virtuous, patriotic citizen. Already Zwingli had claimed, in the context of his classical republicanism, that education meant educating the soul toward a kind of moral resilience or, more traditionally, steadfast virtue (*feste Tugend*) ([1523] 1995b, 229). In the course of the economization of social life, this steadfast virtue – once indicating the steadfast soldier-citizen defending his hometown on the battlefield – came to mean resistance to the seductions of commercial life, luxury, and passion for the private good (instead of the common good). Whereas the more radical exponents of this educational theory in the eighteenth century aimed at banning the commercial way of life altogether by fostering republican virtuous socialization – as did Rousseau in *Letter to d'Alembert* (1759) or *Considerations on the Government of Poland* ([1782] 2005), Mably in *Entretiens de Phocion* (1763), and the young Pestalozzi – it became more and more clear that these virtuous citizens *first had to be made* if they wanted to *conserve their political-ethical ideals in a changing world*. Pestalozzi became the icon of this new educationalized ideology, not least because he often used Lutheran language in promoting his republican aspirations (Tröhler 2013b; 2014b). The aim was to meet the challenges of the modernizing world by making the inwardly steadfast citizen patriotic, selfless, and immune to the temptations of political power and commerce.

The core educational idea was to accept commercial professions other than only the favoured profession of agriculture, precisely by training the soul to be indifferent to the temptations of power and money. Against that background, there was no reason why a tradesman could not be virtuous, as the German translator of Gabriel Bonnot de Mably, Hans Conrad Vögelin from Zürich, suggested in a footnote to Mably's republican treaties *Entretiens de Phocion* (Phocion's Conversations) (Mably 1763) in his translation published in 1764: "Why should they not be industrious and moderate, why should they not be able to have a desire for fame and religion?" And opposing the opinion that agriculture was a considerably more favourable basis for the republic than the trades, Vögelin asked critically, "What then is especially virtuous about the plow, more so than the hammer of the blacksmith?" Regarding the classical republican criticism of tradesmen, Vögelin concluded his remarks that those of the nobility are good, tradesmen are good, and commerce is also good, as long as it can be "correctly modified" (Vögelin note, in Mably 1764, 111).

This idea of modifying, or making virtuous, was interpreted by Vögelin as *inner strengthening* – that is, as strengthening the soul. It is evident that the school curriculum associated with this educational ideology was different from the curriculum in the Lutheran context; it served ideas of equality more, placing less emphasis on the aesthetic idealization of antiquity and more on history and useful or practical sciences. The Reformed Protestant inner strength was the alternative equivalent to the Lutheran aesthetic harmony of the soul as an answer to the challenges of the world. Both conceptions were holistic: *Bildung* as the epitome of the fully and harmoniously developed human potential, and the virtuous citizen acting at the same time as husband, professional (preferably a farmer), politician (self-government), and militia soldier to defend his hometown against aggressors. Accordingly, the German tradition never developed a notion similar to the one of citizen. The normal translation of "citizen" is *Bürger* in German, but that term has always been restricted to the ("mere") economic side of life, and in German sociology it indicated a social class (for instance, in Friedrich Gabriel Resewitz's *Die Erziehung des Bürgers* (The Education of the Citizen), 1776). Later on, the educated citizen, the *Bildungsbürger*, was a class distinct from farmers, workers, and the nobility. The idea of the *Bürger* never reached the social and political holism connected to the idea of the (virtuous) citizen that grew out of the republican form of Reformed Protestantism.

Outlook

This chapter started with the thesis that the educationalized world in which we live – a world that is being interpreted, in terms of individuals' souls, as a place of salvation and therefore as a solution of perceived problems – originated in Protestantism. I have described a time when the uncertain future and the commercialization of politics with its ennoblement of the selfish passions were perceived as problems, and the answer was to promote education, the perfecting of the soul of the individual, enabling people to lead a pious – that is, a virtuous – life in changing times with all of the problems resulting from changing social, political, economic, and ideological conditions. However, the idea of what "virtue" meant, and how individuals were expected to act in social, political, and economic spheres, differed between Lutheran and Reformed Protestantism. Whereas the Lutheran tradition led within a century (the long eighteenth century) to the theory or ideology of *Bildung* – that is, inward aesthetic perfection with reference to a cosmopolitan idea of humankind – the Reformed tradition led to the virtuous citizen, building the city upon the hill, the more or less Christian republic as a distinct political entity (Tröhler 2011).

The idea that education can ensure both the continuous development and the (respective) handed-down or traditional system of moral and political order was the major reason why the overall project of the nineteenth century – building territorially and constitutionally defined nation-states with loyal citizens – focused so strongly on the foundation and expansion of the mass school system. The Prussians took the lead in establishing a comprehensive school system, teacher education, and school administration, trying to avoid empowering future Prussians to become citizens (in the classical and modern republican sense) but, rather, trying to "make" future loyal Prussians bearers of the dominant vision of social and political order (Tröhler 2016). Horace Mann and Victor Cousin admired the Prussian system but adapted it in their recommendations to the United States and France in accordance with their respective value systems (Tröhler, forthcoming). Education had become a self-evident or taken-for-granted technology of nation-states precisely because it was able to build on the personal self-governance of Protestant individuals, accountable to themselves as moral beings, irrespective of whether their moral being was inward (Lutheran) or social-political (Zwinglian). Catholic countries lagged somewhat behind on these educational expansions, but sooner or later they started to invest in education too, and I would like to start my conclusion by reconstructing the way that Catholicism caught up in this particular discourse of the modern world and the modern self.

The example that I want to use to demonstrate this is the newly unified Italian monarchy of 1861, when the liberal statesman Massimo d'Azeglio stated in the new parliament: "We have made Italy, now we have to make Italians" (as cited in Hobsbawm 1992, 44; Carter 1996, 545).[19] D'Azeglio was expressing the fact that Italy had (finally) become a modern nation-state with a constitution of its own, but that a nation-state without loyal citizens has no actual fundaments of existence. Hence, the discourse in which d'Azeglio expresses his worries about the future suggests the very idea that (future) citizens had to be made and that, from the time of the Congress of Vienna or at least the 1830s, the school, with its particular formal architecture (levels, tracks, transition regimes) and curricular order, was the central institution to make the future citizens. Quite clearly, the rise of the modern nation-state with its constitution, which defined the social order and the realms of its legal entities, the citizens, set an ineluctable standard that coerced traditional discourses to adapt sooner or later.[20] The Italian envisioned by political activists was still Catholic, but a Catholic Italian, meaning a Catholic-minded national citizen. Yet, the almost insurmountable problems liberal Italians encountered in expanding the school system and hence in "making" the Italian citizen points to the cultural power of Catholicism to resist ideas of empowerment, especially considering the fact that the model that Italians knew was France and not Germany.

By the last third of the nineteenth century, it had become a truism that a citizen is never born but "made" and that schooling and curriculum were major means of making future citizens, even if those citizens were not citizens in the democratic republican sense. Discovering the regulating power of this technology, Catholic nation-states could not but adapt to these artefacts and had to allocate a different meaning to education than Catholicism had done before. In doing so, Catholicism eventually contributed to the educationalization of the world, and it did so by using an idea and strategy that was genuinely rooted in Protestantism. This does not mean that Catholic intellectuals simply copied and pasted Protestant concepts; they copied the underlying idea that the uncertain future had to be mastered by educating the individual and by doing this foremost at school.[21] A prime example of this "Catholization" of dominant Protestant theories of education may be seen in Otto Willmann, who was a Catholic professor of education at the German University of Prague and the most prominent Catholic Herbartian in Germany, publishing in the last third of the nineteenth century. One of Willmann's most central publications, *Didaktik als Bildungslehre nach ihren Beziehungen zur Sozialforschung und zur Geschichte der Bildung* ([1882] 1889),[22] was, not coincidentally, translated into Spanish,[23] in the realm of the comparatively late establishment of *pedagogía* as an academic discipline in the 1940s, as *Teoría de la formación humana: la didáctica como teoría de la formación humana en sus relaciones con la investigación social y con la historia de la educación* (1948). The translated work provided the standards of academic education in Spain for a long time.[24]

The triumph of Protestantism – a triumph that no one should be proud of – is not that its strategies are implemented in Protestant areas but that they are also implemented in non-Protestant areas. It has become the dominant discourse in defining the Western world, its political and economic order, its perceptions and identification of social problems, and its (educational) recipes to solve these problems by fundamentally educationalizing the modern self. And most often the modern educationalized self is expressed in the language of psychology that no one seems to be able to withstand anymore: It is part of this water that the fish-anthropologist will have such difficulty in recognizing. Talking about education in the modern way, using educational utterances or *paroles*, is to impose Protestant world interpretations and a Protestant way of making sense of the world. After all, words are deeds (Wittgenstein [1953] 2001; Austin 1962; Pocock 1987; Skinner 1988a, 1988b; Tully 1988).

Traditionally, we are inclined to think of modern education as a noble result or even as fulfilment of the Age of Enlightenment and its emphasis on rational human reasoning. This construction, guided by our contemporary interests in understanding ourselves as rational, is evident only if we accept the Protestant influence on the Enlightenment, not only in Germany, and if we accept the degree to which our self-assigned rationality leaves us hardly any alternatives other than to identify or define social, economic, or political problems in order to educationalize them at once. With that, we are in the good company of the dominant discourse and its manifold voices in politics, the economy, and research, which allows hardly any historical reconstruction and systematic deconstruction – which probably would have been the true idea of "the Enlightenment," and which ultimately would lead to the reconstruction of the dominant ways in which we try to understand ourselves and the world.

NOTES

1. An earlier version of this chapter was presented at the Helsinki Collegium for Advanced Studies symposium Legacy of the Reformation: Law, Democracy, Education, University of Helsinki, Finland, 11–12 February 2016.
2. Thinking, for instance, about forest educational trails points to the fact that educationalization is not limited to schooling, even though schooling is the main institutional bearer of this culture. Another non-school-based educationalized practice would be found in different adult education initiatives and programs such as LLL (Lifelong Learning) or in public advertisements focusing on sexual behaviour in connection with HIV/AIDS.
3. "Certains Français ont besoin d'un accompagnement personnalisé en matière d'emploi et d'éducation. L'école c'est le lieu de rendez-vous de la République" (Jakubyszyn 2005).

4   This is not to suggest that Protestantism is a homogeneous doctrine, as will be seen in the identification of different trajectories of the dominant denominations. By these, I refer to those doctrines that became officially taught at the universities and hence found political support. If I hereafter refer to Luther, Zwingli, and Calvin, and foremost to the theologies that derived from them, it is precisely because of this institutionalization, not in order to deny the importance of reformatory precursors such as John Wyclif or Jan Hus or the general reformatory importance, for instance, of humanism, exemplified by Erasmus of Rotterdam.

5   To be sure, the anthropologies of the three reformatory "fathers" (Luther, Zwingli, and Calvin) considered here would not have allowed optimistic faith in education. But there was one very crucial element in their shared soteriological (i.e., referring to the religious doctrine of salvation) emphasis on the individual's soul that, over the course of more than a century, prepared the breeding ground for the "educationalization" discussed in this paper. If I still talk about *different* trajectories, it is foremost because of differing political elements among the three – that is, different visions of the earthly organization of life. Whereas Calvin can be said to have advocated some form of theocracy, Luther was a monarchist, as his motto *Cuius regio, eius religio* (Whose realm, his religion) indicates: it meant that the religion of the (political) ruler was to dictate the religion of those ruled. Zwingli, in contrast, was an advocate of classical republicanism, with the ideal of the virtuous and self-governing citizen (at least for citizens of the cities).

6   To be more accurate, I would also have to make a distinction between the *English* Calvinists and the *Scottish* Calvinists. Under the reigns of Henry VIII and Mary I ("Bloody Mary"), many English Calvinists fled to Zurich and began to orient themselves to the classical-republican Protestantism of Zwingli and especially of his successor, Heinrich Bullinger, and thus transformed Calvin's theocratic political theory into locally democratic congregationalism in England under Elizabeth I. In contrast, due to the weak Scottish monarchy, the *Scottish* (and later Northern Irish) Calvinists (Presbyterians) were never forced to undergo such a political transformation (on all this, see Ryce 2013), and neither was the Dutch Calvinist movement called Arminianism, which then flowed into English Methodism. It is no coincidence that, in the following centuries, Presbyterians and Methodists outside of Europe worked together, not least on questions of schooling – for instance, in the Presbyterian and Methodist Schools Association in Australia. However, since in this chapter I discuss Continental European trajectories, the distinctions mentioned in this note remain relatively unimportant for my purposes.

7 I realize, of course, that the Gallican Church was Catholic (even if it was comparatively autonomous), but the central arguments for the French Revolution did not originate in Gallicanism but rather in French translations of German Protestant natural law theories (foremost those written by Samuel von Pufendorf in Latin) of the Genevan Calvinists (Jean Barbeyrac and Jean-Jacques Burlamaqui). These translations radicalized critical tendencies in France borne by Abbé Saint-Pierre or the young Montesquieu, discussions that were much less secular than the self-perception of the French philosophers would have allowed them to recognize (Becker [1932] /2003), and they contributed to what Dale K. Van Kley (1996) identified as the ultimately Calvinist influence on revolutionary thought in France, which provided a particular (and latent sacred) way to understand progress in history.
8 To be sure, the educational "answer" to the rising influence of money in political and public life affected not only elite education (although it was dominant) but also the education of the very poor in the "charity schools," which, not by chance, started and disseminated first in Protestant parts of Europe (Tosato-Rigo 2014).
9 Irrespective of the fact that the founding "fathers" of the Reformation did not believe in the free will of the human. The relevant issue here is that the "place" or "space" of salvation is in the individual's soul. As soon as the pessimistic anthropology of the original Protestant theology became more optimistic, the soul became the crucial instance of desire of people morally concerned about the transformations and eventually of the educators.
10 This is of utmost importance and in strict contrast to the Catholic Church doctrine of "extra Ecclesiam nulla salus" (outside the church there is no salvation). The *Catechism of the Catholic Church* issued in 1997 reformulated that "positively, it means that all salvation comes from Christ the Head through the Church which is his Body" (http://www.vatican.va/archive/ccc_css/archive/catechism/p123a9p3.htm#IV).
11 In the Lutheran tradition, the distinction between the soul, the conscience, the heart, and the mind is not always very clear; see Luther ([1520] 1982), who seems to use these notions almost as synonyms.
12 *Maxima inde homini dignatio, quod animam obtinet immortalem, lumine intellectus, facultate res dijudicandi & eligendi praeditam, & in plurimas artes solertissimam.*
13 Datur enim perfectio naturalis hominis, qua is distinguitur a rebus omibus aliis.
14 Again, this is not to say that there were no educational activities before that time, in particular in Catholic contexts, and these may have contributed to the configuration of the educationalized world, but the configuration itself presupposes the vision of the individual soul as the "place"

or "space" of salvation. Bettering the world did not mean bettering the Catholic Church but the perfecting of the individual's soul.

15 According to Rousseau, it is in man's "consciousness" of his liberty to choose that "the spirituality of his soul chiefly appears" (Rousseau [1755] 2002, 95).

16 In the context of the First Word War, John Dewey (1915) traced German aggression and that country's political subservience to Kant's German idealism as an expression of Luther's two kingdoms doctrine, according to which freedom is purely inward, whereas in the social realm obedience is expected.

17 This indicates that Zwingli's political theory is embedded in a long tradition with pre-Christian roots, even though he blended it with Reformed Protestant aspects. Zwingli developed the fundaments of this Christian-classical republic in parallel to Machiavelli's ideals, but he was more successful, for he succeeded in convincing the political stakeholders of Zurich of the need for an anti-aristocratic form of government. Both Machiavelli and Zwingli (and his immediate successors, such as Bullinger and Hochholzer) focused their educational theories on virtuous citizens; see Tröhler (2003).

18 The idea of tyrannicide as legitimate political action dates back to classical republican authors such as Plutarch or Cicero. In Switzerland, it has become an unparalleled part of the national myth with the story of Wilhelm Tell.

19 Actually, this famous sentence is a compilation of two sentences, separated by a third. Here the two: "Il primo bisogno d'Italia è che si formino Italiani dotati d'alti e forti caratteri" (The first need of Italy is that Italians are formed with high and strong characters) and "Pur troppo s'è fatta l'Italia, ma non si fanno gl'Italiani" (Unfortunately, we have made Italy but not Italians).

20 At least in education research, the effects of constitutions are largely underestimated. Constitutions – the first was the American, then the French – not only defined the fundaments of the envisioned social order, but they also transformed human beings, inhabitants, working people, and subjects of a defined territory to a previously unknown category: the national citizen (previously, citizenship had been restricted to privileged inhabitants of cities) with particular (sometimes large, sometimes small) rights and duties. The invention of constitutions was the first and fundamental act in what Hacking (1986) calls the "making up people."

21 It is characteristic that the Catholic Church in general and Pope Leo XIII in his *Rerum Novarum* (1891) in particular did not address the so-called social question of the nineteenth century as an educational (or political) challenge but as the sad result of anti-Catholic developments starting with the French Revolution; hence its reaction was aimed at strengthening the Catholic Church while making appeals to the privileged for more mercy toward the poor (Tröhler 2014a). That is not to say that many individual

Catholics were not engaged politically, socially, and educationally to address the (perceived) problems related to the "social question," which indicates that they (already) followed somehow Protestant convictions. A larger educationalization process of the Catholic Church was triggered by the Second Vatican Council (1962–5), which has recently attracted interest (Bruno-Jofré and Zaldívar 2017).

22 The title translates in English as "*Didaktik* as Theory of *Bildung* According to Its Relation to Social Inquiry and to the History of Education." For the difference between the German and Nordic idea of *Didaktik* and the Anglo Saxon idea of curriculum, see Gundem and Hopmann (1988).
23 By Salustiano Dunaiturria, who had studied in Germany.
24 I wish to thank Miguel Pereyra (Granada) for this very helpful information.

REFERENCES

Austin, J.L. 1962. *How to Do Things with Words: The William James Lectures Delivered at Harvard University in 1955*. Oxford: Clarendon Press.
Bahrdt, C.F. 1782. *Briefe über die Bibel im Volkston: Eine Wochenschrift, Band 1*. Halle, DE: Johann Friedrich Dost.
Baron, H. 1955. *The Crisis of the Early Italian Renaissance: Civic Humanism and Republican Liberty in an Age of Classicism and Tyranny*. Princeton, NJ: Princeton University Press.
Becker, C.L. (1932) 2003. *The Heavenly City of the Eighteenth-Century Philosophers*. New Haven, CT: Yale University Press.
Beseke, J.M.G. 1786. "Über Lektüre und Selbststudium." *Deutsches Museum* 11 (1): 360–5.
Bruno-Jofré, R., and J. Zaldívar, eds. 2017. *Catholic Education in the Wake of Vatican II*. Toronto: University of Toronto Press.
Carson, R. 1962. *Silent Spring*. Greenwich, CT: Fawcett.
Carter, N. 1996. "Nation, Nationality, Nationalism, and Internationalism in Italy, from Cavour to Mussolini." *Historical Journal* 39 (2): 545–51. https://doi.org/10.1017/S0018246X00020392.
Dewey, J. 1915. *German Philosophy and Politics*. New York: Henry Holt and Company.
Farner, O. 1931. *Das Zwinglibild Luthers*. Tübingen, DE: Mohr.
Gundem, B.B., and S. Hopmann, eds. 1988. *Didaktik and/or Curriculum: An International Dialogue*. Frankfurt: Peter Lang.
Habermas, J. 1965. "Erkenntnis und Interesse." Frankfurter Antrittsvorlesung vom 28. Juni 1965. *Merkur* 19: 1139–53.
Hacking, I. 1986. "Making Up People." In *The Science Studies Reader*, edited by M. Biaglio, 161–71. New York: Routledge.

Hirschman, A.O. 1977. *The Passions and the Interests: Political Arguments for Capitalism before Its Triumph*. Princeton, NJ: Princeton University Press.

Hobsbawm, E.J. 1992. *Nations and Nationalism since 1780: Programme, Myth, Reality*. 2nd ed. Cambridge: Cambridge University Press.

Horlacher, R. 2016. *The Educated Subject and the German Concept of Bildung: A Comparative Cultural History*. New York: Routledge.

Humboldt, W. v. (1792) 1960. "Ideen zu einem Versich, die Gränzen der Wirksamkeit des Staates zu bestimmen." In *Wilhelm von Humboldt: Werke in fünf Bänden. Band 1*, edited by A. Flitner and K. Giel, 56–233. Darmstadt, DE: Wissenschaftliche Buchgesellschaft.

– (1797) 1960. "Über den Geist der Menschheit." In *Wilhelm von Humboldt: Werke in fünf Bänden. Band 1*, edited by A. Flitner and K. Giel, 506–18. Darmstadt, DE: Wissenschaftliche Buchgesellschaft.

– (1807) 1961. "Über den Charakter der Griechen, die idealische und historische Ansicht derselben." In *Wilhelm von Humboldt: Werke in fünf Bände. Band 2*, edited by A. Flitner and K. Giel, 65–72. Darmstadt, DE: Wissenschaftliche Buchgesellschaft.

– (1809) 1964. "Der Königsberger und Litauische Schulplan." In *Wilhelm von Humboldt: Werke in fünf Bänden. Band 4*, edited by A. Flitner and K. Giel, 168–95. Darmstadt, DE: Wissenschaftliche Buchgesellschaft.

Jakubyszyn, C. 2005. "Contre l'échec scolaire, le premier ministre prône le suivi des élèves et des sanctions parentales." *Le Monde*, 12 January. http://www.lemonde.fr/societe/article/2005/12/01/villepin-implique-les-familles-dans-la-lutte-contre-l-echec-scolaire_716366_3224.html.

Luther, M. (1520) 1982. "Von der Freiheit eines Christenmenschen." In *Martin Luther: Studienausgabe. Band 2*, edited by H-U. Delius, 260–309. Berlin: Evangelische Verlangsanstalt.

– (1528) 1986. "Vom Abendmahl Christi, Bekenntnis." In *Martin Luther: Studienausgabe. Band 4*, edited by H-U. Delius, 13–258. Berlin: Evangelische Verlangsanstalt.

Mably, G.B. de. 1763. *Entretiens de Phocion: Sur le rapport de la morale avec la politique / trad. en grec de Nicoclès; avec des remarques*. Amsterdam: n.p.

– 1764. *Gespräche des Phocion über die Beziehung der Morale mit der Polititk. Aus dem Griechischen des Nicocles. Mit Anmerkungen aus dem Französischen des Herrn Abt Mably übersetzt*. Translated by H.C. Vögelin. Zurich: Heidegger.

National Commission on Excellence in Education. 1983. *A Nation at Risk: The Imperative for Educational Reform*. Washington, DC: Superintendent of Documents, US GPO.

Pocock, J.G.A. 1987. "The Concept of Language and the Métier d'historien: Some Considerations on Practice." In *The Languages of Political Theory in Early-Modern Europe*, edited by A. Pagden, 19–38. Cambridge: Cambridge University Press.

Pufendorf, S. v. 1672. *De jure naturae et gentium, libri octo.* Frankfurt: Knoch.
Raab, F. 1964. *The English Face of Machiavelli: A Changing Interpretation, 1500–1700.* London: Routledge.
Resewitz, F.G. 1776. *Die Erziehung des Bürgers zum Gebrauch des gesunden Verstandes, und zur gemeinnüthzigen Geschäfftigkeit.* 2nd ed. Copenhagen: Heineck und Faber.
Rickover, H.G. 1959. *Education and Freedom.* New York: Dutton.
Rousseau, J.-J. (1755) 2002. "Discourse on the Origin and Foundations of Inequality among Mankind." In *Jean-Jacques Rousseau, The Social Contract and the First and Second Discourses,* edited by S. Dunn, 69–148. New Haven, CT: Yale University Press.
– 1759. *A Letter from M. Rousseau of Geneva to M. d'Alembert of Paris Concerning the Effects of Theatrical Entertainments on the Manners of Mankind, Translated from the French.* London: J. Nourse.
– (1782) 2005. "Considerations on the Government of Poland and on Its Planned Reformation" In *Jean-Jacques Rousseau: The Plan for Perpetual Peace, On the Government of Poland, and Other Writings on History and Politics,* translated and edited by C. Kelly, 167–240. Lebanon, NH: Dartmouth College Press.
Ryce, A. 2013. *The Age of Reformation: The Tudor and Steward Realms, 1845–1603.* London: Routledge.
Skinner, Q. 1988a. "Meaning and Understanding in the History of Ideas." In *Meaning and Context: Quentin Skinner and His Critics,* edited by J. Tully, 29–67. Princeton, NJ: Princeton University Press.
– 1988b. "A Reply to My Critics." *Meaning and Context: Quentin Skinner and His Critics,* edited by J. Tully, 232–88. Princeton, NJ: Princeton University Press.
Spindler, G.D., ed. 1982. *Doing the Ethnography of Schooling: Educational Anthropology in Action.* New York: Holt.
Tosato-Rigo, D. 2014. "Paroles de témoins: Vers une pluralisation du récit historique." *Encounters on Education / Encuentros sobre Educación / Rencontres sur l'Éducation* 15 (4): 137–59. http://dx.doi.org/10.15572/ENCO2014.08.
Tröhler, D. 2003. "Republikanische Tugend und Erziehung bei Niccolò Machiavelli und im Selbstverständnis des Schweizer Stadtbürgertums des 16. Jahrhunderts." In *Anfänge und Grundlegungen moderner Pädagogik im 16. und 17. Jahrhundert,* edited by H.-U. Musolff and A.-S. Göing, 55–72. Cologne: Böhlau.
– 2011. *Languages of Education: Protestant Legacies, National Identities, and Global Aspirations.* New York: Routledge.
– 2013a. *Los Lenguajes de la educación: Los legados protestantes en la pedagogización del mundo, las identidades nacionales y las aspiraciones globales.* Barcelona: Octaedro.
– 2013b. *Pestalozzi and the Educationalization of the World.* New York: Palgrave Pivot.

– 2014a. "The Construction of Society and Conceptions of Education: Comparative Visions in Germany, France, and the United States around 1900." In *The Reason of Schooling: Historicizing Curriculum Studies, Pedagogy, and Teacher Education*, edited by T.S. Popkewitz, 21–39. New York: Routledge
– 2014b. *Pestalozzi y la educationalización del mundo*. Barcelona: Octaedro.
– 2016. "Curriculum History or the Educational Construction of Europe in the Long Nineteenth Century." *European Educational Research Journal* 15 (3): 279–97. https://doi.org/10.1177/1474904116645111.
– 2017. "Progressivism." In *Oxford Research Encyclopedias: Education*, edited by G.W. Noblit. Oxford: Oxford University Press. https://doi.org/10.1093/acrefore/9780190264093.013.111.
– Forthcoming. "Curriculum History." In *The Oxford Handbook of History of Education*, edited by J. Rury and E. Tamura. Oxford: Oxford University Press.
Tully, J., ed. 1988. *Meaning and Context: Quentin Skinner and His Critics*. Princeton, NJ: Princeton University Press.
Van Kley, D.K. 1996. *The Religious Origins of the French Revolution: From Calvin to the Civil Constitution, 1560–1791*. New Haven, CT: Yale University Press.
Willmann, O. 1882, 1889. *Didaktik als Bildungslehre nach ihren Beziehungen zur Sozialforschung und zur Geschichte der Bildung*. 2 vols. Braunschweig, DE: Vieweg.
– 1948. *Teoría de la formación humana: La didáctica como teoría de la formación humana en sus relaciones con la investigación social y con la historia de la educación*. Translated by Salustiano Duñaiturria. Madrid: Cons.Sup.de Inv. Científicas, Inst. San José de Calasanz de Pedagogia.
Winckelmann, J.J. (1755) 1765. *Reflections on the Painting and Sculpture of the Greeks: With Instructions for the Connoisseur, and an Essay on Grace in Works of Art*, translated by H. Fusseli. London: A. Millar.
Wittgenstein, L. (1953) 2001. *Philosophische Untersuchungen*. Darmstadt, DE: Wissenschaftliche Buchgesellschaft.
Wolff, C. 1739. *Theologia naturalis, methodo scientifica pertractata: Pars prior*. Frankfurt: Libraria Rengeriana
– 1746. *Theologia naturalis, methodo scientifica pertractata: Pars sexta*. Frankfurt: Libraria Rengeriana.
Zurbuchen, S. 1991. *Naturrecht und natürliche Religion: Zur Geschichte des Toleranzbegriffs von Samuel Pufendorf bis Jean-Jacques Rousseau*. Würzburg, DE: Könighasuen und Neumann.
– (1523) 1995a. "Auslegung und Begründung der Thesen oder Artikel." In *Huldrych Zwingli, Schriften. Band 2*, edited by T. Brunnschweiler and S. Lutz, 1–499. Zurich: Theologischer Verlag.
Zwingli, H. (1523) 1995b. "Wie Jugendliche aus gutem Haus zu erziehen sind." In *Huldrych Zwingli, Schriften. Band 2*, edited by T. Brunnschweiler and S. Lutz, 215–41. Zurich: Theologischer Verlag.

2 Multiple Early Modernities and "Educationalization": Reframing the Confessional Debate on Education, Politics, and Religion in Early Modern Europe

CARLOS MARTÍNEZ VALLE

In order to understand which characteristics of Protestantism determined modern schooling and politics, this chapter presents a study of the theology of John Calvin and Martin Luther, in particular their soteriological doctrines and the rejection of free will for their conception of the soul, which constitutes the subjectivity and dignity of the human beings. Calvin and Luther rejected free will and millenarianism and instead proposed rigorist, anti-modern approaches to reforming the individual (psychagogies) that opposed the values that supposedly have shaped modernity. In addition, I analyse and compare the theory and ideas of John Milton and those of their enemies, the Jesuits Molina and Suárez. Finally, I explore the divisions in "Catholicism" and "Protestantism" regarding two ideas that were central for many early modern educationalists and republican revolutionary politicians: free will and millenarianism. The comparison of Milton with Molina and Suárez brings to light the intra-confessional differences and inter-confessional similarities that turn "Protestantism" and "Catholicism" into terms of little use for historical analysis because they lead to overgeneralizations.

The Stanford current of neo-institutionalism, which is one of the most interesting theories used to understand the creation of mass schooling and school globalization, explains the creation and expansion of school through the existence of an educational ideology and culture that has become authoritative worldwide in the interstate system. For its authors, this culture is based on the Enlightenment and Protestantism (Boli, Ramirez, and Meyer 1985). Their thesis is further developed in a previous book (2012) and in the chapter in the present volume by Daniel Tröhler, who highlights the specific Protestant origins of the modern educational "languages" as based either on republican ideas of the free individual or on the cultivation of inner life (*Bildung*).

These "ways of understanding education" conceive of education as an instrument for solving social problems – educationalization that has been transferred and received worldwide, thereby moulding the modern understanding of education and educationalization.

With respect to this last argument, I collaborated with Jürgen Schriewer to test the thesis of an authoritative globalized educational discourse from a comparative perspective. In contrast to Stanford's and Tröhler's predictions, our analysis of the main twentieth-century educational journals in China, Russia/the Soviet Union, and Spain did not show the existence of a convergence around Western (North European and American) educational discourses or languages, but rather the re-creation of idiosyncratic educational and cultural references, problems and imaginaries – that is, the use of specific educational languages, which could be construed as part of different, multiple modernities (Schriewer and Martínez Valle 2003).

From a social system theory perspective, educationalization could be useful for analysing the diverging requirements and objectives of society, on one hand, and of the educational subsystem, on the other, a subsystem that has increasingly become functionally differentiated and self-referential (life-long; professionalized and scientized; steered by educational assessments that determine the central objectives in learning). However, education is a primary but still dependent social subsystem, and was even more so in early modern Europe, when social differentiation was just beginning (Luhmann 2002). Historically, it is a known fact that early modern schools supplied basic training for trade, bureaucracy, or armies, and, even when schools did not teach anything, they still provided a place to keep children out of the way. Educationalization, Tröhler maintains, originates in the Protestant emphasis on using schools for saving the students' souls, a social need different from learning. However, a wide academic consensus holds that early modern schooling in "Protestant" and "Catholic" spaces alike was directed to religious indoctrination and therefore, perhaps, the salvation of souls.

In this chapter, I would like to concern myself with the specific Protestant origins of modern educational discourses and educationalization. For Tröhler, educationalization derives from the possibility of the believers' souls communicating directly with God, without church mediation, through reading the Bible in the vernacular – the only way to salvation. Therefore, he argues, Protestantism would bring a new affirmation and cultivation of the self, the dignity of the human being, and would foster an active, responsible, and free human being, personal and social progress, political freedom, and civic culture.

In order to understand how Protestantism or Reformation influenced modern schooling and politics, I studied the theology of John Calvin and Martin Luther and contrast their words with the ideas sketched above. Like most religious currents of the time, Calvin and Luther's doctrine did not focus on schooling. Even if the need to indoctrinate the population into the new faith and to educate priests and civil servants forced religious confessional bodies to open schools, most of them proposed instruments for moulding and reforming the believers (and society) based on traditional ideas and praxis that I call *psychagogies* (i.e., instruments for guiding the soul). I analyse the religious, political, and educational ideas of John Milton and compare them with those of the Jesuits Molina and Suárez. Finally, I explore the divisions within "Catholicism" and "Protestantism" regarding two soteriological ideas that were central for many educationalists and republican revolutionary politicians in the early modern age: free will and millenarianism.

The Anthropologies of Luther and Calvin: *Sola Gratia* and Rejection of Free Will

In Tröhler's words, contemporary educational languages and educationalization as "particular culture," "mental pattern or reflex," or "currently dominant way to understand the world and the self" originated in two ideas from the Reformation that separates it from Catholicism: the "principle of *Sola scriptura* (by scripture alone), stating that God's message of salvation is mediated through the Bible and is, most importantly, in no need of completion by any institutionalized tradition," unlike in Catholicism. "Scripture alone," maintains Tröhler, also in this volume, is complemented "'by faith alone,' which is the idea that the sinfulness of human nature can be cured only by God's will and not by confession, good works," and so on.

This conception of the Bible as a message of salvation and worldly healing that is available to the believer should be, as everything in theology, carefully considered. In Luther's *The Bondage of the Will*, a response to Erasmus and one of Luther's central works, Luther maintains that the meaning and message of the Scriptures are clear: "For what thing of more importance can remain hidden in the Scriptures, now that ... the greatest of all mysteries brought to light, Christ made man: that God is Trinity and Unity: that Christ suffered for us, and will reign to all eternity? Are not these things known and proclaimed even in our streets?" However, he continues, if the scriptures "remain abstruse to many this does not arise from obscurity in the

Scriptures, but from their own blindness or want of understanding." Because "the truth is that nobody who has not the spirit of god sees a jot of what is in the Scriptures," as "the spirit is needed for the understanding of all the Scripture and every part of the Scripture" (Luther 1957, 70–4). Why, then, can human beings not understand the Bible without God's spirit?

The Lutheran principles *sola scriptura, sola fides, sola gratia* are connected on the one side with god's omnipotence and on the other with the conception of the human "enslaved will." God is almighty in the worldly and spiritual realms: "the will of God, which rules over our mutable will, is immutable and infallible ... And our own will, especially our corrupt will, cannot of itself do good." Therefore "whatever I have thought or done, whatever I shall achieve and possess, I see now that it is not the result of my industry, but was ordered long ago by Thy care" (Luther 1957, 81, 70). Therefore, Luther conceives of faith as the acceptance, given also by the spirit, "that god foreknows and wills all things, not contingently, but necessarily and immutably. [Without this acceptance] how can you believe confidently, trust to, and depend upon His promises?" And "if these things [human *servo arbitrio* and God's omnipotence] be not known there can be neither faith, nor any worship of God" (83–4).

God's omnipotence is linked to human *servo arbitrio*: "In things which pertain unto salvation or damnation, he has no 'Free-will' [the reunion of reason and will that allows independent choice and freedom] but is a captive, slave, and servant, either to the will of God, or to the will of Satan" (Luther 1957, 107). Therefore, as human beings are by themselves unable to believe the Gospel and as grace and faith (the Spirit) are freely given and are not gained by human efforts, salvation is by the grace of Christ through faith alone. Luther considers that the understanding of the scriptures cannot depend on human reason or will, which are so depraved and that make the undeserving progeny of Eve incapable of even asking for God's mercy, let alone of collaborating in their salvation.

Furthermore, Luther did not maintain that human nature "can be cured": it always remains sinful. The wrong doing of the chosen are from human nature; their salvation is from Christ, whose sacrifice redeems the soul of the chosen after the final judgment. For Luther, therefore, in pure soteriological terms, no human activity can achieve salvation – not preaching or the reading of the Bible, the cultivation of the soul, the development of discipline, or, for our purposes, schooling. Salvation occurs only at the final judgment. Indeed, nothing human is sound. Nothing human is requested for salvation, as, in his theocentric view, Luther, like Calvin, eliminated human agency or, rather, rejected it as sinful. Free will, if it exists, is sin because it is opposed to faith, and it gives no glory to God.

In his chapter, Tröhler implies that Protestantism liberates individuals from their medieval Catholic-Babylonian captivity, discovering an independent soul and therefore the (modern) self and educationalization: "This idea of the soul as the exclusive 'place' or 'space' of salvation – that is, as the only possible way of saving the soul from sin and its consequences, a way that is in no need of any institutionalized mediation and institutionalized rituals such as confessions or indulgences ... – has proven to be an engine in the educationalization of the world."

However, Luther and Calvin were adamant that the soul is not the place of salvation (whatever it means), because salvation happens only in God's heart. Furthermore, they didn't eliminate the church and the sacraments but continued to consider them necessary for sanctification (Towns 1969) – that's the reason they founded their respective churches. More important is the question of how this "Protestant conception of the soul" – which, according to Tröhler, would become "the crucial principle allowing the educationalization of the challenges or problems [associated with fundamental philosophical, social, and political transformations]" – would look if Luther and Calvin had rejected free will, the individual powers of reason and will. In other words, how could the discovery of the individual and its agency be linked to the rejection of two of its central powers?

Tröhler also maintains that Zwingli's theology, in particular, fostered political freedom and civic culture, as proved by his supposedly new defence of tyrannicide, which resulted in an educational language of the "good citizen." This conception contrasts with the rejection in orthodox Protestantism of free will, but also with the conception of justice resulting from predestination. God should be reverenced and respected even if he justifies or condemns freely without considering the relative merits of the saved and reproved. So, Luther states that God's justice is different from human justice and it is beyond our human understanding. The idea of justice, human agency, and human dignity are connected with free will. Indeed, as Luther himself stated, his theology, or for what matters Calvin's, was not a move "against papacy, purgatory, indulgences and such like trifles," but against free will, "the question on which everything hinges" (Luther 1957, 319; Hamm 1999; Ocaña 2000).

It is possible to more thoroughly analyse the meaning of free will for the magisterial reformers through the work of John Calvin. Although historians have neglected its practical content, Calvin's *Institution de la religion chrétienne* was more than a systematic theological treatise, a conversion method (books 1–3), and a guide for conscience in civil and religious matters (book 4). It was a manual for guiding the soul, a method for "reforming the intellect" and thereby society, a *psychagogy*. Calvin evaluated the different salvation doctrines and stated that he defends enslaved will (a thorough rejection of free will, which is based in the full depravity of human nature) and salvation by grace alone for its political consequences. He maintained that the mere idea of free will – that is, the ability of contention that allows moral rational deliberation about the options for acting responsibly – fosters human pride and rebellion against God's will (Calvin 1964b, 3: 297–308). Drawing on Augustinian anthropology (Bouwsma 1989), Calvin maintained that original sin destroyed human nature (reason and will), and therefore natural law and justice, making all of them fully depraved and abject.

Basing it on this Augustinian anthropology, Calvin proposed a method for reforming the soul, which he calls "penitential doctrine." Calvin asked the reader to compare human nature, which is "dirt and trash," with God. The meditation regarding the perversity of human nature, the sins and the angst of eternal condemnation, forces penitents to hate and reject themselves. This self-hatred leads to rejecting one's animal instincts, appetites, desires, reason, and will and to receiving God's will (the providence and vocation), laws (i.e., the Bible), and grace (theological virtues, in particular faith) (Calvin 1964, vol. 3; 1968). So, God governs the world through the apprehensions or fears of the conscience, evil, and Satan; through people's sins that pay other's sins (so every injustice received is only the payment of one's own wrong doings); through the Bible, vocation, and the providentially chosen churches and civil governments; and through elders and husbands, who should be revered, in accordance with Paul's Epistle to the Romans.

The motto *"sola scriptura"* means that the Bible "alone" – not individual reason, natural law, or papal decree – is the legal-moral binding norm, as in Luther's words in Worms – "imprisoned in God's word" (*gefangen in dem Worte Gottes*). In order to be aware of the perversity of human nature, the reformed believers needed to read the Bible and learn it by heart – that is, by imprinting the law on their heart (the organ of moral apprehension) and internalizing the prohibitions as deterrents of action (Martínez Valle 2008).

By rejecting free will, Calvin and Luther portrayed the rational deliberative conscience as always sinful. They believed that the sinfulness of one's conscience reduces it to a prosecutor of oneself (*accusator sui*); it cannot communicate with God. The rejection of human reason, self-dominion, power, and rational conscience implies the rejection of humans as being

God's image and, therefore, of human dignity. Furthermore, since rights in Calvin's day derived from faculties, rejecting free will implies rejecting the right to reason and know and to have dominion, self-government, and freedom in choosing in accordance with one's own conscience. This is the meaning of Luther's and Calvin's metaphor of the human being as a mule without self-determination, to be ridden either by God or Satan (Luther 1957, 103–4; Calvin 1964b, 3: 228, 240, 354).

Rejecting free will also means rejecting human virtues. Human beings can achieve, only by divine grace, the theological virtues of full faith in God; of hope that utter abnegation is a sign of election; and of charity, which is full abnegation to God and one's neighbour (Calvin 1960). Consequently, Calvin and Luther denied the ability of humankind to achieve the core of republican ideology. For scholars such as Skinner, then, there is nothing Protestant in modern resistance doctrines, as magisterial Protestantism considered that God "put all human beings under political subjection as remedy for their sins" (Skinner 1978, 321).

The equation of a religion of the Bible, schooling, and literacy is compelling. Confessional historiography has maintained the role of the vernacular Bible in Luther's theology as the source of his interest in education and his petitions to municipal authorities and princes to establish and maintain schools. Yet his motivations could have been more terrene. Like Bugenhagen, in his early writings Luther favoured forms of familiar and religious psychagogies (preaching). However, different reasons led him to support education under municipal or principal government. The need for bureaucratic and religious cadres made him support Latin schools and universities, which received much of his attention (Luther 1982). Humanist influence (for example, that of Melanchton or Sturm) was central to this position. People's indifference toward or ignorance of the new confession, and the need to indoctrinate them with Lutheran doctrines against Catholics, Anabaptists, and Calvinists, determined his pleading for vernacular schools. Confessionalization of the population of the evangelical principalities under the motto "Whose realm, his religion" (*cuius princeps eius religio*) was the driving force behind the passing of more than a hundred school rules (*Schulordnungen*), usually within church rules in different principalities and municipalities. These asked to establish or reform existing "German Schools" for girls and boys (Luther 2012; Strauss 1978). The curriculum consisted of the Commandments, the Lord's Prayer, the Creed, Luther's Catechism, and basic reading and writing. Reading or teaching the Bible directly had proven very dangerous. Except for the secular involvement that effectively allowed many of them to be established, these schools were hardly anything new: similar proposals were made, for instance, by the Alcalá Synod, in Spain (1480), and had been requested again at subsequent synods (Cruz and Perry 1992). Confessionalization, more than any religious idea, was the central force behind the educational impulse of the early modern age. However, a direct causal relation is difficult to establish: not only did schools not necessarily follow the introduction of the new confessions but also literacy (a proxy for schooling) seems more strongly determined by socio-economic and political factors. Religion is not an almighty factor. As an example, by the early eighteenth century, literacy rates in lowland Scotland had risen to one of the highest in Europe, thanks to the pressure of the Presbyterian Kirk. This literacy contrasts with the high degree of illiteracy in the Calvinist Cévennes (Furet and Ozouf 1982). Schooling and science were not Calvin's objective, as shown by his words: "I'd prefer that all human sciences would be exterminated rather than let them cool the zeal of the believers taking them from God's path" (Calvin 1964a, 600).

Conversing with God and cultivating the inner spirit were characteristics of the mystics whom Luther and Calvin condemned. Introspection, cultivation of the faith (gratis given), direct communication with God, and modern *Bildung* seem to me difficult to derive from enslaved will (*servo arbitrio*).

The Jesuit Molinists and John Milton: A Comparison

In this section, I compare the soteriology and theodicy, and educational ideas, but not the ecclesiology, of two archetypical expressions of "Catholicism" and "Protestantism": the Jesuits Luis de Molina and Francisco Suárez and the republican "puritan" John Milton, poet and defender of the first modern revolution (Kelley 1941; Hesselberg 1952). Although Molina and Milton prefer the noun "freedom" (freedom, liberty) or the adjective "free" (free individuals) to the term "free will," they define "free will" as an accumulation of different abilities grounding different freedoms. The basic freedom from necessity (Molina 1953; Milton 2017) implies the ability to choose spontaneously between different, contradictory options or to not choose (contradictory choice) ("The Art of Logic" in Milton 1953; Molina 1953). It means that humans are free from having to follow their base instincts and perverted wills, but rather can suspend choice, deliberate about the different options posed, and then choose in accordance with moral reason (deliberative conscience). Consequently, free will implies that humans can restrain their will and examine very different options without the choice being determined by the will (Molina's indifferent equilibrium (Nelli 1982); Milton's "even floor" for choosing (Milton 2017)). Therefore, under free will, reason presents, after deliberation, the greatest (moral) good to be chosen by the will. But to prevent the external imposition of the greater good (which would be the final result of all right free-will choices), Milton and the Jesuits defended freedom from coercion. In contrast to Calvin, Milton and the Jesuits considered that reluctant (*invitus*) choices, such as those elicited under coercion, do not achieve an effective conformity of will but, rather, a divided will (*voluntas divisa*) (Milton 2017; "De doctrina Christiana" and "The Art of Logic" in Milton 1953; Calvin 1964a; Suárez 1918).

For the Jesuits and Milton, this free will is an experiential fact that was accepted by Aristotle and Cicero (Molina 1953; Suárez 1966, 3: 332–3, 326–7) and a precondition for reason, for the cardinal virtues that lead to the theological ones, for human dignity and freedoms, and for God's justice and salvation ("De doctrina Christiana" in Milton 1953). Only free choice permits the existence of reason – "for reason is but choosing" or "reason is but Choice" ("Areopagitica" in Milton 1953, 526) – and of real virtue. Free will is the source of autonomy that constitutes humans as free agents, and in God's image. Therein lies human dignity and the ability to do good works. Merit is earned by the "works of faith," or plainly by "works" or "deeds," for these are the manifestations of obedience (Milton 2017; "The Art of Logic" and "De doctrina Christiana" in Milton 1953; Suárez 1966). Acceptance of free will determines other similarities in their theologies: God's indifferent concourse, inviting grace and prescience (Molina's *scientia media*; Milton's high foreknowledge) (Molina 1953; "The Art of Logic" and "De doctrina Christiana" in Milton 1953).

The main difference between Milton and the Jesuits in anthropology and soteriology is that Milton adopted a fully Pelagian understanding of the free will and considered that humans have enough restraint and that their (educated) faculties are strong enough for attaining perseverance and salvation (Milton 2017: VII). The Jesuits kept the Catholic doctrine of the need for the church's aids and sacraments in achieving perseverance. However, this opinion was debated within the order, as contact with pagans led sixteenth-century Catholic divines to ponder the need for the church's graces and stress salvation by good works (Döllinger and Reusch 1968).

The two Jesuits and Milton followed Cicero by maintaining that "the law is ... right reason." They linked humans' good, right deliberative reason and conscience, infused natural law, and divine law. Milton and the Jesuits considered conscience a probabilistic instrument that applies norms to the contingent reality in a probabilistic way, and maintained that conscience's mandates must be followed even if they contradict positive law. Milton rejects Presbyterian conscience and eternal predestination as cruel and immoral and leading to political submission (Molina 1953; Milton 2017; "The Doctrine and Discipline of Divorce" in Milton 1953; Milton 1991b).

Arbitral or "probabilistic" conscience is based on a prudent and benevolent interpretation of the law, as laws must be proportionate to human forces and directed to human good. God's laws bind because they are rational, good, and fair and they do not ask for overly harsh moral standards. Against rigorism, Suárez and Milton take Cicero's *De Inventione* and develop similar conception of justice as *epiky* (equity) for applying and fixing laws, divine, natural, and positive. Jesuit probabilism and Milton's charity put human freedom first with respect to following the spirit of the law and breaking it when its promulgation or articulation is deficient, when it conflicts with other laws, when it injures the common good, or when it is unfair or too harsh for a single individual. This charity allows Milton to ponder the value of the Bible and the Pauline epistles that state that positive law obligates in conscience and that breaking it is sinful, a basic Calvinist tenet ("The Doctrine and Discipline of Divorce," "Areopagitica," "Tetrachordon," and "De doctrina Christiana" in Milton 1953; Suárez 1918).[1] Upon this human freedom, reasonableness, dominion over oneself, conscience based on rational natural law, and charity-probabilism as an instrument of legal determination, Milton defends freedom of conscience, the rejection of Catholic and Protestant rigorism, and political freedoms. The application of free will by natural law languages following Aquinas (Sentences), Aristotle, Plutarch, or Cicero granted the right to break the unjust law and kill the tyrants – a doctrine followed also among Jesuits, as, for instance, in Juan de Mariana's *De rege et regis institutione*, published in 1598 (Martínez Valle 2008). There is nothing new or particularly Protestant in Zwingli's defence of tyrannicide that Tröhler considers central for a modern republicanism and citizenship leading to educationalization.

Free will and charity/probabilism were also central to the educational theories of Suárez, Molina, and Milton. They proposed a sensualist epistemology (impossible in magisterial Protestantism). Knowledge, which leads to virtue, is acquired from the senses. Following Aristotle, they consider that, around the age of seven or eight, children begin to accumulate the moral notices to begin to make moral choices. The maturation of reason and acquisition of moral experience continues until the coming of age at around thirteen to eighteen, when individuals should be considered responsible for their doings. Education should be guided by love, not fear, of God and humankind to "repair the ruins of our first parents" and to achieve virtuous individuals. Thus, free will, which Milton designates explicitly with the term *proairesis*, is both a precondition for (human nature is ruined but can be mended) and the objective of education. The justice principles of *epiky* and temperance should infuse educational practice, which should be consistent with the forces and abilities of children (Molina 1953; Milton 2016). Instruction should be invigorating and strict but also delightful. The Jesuits even made a conscious use of humour (eutrapelia) (Martínez Valle 2013). All of them drew heavily on humanism for their political and educational proposals (O'Malley 2000). They thought of education not only as a way to the theological virtues but also as a way to achieve worldly virtues in an active life. The Jesuits educated mainly religious and public cadres; Milton's curriculum was devoted to the rural gentry and army. All of them stressed the reading of the classic authors and the Church Fathers (among others, John Chrysostom and Basil the Great). Rhetoric (Cicero) became central in the curriculum (O'Malley 2000; Lewalski 1994).

The Jesuits discovered schooling in Messina (1548) and directed their work to it, but primarily they proposed the mystic enlightening way (*via iluminativa*) of the Spiritual Exercises for guiding the soul (psychagogy). For them, schooling was not only a way to achieve religious indoctrination but also a piece in the power relations between monarchs and churches directed to the construction of the modern state (*Konfessioanlissierung*). Furthermore, the Jesuits' impetus for schooling needs qualification, as in France they took over a net of already existing colleges and schools, whereas in Portugal they followed others' initiatives (Huppert 1984; Alden 1996).

Confessional Schisms and Religious Ideas of Early Educationalists and Republican Liberals: Free Will and Millenarianism

Traditional confessional literature maintains a clear divide between Catholicism and Protestantism based on soteriology (Wolf 1950). However, for obvious reasons of cultural inertia, the different views (Agustinian versus Pelagian) around the role of grace and free will for salvation that existed previous to the Reformation remained on both sides of the "Protestant"/"Catholic" divide. Not all "Protestants" shared Luther's or Calvin's doctrines of enslaved will, predestination, and salvation by grace, nor did all "Catholics" accept ideas about a semi-Pelagian free will and salvation by good deeds, as promulgated by the Jesuits. Radicalization and dogmatic differentiation took place not only between "Catholicism" and "Protestantism" but within them as well, with similar fury. Imposing orthodoxy was impossible, especially in the North, where centralized institutions were less powerful.

In "Catholic" spaces, the dispute around grace, unsettled in Trent, became a schism. The debates and mutual accusations of Pelagianism and Lutheranism between Dominicans and Jesuits continued in France in the seventeenth and eighteenth centuries between *Molinistes* and "Lutheran-like" Jansenists (Groethuyssen 1995).

Similar dogmatic fractures and political clashes took place in "Protestant" areas. In Switzerland, Calvin attacked the humanist rationalist anti-Trinitarians and defenders of free will Servet or the Sozzini. The evolution of the Genevan Church, from Calvin's and Beza's theocracies toward tolerance and intellectual freedom was aided not by Calvinists but by the heirs of the above-mentioned humanists (Trevor-Roper 1984).

In Holland, the appearance of Calvinism generated an immediate reaction. Arminius adopted the views of Erasmus and most probably of Molina's *Concordia*, who was recorded in his library (Bangs 1985; Dekker 1996). The religious-political differences between the Arminian party of Oldenbarnevelt and natural law philosopher Grotius, and the Calvinists led by the Prince of Orange, exploded at the Synod of Dort. The Calvinists held monarchical, absolutist, rigorist, and populist stances. The Arminians adopted republican, federal, tolerant, and morally relaxed positions. The Arminians were executed, imprisoned, and expelled.

In England, Cambridge Platonists adopted free will (Colie 1957). Locke and Milton, usually considered Puritans, were Arminians in soteriology and Arians-Socinians in theodicy. Any view that disregards the intra-confessional rifts falls into a fallacy of overgeneralization. For example, both John Milton and William Prynne have been considered Puritans, although the former was Arminian-Socinian and the latter Presbyterian, and they were ferocious enemies. Milton asked for a republic and the latter fought for a theocratic monarchy; he was lax on morals and asked for education, while Prynne was a rigorist who asked for the imposition of God's law (Martínez Valle 2008). Prynne (1650; 1659) accused the sectarians of being Jesuits in disguise. As in Holland, the defenders of free will and religious rationalism were closer to republican ideals, while Calvinists defended an anointed theocratic monarchy (Armitage, Himy, and Skinner 1995; Coffey 2008).

In Germany, even some of Luther's closest collaborators, such as Melanchton, distanced themselves from his soteriology. Following Melanchton, the Philippisten defended synergism, an "ability to apply to grace" or a concurrence in the conversion to God, which was opposed to Luther's ideas. This kindled a heated debate and violence, the *Synergistische Streit* (1556–61) (Stefan 2006). No wonder that the first "evangelical" defence of the right of resistance, *Die Notwehr Unterricht*, was Melanchthon's work.

Furthermore, the confessional literature ignores mysticism, another pre-reformed religious (soteriological) tradition that became a main actor in modern Europe's intellectual and social evolution. In particular, different forms of pre-millenarianism, in which the believer must pave the way for the second coming, seem to have had an important role for educational thinkers and revolutionaries, from Müntzer to the French *figuristes,* from Comenius to the group that, for the first time in history, asked for universal male voting rights, the Levellers and Diggers (Williams 1992; Fast 1962). Millenarian ideas existed prior to the magisterial reformers who condemned and persecuted millenarianism, as the Catholic Church also did (Cohn 1981).

The Catholic Church campaigned throughout the seventeenth century to suppress mysticism (for example, in its condemnation of Molinos) (Valente 1991). However, Fenelon and other Jesuits promoted a contemplative mysticism (*Quiétisme*), and monarchical-Jesuit repression led many Jansenist to adopt a pre-millennial theology that made the *figuristes* an important force in the Grand Revolution (Adam 1968).

Jon Amos Komenski was a bishop of the Moravian Church, which followed many ideas of the millenarian Jan Huss (Atwood 2009). Trevor-Roper maintains that Comenius and his associates John Dury and Samuel Hartlieb were not only educational writers but "the philosophers of the puritan revolution" (Trevor-Roper 1984).

Synergism and the Moravian Brethren's millenarianism influenced *Pietismus* through Arndt and Zinzendorf. Pietism, not the respective Lutheran churches, provided the ideas and personnel for Prussia's and Scandinavian's early school systems, and it was in this milieu that Pestalozzi was educated (Oelkers and Osterwalder 1995; Van Horn-Melton 1988). However, not the confessions but the absolutist monarchies, such as those of Prussia or the Habsburg Empire, which used religion for state formation, were the real promoters of modern universal schooling.

Conclusion

The utility of the concept of educationalization for studying education prior to functional differentiation is, in my opinion, very limited, since it is clear that the European early modern school, "Catholic" and "Protestant" alike, was meant to solve a social problem by taking care of children for several hours a day.

Schooling predated the Reformation and was advocated primarily by humanism and scholasticism. Most religious thinkers of the early modern period proposed other forms of soul direction (psychagogies) rather than the school. Calvin's and Luther's soteriology and theodicy draw on Augustine and were rather orthodox. Instead of advancing modern political and educational ideas, they advocated a form of anti-modern reformation of the psyche based on the ascetic *via purgativa*, which proposed the penitent's abnegation for "being sacrificed to God" and following God's will and calling (Maréchal 1927). Instead of easing access to the Bible, their schools were devoted to the indoctrination of indifferent or ignorant subjects under the norm *cujus princeps ejus religio* (Whose realm, his religion). Confessional historians tend to consider religion the repository of the central feelings and ideas that influence other ideas and practices of early modern Europe, but this conception should be nuanced. The interconfessional and interstate concurrence and the interrelation of confession and political power (confessionalization more than any soteriology) led churches and states to adopt schooling as an instrument of indoctrination. In many cases, the new religious schools were only the appropriation by these religious entities of existing municipal initiatives and institutions.

Although soteriological ideas alone do not explain schooling, more modern forms of school tended to be advocated by liberal theologians who relied on free will and antinomianism for advocating human educability, schooling, and political freedom. However, modern schools were created by absolutist monarchies for state-building purposes.

The two concepts of "Protestantism" and "Catholicism" do not exhaust the complex religious panorama of early modern Europe and even less the intellectual one. General concepts such as "Protestants," "Puritans," and "Catholics" tend to veil inner differences and historical transformations and changes. Forgetting confessions' internal divisions creates false attributions. So, for instance, while Samuel Puffendorf studied Lutheran theology, he disliked it and used the natural law language and ideas of Grotius and Suarez's Molinism, not Lutheranism, for asserting human dignity (Holland 2017; Müller 2011). Thus, as an example, to consider all Germans from Lutheran territories as Lutherans, and all northern Europeans as Protestants, could be the easiest form of the *post hoc ergo propter hoc* fallacy.

NOTE

1 In *The Doctrine and Discipline of Divorce*, Milton entitles Chapter 14 "That Beza's [Calvin's successor] Opinion of Regulating Sinne by a Politick Law, Cannot Be Sound."

REFERENCES

Adam, Antoine. 1968. *Du mysticisme á la révolte, les jansénistes du XVIIe siècle*. Paris: Fayard.
Alden, Dauril. 1996. *The Making of an Enterprise*. Stanford, CA: Stanford University Press.
Armitage, David A.H., and Quentin Skinner. 1995. *Milton and Republicanism*. Cambridge: Cambridge University Press.
Atwood, Craig D. 2009. *The Theology of the Czech Brethren from Huss to Comenius*. University Park: Pennsylvania State University Press.
Bangs, Carl O., ed. 1985. *The Auction Catalogue of the Library of James Arminius*. Utrecht: HES.
Boli, John, Francisco O. Ramirez, and John W. Meyer. 1985. "Explaining the Origins and Expansion of Mass Education." *Comparative Education Review* 29 (2): 145–70. https://doi.org/10.1086/446504.
Bouwsma, William J. 1989. *John Calvin*. Oxford: Oxford University Press.
Calvin, John. 1960. *Commentaires de Jean Calvin sur le Nouveau Testament*. Vol. 4. *Epître aux Romains*, edited by Paul Marcel. Geneva: Labor et Fides.
– 1964a. "Excuse de Iehan Calvin a Messieurs les Nicodemites." In *Ioannis Calvini Opera que supersunt omnia, Corpus Reformatorum*. Vol. 6, edited by Jean G. Baum, August E. Cunitz, and Edouard Reuss, 591–614. Frankfurt: Minerva.
– 1964b. *Ioannis Calvini Opera que supersunt omnia, Corpus Reformatorum*. Vols. 3–4. *Institution de la religion chrétienne*, edited by Jean G. Baum, August E. Cunitz, and Edouard Reuss. Frankfurt am Main: Minerva.
– 1968. *Commentaires de Jean Calvin sur le Nouveau Testament*. Vol. 2. *Évangile selon saint Jean*, edited by Paul Marcel. Geneva: Labor et Fides.
Coffey, John. 2008. *John Goodwin and the Puritan Revolution*. London: Thamesis.
Cohn, Norman. 1981. *En pos del milenio*. Madrid: Alianza Universidad.
Colie, Rosalie Littell. 1957. *Light and Enlightenment: A Study of the Cambridge Platonists and the Dutch Arminians*. Cambridge: Cambridge University Press.
Cruz, Anne J., and Mary Elizabeth Perry. 1992. *Culture and Control in Counterreformation Spain*. Minneapolis: University of Minnesota Press.
Dekker, Eef. 1996. "Was Arminius a Molinist?" *Sixteenth Century Journal* 27 (2): 337–52. https://doi.org/10.2307/2544137.
Döllinger, Johann, and Ferdinand H. Reusch. 1968. *Geschichte der Moralstreitigkeiten in der römischkatholischen Kirche seit dem 16. Jahrhundert*. Aalen, DE: Scientia-Verlag.
Fast, Heinold. 1962. *Der linke Flügel der Reformation*. Bremen, DE: C. Schünemann.
Furet, Francois, and Mona Ozouf. 1982. *Reading and Writing*. Cambridge: Cambridge University Press.
Groethuyssen, Bernhard. 1995. *La formación de la conciencia burguesa en Francia durante el siglo XVII*. Mexico City: Fondo de Cultura Económica.

Hamm, Bernd. 1999. "What Was the Reformation Doctrine of Justification?" In *The German Reformation*, edited by Charles Scott Dixon, 53–90. Oxford: Wiley-Blackwell.

Hesselberg, Arthur K. 1952. *A Comparative Study of the Political Theories of Ludovicus Molina, and John Milton*. Washington, DC: Catholic University of America Press.

Holland, Ben. 2017. *The Moral Person of the State*. Cambridge: Cambridge University Press.

Huppert, Georges. 1984. *Public Schools in Renaissance France*. Chicago: University of Illinois Press.

Kasa, Deni. 2016. "Arminian Theology, Machiavellian Republicanism, and Cooperative Virtue in Milton's *Paradise Lost*." *Milton Quarterly* 50 (4): 260–76. https://doi.org/10.1111/milt.12189.

Kelley, Maurice. 1941. *This Great Argument*. Princeton, NJ: Princeton University Press.

Lewalski, Barbara K. 1994. "Milton and the Hartlib Circle." In *Literary Milton: Text, Pretext, Context*, edited by Michael Lieb and Diana Treviño Benet, 202–19. Pittsburgh, PA: Duquesne University.

Luhmann, Niklas. 2002. *Das Erziehungssystem der Gesellschaft*. Frankfurt: Suhrkamp.

Luther, Martin. 1957. *On the Bondage of the Will*. Westwood, NJ: Revell.

– 1982. *An den christlichen Adel deutscher Nation*. Stuttgart: Reclam.

– 2012. *An die Ratsherren aller Städte deutschen Landes*. Munich: Grin.

Maréchal, Joseph. 1927. *Studies in the Psychology of the Mystics*. London: Burns, Oates and Washburne.

Martínez Valle, Carlos. 2008. *Anatomía de la libertad*. Madrid: Universidad Complutense.

– 2013. "Jesuit Psychagogies." *Paedagogica Historica* 49 (4): 577–91. https://doi.org/10.1080/00309230.2013.799505.

Milton, John. 1953. *Complete Prose Works*. New Haven, CT: Yale University Press.

– 1991a. "A Defence of the People of England." In *John Milton: Political Writings*, edited by Martin Dzelzainis and Claire Gruzelier, 146–55. Cambridge: Cambridge University Press.

– 1991b. "The Tenure of Kings and Magistrates." In *John Milton: Political Writings*, edited by Martin Dzelzainis and Claire Gruzelier, 204–46. Cambridge: Cambridge University Press.

– 2016. *Of Education*. http://www.dartmouth.edu/~milton/reading_room/of_education/text.shtml.

– 2017. *Paradise Lost*. http://www.dartmouth.edu/~milton/reading_room/pl/book_1/text.shtml.

Molina, Luis de. 1953. *Liberi arbitrii cum gratiae donis ... concordia*, edited by Johannes Rabeneck. Madrid: Sapentia.

Müller, Sascha. 2011. "Samuel von Pufendorfs Stärkung des neuzeitlichen Autonomiegedankens." *Theologische Quartalschrift* 191: 242–59.

Nelli, Sergio. 1982. *Determinismo e libero arbitrio da Cartesio a Kant*. Turin: Loescher.
Ocaña, Marcelino. 2000. *Molinismo y libertad*. Córdoba, ES: CajaSur.
Oelkers, Jürgen, and Fritz Osterwalder, eds. 1995. *Pestalozzi*. Weinheim, DE: Beltz.
O'Malley, John. 2000. "How Humanistic Is the Jesuit Tradition?" *Jesuit Education* 21, edited Martin R. Tripole, 189–201.
Prynne, William. 1650. *The Time-Serving Proteus, and Ambidexter Divine*. London: n.p.
– 1659. *The Re-Publicans and Others Spurious Good Old Cause*. London, n.p.
Schneemann, Gerhard. 1879. *Die Entstehung der thomistisch-molinistischen Controverse*. Freiburg, DE: Herders'che Verlagshandlung.
Schriewer, Jürgen, and Carlos Martínez Valle. 2003. *World-Level Ideology or Nation-Specific System-Reflection? Reference Horizons in Educational Discourse*. Lisbon: EDUCA.
Skinner, Quentin. 1978. *The Foundations of Modern Political Thought*. Vol. 1. Cambridge: Cambridge University Press.
Stefan, Michel. 2006. "Der Synergistische Streit." In *Politik und Bekenntnis*, edited by Irene Dingel, 249–78. Leipzig: Ev. Verlagsanstalt.
Stewart, Michael A. 2000. *English Philosophy in the Age of Locke*. Oxford: Clarendon Press.
Strauss, Gerald. 1978. *Luther's House of Learning*. Baltimore, MD: Johns Hopkins University Press.
Suárez, Francisco. 1918. *De legibus ac Deo legislatore*, edited by José Torrubiano. Madrid: Hijos de Reus.
– 1966. *Disputaciones metafísicas*. 7 vols. Edited by S. Rábade Romeo. Madrid: Editorial Gredos.
Towns, Elmer L. 1969. "Martin Luther on Sanctification." In *Articles*, edited by Elmer L. Towns, 115–22. Ann Arbor, MI: Liberty.
Trevor-Roper, Hugh R. 1984. *Religion, the Reformation, and Social Change*. London: Secker and Warburg.
Tröhler, Daniel. 2012. *Languages of Education: Protestant Legacies, National Identities, and Global Aspirations*. London: Routledge.
Valente, José Angel. 1991. *Variaciones sobre el pájaro y la red*. Barcelona: Tusquets.
Van Horn-Melton, James. 1988. *Absolutism and the Eighteenth-Century Origins of Compulsory Schooling in Prussia and Austria*. Cambridge: Cambridge University Press.
Williams, George H. 1992. *The Radical Reformation*. Kirksville, MO: Sixteenth Century Journal Publishers.
Wolf, Ernst. 1950. "Die Rechtsfertigungslehre als Mitte und Grenze reformatorischer Theologie." *Evangelische Theologie* 9 (1–6): 298–308. https://doi.org/10.14315/evth-1949-1-629.

3 Catholicism and Educationalization

ROSA BRUNO-JOFRÉ

In this chapter, I use a historical perspective to refer to the uses of education by the Catholic Church in the form of schooling, starting from early modernity. The church aimed at various times at cultivating a way of being Catholic, a way to deal with the social illnesses generated by poverty, a way to avoid deviation from the faith, and a means to carve out a Catholic social order within society. In this sense, the church was involved in processes of educationalization of its own, and with its own characteristics and meanings. These were sustained by Catholic conceptions of education. For example, from the late nineteenth century until Vatican II, Catholic education, particularly in North America, aimed at the cultivation of the "Catholic mind," created specific content in which neo-scholasticism was present, and had multiple purposes, some of which converged with the goals of the modern state. Confessionalization was at the core of educational intervention. There were historical shifts and even ruptures (for example, the ultramontane Vatican Council I (1869–70) and the paradigmatic change generated by Vatican II) that emerged from a confluence of internal and external variables over the *longue durée*. External variables included ways of dealing with late modernity, the intersection with the state-led education system, and new socio-economic demands. Even if confessional concerns were the driving force, Catholic schooling and its educational aims took different forms and institutional expressions to an important extent, as a result of the process of differentiation of functions of church and state and the unique contributions and charism of the congregations. Here, I am liberating the concept of educationalization from the specificity it acquired from its use to explain mostly state-directed processes linked to late modern contexts, in which it was mostly applied. I am expanding its use in this analysis in consideration of the variations and spaces within the church across time and place.

I would also like to question the assertion of Daniel Tröhler, in chapter 1 of this volume, that the Catholic Church – meaning here the magisterium – fully mediated the soul. Educationalization processes led by the church and its various congregations were mediated not only by the official doctrine of the church but also by emerging contextual, theological, and social configurations; individual agency (free will) also played a role in moulding educational efforts, in spite of moments of repressive policies. (See Carlos Martínez Valle's chapter for a discussion of free will.) My review of historical turning points is intended to unsettle any notion of "sameness" and uniformity in the church, and thus move us toward understanding it as a multifarious institution. I also assume here that any form of education implies socialization, content, purpose, aims, and practices of self-regulation (Bridges 2008); consequently, the extension of educational practices and pedagogies/andragogies to solve emerging social issues in principle does not appear in contradiction with the teaching of the faith and the social teaching of the church.

To elucidate my points, I will discuss historical moments in the intersection of the church and its plurality of cultural formations with modernity, with educational intervention as a point of reference. The spatial, geographical, and configurative contexts of this chapter are limited to the Western world. The journey goes from early modernity (the sixteenth to the eighteenth centuries) through what is called the long nineteenth century (for the purposes of church history, from the French Revolution to 1958, when Pius XII died (O'Malley 2008, 54)) and concludes with "the long 1960s" (a term coined by Marwick (1998), indicating the period between 1958 and 1974). Starting from the mid-1970s, neoliberalism became extensive in Western politics and economics, and the Holy See reacted against liberation theology – a perspective, emerging from people's experience of oppression in Latin America, that would nourish the movement of popular education in the 1970s and early 1980s with a strong, grassroots, political educational intentionality.[1]

The last part of the chapter discusses the epistemic break in the church in the "long 1960s" and alternative practices in adult education developed by Catholics in Brazil that would use educationalization as a counter-hegemonic political tool. I do not disagree with Tröhler's position that the educationalization of the world, as he says, developed as a mentality, although I do not elaborate on this point.

An Overview of Catholic Thinking and Its Insertion in Early Modernity

As Braudel has put it, "Western Christianity was and remains the main constituent element in European thought – including rationalist thought, which although it attacked Christianity was also derivative from it" (1993, 333). He was referring to the early efforts by St Augustine to bring together faith and intelligence, classical and Christian civilization, and the notion of embracing faith after deep personal reflection, and was pointing to the ethical tenets and the mentality characterizing the Western world. I would further qualify this, by saying that his statement is applicable only up until late modernity.

In the twelfth and thirteenth centuries, a notion of individuality had emerged that took shape in Renaissance humanism in a return to the classics and the discovery of life. The thirteenth century brought the efforts of Dominican theologian Thomas Aquinas (1225–1274), who, as Watson (2005, 330) notes, helped to ground the fundamentals of the West with his attempt to reconcile Christianity with Aristotle and the classics; before Aquinas, the world was perceived as having meanings and patterns only in relation to God. Aquinas brought, at least in principle, the possibility of a natural and secular outlook, by distinguishing between nature and supernature, nature and grace, and reason and revelation; an objective study of the natural order was possible, since there was a natural, underlying order of things (330).[2] Aquinas recovered the classics within a context in which belief in God was a given; he strongly believed that faith and reason could be united (331). The Aristotelian inspiration also underscored the notion of woman as passive "underling," and the rule of men over women, which has been a powerful hallmark of neo-scholasticism and of the Catholic Church. Neo-scholasticism – a form of neo-Thomism – refers to a reading of Aquinas mediated by the magisterium (the Holy See) that would be at the core of Catholic education in the official church discourse of the long nineteenth century.

Whereas Aristotelianism led to the scholastic mind, Platonism provided humanists with a world view (Watson 2005, 397). However, there was no abrupt rupture from medieval Christianity in terms of ideas. Renaissance humanism would have an impact on education and, more specifically, Catholic education, and in particular on the Society of Jesus (O'Malley 2013), especially through Desiderius Erasmus (1466–1536). Erasmus advocated a reform of piety through the interior appropriation of feelings, and a reform of schooling in line with the student-centred and ethically oriented philosophy of the humanists.

The establishment of the Society of Jesus represented a leading moment in the way Catholicism embraced education in its interaction with the modern world after the Reformation. The society, founded by Ignatius of Loyola, was approved by the pope in 1540; within a decade, it had developed education as a ministry, which made it distinctive.

As O'Malley has written, "Ignatius's decision inaugurated a new era in Roman Catholicism for formal education" (2014, 13). Situated within the context of the Reformation, the operation of full-fledged schools (in the case of the society, for any male student) as a primary ministry was followed in time by many religious orders. The schools were complex institutions with classrooms, astronomical observatories, courtyards, and theatres, and were "for everybody poor or rich," according to Ignatius (14). Some Jesuit schools qualified as universities very early on. The influence of Thomism as well as Renaissance humanism was clear in the curriculum: the pagan classics of ancient Greece and Rome, including drama, were studied, and classical rhetoric was important. The *Ratio Studiorum* (the official plan for Jesuit education) showed a combination of scholasticism and humanism; of course, the students studied the classical languages, but some works were translated into the vernacular. An important goal was to think clearly, and the schools' spiritual exercises were rooted in educational principles of self-activity, adaptation to the individual, and mastery of the subject. Discernment (in the Jesuit tradition) as a habit of mind and a spiritual inclination was central to the inculcation of virtues within the parameters of faith.

O'Malley has made the point that, when the Council of Trent (1545–63) met, it was widely believed that "'the well-being of Christianity and of the world would depend on the proper education of youth,' that is, education in the Humanistic mode" (O'Malley 2013, 45). By the time the council closed, the Jesuits already had a network of humanistic schools throughout the Catholic world. The Jesuits' "intended force" behind the network of schools can be understood only in light of the influence of humanism, the impact of the Reformation, the founder's original intuition, and his group's theological explorations.

The Council of Trent was aware of the power of education to regulate life, keep the faithful in the flock, and avoid deviations from Catholic doctrine. The council, which was so reactive and conservative in its decrees, issued a decree in 1547 in response to Luther's teaching of "justification by faith alone." The decree affirmed that both free will and grace (undeserved help from God to respond to the call of the individual) were operative in the soul, although it did not explain how they worked (O'Malley 2014). The failure of the decree to fully explain the issue led to an exploration directed at solving the problem in light of the ideological configurations of the time. For example, the Spanish Jesuit Luis de Molina (of the Salamanca School) published *Concordance of Free Will with the Gifts of Grace* in 1588, which generated a controversy with the Dominicans, who thought that Molina's emphasis on free will was heresy. The point here is that the Jesuits retained a bias toward free agency; they would continue to hold this view even into the nineteenth century, in spite of a shift toward strong conservative positions (O'Malley 2014; Martínez Valle 2007).

Meanwhile, another Spanish Jesuit from the Salamanca School, Francisco Suárez, who wrote *Tractatus de Legibus ac Deo Legislatore* (Treatise on the Laws and God the Legislator, 1612), argued that all power comes from the community, making the community an authority in itself, based on common consent. He also redefined the papal position as a sovereign as being on par with other sovereigns, not above them. Overall, at the time, after the breakdown of Christendom, many sources emphasized the secular side of politics and ideas of individual liberty (Watson 2005).

In the seventeenth century, as a renewed response to the Reformation, efforts at educational intervention through forms of schooling and even pedagogization of the faith began to take shape. Thus, for example, Nicholas Barré, founder of the Institute of Charitable Teachers, as well as his spiritual advisee Jean Baptiste de La Salle, founder of the Institute of the Christian Brothers, developed methods through which to evangelize and instruct in the three Rs. The little-explored thought and work of Barré represent an important moment in the history of Catholic educational intervention, with the purpose being to keep the faithful in the flock and to solve social problems emerging from economic dislocation.

Catholic Popular Schools in Seventeenth-Century France: Situating Nicholas Barré (1621–1686)

The seventeenth century was a time of theological renewal and conflict within the framework of the encounter between religion and politics, as conveyed by disputes related to Jansenism, anti-Jansenism, and theological Gallicanism, which had old roots in the eighth and ninth centuries. Jansenism is a designation derived from Flemish bishop Cornelius Jansen, author of *Augustinus*, published in 1636. Jansen's position needs to be understood within the context of debates over the relationship between God's grace and humans' free will. Jansen intended to restate the fourth-century position on grace advanced by St Augustine, and insisted on the crippling impact of original sin on human will, which needed to be motivated by grace. The movement, which reached beyond France and extended well into the nineteenth and early twentieth centuries, was linked to moral rigorism, an element that persisted over time. This element included the fear of a drastic God and the need for sacrifice and reparation for sins. Current research identifies that, in its origins, Jansenism had modernist/reform elements and was a threat to Rome and Versailles (Sedgwick 1990). In this line of thought, contemporary scholars have interpreted Jansenism as favouring the rights of the individual consciousness, advocating direct contact with the Bible, supporting a major role for women in the church, and understanding the church as an assembly of the faithful (Hildesheimer 1992). Nonetheless, Jansenists were in direct confrontation with the Jesuits, who were accused of putting too much emphasis on reason rather than on scripture, and who used probabilism as their preferred form of moral reasoning, taking a lax approach to morality (O'Malley 2014). Rome condemned Jansenism, but its influence in the form of moral rigorism persisted. As for Gallicanism, Susan Smith has written: "Gallicanism is best defined as a complex of ecclesiastical and political doctrines and practices which sought to restrict papal power in the French Catholic Church, and which advocated that the Pope be subject to ecumenical councils" (2010, 272). Meanwhile, along with processes of colonization, women and men congregations began to move across the Atlantic to the Americas, and even to the Far East, and engage in unexpected processes of educationalization.

The seventeenth century was a complex time of renewal for French theology, beyond the disputes generated by Jansenism, anti-Jansenism, and Gallicanism, although the terms of the debate were in the air. Some of the leading voices, including Nicholas Barré, Jean Eudes, Vincent de Paul, Jean Jacques Olier, and Jean Baptiste de La Salle, among others, saw the need to open to the social needs of the world around them. In addition, it became clear that women religious without enclosure were needed to support the Catholic effort toward the educationalization of the poor. The Council of Trent's decision to exclude consecrated women from the active apostolate and Pius V's decrees of the mid-sixteenth century were still in effect in the seventeenth and eighteenth centuries.[3] In 1661, Nicholas Barré, a Minim friar,[4] initiated a campaign from the pulpit to collect money for popular schools, and called for both male and female teachers. In 1666, he established an Institute of Charitable Teachers in Rouen – the future Sisters of the Holy Infant Jesus – without vows or enclosure, and under the direction of a superior (see article 5 of the statutes of the institute) (Barré 1997).[5] The institute was a way to deal with the church's exclusion of women from the active apostolate. This was not the first time such action had been taken; for example, in 1634, Vincent de Paul had founded the Daughters of Charity, which had annual vows and no enclosure.

Barré had been educated by the Jesuits and kept a strong attachment to processes of "discernment" in his pedagogy, and, in the preparation of his teachers, put great emphasis on the individuality of the child. The latter idea was inspired by the spirituality of the seventeenth century that centred on the infant Jesus, although new notions of childhood had appeared by late medieval times.

What was unique about Barré? He established free schools in villages and small towns. He did not pursue individualized instruction but rather simultaneous instruction graduated by age, and he tried to limit the number of students in a school to a maximum of seventy. He gave importance to records of registration and to information about the girls and boys and their parents. Barré engaged lay teachers, and the teaching was in the vernacular. The schools had a strong religious component, with its materiality expressed in blessed water and religious symbolism and representations, as well as in religious rituals marking daily life in the school. The teachers taught arithmetic (with cards), the alphabet and reading with movable letters to form words, as well as history, geography, singing, and catechism. There were timetables and organized classes, and punctuality was very important. The schools provided practical skills to enable children to have a future place in society, and the schools functioned as catechetical centres after instruction time. There were workshops for women, and Barré opened schools of manual work for girls, as well as Sunday schools for everyone.[6] Institute seminars for the preparation of teachers had the function of what we would come to know much later as normal schools: the Charitable Teachers had to be prepared for their role and be engaged in ongoing religious and instructional studies. These teachers were not subordinated to the clergy, although they were under the overall authority of the archbishop or bishop of the diocese (Bruno-Jofré 2017b).

What was behind Barré's creation of popular schools? The "spirit of the Institute was the salvation of souls and Christian [Catholic] instruction was the means, but the teaching of the doctrine appeared linked to the daily problems of poor people in villages and small towns, to their needs" (Moretti 1935). A practical, utilitarian dimension was clearly expressed in the provision of skills. Moreover, Barré was not the only one with this utilitarian focus, which was a response to the Reformation and processes of de-Catholization but also to the social situation of the time. The schools covered a need, specifically the lack of schooling opportunities for poor girls. It was a form of confessionalization taking on the tones of educationalization.

Barré made a serious attempt to organize the schools using modern elements to achieve Catholic goals, mainly the forming of a Catholic soul. The spirituality of the century permeated the work of Barré and others, as did notions of personal spiritual discernment and of spaces of action, all of which came out of the major debates of the century. The notion of the school as integrated with the community, and as a place of reunion, had to do with the understanding of the church as the centre of the village, which was dominant in the seventeenth century (Dupuy 1997). Barré himself was submerged in a baptismal spirituality, referring to the notion that Christian people can respond to the perfection received when they are baptized.

Other projects also involved the opening of popular schools; some were inspired by Barré, while others emerged as independent projects. These schools were not limited to France. One example is the Pius Schools funded by José de Calasanz, who opened his first school in Rome in 1597. These were elementary free schools, but the teachers were priests and the language of teaching was Latin, thus preparing students for secondary school.

The number of Barré's schools for girls grew rapidly, but he had difficulties succeeding with the male group of Charitable Teachers running the schools for boys that he had founded in 1681. Barré was spiritual advisor to Jean Baptiste de La Salle (1651–1719), and de La Salle received the male Charitable Teachers in his home in 1682. In 1684, de La Salle, after intense correspondence with Barré and a visit with him in Paris in 1683, became the founder of the Institute of the Christian Brothers, which would provide free elementary and religious instruction in the vernacular language to poor boys. De La Salle's schools, still well placed in the system today in various parts of the world, had characteristics similar to Barré's schools, such as teaching in the vernacular, control of space and time, programming, a system of grades organized by age, and the teaching of practical skills.[7] The principles were further developed with the creation of professional training or vocational schools, which offered subjects such as drawing, bookkeeping, agriculture, and mechanics and thereby established the first technical professional schools (Dávila, Naya, and Murúa 2013). The goal was not only to teach skills but also to instil Christian (Catholic) virtues, and historians have referred to *The Conduct of Christian Schools*, a compilation of de La Salle's principles, as Lasallian pedagogy (ibid.).

In contrast to Barré, who is not known in pedagogical circles and whose experience and initiatives have been neglected in the history of education, de La Salle's work and thought are well studied. It may be that the Lasallian schools had greater continuity in terms of their goals and character. Yet the institute created by Barré generated two teaching congregations – the Sisters of the Holy Infant Jesus, St Maur, with a base in Paris, and the Sisters of the Holy Infant Jesus, Providence, with a base in Rouen – which founded prestigious private schools.

It is clear that the sixteenth and seventeenth centuries showed a shift in intentionality with respect to education. Key figures attempted to develop networks of popular schools where the teaching of catechesis was very important. The underlying purpose of Barré and de La Salle and other founders was the protection of the "true faith" and securing salvation. Not unrelated was their commitment to provide practical skills and to improve the social conditions of the poor. The Jesuits started their schools with the goal of attracting boys from all social classes; in this they were initially successful, even though, over time, given their secondary programs, they became known for forming a Catholic intellectual class. However, all the schools I have mentioned here, and many others in Europe and in the United States, as well as sisters' efforts to educate girls within the limitations of consecrated women, integrated components that would characterize the modern school (Bugnard 2006). These include control of time (timetables) and space (classrooms), discipline, norms of life (in the Lasallian and Barré schools, these norms were suited to urban life), obedience to ethical rules, calendars, programs, and teacher preparation (Bruno-Jofré 2017b; Dávila, Naya, and Murúa 2013). Depaepe and Smeyers (2012) refer to the innocence of childhood as being another focus of the modern school. This notion was quite relevant within the spirituality of early modernity in Europe that underlined educational work, in particular among the Jesuits. The network of schools created, although not modern in the sense of modern states, aimed at reforming the intellect and changing social conditions within the framework of confessionalization.

At the Intersection with Modernity: The Church in the "Long Nineteenth Century"

The eighteenth century saw the burgeoning of a scientific and philosophical movement that opposed the church in the name of progress and reason, and, of course, witnessed the experience of 1789 and the years that followed (Braudel 1993). Immanuel Kant (1724–1804) made it clear that while, in the pursuit of knowledge, we can make certain claims *a priori*, they are about reality as it is experienced, thus stressing subjectivity and a moral concept of progress. While he considered Christianity a loving religion and accepted its basic tenets, he opposed its supernatural elements (Watson 2005, 521). In the previous century, René Descartes (1596–1680) had established the first systematic and modern critical appraisal of knowledge in the seventeenth century; but, in the crossing over from the eighteenth to the nineteenth century, as Watson puts it, a threshold was passed that led to modern science and the questioning of prejudice and pre-logical thinking. The idea of knowledge as a virtue advocated by the Enlightenment and the assumption that knowledge had an emancipatory character were further pushed by the educational optimism of Romanticism, starting with Rousseau. There was a change of attitude toward human awareness. The scientific examination of the mind during the Enlightenment was empirical and epistemological, with a focus on the senses and cognitive development; the Romantics, starting with early Romantic Rousseau's *Confessions*, a response to Augustine's *Confessions*, showed an interest in human consciousness, with a sense of self-awareness and the complex nature of the human self (Tarnas 1991).

Voltaire, in *The Century of Louis XIV* (1751), and David Hume, in *The History of England* (1778), each questioned dogmatic Christianity as the central theme of historical change (Watson 2005, 546). The establishment of political economy by the end of the eighteenth century, with Adam Smith's *The Wealth of Nations* (1776), signalled the profound economic changes that were taking place. Following the upheavals of the 1700s, dramatic changes brought about by the Industrial Revolution and accompanied by new forms of capitalism (including banking and financial capitalism), credit, new social classes, widening of world markets, intense processes of colonization, and human exploitation framed the mid-nineteenth century. Modernity took on new shapes by late in the century, and these came along with the dominant presence of science, a revised view of cognition, the critique of knowledge, the theory of evolution, and the international movement of ideas and people. Complex configurations of ideas, social unrest, and movements of people nested the politics of modernity and identity. The church had to navigate through these configurations.

How did the church place itself in this new milieu and in the aftermath of Jansenism and Gallicanism? And how would its positioning influence its educational work, which was becoming extensive? The reaction from the Holy See took shape in the encyclical *Quanta Cura*, with the appended document *Syllabus Errorum* (1864) of Pope Pius IX (1846–72), who took a strong position against the "errors" of the time: socialism, liberalism, rationalism, and separation of church and state. The pope felt that these doctrines were a threat to the papal monarchy (Christensen 2011). The Society of Jesus, which had been suppressed in 1773 by Clement XIV and their schools dismantled, and then was re-established by Pius VII in 1814, supported the *Syllabus*. The Jesuits even helped draft it, in an attempt to avoid a reconciliation of Catholicism with "progress, liberalism, and modern civilization" (McGreevy 2016, 17). (The Jesuits left aside their previous stands of the seventeenth and eighteenth century, when they occasionally sided with bishops, and moved into full loyalty to the pope.) The church's reaction marked the establishment of a neo-scholasticism mediated by the Vatican, which in turn was influenced by sixteenth- and seventeenth-century thinkers who conceived of theology as a "system of thinking." This Aristotelian theology sustained the thesis of an objective divine order and a theology separated from the world and from history (Mettepenningen 2010).

The ultramontane papal-centrist view that dominated the Vatican I Council (1869–70) was expressed in the *Pastor Aeternus* (the first Dogmatic Constitution on the Church of Christ), which declared the teaching authority of the pope on faith and morals to be infallible (Misner 2000; Smith 2010). This position was also supported by the Jesuits, as well as by the constitution *Dei Fillius*, which insisted that the magisterium – the teaching authority of the church – was the authentic interpreter of the Bible and rejected the autonomy of reason. Proponents saw this authoritarian approach as necessary in what the church construed as evil times. Anti-modernist positions did not lose their continuity with Pope Leo XIII (1810–1903), who affirmed that "scholastic philosophy be made the basis of the sacred sciences" (Jodock 2000, 6). Scholars have traced a continuity of thought within the church against rationalism and secularization and increasing centralization (Misner 2000). The Vatican position was fully conveyed in the 1907 Pius X encyclical *Pascendi Dominici Gregis*, in which the pope condemned "modernism" as the "synthesis of all heresies." This broad condemnation "virtually slammed the door on any historical study of the Bible, on theological creativity, and on church reform" (Jodock 2000, 1).

The pope's words exemplified the intention to suppress any expression of modernity and its agnostic, immanentist, and evolutionist criticism (Jodock 2000, 6): modernists were enemies of the church, and endorsing one aspect of a modernist idea implied the endorsing of the whole. The Catholic revival of the nineteenth century took place within this context and acquired its own features. In this process, the language of rights – present since late medieval and early modern Catholic ethical and political thinking, though neglected in the eighteenth century – was completely rejected by Pius IX's *Syllabus* and the Thomist neo-scholasticism that followed. A language of duties took over and, of course, permeated the Catholic language of education.

Leo XIII articulated social Catholicism, already in practice, in his encyclical *Rerum Novarum* (1891). Social Catholicism was relevant to the extension of Catholic education beyond schooling and the building of a political-pedagogical discourse. Social Catholicism had emerged in earlier centuries as part of the struggle of grassroots leaders, congregations, and faithful people with social moral problems caused by economic changes and crisis, and by religious and cultural tensions (Schuck 2005). The encyclical gathered that work. *Rerum Novarum* was traditionalist in character – for example, the pope did not endorse autonomous labour unions but recommended pious associations under the direction of the clergy. This approach was not very acceptable to the modern world because the point of reference would be the hierarchical papal authority (Misner 2000). However, the encyclical played a role in the new shape taken by sectors within Catholicism in many countries from the end of the century, whether it was a Catholic labour movement in rivalry with socialists and communists, lay organizations with socio-educational missions, sodalities related to teaching congregations (for example, the Jesuit Sodality of Our Lady) that did service work, or, of course, political parties (ibid.). In many places the church was an ally of conservative forces, as was the case in Chile at the beginning of the twentieth century, but there were voices and organized activities that, inspired by *Rerum Novarum*, advocated for a just social order. The pastoral social work of Fernando Vives del Solar in Chile, who had great conflicts with the Chilean hierarchy and the Conservative Party, is a case in point. In his view, "a Christian cannot claim to have charity in his or her heart while despising justice" (Bruno-Jofré 2013a, 716).

But it is important to further contextualize the consolidation of neo-scholasticism. The modernist crisis started under Leo XIII and can be defined as the suppression of a theological approach – construed as modernist by the Vatican – the developers of which tried to integrate a historical-critical method into their scientific research (Mettepenningen 2010). In its variations, the new ("modernist") theological approach is understood by historians as an attempt to bring Catholic thought into contemporary times and to partially abandon neo-scholasticism as an exclusive conceptual framework (21). However, the Vatican saw the modernists as a threat to the doctrine of the faith, due to their emphasis on subjectivity, experience, evolution, and relativity of knowledge. Indeed, from *Aeterni Patris* (1879) to the 1920s, neo-scholasticism was established as the church's only accepted intellectual conceptual framework during its time of anti-modernist struggle (ibid.). As McCool (1989, 29) has put it, Leo XIII, in *Aeterni Patris*, recommended the philosophy and theology of St Thomas as the "structuring elements of a Catholic liberal education." The encyclical aimed at the integration of arts and sciences "by the believing mind under the guiding light of theology" (ibid.). This aim was at the core of the idea of the "Catholic mind" that was in line with the notion of Catholic education cultivated by Cardinal Newman, and that was largely fostered by the Jesuits

(Elias 1999; McCool 1989). In this view, people had a rational spiritual nature and a supernatural destiny, transcending every element in the universe (Elias 1999).

This approach was rooted in the dominant Western cosmology and its hierarchies, which, together with the notion of truth at the core of Catholic theology, set the basis for otherness and seeing the other as a victim, as evident in the educational dimension of the processes of colonization. The aim of education was salvation and to enable in students the power of mind and will so that they might reach salvation. In many respects, neo-scholasticism responded to empiricist philosophies of education, which viewed education as instrumental for other purposes. The 1929 encyclical of Pope Pius XI, *Divini Illius Magistri* (On Christian Education), underlined the neo-scholastic position of the church on education and was much in line with *Aeterni Patris*. Article 15 declares that "education belongs preeminently to the Church, by reason of a double title in the supernatural order, conferred exclusively upon her by God" (Pius XI 1929).

One note of caution: there were educational traditions within the church that competed with those of Thomism and neo-scholasticism. Such was the case with the Benedictine and the Franciscan traditions (Elias 1999), which are evident in the characteristics of missionary work in the Araucanía region of Chile, as discussed in chapter 15 by Serrano and Ponce de León in this volume.

In practice, some archdioceses strictly followed the Vatican's instructions (see, for example, the discussion in chapter 7 by Stafford in this volume, in relation to religious education in Ontario), at least in terms of policies. Others, like that in New York City, and specifically in the case of the Corpus Christi School, show us a more complex reality. Dogmatism is reflected in books used in religious education, such as *Bible Studies*, originally published in 1881 and used in high schools in Ontario until the 1950s. It was a book in which prejudice – including statements offensive to the Jewish people – and otherness were explicit. Yet educational practice developed its own contours at its intersection with educational states as well as place and time, and in relation to the charism and agency of congregations and individual leaders. Outside the walls of the Vatican and without its approval, between the 1920s and 1950s, there was a pluralization of neo-Thomism (deviating from official neo-scholasticism) that was accentuated from the 1930s onward, with theologians going directly to Thomas Aquinas's work. Parallel to this development was the growth of phenomenology (in the work of Edmund Husserl) and existentialism (in the work of Martin Heidegger and Carl Jaspers), from which interpretations of perception and experience reached Catholic theology and influenced, in particular, the personalism of Emmanuel Mounier. The movement known as *nouvelle théologie* had its starting point in 1935, when the Dominican Yves Congar wrote an article entitled "Déficit de la théologie" (Deficit in the theology). This theological current, censured by Rome in its early phases, and yet a precursor of Vatican II, reconnected Catholic theology to historical reality and daily life. Its latest phase converged with Vatican II, and several representatives of *nouvelle théologie* were present at the council as *periti* or experts (for example, Congar, de Lubac, and Daniélou).[8]

Until Vatican II, a papal-centralist approach to education grounded in neo-scholasticism was in operation, along with the old integrist notion embodied in the concept of "Catholic mind" that permeated higher levels of education. However, apart from theological developments that often reached beyond strictly theological circles, in spite of a lack of approval from the Vatican, missionary insertion in the field and interactions with cultural and political contexts generated idiosyncratic understandings and practices of education, as well as complex agendas. In other words, we encounter complex idiosyncratic processes that could be conceptualized under the umbrella of Catholic educationalization of the faith. That is the topic of my next segment.

The Intersections of Catholic Directives with Place and Time: The Impact of Field Experience

The nineteenth century witnessed a widespread missionary movement, both Catholic and Protestant. Within the context of processes of colonization, religious missionaries found a space for their vocation, which included a civilizing mission – an educational arm of colonialism – and which also provided education and social and health services to settlers. In a world of missions, a renaissance of older orders, such as the Carmelites, Benedictines (1837), and Dominicans (1839), a restitution of the Jesuits (1814), and an emergence of new male congregations with an international call, such as the Marists, Marianists, Oblates of Mary Immaculate, and Fathers of the Holy Cross, among others, were taking place.

Hundreds of active apostolic congregations were founded, particularly congregations of women, which would move to various parts of the globe to assert Catholic values in a modernizing and secularizing world. In the nineteenth and twentieth centuries, 1,861 religious institutes were founded, half of these in Spain, Italy, and France (Chico 2000). In the end, the original intentionality or "illocutionary force" framed by neo-scholasticism took on various meanings in the process of trying to keep a Catholic social order, by creating moral agents through schooling while interacting with modernity and assuming local Catholic agendas (Bruno-Jofré 2013a). Catholics engaged in a confessional form of subjectification that aimed at cultivating relational pastoral power.

The establishment of public schooling in Canada in the mid-nineteenth century was one of the administrative mechanisms involved in the process of developing a modern state and in the realization of a project that Ian McKay (2000) has conceptualized as one of liberal rule that, in its articulation, preserved, cancelled, or transformed many social and political realities. Curtis (1992, 5) has defined this period as one of centralization and state formation, involving the creation of systematic social policies (bureaucratization), often using local government bodies and management agencies. Public schooling in Canada was rooted in a Protestant world view and had an assimilationist thrust, with a view, for example, to building a Canadian heritage centred on Canada as a member of the "great British Empire." The example of a counter-discursive process of educationalization that I will use here is the resistance in Franco-Manitoban communities (in the province of Manitoba), where, in 1897, public funding for confessional schools ended, along with the official status of French in the province as the language of one of the "founding" nations. Community leaders and the church made an organized effort to carve out a space in the system and keep the French language and the Catholic faith, as well as build a French-Canadian identity. Facilitated by an administrative structure that was divided into hundreds of school districts in rather homogeneous communities, teaching congregations such as Notre Dame des Missions / Our Lady of the Missions and the Oblate Missionary Sisters of the Sacred Heart and Mary Immaculate, among others, were able to be in charge of public schools in rural areas (Bruno-Jofré 1998/9; 2005). The congregations were inserted in the social imaginaries of the communities – in other words, in their ways of imagining social existence, and in the normative notions and images underlying expectations (Taylor 2007, 171–2). But, even more so, the schools were part of a provincial and national institutional network, created by the French-Canadian clergy with the support of professionals, that was an instrument of collective action for the project of French Canada in minority settings outside Quebec (Martel 1997, 20). This is but one example of the educationalization of a national political issue as a means of resistance to state policy. Children educated in such circumstances were formed as Catholic moral agents carrying the true faith and exposed to a language of obedience, docility, sacrifice, and fear of God within the context of the church. But they were also formed as political agents who went through a process of citizen formation. Thus, this process had an open oppositional dimension that was part of a movement around language and faith understood as rights issues (Bruno-Jofré 2013c).

Another case of educationalization, pedagogization, and confessionalization of cultural identity was the joint work of the federal government and teaching congregations in residential schools for Indigenous children across Canada, a project representing the darkest side of schooling and religion. Salvation was the "intended force" or intentionality behind removing children from their families and placing them in residential schools. As a specific example of this church/state intersection, I will refer here to the brief work of the Religieuses de Notre Dame des Missions (RNDM) / Sisters of Our Lady of the Missions in Lac Croche, Saskatchewan, at an industrial school run by the Oblate Fathers, to whom the sisters did not want to be subordinated (Bruno-Jofré 2016).

The RNDM had inherited from its founder, Euphrasie Barbier (1829–1893), some vicarious familiarity with the thinking of Pestalozzi and Froebel, and, within the context of the Gospel, the congregation had a commitment to a child-centred approach, albeit one situated in relation to the inculcation of universal truths, the only true faith, and a particular way of life (Bruno-Jofré 2017c). The notion of child centredness was hollow in this case because the actual practice dehistoricized the Indigenous child. Further, the recollections of the individual RNDM, as well as journals kept by the Missionary Oblate Sisters, who were auxiliary to the Oblate Fathers for decades, are a testimony of the cultural (religious) process of the socialization of the children's body and soul that occurred (Anonymous 1926, 45–6; Bruno-Jofré 2005). In the case of the residential schools in Canada, churches (Catholic and Protestant alike) joined the state policy with different intentionalities (mainly conversion), which converged in the process of colonization of the Indigenous peoples and their culture – and, as Phillips (1990) has argued, in the goal of ending Indigenous claims for land that were not compatible with the settlement and economy of western Canada.

I now turn to a very different example, situated in the United States in the late 1930s, that makes clear not only the power of context, but also the disrupting power of the concept of self-agency in the intersection of education and Catholic confessionalization. The Corpus Christi School, which enrols children from kindergarten through eighth grade, is situated in a densely populated area of New York City, on West 121st Street with Columbia University directly to the south. The school, of course, as all other Catholic schools, followed official curricula mediated by Catholic conceptions. The 1930s was a time when the Vatican's approach to Catholic education was quite restrictive, in keeping with Pius XI's 1929 encyclical "On Christian Education." Father George Barry Ford, who was assigned the Corpus Christi parish, oversaw the erection, in 1936, of a church, school, convent, and social centre. Father Ford, who had been the Catholic chaplain at Columbia University, and who was an early crusader for civil rights and ecumenism, invited the Dominican Sisters of Sinsinawa, Wisconsin, as teachers, to put together what an informational pamphlet called a "new education in Catholic living" (Corpus Christi Church and School n.d.; Gans 1938; Holzhauer 1952). The parochial school was free, supported by members of the parish, and was open for a fee to non-Catholics. It was grounded in a philosophy of living and a Catholic philosophy of life, and John Dewey's central concepts of education were explicit in the school's curriculum, the school's design, and the principles governing the school. At the school, William Kilpatrick's project methods, according to which the emphasis should be on applying specific knowledge and skills (Kilpatrick 1936), were on full display. The children's work was based on cooperation (that is, the notion of working together). In the school at large, the focus was not on competition; religious concepts were applied to labour problems, social justice, housing, and employment practices (well before Vatican II); and there were no report cards or after-school activities. Students were encouraged to express themselves freely, and a democratic ethos was openly cultivated. Even as other Catholic schools in the United States used active methods of teaching and learning, the ethos and epistemology underlying the school's work went beyond the Vatican's concerns with democracy and inquiry.

Democracy was at the core of the school, as expressed in this excerpt from an undated brochure outlining the school's mission statement: "The children of Corpus Christi School through living in a democratic way are learning to live in and appreciate their democracy. By furnishing opportunities for the pupils to think for themselves, to work for the common good, to be resourceful, to inculcate ideals of practical Christian life, the school is helping to develop good, sound citizens" (Corpus Christi School n.d.).

Needless to say, Ford's liberalism often led to a conflict with the Catholic hierarchy; at one point, in 1938, in a letter to Mother Samuel, the principal of the school, Ford wrote:

> In dealing with a few close to the centre of authority in the New York Archdiocese, it is distressing, if not alarming, to observe that they are literally fiddling while Rome is burning. Preoccupied with minutia, imperative needs and issues remain unseen and, of course, unsolved. Inaction

invites approval. Any undertaking that diverges in the slightest degree [from] what has been and from the small thinking of those in authority provokes disapproval and persecution. (Ford 1938)

Perhaps not surprisingly, Ford was chastized by Cardinal Spellman (Ford 1969). However, the school continued its journey, and Father Ford was later bestowed with the John Dewey Award.

The Epistemic Breaks of the Long 1960s: Vatican II

The long 1960s brought overlapping *conjonctures* – products of the convergence of medium time-length developments, according to Braudel's use of the term (1980, 7). These *conjonctures* were theological and institutional, as well as socio-economic and political. Vatican II crystalized theological developments that were taking place outside the Vatican walls; the latest phases of *nouvelle théologie* had gone through a process of internationalization and gave impetus to the themes of Vatican II (Mettepenningen 2010). Vatican II itself provided a new paradigm. The church moved away from neo-scholasticism and Thomism in its variants, and from reliance on the classical tradition as well as from the notion of the church as the depositary of an unalterable truth. There was an opening for democracy, albeit within patriarchal boundaries. Vatican II relativized the church's positioning in a pluralistic world, and, in the midst of the religious crisis of the 1960s, situated the church in dialogue and cooperation with the world. It recognized the commitment to social justice as an imperative of the Gospel (Baum 2011). It opened the door for congregations and lay organizations to think of a reignocentric, or need-centred, mission, rather than the ecclesiocentric (church-centred) one that had been organized in the 1930s and 1940s through Catholic Action.

Catholic education was profoundly affected by the implications of a number of concurrent constitutions and decrees, in particular, the Pastoral Constitution on the Church in the Modern World (*Gaudium et Spes*), the Dogmatic Constitution on the Church (*Lumen Gentium*), and, given the implications on the teaching congregations' mission and its resignification, the Decree on the Appropriate Renewal of Religious Life (*Perfectae Caritatis*) (Abbot 1966, 462–85). However, the Declaration on Christian Education (*Gravissimum Educationis*), a document that did not bring clarity or direction, was not as influential.

The long 1960s opened a new historical moment in the history of Catholic education and its intentionality. The responses from the teaching congregations also took place at this intersection, resulting in a dramatic decrease in the number of vocations, a crisis of identity, and changing socio-economic conditions, as well as educational paradigms that required drastic accommodations. Many communities moved to a very broad concept of education beyond schooling to accommodate their new ministries (Bruno-Jofré 2017c).

At the same time, a socio-economic and political *conjoncture* influenced the church in various ways. The immediate postwar era that led to the long 1960s opened up a process of social and political change; it was a moment of break, of rupture (Rodgers 2011). The social movements of this period brought with them a concern for critical mindedness, rights, and the common good, and they introduced new relationships between epistemology, politics, and counterculture (Bruno-Jofré 2017c). Intellectually, in the 1970s and early 1980s, feminists and post-structuralists in the Western world pursued epistemological searches that challenged traditional humanistic scholarly work. Within this context, the renewal process in Catholic congregations took different shapes amid processes of decolonization and the emergence of post-colonial critiques affecting missionaries, the development of feminist theology, and the questioning of Western cosmologies. Important sectors of the church reflected these critiques.

Education and the uses of education took on new meaning. Catholics entered into the contemporary process of educationalization from various standpoints, depending on their theological and cosmological positioning. Thus, in Latin America in the early 1960s, there was a particular *conjouncture* in which the Cuban Revolution (1958), revolutionary utopias, critiques of US interventions in Latin America, and the emergence of liberation theology were components that incubated, particularly in Brazil, an epistemic breaking point in conceptions of education. These were rooted in cultural and social movements and in related peasant leagues and literacy campaigns, in which Brazilian bishops had a relevant role. Paulo Freire, a Catholic philosopher of education, was one of the educators of the time; his approach to adult education implied a new conception of education grounded in a language of justice and liberation, and of problem posing, thus opening up a different understanding of the educationalization of social problems. This understanding saw the development of political consciousness as forming inside the political subject rather than being externally revealed – be it by a political party or by agencies of the church.

The 1970s and 1980s witnessed the consolidation of neoliberalism, the notion of market as regulator, and the stress on individualism; the notion of the common good was now understood as an aggregation of individual interests. Meanwhile, there was an intense process of globalization fed by technology. Claims for the recognition of diversity in a fractured world took centre stage. In this setting, the approach to Catholic education and the uses of education can be placed along a wide-ranging theological and ideological spectrum that deserves further exploration.

Conclusion

Christianity during Christendom (roughly from the fourth century) played a strong role in moulding Western thought. The end of Christendom that came with the reformations opened various directions for Christianity. The Catholic Church's positioning from early modernity on education and educational intervention through networks of schools as a method to solve their own problems – keeping the faithful in the church, preventing deviations from Catholic doctrine, developing and operationalizing a Catholic understanding of education – and to alleviate the social misery observed in the parishes was not surprising. For many centuries, the church and its various organizations had carried out some kind of education in monasteries and cathedrals, as well as in catechetical schools. This chapter has put forward the idea that, if we use the concept of educationalization heuristically to capture the movement toward extending forms of education and schooling to solve a variety of problems (or even if we understand educationalization as a mentality; see Tröhler's chapter in this volume), we need to explore the contextual conditioning of specific discursive practice, in this case of the Catholic Church and its formations.

I also argue that, when analysing the church's work, we cannot assume uniformity conforming to the official discourse from the Holy See. If the church tried to mediate interpretations of the Bible and humans' relationship with God, the socio-cultural context and the self (the agency of members of the clergy, congregations, and theologians – the exercise of free will) created disrupting complexities. Indeed, theological explorations conducted outside the Vatican and without its approval in the 1930s and 1940s led to the articulation of the documents of Vatican II. The Catholic Church with all its cultural formations has been fully engaged in processes of educationalization on its own since early modernity, with its purposes acquiring different meanings over time.

The church's ultramontane discourse during the long nineteenth century and its anti-modernist and anti-liberal stances constitute its responses to both the opposition it encountered and to the new emerging world and its attempt to carve out a place in that world. However, this discourse created tensions deriving, in some cases, from resistance, from desires to open to the world, and/or from accommodations that were necessary in order to deal with the context. These tensions were often creatively resolved by exercising free will, nourished by the persistence in the church of long-term traditions of consciousness and individuality. In this chapter, the focus has been Western-centric, as was the extension of education through sending missions around the world, even as the field influenced the character of those missions.

NOTES

1 This is theological reflexion from praxis and "collapsed the distinction between sacred salvation history and secular earthly history, while simultaneously insisting that the two are not synonymous" (Smith 1991, 39).
2 Here Peter Watson (2005) refers to Colin Morris's *The Discovery of the Individual, 1050–1200*.
3 In 1563, the Council of Trent defined women devoted to religious life as enclosed, denying them the opportunity to conduct apostolic work outside the cloister. This was followed by Pius V's *Circa Pastoralis* (1566) and *Lubricum Vitae Genitus* (1568), which made enclosure a prerequisite for female communities claiming religious status. It has been argued, however, that enclosure was not so hermetic. See Lux-Sterrit and Mangion (2011).
4 He belonged to the Order of Minim, founded by St Francis of Paola in the fifteenth century. It was characterized by its asceticism, humility, and poverty.
5 "Estatutos y Reglamentos de las Escuelas Cristianas y Caritativas," in Barré (1997, 170–8). These statutes were written in 1677.
6 "Reglamentos para hacer observar en las escuelas de trabajo manual por las hermanas maestras de las escuelas caricativas del Santo Niño Jesús," in Barré (1997, 140–6). These rules were written in 1679.
7 De La Salle Schools have been well analysed. This is not the case with the Charitable Teachers. See García Ahumada (2002); Valladolid and Dávila (2012); and Dávila, Naya, and Murúa (2013).
8 Jacques Maritain, a neo-Thomist, did not go directly to Thomas Aquinas, but referred to scholastics from the sixteenth and seventeenth centuries. He developed the concept of integral humanism, in which the human person is ascribed a natural purpose, to be achieved through politics, and a supernatural purpose, to be achieved through religion and ethics. He was very influential in Latin America in the 1930s and 1940s, and on groups involved in Catholic Action (Mettepenningen 2010).

REFERENCES

Anonymous. 1926. *Petit historique de nos fondations au Canada, 1898–1923*. Lyon: Maison de recrutement pour les missions.

Baum, Gregory. 2011. "Vatican Council II: A Turning Point in the Church's History." In *Vatican II: Canadian Experiences*, edited by Michael Attridge, Catherine Clifford, and Gilles Routhier, 360–77. Ottawa: University of Ottawa Press.

Barré, Nicolás. 1997. *Obras Completas*. Introduction by Michel Dupuy. Translation into Spanish by Ma. Assunción Brandoly Montañes, Ma. Núria Gelpi Vintró, and Pilar Tarazaga Brillas. Barcelona: EDIM.

Braudel, Fernand. 1980. *On History*. Chicago: University of Chicago Press.

– 1993. *A History of Civilization*. New York: Penguin Books.

Bridges, David. 2008. "Educationalization: On the Appropriateness of Asking Educational Institutions to Solve Social and Economic Problems." *Educational Theory* 58 (4): 461–74. https://doi.org/10.1111/j.1741-5446.2008.00300.x.

Bruno-Jofré, Rosa. 1998/9. "Citizenship and Schooling in Manitoba, 1918–1945." *Manitoba History* 36: 26–36.

– 2005. *Missionary Oblate Sisters: Vision and Mission*. Montreal and Kingston: McGill-Queen's University Press.

– 2013a. "The Catholic Church in Chile and the Social Question in the 1920s: The Political Pedagogical Discourse of Fernando Vives del Solar, SJ." *Catholic Historical Review* 99 (4) (October): 703–26. https://doi.org/10.1353/cat.2013.0194.

– 2013b. "Introduction. Catholic Teaching Congregations and Synthetic Configurations: Building Identity through Pedagogy and Spirituality across National Boundaries and Cultures." *Paedagogica Historica* 49 (4): 447–53. https://doi.org/10.1080/00309230.2013.799498.

– 2013c. "The Missionary Oblate Sisters of the Sacred Heart and Mary Immaculate (MMO) and the Sisters of Our Lady of the Missions (RNDM): The Intersection of Education, Spirituality, the Politics of Life, Faith, and Language in the Canadian Prairies, 1898–1930." *Paedagogica Historica* 49 (4): 471–93. https://doi.org/10.1080/00309230.2013.799499.

– 2016. "The Situational Dimension of the Educational Apostolate and the Configuration of the Learner as a Cultural and Political Subject: The Case of the Sisters of Our Lady of the Missions in the Canadian Prairies." In *Education, Identity, and Women Religious, 1800–1950: Convents, Classrooms, and Colleges*, edited by Deirdre Raftery and Elizabeth M. Smyth, 160–83. New York: Routledge.

– 2017a. "Pedagogies in a Fluid Digital Age, Comments from the Editor." *Queen's Education Letter* (Spring/Summer), 1–3.

– 2017b. "The Sisters of the Infant Jesus in Bembibre, León, Spain, during the Second Stage of Francosim (1957–1975): The School with No Doors." In *Catholic Education in the Wake of Vatican II*, edited by Rosa Bruno-Jofré and Jon Igelmo Zaldívar, 111–34. Toronto. University of Toronto Press.

– 2017c. "The Sisters of Our Lady of the Missions in Canada, the Long 1960s, and Vatican II: From Carving Spaces in the Educational State to Living the Radicality of the Gospel." In *Catholic Education in the Wake of Vatican II*, edited by Rosa Bruno-Jofré and Jon Igelmo Zaldívar, 190–209. Toronto: University of Toronto Press.

Bugnard, Pierre-Philippe. 2006. *Le temps des espaces pédagogiques: De la cathédrale orienté à la capitale occidentée*. Nancy, Fr: Presses Universitaries de Nancy.

Chico, Pedro. 2000. *Institutos y Fundadores de la Educación Cristiana*. Valladolid: CVS.

Christensen, Drew, SJ. 2011. "Commentary on *Pacem in Terris* (Peace on Earth)." In *Modern Catholic Social Teaching: Commentaries and Interpretations*, edited by Kenneth R. Himes, O.F.M., 217–43. Washington, DC: Georgetown University Press.

Corpus Christi School. n.d. Brochure. Compiled with the Assistance of the Student Council. New York: Corpus Christi School.

Curtis, Bruce. 1992. *True Government by Choice Men? Inspection, Education, and State Formation in Canada West*. Toronto: University of Toronto Press.

Dávila, Paulí, Luis M. Naya, and Hilario Murúa. 2013. "Tradition and Modernity of the De La Salle Schools: The Case of the Basque Country in Franco's Spain (1937–1975)." *Paedagogica Historica* 49 (4): 562–76. https://doi.org/10.1080/00309230.2013.799500.

Depaepe, Marc, Frederik Herman, Melanie Surmont, Angelo Van Gorp, and Frank Simon. 2012. "About Pedagogization: From the Perspective of the History of Education." In *Between Educationalization and Appropriation: Selected Writings on the History of Modern Educational Systems*, edited by Marc Depapepe, 177–200. Leuven, BE: Leuven University Press.

Depaepe, Marc, and Paul Smeyers. 2012. "Educationalization as an Ongoing Modernization Process." In *Between Educationalization and Appropriation: Selected Writings on the History of Modern Educational Systems*, edited by Marc Depaepe, 167–76. Leuven, BE: Leuven University Press.

Dewey, John. (1916) 1997. *Democracy and Education*. New York: Free Press.

Dupuy, Michel. 1997. "Introducción." In *Obras Completas*, by Nicolás Barré. Barcelona: EDIM.

Elias, John. 1999. "Whatever Happened to Catholic Philosophy of Education?" *Religious Education* 94 (1): 92–100. https://doi.org/10.1080/0034408990940108.

Ford, George B. 1938. Letter to Mother Samuel, Corpus Christi Rectory, New York. 8 August, Dominican Archives, Sinsinava, WI, 1/ 060.

– 1969. *A Degree of Difference: Memoirs of George Barry Ford*. New York: Farrar, Straus and Giroux.

Gans, Roma. 1938. "The New Education in Catholic Living." *Religious Education: The Official Journal of the Religious Education Association* 33 (2): 93–9. https://doi.org/10.1080/0034408380330205.

García Ahumada, Enrique. 2002. "350 años del natalicio de San Juan Bautista de La Salle." *Annuario de historia de la iglesia* 11: 375–81.

Hildesheimer, Françoise. 1992. "Le Jansénisme, l'histoire et l'heritage." In *Petite encyclopédie moderne du Christianisme*. Paris: Desclée de Brouwer, 8–10.

Holzhauer, Jean L. 1952. "Parish School Tries Old-with-New Experiment to Make Better Christians and Citizens for Tomorrow." *Catholic Herald Citizen*, 25 October, 12–14.

Jodock, Darrell. 2000. "The Modernist Crisis." In *Catholicism Contending with Modernity: Roman Catholic Modernism and Anti-Modernism in Historical Context*, edited by Darrell Jodock, 1–19. Cambridge University Press.

Kilpatrick, William H. 1936. *Remaking the Curriculum*. New York: Newson and Company.

Lux-Sterrit, Laurence, and Carmen M. Mangion. 2011. "Introduction: Gender, Catholicism, and Women's Spirituality over the *Longue Durée*." In *Gender, Catholicism, and Spirituality: Women and the Roman Catholic Church in Britain and Europe, 1200–1900*, edited by Laurence Lux-Sterrit and Carmen Mangion, 1–19. London: Palgrave Macmillan.

Martel, Marcel. 1997. *Le deuil d'un pays imaginé: Rêves, luttes, et déroute du Canada français: Les rapports entre le Québec et la francophonie canadienne, 1867–1975*. Ottawa: Les Presses de l'Université d'Ottawa.

Martínez Valle, Carlos. 2007. "Anatomia de la libertad el libre arbitrio y el pfundamentalismo protestante el antirrigorismo escolastico y el republicanism humanista, 1559–1649." PhD diss., Universidad Complutense de Madrid. https://www.researchgate.net/publication/39161028.

Marwick, Arthur. 1998. *The Sixties: Cultural Revolution in Britain, France, Italy, and the United States, c. 1958–1974*. Oxford: Oxford University Press.

McCool. Gerald A. 1989. "Spirituality and Philosophy: The Ideal of the Catholic Mind." *Sacred Heart Review* 10 (1), Art. 3. http://digitalcommons.sacredheart.edu/shureview/vol10/iss1/3.

McGreevy, John T. 2016. *American Jesuits and the World: How an Embattled Religious Order Made Modern Catholicism Global*. Princeton, NJ: Princeton University Press.

McKay, Ian. 2000. "The Liberal Order Framework: A Prospectus for a Reconnaissance of Canadian History." *Canadian Historical Review* 81 (4): 616–78. https://doi.org/10.3138/chr.81.4.616.

Mettepenningen, Jürgen. 2010. *Nouvelle Théologie – New Theology: Inheritor of Modernism, Precursor of Vatican II*. New York: T. and T. Clark International.

Misner, Paul. 2000. "Catholic Anti-Modernism: The Ecclesial Setting." In *Catholicism Contending with Modernity: Roman Catholic Modernism and Anti-Modernism in Historical Context*, edited by Darrell Jodock, 56–88. Cambridge; Cambridge University Press.

Moretti, P. Genaro. 1935. *Un pedagogo santo: El Padre Nicolás Barré de la Orden de los Mínimos. Fundador de las escuelas de caridad del Santo Niño Jesús*. Translated from Italian by P.G. Pbro. Barcelona: Balmes.

Morris, Colin. 1972. *The Discovery of the Individual, 1050–1200*. London: SPCK.

O'Malley, John W. 2008. *What Happened at Vatican II*. Cambridge, MA: Belknap Press of Harvard University Press.

– 2013. *Trent: What Happened at the Council*. Cambridge, MA: Belknap Press of Harvard University Press.

– 2014. *The Jesuits: A History from Ignatius to the Present*. London: Rowman and Littlefield.

Phillips, Paul. 1990. "Manitoba in the Agrarian Period: 1870–1940." In *The Political Economy of Manitoba*, edited by Jim Silver and Jeremy Hull, 3–24. Regina, SK: University of Regina Press.

Pius IX. 1864. *Quanta Cura* (Condemning Current Errors). Promulgated 8 December. http://www.papalencyclicals.net/Pius09/p9quanta.htm.

Pius XI. 1929. *Divini Illius Magistri* (On Christian Education). Libreria Editrice Vaticana. http://w2.vatican.va/content/pius-xi/en/encyclicals/documents/hf_p-xi_enc_31121929_divini-illius-magistri.html.

Rodgers, Daniel T. 2011. *Age of Fracture*. Cambridge, MA: Belknap Press of Harvard University Press.

Schuck, Michael J. 2005. "Early Modern Roman Catholic Social Thought, 1740–1890." In *Modern Catholic Social Teaching: Commentaries and Interpretations*, edited by Kenneth R. Himes and Lisa Sowle Cahill, 99–126. Washington, DC: Georgetown University Press.

Sedgwick, Alexander. 1990. "Jansen and the Jansenists." *History Today* 40 (7): 36–42.

Smith, Christian. 1991. *The Emergence of Liberation Theology: Radical Religion and Social Movement Theory*. Chicago: University of Chicago Press.

Smith, Susan, RNDM. 2010. *Call to Mission: The Story of the Mission Sisters of Aotearoa, New Zealand, and Samoa*. Auckland, NZ: David Ling Publishing.

Tarnas, Richard. 1991. *The Passion of the Western Mind. Understanding the Ideas That Have Shaped Our World View*. New York: Ballantine Books.

Taylor, Charles. 2007. *A Secular Age*. Cambridge, MA: Belknap Press of Harvard University Press.

Valladolid, José María, and Paulí Dávila. 2012. *Estudio crítico, notas y bibliografía a la edición en Español de la Guía de las Escuelas*. Madrid: Biblioteca Nueva-Siglo, vol. XXI.

Watson, Peter. 2005. *Ideas: A History from Fire to Freud*. London: Weidenfeld and Nicolson.

4 Antigonish, or an "Education That Is Not Educationalization"

JOSH COLE

Live with your century, but do not be its creature.

– Friedrich Schiller

You have to bootleg education.

– Myles Horton

In this chapter, I take a different tack from my Theory and History of Education Research Group (THEIRG) colleagues. Like them, I respond to Daniel Tröhler's provocative theory of the "educationalization" of modern societies, while trying to expand its parameters by moving its frame of reference to Canada – more particularly, to eastern Nova Scotia in the 1920s and 1930s – and away from the education of children (the primary subjects of educationalization in Tröhler's model). Instead, I examine the intellectual underpinnings of adult education as conceptualized by the famous (and fabled) "Antigonish movement." Here we see a move away from educationalization narrowly defined and toward something fundamentally different: a form of "counter-educationalization" rooted in rural and Catholic concerns, utilizing techniques of mass-mediated education that broke down the artificial distinctions between "school" and "society." Indeed, it was – and was intended to be – an "education that is not educationalization," one geared toward grassroots democracy.[1] Through the writings of M.M. Coady, Antigonish's most systematic thinker, I will draw out the similarities and the deep differences between these two conceptions of education's place in the modern world.[2]

Tröhler's theory of educationalization is a theory of modernity. But what is modernity? It entails the transformed economic relations of corporate capitalism and their spatio-temporal consequences, as the forces of economic production, distribution, and exchange are all transformed beyond recognition, as are the social relations associated with them. It calls into question the proper role of the state, whose structures and functions are expanded far beyond their previous limits. It entails a future-oriented perspective toward time, which makes for a sharp impatience with mere tradition – especially for those who wish to safeguard the autonomy and dignity of the individual. It means a cultural revolution – an awareness of the extent to which the individual might be alienated and undermined by the coldness and impersonality of modern life and an equally sharpened sense that conditions of modernity allow for unprecedented freedom of individual expression. It means a deep respect for science and the social sciences as sources of knowledge about these daunting developments and as a support for more comprehensively planned systems of governance. And, finally, it entails an implicit (and at times explicit) utopianism: the putting forth of ideals (such as the universal human right to education and its attendant processes) whose radical implementation might well be at odds with popular "common sense," but on whose expression the survival of freedom depends, and that serve to highlight the imperative need for the existing order to change (Giddens 1991, 83; Berman 2010, 7; Bauman 2007, 7; Löwy and Sayre 2001, 17–19).

For Tröhler, educationalization is a central – if not *the* central – response to this world of transformation. As he writes: "Since the eighteenth century the construction of … progress [toward an] open future depends on an idea of education that promises to be the engine of modernity by means of (new) and broadly disseminated knowledge and technologies and, at the same time, an instance of moral reassurance empowering the individual exposed to these modern conditions and their moral hazards to act morally or virtuously." This educationalization of modern problems presupposes a "linear way of thinking" ("progress"), which replaced the cyclical, pre-modern one ("an eternal cycle of events"). If the forces of modernity were contained and harnessed by the processes of educationalization, humanity would inevitably move toward "peace, justice, and bliss" as traditional "political conditions that [impede] this progress [were] destroyed." Further, for Tröhler, educationalization is a means of reconciling (seeming) irreconcilables: modern political citizenship (along classical republican lines) and the anarchic (and equally modern) energies of capitalism, which has its productive (and destructive) roots in uncontrolled human "passions." The "key" to squaring these contradictory forces is to work intensively on modernity's "danger zone" – the human soul – through the educationalization of social problems. Large-scale "sovereign" gestures (compulsory mass schooling and the expansion of tertiary education) as well as "minor procedures" ("training" and "re-training" exercises of all sorts, "public education" advertising campaigns, and so on) would maximize *and* tame modern individualism, and, by extension, the modernity that unleashed it (Tröhler 2016; see also Tröhler's chapter in the present volume). In short, to be modern is to be formally educated in all things – ideally forever.

Tröhler is surely on to something. Educationalization has much to recommend it as a means of understanding how societies grapple with a modernity in which "all that's solid melts into air" (to quote Marx) endlessly. I aim not to bury the thesis, but to expand its scope and parameters through an examination of adult education in eastern Nova Scotia, as embodied in the Antigonish movement. Differences between Tröhler's take on educationalization and what I elaborate below as an "education that is not educationalization" are immediately apparent. Educationalization is primarily an urban conception, originating in the salons and other public spheres of eighteenth-century France, and in London, England, through the founding of the Bank of England in 1694. Antigonish, on the contrary, was primarily a rural movement for self-improvement, not "improvement" from the "top-down." The teachers and students of Antigonish were Catholic, whereas Tröhler's actors were Protestant. The educators of Antigonish were deeply wary of the economic and social effects of capitalism, and did not want to "improve" it per se, but rather to supersede its "possessive individualist" underpinnings, replacing these with a cooperative model of economics that would be mirrored in it educational endeavours.[3] Finally – and most fundamentally – educationalization is primarily centred on the education of children and young people ("pedagogy," or the "leading of children"), while Antigonish was a grassroots movement that was exclusively concerned with the education of adults (known as "andragogy").[4] Actually existing democracy, not social control, was its ultimate goal – the latter being difficult to disentangle from Tröhler's conception of the educationalization of social problems.

The experiments in adult education carried out in Antigonish, Nova Scotia, are among the most famous that Canada has produced, yet they are – as historians Michael Welton and Peter Ludlow argue – among the most "mythologized" as well (Welton 2003; Ludlow 2013). Yet there is considerable truth behind this "myth." The Antigonish movement came into being in the 1920s, spearheaded by three important Catholic intellectuals and activists: James Morrison, Jimmy Tompkins, and M.M. Coady. Tompkins is the central figure in Antigonish's initial phase.[5] He studied at St Francis Xavier University (informally known as "St F.X.") before departing for Rome and the Urban College of the Congregato de Propaganda Fide. There he discovered the "Social Question" being vigorously debated in European Catholic circles – centred on "modernizing" Catholicism as a means of beating back the excesses of the contemporary era, particularly its generation of a possessive individualist citizenry.[6] After being ordained in 1902, he returned to St F.X. as an administrator, later becoming vice-rector and, by the end of the decade, vice-president. In the latter position, he was able to explore some of the most notable national and transnational educational experiments of the early twentieth century. These included the University of Wisconsin's adult extension activities (where "the people, their needs and capacities, and the circumstances of their lives are studied at close range") (Tompkins 1963, 98), the British Workers' Education Associations, as well as Danish folk schools, Swedish discussion circles, and "programmes throughout Scotland and Ireland designed for people without access to traditional, university-based education" (Dennis 2014, 63–4). Within Canada, agricultural programs at the University of Saskatchewan and Quebec's agricultural colleges added more fuel to Tompkins's dissatisfaction with traditional schooling and tertiary education and, underlying this, a slow-burning hostility to educationalization writ large.

Tompkins was transformed by these educational encounters in ways that would reverberate through the Antigonish movement, shaping its cultural and educational politics. Even before these encounters, he had been deeply concerned with school reform – particularly with raising the level of "skilful teaching, equal provision in buildings and equipment, and professional direction" (Tompkins 1963, 101). This might be considered Antigonish's "educationalization moment." Eastern Nova Scotia's social and economic problems would be ameliorated by more and better schools, which would be properly planned (the word he uses is "direction") and subject to "sympathetic and close supervision" by well-meaning technocrats in order to ensure that all children were equally able to climb the "ladder" of liberal education to educational and economic success (ibid.).

Later, Tompkins's attitude to education shifted and deepened, as he gravitated toward adult leaners in rural contexts. He created "an annual people's school" at St F.X., inspired by Danish folk schools he observed on his educational travels. It focused on "cooperativism, leadership, and the liberal arts" (Remes 2010, 61). This modest effort – stymied by a sceptical James Morrison, the archbishop of Antigonish – was conceived as a means of combating the "atomization of the countryside, [and] the 'lack of organization and cohesion' that left [rural people] prey to the better organized interests around [them]" (Rodgers 1998, 352). Tompkins also waged battles over university consolidation, which did nothing but anger his superiors (he favoured a Carnegie Corporation proposal to unite the province's small colleges into a non-sectarian university in Halifax, to "create more educational opportunities for the ordinary people of the Antigonish diocese" (Remes 2010, 62–3). He lost this battle, and his newfound interest in democratically oriented andragogy did nothing to ingratiate him to his more traditionally minded colleagues.

As punishment, he was sent to "out-of-the-way Canso" in 1926 – a parish of a mere 400 people (out of 1,626 living in the region). Ironically, it was here (and in nearby Little Dover) that Tompkins's – and Antigonish's – adult education philosophy truly took shape. In Canso, he encountered "a fishing industry [in] a state of crisis, with fishers facing stiff competition" from larger "modern," industrial concerns (64).[7] In response, drawing once more on his travels from Sweden to Saskatchewan, Tompkins prioritized adult education as a means of empowerment, encouraging "his parishioners to form study clubs, in which they taught themselves about their problems and found ways to solve them" (65). As historian Jacob Remes notes, on Dominion Day, 1927, "rather than celebrating the 60th anniversary of Canadian Confederation," the Catholics of Canso rallied in protest, asking loudly "what Confederation had done for them?" (ibid.).

It was a rhetorical question, of course – and, in any case, Tompkins and his fellow critics were able to draw upon the Royal Commission on Maritime Claims (tabled in 1926) to answer it. The commission recommended "that a fund be created to improve the social well being, recreation, and living conditions of Nova Scotia's coal miners" and, by extension, all workers in the embattled province (Dennis 2014, 72). This commission – scuttled by the federal government of William Lyon Mackenzie King – was followed by the Royal Commission on Fisheries, which, with more force (and in the light of a global capitalist system barrelling toward the Great Depression), put a spotlight on "the grim conditions of life in the fisheries" (ibid.). It reinforced Tompkins' conviction that things could be improved in eastern Nova Scotia only by "bring[ing] education to people traditionally excluded from the university's purview," through an expanded system of university extension work (ibid.).

At last, the powers that be – driven by a measure of palpable desperation – acquiesced to these demands in 1929, ushering in the "Antigonish movement," to be housed in St F.X. Tompkins, joined by his cousin M.M. (Moses) Coady, set to work on improving the "social, economic and educational" situation of eastern Nova Scotians by wedding "temporal and earthly interests" to "spiritual" and cultural concerns (Dennis 2014, 73). Coady took things further than Tompkins by explicitly welding together the "temporal" (economics) and the "spiritual" (culture and education) in the Antigonish movement, as we shall see.

If Tompkins gave birth to Antigonish, Coady, as its leading "organic" thinker, gave it its theoretical expression. He was born in Nova Scotia in 1882 and trained as a teacher in Truro before becoming the principal of Margaree Forks High School in 1901. He then attended St F.X. in Antigonish, before entering the priesthood in 1905. Under the influence of Tompkins, he studied at the Urban College of the Congregato de Propaganda Fide, where he earned both a doctorate in divinity and a PhD in philosophy. After teaching briefly at St F.X., he was sent by Morrison to the Catholic University of America for graduate study, this time in education. Upon his return, he became the principal of the St F.X. High School and professor of education at St F.X. University. He became enmeshed in educational politics through work on behalf of the Provincial Educational Association, ushering that group toward unionism (though his interest in the union movement has its limits, as deeper analysis of his mature philosophy will make clear). In the 1920s, with Nova Scotians leaving the province in droves in search of better economic prospects elsewhere, he began to conceive of an adult educational program that would buck the excesses of capitalism. In 1928, he was appointed head of St F.X.'s Extension Department, with an explicit mission to "organize the fishermen" of eastern Nova Scotia and beyond. In 1939, as Antigonish became recognized provincially, nationally, and internationally for its educational approach to economic problems, he penned his only book – *Masters of Their Own Destiny* – immediately recognized as a global classic in adult education. I will draw on this and other writings to elucidate his conception of an adult education that was explicitly not a form of educationalization.

As he makes clear at the beginning of *Masters of Their Own Destiny*, the Antigonish movement was born in eastern Nova Scotia and owed little (if anything) to the metropolitan educationalizers of Paris or London. Instead, like Raymond Williams, another innovative thinker on andragogy, he insisted that education is "ordinary" and must have its beginnings in local (rather than national or global) settings. To be educated in the style of Antigonish is to "write" oneself out of, and then back "into the land" through "active debate and amendment, under the pressures of [localized] experience, contact, and discovery" (Williams 1993, 90). Places like Antigonish or Little Dover may have been modest, but they also expressed the "beauty and grandeur" of northern North American nature, and through it, the hand of God. Even humble Canso could, if viewed in the correct light, serve as a "divinely hewn portal of inspiration, stirring men's hearts to noble and lofty ideals" (Coady 1939, 15). For Coady, eastern Nova Scotia – "nature's masterpiece" – could double as "the great social laboratory" of the twentieth century as well (ibid). To emphasize the beauty and andragogical promise of these "ordinary" connections between environment, culture, and God's work, Coady took to poetry:

> Divine mosaic by a Master hand,
> Inlaid with stream and meadow, rugged hill
> And dusky woodland round a mirror lake,
> With all the colors of the world aglow,
> By all its quiet dimness soothed and toned,
> Exquisite picture framed in ancient stone,
> The rugged bulwark of old Acadie,
> These are the Maritimes. This bright façade
> That fronts the greatest structure yet to be
> Was wrought in eons past, a work of art
> Minute and perfect as the last green frond
> Of fern that opens. Rugged as the swell
> Of all the broad Atlantic and its roar.
> Who would not love this land for what it is?
> For what it yet will be not love it more?
> Young and unsullied by the baser man,
> Fresh from the mind of God. Tread lightly, then,
> Lest human blunder wreck the perfect plan,
> Displace the pattern of Omnipotence.
> 'Tis but a setting for the things to be,
> When every little hill shall be a torch
> And hold a beacon fire high to light
> The world with love and beauty, goodness, truth.
> The homely, rugged tasks we do today,
> As jostled by the crowds that buy and sell,
> We raise our voices in the market place,
> Are not our goal, are but the solid ground
> That holds our feet the while we build our wings.
> In temperate mood God raised these lowly hills,
> With calm and moderation shaped our land,
> So while the world goes mad, it stands serene
> In quiet pledge of everlastingness
> That dares to flash its hope to all mankind. (15–16)

What took eastern Nova Scotia "fresh from the mind of God" toward "human blunder" was a capitalism spun out of control. As Coady saw it, it had not always been this way. There had been a form of civilized commerce before modern capitalism – a "small log shack" that preceded that "blazed forest trail" (19). What was lost in the transition was not just community and nature in delicate balance, but an organic individuality infused with an attendant sense of responsibility that kept those forces in equilibrium. "While the rest of the pioneers were busy pulling and burning stumps, one who did not fancy such hard work foresaw the possibilities of supplying them with the necessities of life. With an eye to future real estate values, he chose the best corner and set up a small store [then] a wholesale, a bank, an insurance office, until the common man found himself surrounded by a host of agencies eager to service him, to do for him all the offices he had hitherto done for himself" (ibid.). He added that the people of eastern Nova Scotia – considered "primitive" antimoderns, not genuine "individuals" in the modern sense – were frozen out of this process. As Coady notes, "there was no contract drawn up and signed by both parties ... which [amounts] in reality [to] no contract at all" (ibid.). As the community busied itself with traditional work, outsiders created "mills and factories," mines, and modern fishing operations. Coady indicted industrialist outsiders for this state of affairs, but he did not let the "common man" off the hook. If anything, the latter shouldered most of the blame for this "modern" decimation of traditional life, for these people chose to remain "blind to the significance of the economic system that was growing up" (22). As a result of their bad faith, they allowed "a convenient theory – the theory of laissez faire" to roll over them and the land that they cherished (ibid.).

Coady and the educators of Antigonish sought to teach people a better way of dealing with the disruptions of modernity through cooperative economics. Through that alternative system, they sought to harness modernity for their own ends, creating a dynamic form of economic production, distribution, and exchange that enhanced, rather than eroded, local communities and their traditional cultures. Capitalism was not opposed in principle but was rejected for its effects. It pitted community and against community, individual against individual, producer against consumer, and humanity itself against the natural environment. Its core was the self-immolating logic of possessive individualism, and this made it, for Coady and his fellow educators, "unscientific." As he wrote, one might as "well try to fix a watch with a crowbar as to regulate the delicate economic machine with competition" (22).[8]

The "Industrial Revolution destroyed the domestic system," sweeping "away community industries and [taking] from the common man any chance he had of control in a large sector of production" (70). Cooperative economics, on the other hand, would slowly create new forms of community control to rival the hegemony of competitive capitalism. According to Coady, this counter-hegemonic move would begin with those social institutions – "stores, banks, and various kinds of service agencies" – still held in common (ibid.). Once these were secured, good, services, and resources would slowly shift back toward community control. From then on, the sky was to be the limit, according to Coady. No economic endeavour – no matter how large, complex, or alienating – would be out of reach.

This was not just abstract theorization. This process, Coady argued, was well underway in eastern Nova Scotia by the 1930s. As a result of Antigonish's endeavours, the first cooperative store opened in Canso in 1934. By 1937, Nova Scotia's cooperators had generated $2,099,357 in profits. In 1935, a cooperative lobster factory was established in Ballantyne's Cove. The resulting experience was a moral and educational, one according to Coady. Acting in concert in this way "develops the right type of human character" by making people "honest" through the "brotherhood that it engenders and the group sanction that is attached to it" (83). Although Coady insisted that cooperative economics and adult education alike should begin "on the ground," his thought was also deeply utopian. Thus, be considered economic and social cooperation to be an "inevitability" – the first step toward a reclamation of "rights by the people" in a "new order" (26). (Phrases such as these have a Marxist ring, but Coady vigorously rejected that body of thought: Marxism might constitute an "intriguing" social program, but it was ultimately a "myth and a delusion" based on collective violence, and thus had to be rejected) (137).

If cooperation was one pillar of the Antigonish approach to social justice, Catholicism was another. Tröhler's educationalizers based their pedagogical aims and objectives on Protestant ideals, although they often attempted to bury this aspect of their efforts – in this sense, educationalization is deeply ideological. Coady and his fellow adult educators put their faith front and centre, tying it to cooperative economics and utopian andragogy. It was, in short, an eastern Nova Scotian response to the "social question" in Catholicism. As Coady proclaimed, "Properly considered, cooperation postulates more, not less religion" (140). This is because all forms of cultural life – including material production – entail "charity and justice," which "have their foundation in religion" (ibid.). Coady rejected the notion, shared by Marxists and many Protestants, that Catholicism was anti-social, an "opiate of the masses." Instead, "it is food and drink ... more vivifying and more energizing than the thin gruel of materialistic philosophy" (142–3). Under the economic and social conditions of competitive capitalism, people "grow fat, lazy, stupid, and easy victims of the bargain-dealers and quacks who would be happy to use [them] for their own unworthy ends" (143). Materialism was not to be rejected (it was not *just* "thin gruel"), but rather was to be articulated with a socially minded Catholicism, which would "quicken" workers "with that divine discontent which urges man onward to loftier and more noble ... heights" (ibid.). Liberal capitalism "delude[s]" people into "contentment with less than the greatest good" (ibid.). The resulting economic, spiritual, and educational fall-out constituted, for Coady, "the sin of our age." Yet, a reversal was possible (if not inevitable), quickened by the utopian thrust of cooperative economics and socially just Catholicism. Antigonish began with the material but used it "as it ought to be used, a means to a higher end" (ibid.).

This led to the catalyst that would allow cooperative economics and Catholic social justice to flourish: adult education, or an education that is not educationalization. This approach proceeded on three interlocking fronts opposed to educationalization, as conceived by Tröhler: dissatisfaction with traditional schooling and tertiary education; a desire to root adult learning in everyday economic activities; and andragogical techniques (immediate and mass mediated) that would bring about genuine democracy in Nova Scotia, Canada, and (so Coady thought) the world.

Coady began his analysis of the economic and spiritual advantages of adult education with a refutation of traditional schooling and traditional tertiary education – what we might call educationalization, for short. He wrote: "Our movement has grown in large part out of the dissatisfactions of great numbers of people with the formal education we have had" (2). Eastern Nova Scotians were subjected to "every traditional effort" that modernity threw up in its wake, and they were all found wanting. As well-intentioned as educationalizers were, and however much they contributed to public knowledge, their efforts fell far short of what a place like Canso, under assault from the pressures of liberal-capitalist modernity, required. As Coady asserted, "the people generally loved learning, [but] they suffered from many serious economic maladjustments," which threw the limitations of "official" education into sharp relief (ibid.). "Our elementary and secondary education did not prepare for life. Our colleges were too much concerned with the education of people for the professions" to be of much help either (ibid.). Thus, the adult educators of Antigonish rejected *avant la lettre* the utilitarian (or "administrative progressive") basis for Tröhler's theory of educationalization.

According to Coady, the true goal of education should be to "enable a man to realize his ... human potentialities" in economic, spiritual, and cultural (and educational) terms (111). Educationalization in Canada – "a demanding, regulated, and standardized course of study" granted to children and young people exclusively – left this process radically incomplete (Axelrod 2003, 46). In order for education to release to the "fullest possible extent all latent [adult] powers" educationalization would have to give way to adult education along the lines put forth by Antigonish (Coady 1939, 111). The first move in this direction was the most crucial. The desire to learn, as Coady argues, does not stop after "school-leaving" age. For the educators of Antigonish, the desire to learn is a lifelong one – it is "hard-wired" into people – and so, in the words of Jürgen Habermas, "*not-learning* is the phenomenon" that is fundamentally unnatural, and thus calls out for critique and analysis (Habermas 2005, 15). Further, Coady insisted that the epistemic split between teacher and student was a false one. That such a split exists at all is a "pedagogical myth" dividing intelligence and learning ability into an "inferior" and a "superior" version. (Rancière 1991, 7). This too was jettisoned by Antigonish. As Coady, channelling Tompkins, wrote, "You must have faith that [the] uneducated ... can learn and can educate themselves. You must have faith that the people will develop their own leaders. You just have enough faith to trust the average man for the general direction of his own activities" (Landis 1950, 196).

In order to realize "symmetry" in the (adult) educated subject, Coady argued that an education that is not educationalization had to begin where the people were: on the ground. As he wrote, "We have indicated what we believe to be the correct point of departure and the right course to follow where the masses are concerned. We consider it good pedagogy and good psychology to begin with the economic phase" as the basis of "the eternally right and basic relations of man to man in society" (Coady 1939, 112). Conceptions of pedagogy tracing back to Plato – ones that we, once again, might label educationalized, had to be jettisoned, for they were "idealist [and] impressed by the permanency and universality of ideas" (116). That influential (and, for Coady, deeply misguided) ancient philosopher distrusted the "the transient, mutable things of the earth that we see about us," and this would not do for the adults of eastern Nova Scotia. Instead, Antigonish championed Aristotle – "the great realist" – in knowledge and education. For Aristotle and Coady, all things in this world worth knowing are "derived through the material senses from the material world," which are then, through a "process of abstraction, refining, and patterning," turned into objects of abstract reasoning (ibid.). The educators of Antigonish also rejected Plato's ultimate goal for education: putting hyper-educated elite "Guardians" in charge of lesser social actors who were "educated" to accept their inferior status. The rule in Antigonish was equality and "mutual aid," not social and educational stratification.

As Coady asserted, it is "good pedagogy, from several viewpoints, to begin with the economic phase" for people "learn best when [their] interests are keenest; and [their] needs determine [their] interests" (112). To be "realistic" in education was to demonstrate how teaching and learning – by and among adults – could improve life immediately; then, and only then, could more abstract considerations be entertained. "Study for study's sake is too much to ask of the masses in the beginning ... Why present them with new difficulties or hypothetical cases that have little or no meaning for them?" (113). For those without much formal education (and those who rejected educationalization as stifling and irrelevant), a grounding in relevant economics was the crucial first step. Once given an entry-point into an education that is not educationalization, people would, Coady was confident, taste "the sweets of thinking" and inevitably seek new educational fields to "conquer" (ibid.). What might have seemed "mad" to people at one point would become a real possibility. Coady then stated this philosophy of education bluntly: "If we are to make an idealist of him [i.e., the adult learner] we must first satisfy his realism" (114).

Coady and his compatriots were "realistic" – that is, Aristotelian – in more than just theory. They created techniques that would empower adults to "do for themselves" what "governments [have failed to] do for them" (Landis 1950, 196). The educators of Antigonish employed techniques that were "practical, inexpensive, [and] widely applicable" and that would steadily fan "out into the higher levels of culture," without "handing out doles or treating [adults] as inferiors or grown-up babies" (Coady 1950, 198–9). This andragogy was based primarily on the mass meeting and the study club. In these forums, adults would establish "needs" and "objectives" as they saw fit, "leadership and facilitation roles" would be "passed from learner to learner," and not monopolized by a powerful teacher-figure. The aims and objectives of this process would be dialectical, involving "reflection upon activity, collaborative analysis of activity, new activity, further reflection and collaborative analysis, and so on" (Coady 1950, 200; Brookfield 1986, 9–11). Throwing another ancient educational figure into the mix, Coady noted that, in the educational space envisioned by the adult educators of eastern Nova Scotia, the mass meeting and study club would constitute a modern take on the "Socratic method of learning" – one "brought up to date and laid against the harsh realities of life" (Coady 1950, 200). With its "men in overalls and women in aprons discussing the everyday difficulties of their livelihood, instead of rich young men of leisure arguing about the essence of truth and beauty," this education that is not educationalization could not be further removed from the origins of the latter educational program in the salons of France or among the proto-bankers of England (ibid.).

Equally significant was the Antigonish movement's determination to extend the mass meeting and the study club through various forms of media, new and old. This was an early attempt to create a "school without walls" before this conception was popularized in the 1960s. More directly, it anticipated the work of the Canadian Association of Adult Education's Farm Radio Forum and Citizen's Forum (launched in 1941 and 1943, respectively). Coady described new media like radio as a "a great wand" able to transcend "unalterables of Canadian life-space" (distance and locality) to address not individuals or "mass audiences" but "groups" forming and re-forming themselves into new educational "communities" capable of solving modern social, cultural, and economic problems (Coady 1950, 201; Sim 1963, 215; 217). Antigonish's experiments in mass-mediated andragogy were to be a "truly democratic" system of two-way communication that added up to a "structure wherein [adult learners] could voice their thoughts and have them heard" (Sim 1963, 217). That structure was both simple and effective: Antigonish dispersed pamphlets to subscribed learners. These learners, in groups drawn from friends and family, then took in radio programs like "Life in These Maritimes." After this, they collectively discussed the issues raised by the program and the pamphlet material. Finally, they gave Antigonish feedback on what they learned, and what could be improved (Coady 1950, 200–1) This is what Nancy Fraser calls a "counterpublic sphere" – a "discursive aren[a]" in which "members of subordinated social groups invent and circulate counterdiscourses, which in turn permit them to formulate oppositional interpretations of their identities, interests, and needs" (Fraser 1990, 67). This would be – and Coady was sure on this point – the beginning of a more democratic approach to education and politics in the modern world.

Which brings us to the real end of Antigonish's efforts: a more genuinely democratic society filled with active citizens prepared for the multifarious challenges of modern life. This, perhaps ironically, leads us back to the beginning of Antigonish's self-imposed mission: a form of education (that is not educationalization) that would improve life in eastern Nova Scotia (and beyond) from the "ground up." As Coady argued, this immediate/mass-mediated counterpublic sphere would start with "digging coal, catching fish, or planting seed" but would end with a "new society," one infinitely more just than the one promoted by the educationalizers, the liberal capitalists with whom they were aligned, or the Marxists whom they saw creeping up on their left flank. As Coady asserted, it could be no other way: if ordinary people do not "bestir themselves to bring [grassroots democracy] about, no one else will" (1939, 17–18). This type of democracy would render all "dictatorial system[s]," "directing energy ... from the top," as objects of derision, for they stood directly in the way of a "people's enlightenment" (18). Events and the interpretation of events would instead move in the opposite direction, creating "a new society where all men are free," first in miniature (in eastern Nova Scotia), then on an ever-widening scale. The result would be "a social architecture" entailing a modern (yet moral) "re-making of society" (40–1).

Through adult education and cooperation, underlaid by a Catholicism that took the "social question" fully on board, Coady insisted that, after having "established *themselves* as full-fledged citizens, the people can participate in ... other general types of social action which logically follow it" (126; my emphasis). They would, at last, be purveyors of "intelligent political action" on contemporary issues. As Coady wrote, they would move beyond apathy and "neutrality in politics" in general to act upon the world thoughtfully and thoroughly (ibid.). By contrast, educationalization would have channeled their political energies in socially controlled, apolitical directions. Adult education, cooperative enterprises, and the Catholic "social question"' would involve them in "the affairs of the political state" on a deeply personal *and* public level (ibid.). They would then, as enlightened citizens, spread the goods of andragogy ("a democratic way of life and way of thought") to those around them, in multiplying concentric circles. "Couldn't we help the people literally to march towards the good things of life?" Coady asks rhetorically (2). "The people generally are for democracy ... Let us mobilize these attitudes ... and help the people to build greater and better democratic institutions than we have ever had before" (2–3). What Antigonish could teach them was an approach to life as experimental as democracy itself. This approach, through "trial and error," was how democracy itself moved. Through the Antigonish movement, "ideas [are] not only being generated and sifted, but a body of able men [are] themselves being educated and [are] learning to think and work together" (9). Democracy was the beginning and end point of Antigonish, and its drive for "an education that is not educationalization" was the "very life blood" of that endeavour (9–10).

Daniel Tröhler's take on the "educationalization" of modern societies is a major interpretation of education's role under the conditions of modernity. In this chapter, I have drawn upon the Canadian Antigonish movement and, in particular, the writing of its most important "organic intellectual," M.M. Coady, to show how these adult educators worked to create a very different, grassroots form of educationalization – or, an education that is not educationalization – in response to modernity and its expression as liberal-democratic capitalism. What the educators of Antigonish produced, and what was theorized in Coady's work, pushes us to see educationalization in a far different light than that offered up by Tröhler's theory. Ultimately, educationalization, like all constructive theories, will prove its worth over time by its elasticity and adaptability to challenges like that represented by the adult educators of eastern Nova Scotia.

NOTES

1. I owe the phrase an "education that is not educationalization" to the philosopher (and THEIRG member) Chris Beeman. My thanks to Chris for this insight.
2. This is far from being a comprehensive history of the Antigonish movement. Rather, it is what Ian McKay calls a "reconnaissance." This scholarly strategy is "several steps down the ladder of comprehensiveness from a ... final synthesis" on the subject. Instead its a "preliminary examination or survey, as of the territory and resources" of this history. The goal is not to produce the "final word" on Antigonish, but rather to "awake us [to its] little explored realities." In this case, I offer a survey of Coady's writings in Antigonish as an "education that is not educationalization" (I. McKay 2008, 1–3). Fuller accounts include Lotz (2005); Lotz and Welton (1997); Welton (2001); Alexander (1997); Sacouman (1976); and MacInnes (1978), among others.
3. The term "possessive individualism" originates with the Canadian philosopher C.B. Macpherson. It denotes what he saw as a fundamental flaw in liberal ideology – that its most cherished tenants (individual freedom, free speech, formal equality, and so on) are fundamentally undermined by the logic of capitalism. As he writes, modern liberalism's "life began in capitalist market societies, and from the beginning, it accepted their basic unconscious assumption, which might be paraphrased as 'Market maketh man.'" (Macpherson 1988, 1).
4. On the difference between pedagogy and andragogy, see Knowles (1980).
5. For a dissenting take, see Ludlow (2013; 2015).
6. In late nineteenth- and early twentieth-century Canada, Protestants, despite being vastly outnumbered by Catholics, sat at the very centre of the modern Canadian state-apparatus. An important exception was Quebec, in which the state followed the dictates of Ultramontane Catholicism until the 1960s (I. McKay 2008, 223–4). Many "moderns" in this period – and many historians subsequently – have considered Catholicism a reactionary force in Canada: Protestantism was "progressive"; Catholicism was intellectually, socially, and economically backward. An important, often unspoken, claim underlies these assessments: that Canadian Catholics were unconcerned with change in this world, their eyes instead fixed on Rome and the "eternal reality located outside of graspable time and space" (ibid., 223).

This was not so with the educators at Antigonish. While indeed focused on that eternal reality, they never lost sight of concrete social and economic circumstances "on the ground" in eastern Nova Scotia. Antigonish was (in part) an eastern Nova Scotian answer to debates over the "social question" – or how Catholics should respond to the upheavals of liberal modernity. As historian Robert Dennis explains, the question broke down along three interconnected lines. Advocates of "corporatism" conceived of human nature in terms of "natural law" – or, religious truth as derived from God, mediated by the church, and embodied in human reason. "Distributionism" was a more concrete attempt to stave off the excesses of liberal capitalism through "schemes of social credit, co-operatives, [and] back-to-the-land projects." At the heart of the latter was the "Just Wage" – the demand that workers be paid enough to keep their families and communities afloat in the face of industrial expansion. "Self-reliance" was also key. Political and economic activity would emerge "from the ground up," rather than being imposed by any outside, temporal force. The third response was "Personalism." Personalists sought to put individuality on a more expansive footing than that allowed under capitalism. These individuals would become "committed witnesses to the truth, who through their own interior renewal and living faith would galvanize the masses into a new communal structure" gathered together under the auspices of the church (Dennis 2014, 19, 17–22).

7 The Maritimer and socialist Colin McKay was eloquent about what the traditional Nova Scotian worker lost under the new industrial capitalist order:

> The shore fisherman in his own little boat is his own master, the regent of his actions, pursuing his calling according to his fancy on a sea that from infancy he had regarded as his own. [Now, instead] of being masters of craft, free on a little boat operated with the aid of a son or two, the fishermen are more and more being incorporated into the machine process, converted into cogs of a wheel, units of a process which is regulated by [an] ever-expanding series of requirements ... Schedules of time, place and circumstance more and more rule the activities of men, and the personal initiative and independence which were the birthrights and prized privileges of generations of [fishermen are disappearing into] limbo. (C. McKay 1996, 245–6)

8 The cooperative idea was first promoted by utopian socialists in France and England in the 1820s and 1830s. It was imported into Nova Scotian mining communities in the 1860s, later spreading to Ontario and Quebec in the 1880s. Cooperative advocates sought an alternative to the possessive individualist logic of capitalism through "democratic member control" of work, the distribution of surpluses (profits) "according to member use,"

"co-operation among co-operatives," and ultimately "support for sustainable community development." The reified worker and the alienating (and alienated) boss alike would become outmoded, as artificial hierarchies were replaced by "a vigorous form of self-help ... in which the co-operators mutually lifted themselves up by their combined resources and character." Finally, education would be central to "co-operatizing" social life itself. Work spaces would become educational spaces, which would then become "organizing node[s]" for an actually existing democracy – a "new system of truthful and social commerce." The import of this line of thought for the Antigonish movement is clear (Rodgers 1998, 326, 329–30, 330).

REFERENCES

Alexander, A. 1997. *The Antigonish Movement: Moses Coady and Adult Education Today*. Toronto: Thompson Education Publishing.

Axelrod, P. *The Promise of Schooling: Education in Canada, 1800–1914*. Toronto: University of Toronto Press.

Bauman, Z. 2007. *Liquid Times: Living in an Age of Uncertainty*. Cambridge: Polity Press.

Berman, M. 2010. *All That Is Solid Melts into Air: The Experience of Modernity*. London: Verso.

Brookfield, S. 1986. *Understanding and Facilitating Adult Learning: A Comprehensive Analysis of Principles and Effective Practices*. San Francisco: Jossey-Bass.

Coady, M.M. 1939. *Masters of Their Own Destiny: The Story of the Antigonish Movement of Adult Education through Economic Cooperation*. New York: Harper and Row.

– 1950. "Mobilizing for Enlightenment." In *Adult Education in Canada*, edited by J.R. Kidd, 198–203. Toronto: Canadian Association for Adult Education.

Dennis, R.H. 2014. "The Via Media to Vatican II: Liberalism, Socialism, and Transatlantic Catholic Social Thought in English Canada, 1912 to 1961." PhD diss., Queen's University.

Fraser, N. 1990. "Rethinking the Public Sphere: A Contribution to the Critique of Actually Existing Democracy." *Social Text* 25/26: 56–80. https://doi.org/10.2307/466240.

Giddens, A. 1991. *The Consequences of Modernity*. Cambridge: Polity Press.

Habermas, J. 2005. *Legitimation Crisis*. Boston: Beacon Press.

Knowles, M. 1980. *The Modern Practice of Education: From Pedagogy to Andragogy*. 2nd ed. New York: Cambridge Books.

Landis, B.Y. 1950. "Little Dover." In *Adult Education in Canada*, edited by J.R. Kidd, 195–8. Toronto: Canadian Association for Adult Education.

Lotz, J. 2005. *The Humble Giant: Moses Coady, Canada's Rural Revolutionary*. Ottawa: Novalis.

Lotz, J., and Welton M.R. 1997. *Father Jimmy: Life and Times of Jimmy Tompkins*. Wreck Cove, NS: Breton Books.

Löwy, M., and Sayre, R. 2001. *Romanticism against the Tide of Modernity*. Durham, NC: Duke University Press.

Ludlow, P. 2013. "Saints and Sinners: Popular Myth and the Study of the Personalities of the Antigonish Movement." *Acadiensis* 42 (1): 99–126. https://journals.lib.unb.ca/index.php/Acadiensis/article/view/20291.

– 2015. *The Canny Scot: Archbishop James Morrison of Antigonish*. Montreal and Kingston: McGill-Queen's University Press.

MacInnes, D. 1978. "Clerics, Fishermen, Farmers, and Workers: The Antigonish Movement and Identity in Eastern Nova Scotia, 1928–1939." PhD diss., McMaster University.

Macpherson, C.B. 1988. *The Life and Times of Liberal Democracy*. Oxford: Oxford University Press.

McKay, C. 1996. *For a Working-Class Culture in Canada: A Selection of Colin McKay's Writings on Sociology and Political Economy, 1897–1939*. Edited by Ian McKay. St John's, NL: Canadian Committee on Labour History.

McKay, I. 2008. *Reasoning Otherwise: Leftists and the People's Enlightenment in Canada, 1890–1920*. Toronto: Between the Lines.

Rancière, J. 1991. *The Ignorant Schoolmaster: Five Lessons in Intellectual Emancipation*. Stanford, CA: Stanford University Press.

Remes, J. 2010. "In Search of 'Saner Minds': Bishop James Morrison and the Origins of the Antigonish Movement." *Acadiensis* 39 (1): 58–82. https://journals.lib.unb.ca/index.php/Acadiensis/article/view/15384/16523.

Rodgers, D.T. 1998. *Atlantic Crossings: Social Politics in a Progressive Age*. Cambridge, MA: Belknap Press of Harvard University Press.

Sacouman, R.J. 1976. "Social Origins of Antigonish Movement Co-operative Associations in Eastern Nova Scotia." PhD diss., University of Toronto.

Sim, A. 1963. "Farm Radio Forum." In *Learning and Society: Readings in Canadian Adult Education*, edited by J.R. Kidd, 213–22. Toronto: Mutual Press.

Tompkins, J. 1963. "Knowledge for the People." In *Learning and Society: Readings in Canadian Adult Education*, edited by J.R. Kidd, 93–106. Toronto: Mutual Press.

Tröhler, D. 2016. "Educationalization of Social Problems and the Educationalization of the Modern World." In *Encyclopedia of Educational Philosophy and Theory*, edited by Michael A. Peters, 1–10. Singapore: Springer. https://orbilu.uni.lu/bitstream/10993/26835/1/Troehler_Educationalization%20of%20Social%20Problems%20and%20the%20Educationalization%20of%20the%20Modern%20World.pdf.

Welton, M.R. 2001. *Little Mosie from the Margaree*. Toronto: Thompson Educational Publishing.
– 2003. "Decoding Coady: Masters of Their Own Destiny under Critical Scrutiny." *Studies in Continuing Education* 25 (1): 75–93. https://doi.org/10.1080/01580370309283.
Williams, R. 1993. "Culture Is Ordinary." In *Border Country: Raymond Williams in Adult Education*, edited by J. McIlroy and S. Westwood, 89–103. Leicester, UK: National Institute of Adult Continuing Education.

PART II

Catholicism, Spirituality, and Educationalization

intersecting portals observed © Alan R. Wilkinson

5 Educationalization of the Modern World: The Case of the Loretto Sisters in British North America

ELIZABETH M. SMYTH

In his 2016 *Encyclopedia of Educational Philosophy and Theory* entry, Daniel Tröhler (2016, 1) defines educationalization as the "idea of education that promises to be the engine of modernity by means of (new) and broadly disseminated knowledge and technologies and, at the same time, an instance of moral reassurance empowering the individual exposed to these modern conditions and their moral hazards to act morally or virtuously." Further, he argues that "the educationalization of the modern world ... is key to understanding the cultural (and ultimately Protestant) construction of modernity and the modern self as a self-reflective lifelong learner in a system of thought that embodies fears and the hope for redemption at the same time" (ibid., 9). This chapter argues that the large and growing presence of Roman Catholic teaching orders of men and women religious that emerged during the long eighteenth and nineteenth centuries played a critical role in the transnational expansion of education systems within empires. As Marc Depaepe (2012) has explained, the expansion of state-wide systems of education in the course of the nineteenth century served many purposes, moving from social control through the moulding of citizen-pupils to the creation of an industrial workforce. This chapter argues that, aligned with the state, teaching religious orders held the same goal articulated by Tröhler of "strengthening the soul towards (civic) virtue" (2016, 6). Based on an analysis of the Institute of the Blessed Virgin Mary (the Loretto Sisters) based in Toronto, Ontario, this chapter outlines how, through curriculum, instruction, and teacher development, Roman Catholic religious orders (and, ultimately, pupils and parents) were engaging with modernity. During the 1870s, the Toronto Loretto Sisters actively, but not without both internal and external r esistance, restructured their curriculum and thereby the education they delivered of their pupils.

Their goal was to educate pupils to meet the state-regulated credentials for admission to the emerging professions. Ultimately, the Loretto Sisters established a women's college affiliated with the non-denominational University of Toronto. It was, in the words of Jill Ker Conway, one of many such learning spaces of special significance that served as "intellectual centres within which the question of knowledge and faith had to be reconciled" (2002, 13).

Women Religious: A Unique Cohort of Teachers

In Canada, the history of education is inextricably bound with the history of Roman Catholic teaching orders. On 4 July 1639, Marie Guyart, known in religion as Mother Marie de l'Incarnation of the Order of St Ursula of Tours (the Ursulines), disembarked in New France with four companions. They were Canada's first women teachers. The Ursulines were the first of the teaching orders in the colony; they would certainly not be the last. At the order's zenith in 1965, the Census of Religious Sisters of Canada reported that there were 183 congregations of women religious in Canada, 60 per cent of which were French in origin. Their membership comprised some 65,254 women (Lessard and Montminy 1966), who operated 2,345 or 76 per cent of the 3,100 Catholic educational institutions in the country (Lacelle 1987). These vowed women worked in all sectors of education. They were employed as classroom teachers, school principals, and superintendents of schools; university professors in all fields, including theology; college and university presidents; and postsecondary instructors in the health care and social service sectors, including at schools of nursing; and they were authors of textbooks and writers of public policy.

"Women religious" is the umbrella term for nuns and sisters – women who bind themselves to living in community under publicly proclaimed vows of poverty, chastity, and obedience. Each community has a charism – a unique way of living out their lives of service to God. As a result, some orders take a fourth vow that is directly related to their charism. In the case of an order dedicated to education, that vow would be one of teaching.

Admission to an order is a long and regulated process. A candidate must be in good health and, for most of the previous centuries, had to be of legitimate parentage. She must come with the recommendation of her parish priest. After an interview with the Mother Superior, she enters the congregation as a postulant, generally for a relatively short period of some three to six months, during which time she is observed by the community leadership. If she is deemed acceptable, she receives the habit, is given a name in religion, and, as a novice, begin the multi-year journey in prayer, studies, and work in order to become a fully professed religious. For a teaching sister, her time as a novice is also a time to learn how to teach. As well as reporting to the mistress of novices, a teaching sister in training begins an association with the directress of schools, who, throughout the sister's career as a teacher, would provide a parallel structure of inspection to that already in place through the state at a school or other institution to which the teaching sister's services were assigned.

In the period before the massive changes in religious life resulting from the Second Vatican Council (1961–5), the life of a teaching sister was highly regulated. The vow of obedience removed from her the power over career and personal decision-making. The vow of poverty removed financial independence. The vow of chastity eliminated the choice of pursing intimate relationships or even "particular friendships" – code for any close friendship. Each community had books of constitutions and customs that listed, in breathtaking detail, how a teaching sister was to live her life; how she was to spend all of her waking hours; how she was to dress and deport herself. As stated in the *Constitution of the Sisters of St Joseph of Toronto* (1881), a woman entering that religious order surrendered herself to the "service of God through the service of neighbour."

The Loretto Sisters in Ontario

Teaching sisters came to Ontario almost 300 years after the arrival of the Ursulines in Quebec.[1] Prior to the passage of the 1841 Common Schools Act (and, indeed, even later in some areas of its vast territory), the region known variously as Upper Canada and Canada West, and now the province of Ontario, had a complex history in the provision of private, secular, and denominational schooling – both formally and informally constituted. Jane Errington's (1995) work on women teachers as entrepreneurs and Patricia Kmeic's (2015) research on the plethora of interdenominational Protestant institutions for the promotion of literacy among both school-aged children and adults attest to this rich history. Within the Diocese of Toronto, which was created in 1841, with Michael Power as its first bishop, attention focused on the provision of denominational schools for the Roman Catholic population. Power invited communities of men and women religious, lay brothers and secular priests, to his massive diocese. Appeals to several European congregational motherhouses yielded personnel. In 1847, five members of the Institute of the Blessed Virgin Mary (Loretto Sisters) came to Toronto to teach in the separate (i.e., Catholic) schools and to establish a private school for the education of girls and young women.

The Loretto Sisters are also known as the Irish Daughters of Mary Ward. Ward (1585–1645) was born into a prominent and devoutly Catholic family in Yorkshire, England. Growing up in turbulent years of inter-religious conflict, she was privately educated. As a young woman, she was determined to establish a religious order modelled on the male Society of Jesus (the Jesuits). Her vision was of an order dedicated to the education of girls and young women. Like the Jesuits, her sisters would follow the spirituality of Ignatius Loyola, would be international and have a unitary administrative structure based on a General Superior, and would deliver a curriculum parallel to that outlined in the *Ratio Studiorum*.[2] Ward's ideas were neither encouraged nor welcomed by either the Jesuits or the hierarchy of the Roman Catholic Church. She continued to work in exile, and she and four companions established a house and school in Flanders. Her actions led to her being summoned before the Inquisition, and she was imprisoned and excommunicated from the Roman Catholic Church for her heretical views on the role of women. She bequeathed to her community a tumultuous early history; indeed, she herself was suppressed as the foundress of the Institute of the Blessed Virgin Mary until the early twentieth century. Yet, in spite of these challenges, the order flourished beyond her death and spread throughout Europe, and ultimately around the world, as a congregation of vowed women dedicated "to our own perfection and salvation, under the influence of God's grace, but, with the same divine assistance, earnestly to endeavour to promote the perfection and salvation of our neighbour by the instruction of the female sex" (*Rules of the Institute of the Blessed Virgin Mary*, cited in Cooper 1993, 95).

In 1814, Daniel Murray, bishop of Dublin, encouraged Dublin heiress Frances Ball to enter the Institute of the Blessed Virgin Mary in York, England, with the goal of establishing an independent foundation in Ireland. By mid-century, the congregation was flourishing, and Ball sent sisters out on teaching missions to Calcutta (1841), Mauritius (1844), and Gibraltar (1845). After numerous requests in writing, and ultimately a visit in person, Mother Ball yielded to Bishop Power's invitation to Canada West and in 1847 dispatched sisters to his fledgling diocese. Power had been candid with Ball. He told her that conditions would not be ideal. In the colony, they would find a poor Irish population that would be served in a parish school; a small Catholic middle class that required a select school for their daughters; and, he stated, bigoted Protestants who, when they saw the superior education delivered by the sisters, would want to send their daughters to be educated at Loretto. Despite the challenges, the mission carried great potential. Ball sent five sisters across the Atlantic to staff this fourth international mission. One of the five pioneering sisters was Ellen Dease (1820–1889), in religion Mother Teresa Dease, an experienced teacher who was asked to go – not sent, as the Loreto rule would read, under holy obedience.

Mother Teresa Dease

Like Mother Ball, Mother Teresa Dease was an Irish woman born of privilege. Dease's family had benefited both from Catholic Emancipation and an association with imperials structures. Her father was from a line of surgeons – her grandfather, who, although a Catholic, had served as a professor of surgery, was memorialized by a statue in the Royal Irish College of Surgeons. Her father had studied at Trinity College and then had joined the army. Upon retirement, he returned to Dublin to serve as surgeon at the Westmoreland Lock Hospital. He died in 1821, leaving his wife, three daughters (including an infant Ellen), and two sons. His wife died soon after him. The three orphaned girls were taken in by the maternal family and were privately educated, with time living abroad to give them an education in "the accomplishments" (Costello 1916). Anna, the eldest, entered the Loreto Order in the town of Fermoy, Ireland and, as Mother Eucharia, rose to be the superior of that community. She was described as a "highly gifted superioress" (Obituary of Miss Bridget Dease n.d.). While remaining a single, lay woman, Bridget, the middle daughter, lived with the Fermoy community until her death in 1867. Ellen, the youngest, entered the Loreto Order in Dublin in January 1845 and received the habit and her name in religion, Sister Teresa, in October 1845. She became a full member (professed) on 3 August 1847, and, just two days later, she set off for the mission in Canada, where, given her musical, linguistic, and artistic skills, she would serve as a teacher.

Four years later, Dease was the only member of the initial group still alive in Canada. Neither Mother Frances Ball nor Bishop Michael Power could have foreseen the horrors of 1847 – leaving behind the Great Famine in Ireland, the sisters arrived in Toronto in the midst of a typhus epidemic. Power, their ecclesiastical superior, succumbed to the epidemic within three weeks of their arrival. They themselves were ailing, and the Canadian winter had not even begun. Power's successor, Armand de Charbonnel, would later write:

> These good ladies have suffered more than I can say. Deprived of a bishop, of a house and of many things during three years, I am amazed at their

> having got through the numberless difficulties they contend with ... There is a good spirit in the house, they are esteemed and cherished by their pupils and all who are acquainted with them; they have done and will do much good among the Catholics and Protestants ... Still the members of the house are few; Reverend Mother is very delicate; Sister Gertrude keeps to her bed [she had a foot amputated because of frost bite]; one has died; in fact they are overwhelmed ... They have suffered heroically; they are sinking under the hardships of their situation. (Quoted in McGovern 1989, 97)

Shortly after this letter, Mother Ignatia Hutchinson, the founding superior died. Dease was cast unwillingly into the role of leader of a seemingly doomed enterprise. In 1851, she had no choice but to close their struggling boarding school. Writing to Dublin, she suggested to Mother Frances Ball that the whole mission be closed and the sisters return to Ireland. Ball firmly directed her to stay. Soon thereafter, their fortunes changed. Canadian women began presenting themselves as postulants, and a few additional sisters arrived from Ireland. By 1859, thirty-one women had joined the community. The order was on a more solid footing and would grow in numbers as an ever-expanding number of women presented themselves as postulants. The community would also expand geographically, establishing a network of schools throughout Ontario, Saskatchewan (1921), British Columbia (1958), and into the United States, in Illinois (1880), Michigan (1896), California (1949), and Arizona (1950). Some of the schools had brief existences; others lengthy ones. Yet, it is important to note that the expansion of the community in no way kept pace with the demands for their services as teachers.

Dease spent over forty years in Canada, returning twice to Ireland to visit her blood and religious families. She died on 1 July 1889. As a teacher and general superior, she shaped the history of the order in Canada. She lived through the beginnings of the Dominion of Canada in 1867 and the implementation of the country's constitution, the British North America Act. Sections 91 and 93 of that act are of special significance. They defined education as a provincial jurisdiction (with the exception of the education of Indigenous peoples, which was the responsibility of the federal government), recognizing the linguistic and religious rights of English and French, Catholic and Protestant. As a result, in Ontario, two parallel publicly funded school systems emerged: one Roman Catholic ("separate") and one non-denominational. In effect, the separate educational system in which Dease taught was further bifurcated into publicly funded and privately funded schools – with publicly funded Roman Catholic separate schools and privately funded Catholic elite schools (also known as select schools or academies) that, ironically, enrolled a multi-denominational student population.

Dease was a teacher at heart. Throughout her long life, she taught a number of subjects in the congregation's academies: English, Italian, and French (a language in which she conducted some of her correspondence) as well as drawing, painting, and music (piano, harp, and organ). She also taught religion. She had to personally wrestle with the thorny issue of the purpose of education for girls and young women. Strongly vested in the "accomplishments" curriculum[3] that she had pursued as a young woman, her views, at times, ran counter to those of other members of her congregation. Yet, under her leadership, her congregation came to be at the forefront of one of the most significant debates in the educationalization of Catholic schooling in the province with the decision she ultimately made as general superior to change the content of the curriculum delivered in the private Loretto academies to align with that of the provincial schools.

The Convent Curriculum and Modernity

Ultimately, and in some ways reluctantly, Dease changed the course of the history of Loretto. Her actions had a significant impact on all religious congregations that administered secondary (and, indeed, elementary as well) schools in the province of Ontario. Once Dease chose to engage with the state by aligning the curriculum of her schools to prepare girls for the emerging professions, she set her congregation on the path to transform their convent-academies into college-oriented institutions of learning. Further, these changes enabled convent schools to also align their curriculum with the needs of external agencies, thus permitting convent school graduates to gain access to teacher education, music certification, and business certification programs.

Dease was forced to confront her own philosophy of convent education when she agreed to send sisters to the small rural community of Lindsay, Ontario, in response to the persistent advocacy of a socially reforming priest, Michael Stafford. Congregational oral tradition tells that Toronto archbishop J.J. Lynch was supportive of this move, in spite of Dease's personal reluctance. Perhaps the chance to oversee a curriculum alignment in a small town located at some distance from Toronto was an advantage. Perhaps, too, the support of the eager and highly educated pastor who had a proven track record in social change led Lynch – and ultimately Dease – to support this change in curricular orientation.

The town of Lindsay is located in the Kawartha Lakes region, about 130 kilometres northeast of Toronto. Its population in 1871 was some 4,000 residents, the majority of whom were Irish and Roman Catholic.[4] The local pastor, Michael Stafford (1832–1882), was a crusader for temperance and education.[5] He was educated in public schools in the Ottawa

Valley, the francophone Collège de St Thérèse, and Regiopolis College, a diocesan college located in Kingston, Ontario, that acquired the power to grant degrees in 1866. As a twenty-five-year-old newly minted priest, he was appointed professor of philosophy and director of his alma mater Regiopolis, a position that he held until the heart disease that would ultimately kill him first presented itself. Travel to warmer climes was prescribed – first to the southern United States and then to the British Isles, Italy, and France. He then returned to the Kingston area, taking charge of a number of parishes before moving to St Mary's Parish, in Lindsay, in 1868. There, he found a town where "taverns were multiplying and schools growing inefficient" ("The Rev. Michael Stafford" n.d., 1). He had tremendous success organizing a temperance society, whose membership grew to nine hundred members (about one-quarter of the population the town). Once he had achieved that goal, he turned his attention to fundraising for a school and convent building, raising some $40,000 (over $700,000 today) to build a convent and school that eventually would serve "300 young lady pupils" in a day and boarding school (3). With the support of Toronto Archbishop Lynch, Stafford approached the Loretto community to establish two schools in Lindsay: an elementary school associated with the parish church (St Mary's Separate School) and a "Select School for the Education of Young Ladies" (Loretto Lindsay). In 1874, Mother Dease committed her community to this mission and placed it under the leadership of Mother Dosithea Gibney.

Like Dease, Frances Gibney – in religion, Mother Dosithea Gibney (1842–1917) – was born in Dublin. As a child, she immigrated with her parents to Guelph, Ontario. There, she attended Loretto Academy, and, as barely a teenager, she entered the order at age fourteen (something that was rare and would later be prohibited under changes to the Code of Canon Law and revisions of the Loretto constitution). As a novice and junior professed sister, she acquired her teaching skills through apprenticeship and mentorship from senior sisters. In 1862, Gibney was one of the five sisters[6] named in a provincial statute, the Act to Incorporate the Sisters of Our Lady of Loretto of the town of Guelph.[7] That act described the sisters as operating "an institution for the instruction and education of young persons of the female sex." Yet, the statute represented more than that: it was in fact an attempt at structuring the Loretto Sisters in North American along diocesan lines. Unlike the school, this venture was to be short lived. The motherhouses in Toronto and Dublin quickly intervened, and Loretto Guelph reverted to being a mission of Toronto and not an independent foundation. Gibney would have learned much about congregational governance from this experience that would serve her well in her future roles.

Gibney grew to have the confidence of the Toronto community. She served as a delegate to the meetings of the provincial and general chapters of 1877, 1883, 1910, and 1911, thus playing a formative role in the transition of the Toronto motherhouse from a province of the Irish motherhouse to an independent foundation. Gibney served the Lindsay community for the first four years of its existence and then was appointment as the founding superior and principal of schools in Joliet, Illinois (1880), principal of the high school in Chicago, and teacher at Loretto Niagara and Loretto Guelph. She also was a member of the congregational leadership team, serving on the General Council for fifteen years.

Other talented teachers followed Gibney to Loretto Lindsay. The community remained there until 1890, when, in one of the frequent fires that roared through the town, their convent was destroyed. Community oral history recalls that the rebuilt convent was not appropriate to their needs, and they therefore turned their schools over to the Sisters of St Joseph in nearby Peterborough.

Loretto Lindsay was a source of many vocations, including for three of the five nieces of Father Stafford who attended the school. The first of the Stafford women to enter the sisterhood was Elizabeth Margaret Stafford (1862–1930; in religion, Mother Irenea Stafford), who entered the convent in 1886 at age twenty-four. Even after the Loretto sisters left the community, two Stafford women chose to enter Loretto: the blood sister of Mother Irenea Stafford, Mary Anne (Annie) Stafford (1865–1947; in religion, Mother Alacoque Stafford), who entered in 1896 at the age of twenty-four, and her cousin Elizabeth Ann Stafford (1872–1910; in religion Mother Emerita Stafford), who entered in 1891. All three of these women went on to have careers in the Loretto academy schools of Canada and the United States, as well as in the separate schools of Ontario.

Dease's decision to support a state-aligned curriculum was significant for many reasons. First, it took control of the curriculum from the hands of the religious order. Loretto, like many other congregations such as the Ursulines and the Religious of the Sacred Heart advertised to their potential clients an international curriculum that formed the heart of their identity and shaped their pupils. Yet, by subsuming their curriculum under that of the state, their pupils were armed with credential to enter the professions. Initially, they were eligible to begin the process to be certified as teachers; later, they were able to present themselves for admittance to other state-regulated institutions of higher learning: schools of nursing and universities to name just two. Loretto would lead the way in carving new paths that would eventually lead to their schools offering credentials in the newly emerging fields of secretarial studies and the traditional fields of the visual and performing arts. Some congregations, including the Ursulines and Sisters of St Joseph would follow the Loretto example and would eventually create federated women's colleges within the publicly funded and non-denominational university sector; others, like the Religious of the Sacred Heart's foundation in London, Ontario, would not. Yet it is important to note Dease's opposition to the idea of embracing the provincial curriculum. Her attitude is apparent in a 1877 letter to the Dublin motherhouse: "Our (sisters) have plenty to do, they work hard, *too* hard, but there is no avoiding it. Education here is carried to excess and I think they will find such is the case" (McGovern 1989, 156). She was even more explicit in another, undated, letter: "It seems rather depreciation of our institution to propose to our becoming affiliated to the Art School of the Normal School, as if we needed to be propped up by the world in which we are appointed to give aid we do not receive. The idea that we should convey with truth is that our convents are superior to those worldly art schools."[8] Yet, despite her misgivings, she enabled the Lindsay congregation to work with the vision of modernity constructed by Father Stafford.

Stafford was described as a significant motivating force for Ontario Catholics: "He succeeded in arousing and stimulating in Catholics of Ontario a laudable ambition, an impatience with mediocrity and impressed upon them how much he expected from them because they were Catholics" ("The Rev. Michael Stafford" n.d., 5). He endowed prizes for Catholics seeking teacher education including one of "$100 for the first successful Candidate for the Normal School First Class Teachers' Certificate [that] was obtained by the late Dr J.F. White who for many years was Principal of the Lindsay Separate School" (ibid.). The pamphlet celebrating his life concludes: "The causes of temperance and education have advanced so much since Father Stafford's time. It is difficult, now, to realize the obstacles he encountered in his promotion of these two great benefits to humanity, but he made possible the improvement of today; he did pioneer work and laid the solid foundation for today's advancement" (8). The author of the pamphlet notes that both public and separate school pupils attended his funeral. It also notes that he was offered the principalship of the Ottawa Normal School.

Stafford saw that Catholic education needed to be altered if Catholic pupils were to gain access to the emerging professions. Without the inclusion of "the profane" subjects of mathematics and sciences, for example, paths to social mobility would not be open to all. Committing members of her congregation to work in the schools of Lindsay required Dease to ensure that her sisters had the required credentials – that they themselves held normal school qualifications and could demonstrate that they were certified teachers. This, in itself, challenged the traditional ways in which teaching sisters were formed.

The constitutions of teaching orders, including Loretto, had clearly defined roles and responsibilities aligned with learning to become a teaching sister. The superior and her council made the decisions about who would teach and who would undertake other duties in the convent. Many orders had classes of sisters, differentiated by habits that outwardly demonstrated their ranks. Choir sisters were the professional class, so named for their ability to recite the Divine Office in Latin, and they wore a higher standard of religious garb. The lay sisters performed domestic chores. Their habits reflected their manual labour. They were considered second-class members of the congregation, and they were relegated to separate spaces for dining and recreation. For community penitential practices, such as the Chapter of Faults, where sisters publicly announced their transgressions, the lay sisters went first and left before the choir sisters began to recite their flaws. Undertaking to change the curriculum and have it delivered by teachers who were credentialed by external agencies challenged this entire system, adding another dimension to internal decision-making: the congregations would either need to amend their admission criteria to include applicants who had completed a teaching credential or alternatively, the congregation would have to bear the cost of sending a novice to school, thereby eliminating her from the employment pool.

Constitutions also outlined the order's expectation of the teaching sister. Her life was described as one "full of difficulties requiring much exertion of the voice and great application of the mind." Superiors were cautioned that "the choice of the sisters who are destined to be teachers should be to the congregation a special object of solicitude ... [They should possess] common sense and good judgement ... Their natural disposition must be mild and inclined to virtue; hence those shall not be received who have a violent temper, are haughty, stubborn, frivolous, inconsistent, proud, idle" (*Constitutions of the Sisters of St Joseph of Toronto* 1881, 32). Teaching sisters were told that they should undertake their duties seriously, with systematic planning: before appearing before their pupils, they should "previously prepare lessons ... so that while understanding perfectly what they teach, they may be able to communicate it to their pupils with clearness and precision ... [They should] devot[e] to their own improvement all the time that is necessary, but they shall not study any other [subjects] than those prescribed by the Superior or Directress [of Schools] in order that their progress in science may be accompanied by their progress in humility and obedience" (ibid., 90–1).

In short, with the decision to have teaching sisters regulated by the state, religious orders were subjecting themselves to parallel structures of recruitment, formation, and inspection. This opened an array of opportunities and challenges for congregational leaders and their members.

Learnings from the Loretto Lindsay Case

The Loretto Sisters were only one of a number of congregations of women religious in Ontario whose histories were reshaped by the decisions to align their curriculum with that of the state. As a result of such decisions, women religious became more integrated with the larger population of teachers and were no longer isolated within their convent walls.

There was never an institution of teacher education sponsored by a religious congregation in Ontario. (The nearest example is the establishment of a short-lived English-language teachers' college established by the Sisters of St Joseph of Pembroke in an English-language enclave of Chapeau, Quebec, in the 1960s.) Fascinating tales of the experience of novices in provincial teachers' colleges appear in the archives of the congregations and oral histories. In Peterborough, for example, the "ladies in the costumes" were asked to sit at the back of the classroom, as their veils blocked the view of students sitting behind them. A 1950s version of the "burkini" was created so that novices could take to the pool, as they were required to pass a swimming test in order to get a teaching certificate. For some non-Catholic teachers in training, it was the first time they met vowed women, and some went on to form lifelong friendships. Teaching sisters went on to pursue doctoral studies in education, including Toronto Sister of St Joseph Antoinette Sheehan, who wrote her dissertation on sister principals. She went on to teach education administration in the Faculty of Education at the University of Toronto.

The move to engagement with the public sector gave sisters many opportunities, including the chance to participate in teachers' organizations. Sister Mary Lenore Carter, sister of the two Carter brother bishops who played a significant role at Vatican II (Gerald Emmett Cardinal Carter, cardinal archbishop of London and Toronto, and Alex Carter, Bishop of Sault Ste Marie, became president of her local unit of the Ontario English Catholic Teachers' Association (OECTA) and ultimately was provincial president of the OECTA and the first religious to be president of the Ontario Teachers' Federation. Further, teaching sisters sat on provincial royal commissions. Of particular note was Sister Alice Marie Macdonald, a Sister of St Joseph of London, who was a member of the Hall-Dennis Commission, whose report, *Living and Learning*, contributed to the restructuring of Ontario education in the 1960s.

Congregations actively engaged with the curriculum-development process, sending representatives to work on curriculum-writing teams and to become authors of textbooks. For example, Richard Litch, the managing director of the textbook publisher Ginn, wrote to the superior of the Sisters of St Joseph of Toronto to expresss the admiration he had for the Toronto Lorettos and the extent to which the congregation supported their sisters as authors: "The Lorettos have made a most outstanding contribution to the teaching of reading through Mother Clement ... a Lady of Loretto ... [who] has been released from her teaching duties to carry authorship."[9]

One of the most significant developments that ultimately resulted from the alignment of curriculum was the decision of the Loretto Sisters to establish a women's college. Beginning in the first decade of the twentieth century, the congregation began its planning, which brought it into competition with two other orders – the Sisters of St Joseph of Toronto and the Ursulines of the Chatham Union. The archival record documents the lobbying they engaged in, having one of their benefactors, Dr J.J. Cassidy, appeal to the superior of the Congregation of St Basil, the male order that ran St Michael's College at the University of Toronto:

> *Only the community of Loretto is qualified to teach the higher education* ... Loretto Abbey is competent to carry out the training ... The Ladies of Loretto are exclusively a teaching body and are affiliated with various universities abroad ... It would seem almost that it is a part of their system. I am very much interested in promoting this affiliation and I trust as a friend of mine and also for the advancement of higher Catholic Education you will aid me in the completion of their work.[10]

Ultimately, the two Toronto orders – St Joseph's and Loretto – established women's colleges that affiliated with the University of Toronto under the umbrella of St Michael's. The Ursulines would establish Brescia College at Western University – the only one of the three that today is still a teaching university-college. The women students of these colleges clearly knew that their purposes was dual – projecting the faith and engaging with the professions, as the 1919 convocation speaker advised:

> As I sat here I wondered what our grandmothers would think of this higher education, I am inclined to think they would be rather scandalized. But we must realize, whether we like it or not that higher education is here and is here to stay. And if it is a fact in the life of to-day, if we have to

consider higher education for the women of the country, there is no one bold enough to say that Catholic women should not be in the forefront of that higher education. ("Convocation" 1919, 24)

It is not an exaggeration to say that all of these developments and this engagement with modernity were directly traceable to the decision that Mother Teresa Dease made to deliver the Ontario curriculum to the young ladies of Lindsay, Ontario, almost four decades earlier.

NOTES

1 In 1841, at the invitation of Bishop Alexander Macdonnell, the Montreal-based Congrégation de Notre Dame established a school for girls in Kingston, Ontario. It is still in existence as the co-educational Regiopolis–Notre Dame High School.
2 *Ratio atque Institutio Studiorum Societatis Jesu* (Method and System of the Studies of the Society of Jesus) was originally written in the sixteenth century and modified over the centuries, especially in the wake of the re-establishment of the Jesuits in the nineteenth century. While it is a guide for both content and pedagogy, it also stressed the necessity of adapting curriculum and instruction to local needs.
3 The seminal article on this topic remains Marjorie Theobald's "Mere Accomplishments? Melbourne's Early Ladies' Schools Reconsidered" (1991).
4 For 1861 and 1871 census data, see www.ontariogenealogy.com/Victoria/lindsaytown.html.
5 Curiously, Stafford does not have an entry in the *Dictionary of Canadian Biography*. Files within the Institute of the Blessed Virgin Mary, Canadian Province Archives, document his life and work, through fragments of letters and newspaper articles and a privately published eight-page biographical pamphlet.
6 The act lists the legal names of the five women: "Mesdames Catherine, Henegan, Superior of the said Society, Louise Murcaini, Frances Gibney, Ellen Doyle and Eliza Breen."
7 An Act to Incorporate the Sisters of Our Lady of Loretto of the Town of Guelph, 1862, Cap. 91, Statutes of the Province of Ontario, 261, http://eco.canadiana.ca/view/oocihm.9_02779/2?r=0&s=1.
8 Fragment of an undated letter, Institute of the Blessed Virgin Mary, Canadian Province Archives, Superiors General: Rev Mother Teresa Dease, file 4.1-46.
9 R. Litch to Mother Maura McGuire, CSJ, 11 February 1966, Congregation of the Sisters of St Joseph of Toronto Archives, Sister Mary Alban Bouchard personal papers.

10 Dr J.J. Cassidy to Rev. Marijon, 11 December 1911, Congregation of the Sisters of St Joseph of Toronto Archives, Loretto College Box 6A (emphasis in original).

REFERENCES

Constitutions of the Sisters of St Joseph of Toronto. 1881. Toronto: Sisters of St Joseph. Congregation of the Sisters of St Joseph of Toronto Archives.

"Convocation." 1919. *St Michael's College Yearbook.* University of St Michael's College Archives.

Conway, J.K. 2002. "Faith Knowledge and Gender." In *Catholic Women's Colleges*, edited by T. Schrier and C. Russett, 11–17. Baltimore, MD: Johns Hopkins University Press.

Cooper, B. 1993. "A Re-examination of the Early Years of the Institute of the Blessed Virgin Mary (Loretto Sisters) in Toronto." In *Catholics at the Gathering Place*, edited by M. McGowan and B. Clarke, 89–105. Toronto: Canadian Catholic Historical Association.

Costello, B. 1916. *Letters of Rev. Mother Teresa Dease.* Toronto: McClelland and Stewart.

Depaepe, M. 2012. *Between Educationalization and Appropriation: Selected Writings on the History of Modern Educational Systems.* Leuven, BE: Leuven University Press.

Errington, E.J. 1995. *Wives and Mothers, School Mistresses, and Scullery Maids: Working Women in Upper Canada, 1790–1840.* Montreal and Kingston: McGill-Queen's University Press.

Kmeic, P. 2015. "More than Sunday's Lessons: Sunday School Education in Upper Canada, 1811–1850." PhD diss., University of Toronto.

Lacelle, C. 1987. "L'apport social des communautes religieuse catholique presentes au Canada avante 1940." Unpublished manuscript prepared for Parks Canada, Ottawa.

Lessard, M. and P. Montminy. 1966. *The Census of Religious Sisters of Canada.* Ottawa: Canadian Religious Conference.

McGovern, K., IBVM. 1989. *Something More than Ordinary.* Richmond Hill, ON: The I Team.

Obituary of Miss Bridget Dease. n.d. Institute of the Blessed Virgin Mary, Canadian Province Archives, series 4, North American Superiors general, R.1/Sh.6/Box 16, file 1 (file 4,1,1,13).

"The Rev. Michael Stafford." n.d. Pamphlet. Institute of the Blessed Virgin Mary, Canadian Province Archives.

Theobald, M. 1991. "Mere Accomplishments? Melbourne's Early Ladies' Schools Reconsidered." In *Women Who Taught: Perspectives on the History of*

Women and Teaching, edited by A. Prentice and M. Theobald, 71–91. Toronto: University of Toronto Press.

Tröhler, D. 2016. "Educationalization of Social Problems and the Educationalization of the Modern World." In *Encyclopedia of Educational Philosophy and Theory*, edited by Michael A. Peters, 1–10. Singapore: Springer. http://orbilu.uni.lu/bitstream/10993/26835/1/Troehler_Educationalization%20of%20Social%20Problems%20and%20the%20Educationalization%20of%20the%20Modern%20World.pdf.

6 New Educational Approaches of Women Religious in the Global South, 1968–1980

HEIDI MacDONALD

In the mid-1960s, the Sisters of Charity–Halifax taught in more than a hundred Catholic and public schools in eastern Canada and the United States.[1] Two-thirds of the almost 1,700 members of the congregation were primary and secondary school teachers, while the second-most common area of work, health care, engaged 7 per cent of members. This specialization in institutional education had evolved from the Sisters of Charity's charism – that is, the spirit of and purpose of their founding – to educate the poor in the spirit of Elizabeth Seton and St Vincent de Paul. That evolution mirrors the dominant North American and European educationalization of social, political, and economic problems through the institutional schooling of children, which David Bridges, Daniel Tröhler, and others have theorized.[2] In other words, the sisters accepted that teaching Roman Catholic children in large numbers was the most effective way to respond to various problems common to many nineteenth- and twentieth-century North American Catholics. Following the encouragement of the Second Vatican Council (1962–5) to renew their mission, the Sisters of Charity expanded their pedagogical approach to empowering people in the Global South and encouraging grassroots democracy. This chapter extends Josh Cole's classification in chapter 4 of the Antigonish movement as an "education that was not educationalization," by examining how a group of Nova Scotia women religious applied a variety of concepts – including those of the Antigonish movement and liberation theology – as part of their response to the social problems of the Global South.

When the Congregation of the Sisters of Charity was founded in 1856, the Roman Catholic population of Nova Scotia held minority status, minimal political influence, and below-average income levels; they suffered from broad-based anti-Catholic sentiment.[3] The archbishop of Halifax invited the Sisters of Charity–New York to assist in responding to these problems by giving Catholic students an institutional education that would allow them to take a larger role in politics, the professions, and business.[4] A century later, in a very different socio-political, post–Second Vatican Council context, the sisters questioned whether this form of educationalization of local social problems of Roman Catholics was still necessary, especially in comparison to the exponentially worse social problems of Latin America. In a shift reminiscent of Moses Coady's own refutation of traditional schooling, the sisters engaged in a process parallel to their century-long tradition in institutional teaching, empowering citizens of the Global South through education. As with the broader intellectual thrust of the Antigonish movement, the sisters' modified application of that movement's principles – along with those of liberation theology and Vatican II renewal – is a form of education that exists outside the definition of educationalization.

As Canadian theologian Gregory Baum (2011, 374) explained, the Second Vatican Council made "social justice ... an imperative of the Gospel." The Sisters of Charity's reassessment of their purpose in light of this social justice imperative and the global socio-economic context of the late 1960s, drew them to educating the poor in the Global South, where social inequality was severe and governments were unstable. This form of education embraced the "preferential option of the poor" and thorough missionary training. This chapter focuses on the sisters' post–Vatican II missions near Chiclayo, Peru, which began in 1968, and in Bani, Dominican Republic, which began in 1970, highlighting how their congregation discerned the viability of and need for these two missions, the Antigonish-inspired adult education approach of the missions, and how two sisters – one in each mission – fulfilled their pastoral and educational roles to teach adults about self-realization in informal situations outside state sponsorship. The Sisters of Charity's decision to send sisters to Latin America was part of a larger phenomenon. By 1971, almost 2,000 Canadian missionaries served in Latin America (Smyth 2017, 156n1), and the United States sent an even larger number.

Vatican II and Latin American Contexts

The impetus for the Roman Catholic Church's monumental Second Vatican Council – considered second in importance only to the Council of Trent (1545–63) – was to bring the Catholic Church "up to date." Among the main conclusions of the sixteen documents produced by the council was the church's responsibility to work more directly with the poor, particularly in areas of the Global South, such as Latin America, where poverty and corruption were so extreme and where bishops had been requesting assistance for some time. "A preferential option for the poor" became a catch-phrase of the post–Vatican II era, a mandate rooted in Biblical teachings on Jesus's preference for spending time with marginalized people and developed by liberation theologians, particularly Gustavo Gutiérrez in *A Theology of Liberation* (1968).

The church, of course, had a long history of missionary activity and had produced five encyclicals related to missions just in the four decades preceding Vatican II (Hogg 1967, 286). According to American theologian Richey Hogg, part of what made *Ad Gentes: Decree on the Mission Activity of the Church* (1965) so remarkable in comparison to earlier encyclicals was that its first draft, *Missions Schema*, presented by Pope Paul VI himself, was rejected by 1,601 of the 1,912 bishops at the Second Council, because they "demanded a theologically fresh response to the new situation in mission" (290), rather than a reiteration of past mission encyclicals.[5]

Ad Gentes not only affirmed the primacy of missionary activity in the church, the necessity of all Christians to engage in missionary activity, and the particular duty of both male and female religious to contribute to missionary activity, it also laid out "best practices" for missionaries (Bevans and Gros 2009, 46). For example,

> 26. From the very beginning, their [i.e., missionaries'] doctrinal training should be so planned that it takes in both the universality of the Church and the diversity of the world's nations. This holds for all of their studies by which they are prepared for the exercise of the ministry ... For anyone who is going to encounter another people should have a great esteem for their patrimony and their language and their customs ... [and a] thorough knowledge of the history, social structures, and customs of the people ... Let the missionaries learn the languages to such a degree that they can use them in a fluent and polished manner ... Furthermore, they should be properly introduced into special pastoral problems. (*Ad Gentes* 1965, 26)

These best practices, which were intended to transform the colonizing missionary style of much of the pre–Vatican II era, were underscored by the Conference of Latin American Bishops at Medellín, Colombia, in 1968. Medellín was, in part, connected to Pope Pius XII's establishment of the Pontifical Commission for Latin America in 1958, and a continuation of the 1959 Inter-American Episcopal Conference, called by the papacy to strengthen the North American Catholic Church's work in South America, especially around communism and the spread of Protestantism (Garneau 2001). The Medellín Conference of 1968 went much farther than the 1959 conference, however, including by marking the "emergence of the new Latin American Church, deeply influenced by the new ideas of inculturation, liberation theology, and conscientisation" (Klaiber 2009, 410). Medellín supported liberation theology as the best response to "structural sin" and "institutionalized violence" that so many Latin American governments had allowed to fester. While liberation theology empowered the poor to stand up for themselves, it also acknowledged the impenetrable depth of corruption and racism among the elite, therefore teaching how "people should create new forms of power for and by themselves" rather than trying to take over the state (Skidmore, Smith, and Green 2014, 384). These new forms of power would come from education, the raising of conscientiousness, self-fulfilment, and reading the Bible from the perspective of the poor.[6] The missionaries who taught liberation theology diverged from the dominant form of education, which had become so obviously insufficient, and were echoing the aims of the Antigonish movement, first proposed by Father Jimmy Tompkins in the 1920s.

Peruvian priest and theologian Gustavo Gutiérrez had been in the background of the Medellín Conference. His *Theology of Liberation* along with Paulo Freire's *Pedagogy of the Oppressed*, also published in 1968, became touchstones for liberation theology and conscientization, and were incorporated into the pre-missionary training for many of the approximately four thousand missionaries who served in Latin America in the 1960s and 1970s. According to Gutiérrez, "The goal is not only to better living conditions, a radical change of structures, a social revolution; it is much more: the continuous creation, never ending, of a new way to be a man, a *permanent cultural revolution*' (Gutiérrez [1968] 1973, 32; emphasis in original). Liberation theologians challenged the church to stand up to injustice, including structural injustices perpetuated by governments. As a movement, liberation theology grew more radical than what the bishops at Medellín had sponsored. As Rosa Bruno-Jofré and Ana Jofre have noted, "Medellín kept continuity with the Council, which had been an expression of liberal progressive thought adapting the Church to developments in the Western world and within the capitalist system. Liberation theology aimed at a new model of society" (2015, 40). On this political continuum, the post–Vatican II papal encyclical *Populorum Progressio* (On the Development of Peoples) (Paul VI 1967) was less progressive than Medellín, and not radical in the way that liberation theology was. Still, *Populorum Progressio* showed the Vatican's support for reform in South America. Among its eighty-seven points was the following, under the heading "The Ultimate Purpose": "Organized programs ... should reduce inequities, eliminate discrimination, free men from the bonds of servitude, and thus give them the capacity, in the sphere of temporal realities, to improve their lot, to further their moral growth and to develop their spiritual endowments" (Paul VI 1967, s. 34). Such language signalled that *Populorum Progressio* was in keeping with the theories of the Antigonish movement (as described by Josh Cole in this volume).

The synergy of two particular Vatican II documents – one not directly related to missions – strongly affected the decision to send so many North American male and female religious to the Global South in the post–Vatican II era. *Ad Gentes* (Decree on the Mission Activity of the Church) (Paul VI 1965a), which called for male and female religious to seriously and prayerfully consider serving as missionaries,[7] was promulgated just two months after the key Vatican II document for religious, *Perfectae Caritatis* (Decree on the Adaptation and Renewal of Religious Life) (Paul VI 1965b), which required congregations to reconsider their purpose in light of the needs of the modern world. Thus *Ad Gentes*'s request for religious for the mission field became a practical option for congregations and individual religious reconsidering their work, including those in congregations in Canada. While the Sisters of Charity's original charism centred on educating the poor, their work had narrowed almost exclusively to institutional schooling, largely due to bishops' insatiable requests for teachers in Catholic schools. Their revaluation of their charism, not surprisingly, included a return to educating the poor in an area of the world recognized for its great need and where the welfare state remained relatively weak, especially in comparison to Canada.

The response of religious congregations to the Latin American appeal was swift and significant. By 1975, 2,414 Canadian women religious were serving abroad, of whom 884 (37 per cent) from 65 religious congregations were in Latin America (Goudreault 1983, 374, 377). (Other popular regions for missionaries were Africa, Asia, and the Caribbean.) At that time, the total number of women religious in Canada was 44,127, of whom 33,488 were under sixty-five years of age. In other words, more than 7 per cent of Canadian women religious under sixty-five were serving in mission fields in 1975. Meanwhile, a decreased number of sisters (26.2 per cent) continued in institutional education in North America, while 28 per cent worked in congregations (as superiors, bursars, and so on), and 24 per cent were retired (Canadian Religious Conference 1975, 372, 374).

Sisters' Reception of Council Documents

The sisters' engagement with various Vatican II documents influenced their response to social issues in the Global South. Indeed, one cannot appreciate post–Vatican II congregational social justice initiatives, including those in Latin America, without understanding the dynamic of renewal concurrently underway in congregations. The apostolic letter *Ecclesiae Sanctae II* (1966) contained instructions that ensured a deep level of engagement around *Perfectae Caritatis*: that adaptation and renewal be negotiated within general chapters (that is, in congregations' governing meetings, usually held every four years), that a special general chapter be convened within two years to promote adaptation and renewal, and that all members be consulted in preparation of the chapters of renewal. The Sisters of Charity took these guidelines very seriously. In the fall of 1966, every sister received an "Explorations for Renewal" package, consisting of ten pages of worksheets on potential agenda items for the chapter of renewal. Instructions for the follow-up 1967 questionnaire stated: "Each sister is encouraged to express herself as fully as she wishes. The more spontaneous and complete the answer, the more helpful it will be ... Our aim is to ascertain the sisters' uninhibited thinking, the questionnaires need not be signed" (McKenna 1998, 106).

In all, the 1,629 members of the Sisters of Charity submitted over a thousand proposals to the chapter of renewal. The most common recommendation was for decreasing superiors' authority over individual sisters' daily lives, including discontinuing standardized bedtimes and recreation periods, as well as censorship of correspondence and control of radio and television use. This campaign for more autonomy is relevant to the sisters' ministries in Latin America and the Caribbean. Many sisters believed themselves to have been oppressed within their convents. They identified easily with economically and politically oppressed Latin Americans. The fifty-four elected chapter delegates met for eight to ten hours a day, six days a week, for six weeks in the summers of both 1968 and 1969, creating dozens of new congregational policies ("Chapter Communications and Explorations for Renewal" n.d.; McKenna 1998, 106). Such unprecedented consultation and deliberation among the sisters regarding changes in the congregations' governance, purpose, and character (spirit) were comparable to Paulo Freire's concept of "conscientization." Sisters could not have engaged in the global social justice movement had their own congregations not examined their hierarchical structures and the lack of autonomy of members and not undergone their own transformation.

Discerning the Missions

The interest in missions grew quickly among the Sisters of Charity after Vatican II. At least a dozen proposals submitted for the Sisters of Charity's chapter of 1968 supported establishing Latin American missions.

The leader of the congregation, Mother Maria Gertrude (Sister Irene Farmer) (1913–2003) was moved by *Ad Gentes*'s request for religious to work in missions. Her predecessor, Mother Stella Maria, had refused two bishops' requests to send sisters to Latin America in 1960, saying she could not spare any sisters (McKenna 1998, 179), but the post–Vatican II priorities of the congregation were much different.

Even before the sisters' chapter of renewal started in 1968, Mother Maria Gertrude announced that the congregation would send four sisters to Latin American before the end of 1967.[8] In preparation for continuing that discussion, every sister in the congregation was asked to study two encyclicals: *Ad Gente:* and the recently proclaimed *Populorum Progressio*. Mother Maria Gertrude had a good relationship with Archbishop James Hayes (1924–2003), the young and progressive local bishop, and the two talked often about how best to participate in the Latin American missions. At Mother Maria Gertrude's initiative, the Sisters of Charity formed a formal partnership with the Archdiocese of Halifax to send a team of sisters and priests to Latin America.

Mother Maria Gertrude, Archbishop Hayes, two other Sisters of Charity (Sisters Gabriela Villela and Sister Ellen Francis Meagher), and a diocesan priest (the Reverend George Hooper) went on a month-long, fact-finding tour of ten Latin American dioceses from which they had received invitations to serve. While Mother Maria Gertrude noted widespread poverty and need, she wrote, "If we had thought that there was poverty in the other [Latin American] countries, we know now that it is multiplied a thousand times in Peru" (McKenna 1998, 183n10). Economist John Sheahan affirms this impression, explaining that, in the 1960s, Peru had severe income inequality: employment opportunities were limited for the impoverished citizens while political structures protected the elite. Although Peru was rich in primary resources, especially minerals, there was little industrialization. Most of the ore was exported in raw, unprocessed form. Processing and manufacturing jobs did not exist. Coca leaves, used to produce cocaine, were the most profitable export in the 1970s, but were, of course, linked to violence. Conflict between dominant European minorities and the Indigenous and mixed-race majority was layered on top of other social inequalities; a caste system was still in place in the 1960s and 1970s (Sheahan 1999, 1–5; see also Skidmore, Smith, and Green 2014, 149; Reid 2007, 69).

Mother Maria Gertrude and Archbishop Hayes decided that the first Archdiocese of Halifax mission would be in the Diocese of Chiclayo, in the Province of Lambayeque, in northern Peru. In addition to Mother Maria Gertrude's impression that Peru was the most impoverished of the ten Latin American countries she visited, Archbishop Skinner of

St John's, Newfoundland, had lobbied Archbishop Hayes to consider a cooperative project in Chiclayo, where Newfoundland priests and sisters had served since the early 1960s. Skinner argued firmly that the Halifax missionaries could benefit from the experience and support the Newfoundland missionaries would be pleased to provide ("The Sisters of Charity in Peru" n.d., 3). Skinner offered further advice that Archbishop Hayes and Mother Maria Gertrude visit Lima and Monsefu: "This should be done before any planning to send a group of Priests and Sisters to Peru. You must meet and talk with the right people first. I believe this is extremely important for the future success of any foundation."[9] So, it was undoubtedly with Skinner's advice that the Latin American tour was arranged. On that tour, the Halifax group received a "warm reception" from the Bishop of Chiclayo, and they learned that the main town in which they would eventually serve, Victoria Nuevo, had 30,000 residents but no Catholic priest (ibid., 6). Four sisters were chosen from the seventy-seven who volunteered, including Sister Gabriela Villela, who was born in Guatemala and was the congregation's only native Spanish-speaker and the translator on the ten-diocese tour (McKenna 1998, 180, 184).

Pre-mission Training

Unlike some congregations who sent religious into the missions relatively unprepared, the four Sisters of Charity destined for Peru in 1968, and those destined for the Dominican Republic in 1970, participated in pre-mission training programs, including those offered by the Scarboro Missionary Fathers at St Mary's, Ontario, and by the Coady International Institute at St Francis Xavier University in Antigonish, Nova Scotia.

The Scarboro Fathers had themselves served as missionaries in Latin America since 1944, and in Asia since 1919.[10] Notably, one of their priests serving in the Dominican Republic, Father Art MacKinnon (1932–1965), had been murdered by a soldier for supporting the rebels (MacKinnon 2005).[11] (The Catholic Church in Latin American had been supporting locals' civil disobedience and had become targets themselves of the government's ire (Lernoux 1991, 246).) With the Scarboro Fathers' relatively long missionary experience, and Vatican II's strong encouragement of and guidelines for missionary work, their pre-missionary program offered to male and female religious and diocesan staff, beginning in 1964, was well respected in Canada (Scarboro Fathers 1968). The Scarboro Fathers advertised that their course, led by "veteran missionaries," would prepare participants to be "competent on arrival in the missions" ("Scarboro Pre-Mission Training" 1968, 16).

Sister Gabriela Villela participated in the Scarboro Fathers' "sociocultural orientation" course intended to "adjust future missionaries to cultural differences in Latin America countries" ("Orientation Program" 1968, 18). The first part of the program was divided into seven areas: cultural anthropology; sociology; social psychology; economics; public health, sanitation, and nutrition; pastoral theology; and history. Tuition was $200 per participant ("Culture at the Service of Faith" 1968, 30; "The Spanish Language Course" 1968, 20–1). Rather than send additional sisters to this course, the congregation determined – on Villela's advice – that more relevant training could be attained in Peru itself; they sent the other three Peru-destined sisters to Lima to participate in cultural and language pre-missionary training offered by priests from the Archdiocese of Boston.[12]

All of the Sisters of Charity sent to both Peru and the Dominion Republic in the 1960s and 1970s received training at the Coady International Institute in Antigonish, which was only a two-hour drive from the Sisters' Motherhouse in Halifax, where they engaged with Father Moses Coady's economic and democratic teachings (for greater detail on these teachings, see chapter 4 by Josh Cole in this volume). At the turn of the century, St Francis Xavier University, the pre-eminent Catholic postsecondary institution in the region, had responded to the poverty and significant outmigration of young people from the region with "useful education" courses for farmers developed by Father Jimmy Tompkins. In 1928, Father Moses Coady began to work with fishermen through the Department of Extension (Alexander 1997, 65). The two trademarks of the Coady Institute's Antigonish movement were the study group and the mass meeting. In the 1930s alone, more than a thousand study groups were formed. Cooperatives and credit unions were regularly developed as extensions of the study clubs (ibid., 79–85). The six principles of the movement, which were identified in 1944, had much in common with liberation theology developed in the 1960s:

- the primacy of the individual
- that social reform must come through education
- that education must begin with the economic
- that education must be through group action
- that effective social reform involves fundamental changes in social and economic institutions
- that the ultimate objective of the Movement is a full and abundant life for everyone in the community. (ibid., 78n2)

While these principles had evolved somewhat by the 1960s, when the sisters studied at the Coady International Institute, the basic principles were considered timeless in development work. Moreover, the socio-economic problems of the Maritimes in the 1930s were, to a significant extent, comparable to the economic problems of Peru and the Dominion Republic in the 1960s: foreign ownership, difficult-to-break cycles of debt and poverty, structural inequality, and uneven access to education. Just as the early twentieth-century Catholic Church in the Maritimes was involved in building alternative economic systems, especially through cooperatives and credit unions, so the 1960s church hoped to improve the lives of Peruvians and Dominicans by respecting individual rights and providing alternative economic systems. According to Sister Gabriela Villela, who participated in the Coady International Institute's summer pre-missionary training with seventy other students from a total of forty-eight countries, the emphasis was on "missionary activity" based on cooperatives. And so the Sisters of Charity brought to Latin America, and later to the Caribbean, a Catholic Nova Scotia–grown philosophy that they were at least somewhat familiar with outside the classroom, having lived in the Maritimes. Whereas some congregations sent sisters to Latin America quite unprepared, the Sisters of Charity ensured their missionary sisters had solid academic and language pre-missionary training both in Canada and Latin America.

The Approach to the Missions

In May 1968, Archbishop Hayes and Mother Gertrude issued a joint decree whereby the sisters and the diocese would consider "the barida of Victoria Nueva in the Diocese of Chiclayo as one of its own" (McKenna 1998, 185). A few months later, the four sisters joined two diocesan priests to form two teams in neighbouring parishes in the pueblo of Reque (800 inhabitants) and the barrio of Victoria Neuva (30,000 inhabitants), near Chiclayo in northern Peru (184).[13] A third priest from Newfoundland, the Reverend David Alward, soon joined the team.

When and where the Sisters of Charity began their Latin American missionary work is very important. The four Sisters of Charity arrived in Peru on 3 October 1968, the very day that General Juan Velasco Alvarado (1910–1975) led a military takeover. This unforeseen development ultimately benefited the sisters' – and all religious congregations' – work in Peru, at least for the first five years of Velasco's rule, because the new military leaders and the missionaries held some goals in common. Just as the sisters were motivated by *Ad Gentes*'s argument that Christians needed to stand up to unjust social and economic structures, so the revolutionaries aimed to eliminate government corruption and the pooling of wealth among a small Peruvian elite. Velasco and his associates blamed Peru's social and economic crisis on the previous government's heavy reliance on foreign capital and unwillingness to share power; its new program of nationalization called for more autonomous economic development and a redistribution of wealth that were broadly complementary to the new missionary ideology of the Roman Catholic Church. The new military government adopted aspects of the Catholic teaching of Thomas Aquinas and Pope Leo XIII and the papal encyclical *Populorum Progressio* (Klaren 2000, 341). The sisters' pre-missionary training had taught them to have confidence in those same ideals.

The first major initiative of the new military government was a radical program of agrarian reform that expropriated land from wealthy landowners and redistributed it among the workers. According to historian Peter Klaren, "the goals were threefold: to eliminate the traditional landed aristocracy ... ; to remove the peasants' discontent and insurgency ... by redistributing income; and to improve the productive efficiency of agriculture" (2000, 346). While these reforms improved the livelihoods of former hacienda workers, they did not extend to the more impoverished highland peasants, with whom the sisters intended to live and work (346–7). In their next phase of reform, the revolutionary government created the Sistema Nacional de Apoyo a la Movilización (SINAMOS), whose main aim was "to achieve conscious and active participation of the national population in the tasks demanded by economic and social development" (349). SINAMOS would facilitate the aims of the revolutionaries while not negatively affecting the sisters' work.

This is not to say the sisters' work was easy or that either the sisters or the revolutionaries achieved all their goals – they did not – but, compared to the intense conflict of sisters with the governments of El Salvador and Guatemala in the 1970s, or the Dominican Republic in the 1960s, the government of Peru was largely sympathetic to and appreciated the sisters' work. Overall, the relationship between the revolutionaries and the many religious congregations in Peru in the late 1960s, relations were "cordial" (Klaren 2000, 352).[14]

The two three-member teams (two sisters and a priest) from the Diocese of Halifax were among twenty-five new missionary groups to arrive in Peru between 1960 and 1984 (Bruno-Jofré 2019, 5n8).[15] For example, the western Canadian branch of the Religieuses de Notre Dame des Missions (RNDM) arrived just two months after the Sisters of Charity, while the Newfoundland Sisters of Mercy had come to Monsefu, Peru, and the London, Ontario, Sisters of St, Joseph had come to Cayalti, Peru, in the early 1960s (Villela 2001, 21–3, 31). In total, fourteen congregations of women religious – some Peruvian and some North American – served in the Diocese of Chiclayo in the late 1960s (ibid., 37). In the post–Vatican II era, sisters and priests usually worked in parishes where they provided services in the barrios (called *pueblos jovenes* – young towns – after Velasco took power), such as a "medical post, soup kitchen, vocational training centre, and children's education centre" (Klaren 2000, 351). According to Susan Fitzpatrick-Behrens, these foreign missionary projects worked in tandem with the state, funded by the American government, the Peace Corps, and the Alliance for Progress. Most Peruvians resented foreign government aid but accepted aid from the church (Bruno-Jofré 2019, 9–10n7). This was the template into which the Sisters of Charity entered through their Peruvian mission.

Victoria Nueva

As noted, Sister Gabriela Villela was one of the first four Sisters of Charity missioned in Peru. She had been raised in Guatemala in a prosperous family before moving to Halifax at the age of seventeen to study at the Sisters' Mount St Vincent Academy for a year. After briefly returning home to Guatemala to bid her family farewell, she became a Sister of Charity in 1953 at the age of twenty-one, against her father's will. Once she completed her formation as a Sister of Charity, she worked for eleven years at the Halifax Infirmary (a hospital owned and operated by the Sisters of Charity), first as an assistant to the hospital's accountant and then secretary to the administrator and assistant administrator.[16]

After volunteering and being chosen as one of the first sister-missionaries for Peru, Villela embarked on significant preparation for her new role. Because she was a native Latin American, the congregation asked Villela to attend the four-week orientation to Latin America program run by the Scarboro Fathers in St Mary, Ontario. After her Scarboro Fathers course, she attended another four-week course at the Coady International Institute in 1968. Her further preparation before moving to Chiclayo, Peru, her intended mission, included spending a few weeks living with the Immaculate Heart of Mary Sisters (from Philadelphia) in Lima and with the Grey Nuns (from Pembrooke, Ontario) in Santo Domingo, Dominican Republic, as well as nine months living with the Sisters of Mercy (from Newfoundland) in Monsefu, Peru, while waiting for the other Sisters of Charity to arrive (Villela 2001, 21–4). Villela was an unusually well-prepared missionary.

The congregation also arranged for Villela and the other sisters bound for Peru to take a hairdressing course, so that that they could "help each other" with their hair, as well as to observe the deliveries of three babies (Villela 2001, 28). This somewhat random training suggests the congregation really did not know what to expect in Peru. Villela did not find all of her training useful, but she did benefit from the two missionary courses. In her own words, the purpose of the courses "was for us to learn as much as possible about mission life and the respect missionaries owe to the people with whom they are going to serve and minister" (5).

Soon after arriving in Victoria Nueva, some members of the team, including Villela, met the local bishop (Bishop Ignacio Maria de Orbegonzo y Goychochea) and explained to him that they wanted to "focus their ministry on the development of the people through a program of adult education" (Villela 2001, 31). In the spirit of supporting local leadership, and following the model of the Coady Institute, the first parish council was organized, with ten local men and women. Demonstrating the philosophy of her Coady Institute training, Sister Gabriela explained that the council benefited from "outstanding" men and women who took the roles of chairperson and councilors and who were "ready to take co-responsibility and work with the priests and sisters'" (ibid., 39). The council met weekly. According to Sister Gabriela, the philosophy was to build a community before building any church or community buildings (12).

The ministry team met every morning for prayer and once a week for evaluation and planning-team meetings (Villela 2001, 38). The team emphasized getting to know the people. According to *Populorum Progressio*, "The people of a country soon discover whether their new helpers [i.e., foreign missionaries] are motivated by good will or not, whether they want to enhance human dignity or merely try out their special techniques. The expert's message will surely be rejected by these people if it is not inspired by brotherly love" (Paul VI 1967, s. 71). In this vein, for the first two years of their mission in Victoria Nueva, the pastoral teams focused on visiting people in their homes and providing Sunday services, rather than starting larger formal programs. According to Villela, "Victoria Nueva was frequently visited by invasions of families from the mountains that, looking for new life, erected their dwellings with *esteras* (straw mats) as temporary houses, possibly for months or years ... A sister and a priest took responsibility for [visiting homes in] one area and shared results with the team during our weekly sessions ... I believe that the personal contact of those visits made the people of Victoria Nueva realize that we were there for them" (2001, 40).

Once the sisters had established a level of trust, they encouraged local residents to establish community groups "such as the Cruzada Social de Damas Victorianas (the Victoria Social Women's Crusade), which set up a medical clinic and improved access to water and electricity" (Villela 2001, 40). An offshoot of this group learned straw weaving, a tradition that some women wanted to preserve for future generations. They also made sandals to sell. The sisters organized other small groups of women to meet in a municipal education centre, the Centro de Educación para el Desarrollo Comunitario (CEDEC). This is an example of how the sisters' parish work was supported by state infrastructure, with the sisters holding programs in a state-owned and -operated education centre. Sister Gabriela suggested that this combination worked well because the centre lent credibility to the women's group, and she built on the opportunity by inviting women teachers from semi-private women's teacher-training academies in Chiclayo to teach the women of the barrio classes in home management and crafts in exchange for practicum credit. Sister Gabriela explained: "What began as a small seed became a large tree in which more than eighty women with families participated in the CEDEC community classes each year ... Each time before the women went home, we spent a few minutes in silent reflection and then sharing their experience of the afternoon. We finished each time with shared prayer or by reflecting and sharing on an appropriate passage from the Scriptures" (2001, 42).[17] This approach mirrored the Coady Institute's model of study groups encouraging local economic development and self-fulfilment that was consistently overlaid with – or potentiated by – the development of participants' faith. Whether Villela emphasized liberation theology by reading the Bible from the perspective of the poor is not certain but likely.

Over the first five years of the mission, two more community development groups were organized, including the Frente Civico Victoriano (Victoria Civic Front), one of whose projects was building a park across from the parish building. Out of that project an art club was formed, which then evolved into a Young Christian Students group. The pastoral team supported the creation of a savings and loan credit union, which was based on cooperative initiatives the pastoral team had studied at the Coady International Institute. Fulfilling their goal of providing advanced education, the team sponsored a local young man's study at the Coady International Institute in Nova Scotia in the mid-1970s and a local young woman's study of catechetical courses in Lima. In both cases, the goal of the ministry team was to empower local adult education leaders.

All of these initiatives in the early years of the Peruvian mission were guided by the sisters' and priests' strong missionary training, which stressed adult education's philosophy of "developing" the individual person *and* his or her society (Roberts 192, 5). In keeping with this philosophy, they practiced a form of education that cannot be called educationalization. Most notably, they aimed to avoid the traditional hierarchy between "teacher" and "student" by seeking their direction from the local people. This was a 180-degree shift away from the sisters' dominant historical educational premise, which had minimal negotiation between students and teachers in determining solutions to social problems.

Due to a shortage of priests in Halifax, the two priests left Peru in 1972, but the sisters remained until 1993, adding a second mission in Cajamarca (150 km southeast of Chiclayo) in 1983 (Villela 2001, 34). Even though the Sisters of Charity were short-staffed in their Nova Scotia commitments in the early 1970s, they prioritized ongoing participation in the Peru mission. While the sisters' work was appreciated by the locals, the reforms promised by the 1968 revolution did not succeed. Poverty increased in Peru in the 1970s and continued to increase in the 1980s. This did not nullify the sisters' work. In the spirit of *Ad Gentes*, *Perfectae Caritatis*, *Populorum Progressio*, liberation theology, and the Coady Institute's teachings, the sisters' primary goal was to support the people in whatever conditions they might find themselves.

Bani

The Sisters of Charity's second mission to Latin America began in 1970 in the Dominican Republic. The context was quite different than Peru: the sisters were initially not part of a diocesan mission; they had specifically been asked to administer a hospital rather than do parish work; and the socio-economic and political circumstances in the Dominican Republic were more volatile. On the other hand, the new mission in the Dominican town of Bani was still strongly aligned with the relevant Vatican II social justice and development encyclicals; the three sisters sent to Bani received missionary and language training, and they were connected to a parish team of Scarboro Fathers who had twenty years experience in the Dominican Republic.

The Sisters of Charity came to Bani during a period of political and economic upheaval. Canadian companies were among those tied to controversial foreign investments. After a three-decade dictatorship, President Raphael Trujillo was assassinated in 1961, and progressive Juan Bosh became his democratically elected successor until ousted by a military coup in 1963. The military governed the country until 1965, when the Americans, in response to fears of rising communism and the development of a "second Cuba," invaded the country. The US invasion also served to safeguard American financial investments in the Dominican Republic. The Americans financially backed President

Joaquin Balaguer, who was elected in 1966. Though he would be democratically re-elected twice and survive twelve years as president, Belaguer would govern increasingly as a dictator (Higman 2011, 260).

Along with the Americans, the Canadian government and Canadian companies also had a stake in the Dominican Republic. The Canadian government had established diplomatic relations in 1954; two Canadian banks, the Royal Bank and the Bank of Nova Scotia, had established themselves in the Dominican Republic in the second decade of the twentieth century; and the Canadian-owned nickel mining company Falconbridge Dominicana was, by the mid-twentieth century, the single-largest investor in the country. According to historians Stephen Randall and Graeme Mount, in 1971 the Belaguer government sent soldiers on behalf of Falconbridge Dominicana "to break a strike so that the company could salvage its $195 million investment," for which the Canadian mine owners expressed gratitude (1998, 124). Against this complicated political backdrop, and as in other countries of the Global South, the disparity between the rich and poor grew. Human rights also suffered, justified by the need to keep communism under control. At least three thousand of Balaguer's political opponents were killed during his twelve-year rule. Although his government invested heavily in infrastructure – roads, hospitals, and schools – much of it paid for by the United States – very few of the benefits reached the poor who would be served by the Sisters of Charity.

It is not explicit in the sisters' historical record why they accepted the request to go to Bani in 1970, but the combination of intense poverty, a Canadian diplomatic presence, Canadian financial investment, the Scarboro Fathers' history in the area, and a personal invitation from President Belaguer must have all been taken into consideration when evaluating the viability of a mission in the Dominion Republic. During their 1968 tour of Latin American countries, the Halifax delegation had met with the controversial president, who had encouraged the team to set up a mission in Dominican Republic. This invitation must have assured them they would be treated well by the government, despite fairly well-known accounts of religious congregations – including the Scarboro Fathers – having been severely reprimanded for perceived interference. Once the sisters arrived, they met with Belaguer again on 4 September 1970, and he assured them of his cooperation; two months later, he responded to the sisters' appeal for supplies for their hospital and a tax reduction on their vehicle (Villela 2001, 21).[18] Clearly, the sisters were fortunate in their mission beginning during a period of relative stability in the Dominican Republic, before Belaguer's human rights abuses mounted. The government may not have considered the sisters a threat, because they were taking over the administration of the 150-bed

Nestra Senora Hospital, which had been built by the Dominincan government in 1959 but had fallen into disrepair, rather than engaging in less-defined, and potentially more threatening, development work.[19]

The sisters' second mission in the Global South had a different intention than their Peruvian mission of 1968. The Bani mission began as an institutional project, set up as an extension of their work in the Halifax Infirmary. The sisters received a petition from the people of Bani requesting them to administer the increasingly decrepit local hospital. With their experience running six small- to large-sized hospitals in Nova Scotia and Alberta, the congregation had the expertise to fulfil the Bani request, though it came at a time when many sisters were seeking dispensations and leaving the congregation. Following their pre-missionary training, three sisters arrived in Bani and spent their first six months getting the 150-bed hospital organized, including coordinating literally tons of donated and purchased supplies.[20]

Sister Catherine McGowan (b. 1927) was one of the three Sisters of Charity who volunteered and was selected to serve in Bani. Having grown up in Halifax, she attended Mount Saint Vincent Academy and then Mount Saint Vincent College, both run by the Sisters of Charity. After graduating with a home economics degree, McGowan worked for a year with the Nova Scotia Department of Agriculture in extension work with farm women. She joined the Sisters of Charity in 1949, at the age of twenty-one, and subsequently taught home economics in two Cape Breton schools and at Mount Saint Vincent College before becoming a dietitian at the Halifax Infirmary.[21] McGowan did the same pre-missionary training with the Scarboro Fathers that Villela did a few years earlier. She then spent five months in Chiclayo, Peru, at her congregation's mission, learning about Latin American culture and studying the Spanish language. Then, in April 1970, she joined the other Sisters of Charity missionaries at the Bani hospital McKenna (1998, 188).

After just six months of working in the hospital in Bani, McGowan requested a role that leaned more toward adult education and parish work than the institutionalized hospital setting. As she explained in an oral interview,

> When I would be visiting around the hospital, seeing what was what, I used to see so many malnourished children. It just used to break my heart. And I said there must be some way that we can do it, so after six months in the hospital ... I asked the congregation if I could be free to work with women. And particularly those with children to try to keep them out of the hospital. They were dying, so many died, and so they said yes. And in the meantime, the priests down there were Scarboro priests, and they invited me to join their pastoral team.[22]

McGowan felt strongly that the best way to help the people of Bani was by teaching the mothers how to improve infant nutrition. She was, on the one hand, engaging in educationalization, to the extent that she was responding to a social problem (infant malnutrition) through education. On the other hand, echoing Josh Cole's argument that not all education is educationalization, McGowan's method was influenced by liberation theology, the theories of the Antigonish movement, and her Scarboro Fathers colleagues in Bani, which all promoted an anti-hierarchical approach. She did not impose her views on the local women; she visited them in rural areas and asked them what they would like help with. They replied, "sewing."[23] So, rather than following her own preference to immediately treat infant malnutrition, which could have more accurately fit with the definition of "educationalization," McGowan accepted direction from the local women she was trying to empower and organized sewing lessons, which attracted a hundred women a week.

After a few months, the Bani women not only learned to sew, but they gained confidence in McGowan. When she asked them what they wanted to do next, they asked for guidance in health. McGowan saw an opportunity for hygiene education, particularly about hand washing and using clean needles for injections. Over the next seven years, this work evolved into establishing well-baby clinics focusing on nutrition. Through the congregation's affiliation with Mount Saint Vincent University in Halifax, connections were made with their Department of Home Economics and with Dr Alleyne Murphy, a professor of nutrition, who successfully applied for a Canadian International Development Agency (CIDA) grant, which supplied materials and research support for the well-baby program in Bani in several years (*Sisters of Charity–Halifax in the Dominican Republic* 2011, 5). In this, the Sisters of Charity partnered with the Canadian state to bring aid to the Dominican Republic.

McGowan explained how they operated the well-baby clinic:

> First we would do the health record on them, to see what they needed, and then we had a special regime for feeding them; because so many were severely malnourished, we had to get to what we called the weak ones and then strengthen them up as they went, and keep a record of how they progressed ... We came up with a good menu, we can say that, as well as teaching the mothers good hygiene, and [the menu] was based on only food that the mothers could duplicate in their home, otherwise they would think it was the special things like the meat that was curing them, but it wasn't that at all, it was the vegetable protein. We had everything analysed so we knew they got the proper nutrition. It has become famous now, the green leaf soup. The soup is made of pasta and vegetable leaves, nutrition

was very high, sweet potatoes, squash, yuka, sweet yuka. The leaves were very high in nutrition. So that's what we had, the green leaf soup.[24]

As in Peru, this work in the Dominican Republic was steeped in the ideals and goals of Vatican II, including ecumenism, education, and serving the poor. It transcended traditional understandings of social service, adult education, and educationalization, and entered the realm of social justice when the sisters, in consultation with the local people, worked toward changing the patterns and structures that perpetuated the problem – in this case, of malnutrition – through adult education and by working within a high-profile secular group such as CIDA. While McGowan responded to social problem through education, her practice cannot be categorized as educationalization.

Conclusion

Before Vatican II, the Sisters of Charity, like many North American congregations of women religious, were quite entrenched in their work as teachers. From the time of their founding in 1854 until Vatican II ended in 1965, the Sisters of Charity had taught close to a million children and young women at all levels in North America. Good-quality institutional education was highly regarded for its perceived benefits in forming children and youth into moral and competent Catholics and citizens. In many ways, the sisters' work educationalized Catholic social problems. Following the Vatican II documents *Perfectae Caritatis* and *Ad Gentes*, both proclaimed in 1965, the sisters reconsidered their purpose and work, and asked how they might best serve the most vulnerable in the modern world. According to an official history of the congregation, in 1968 delegates to the Sisters of Charity's governing chapter "argued that because of increasing participation of government at provincial and federal levels in providing financial assistance to hospitals and higher educational institutions, the time had come to break new ground and reach out to the unmet needs of present-day society" (McKenna 1998, 241). In a global comparative context, the congregation no longer considered North American school children particularly vulnerable. It is doubtful that the Sisters of Charity would have served in Latin America and the Caribbean without strong encouragement to leave some of their institutional teaching.

When asked, seventy-seven sisters volunteered in 1967 for the first Latin American mission. As a congregation that held great respect for education and the process of discernment, missionary sisters were sent for the best available training provided by the Coady Institute in Nova Scotia and the Scarboro Fathers in Ontario, both of whose influences are clear in the sisters' missionary adult education projects. The two sisters featured in this chapter held a firm pedagogical intent to take their cues from the local people. Sister Gabriela Villela and Sister Catherine McGowan discerned their work over many months. In Peru, Villela taught religious education to all ages and also facilitated the CEDEC program for the local women through which they made mats and sandals for sale. She worked in Peru for seven years before returning to Halifax to complete her BA, earn an MA in Family Studies at St, Paul University in Ottawa, and then translate the congregation's constitutions into Spanish. The Chiclayo mission continued another eighteen years after Villela left it. McGowan continued working in the Bani community centre and well-baby clinics for forty years, until she was eighty-three and her congregation encouraged her to retire in Halifax.[25]

Both sisters worked in complex political environments. In oral interviews, neither commented on how they negotiated these political circumstances. Undoubtedly, they drew on the ideals of liberation theology in supporting local people while not openly criticizing the government. This was surely a conscious choice that not all religious congregations made. For example, another Maritime congregation, the Sisters of St Martha (from Charlottetown, Prince Edward Island) were deported from the Dominican Republic in 1984 for criticizing American government intervention, and, as we have seen, in 1965 a Scarboro father from Cape Breton was murdered in the same country for his critique of the American invasion of 1965 (Diocese of Charlottetown 2006; MacKinnon 2005).

As intense as the sisters' pre–Vatican II schoolteaching had been, their foray into education in the Global South was infinitely more complex. David Bridges argues that while education has been a great success over a long period of time, educationalization has failed by pushing education "beyond its scope" (as quoted in Labaree 2008, 448n2). The Sisters of Charity who served in Peru and the Dominion Republic probably would have agreed with David Labaree's further argument that educationalization "gives us a mechanism for expressing serious concern about social problems without actually doing anything effective to solve those problems" (ibid., 459). The sisters, having spent much time reflecting on Vatican II principles, liberation theology, and the Antigonish movement, were committed to improving social problems by empowering people and avoiding hierarchical learning environments. On a large scale, one might question their success: the social revolution that liberation theology intended and the sisters hoped for did not occur. In that same vein, as Penny Lernoux wrote in 1989, the Roman Catholic Church ultimately refused to accept the pluralism in the church that liberation theology had promoted. According to Lernoux, the church was "the only power able to withstand military persecution in Latin America," but it stopped doing so in the mid-1980s when Cardinal Ratzinger (subsequently Pope Benedict) led the Vatican's attack on liberation theology (91, 90–102). It seems that the sisters' form of education saw success in empowering local people, but, without the larger infrastructure that the church had initially provided and then drastically scaled back, larger-scale success in alleviating social problems was impossible.

ACKNOWLEDGMENTS

I wish to thank the Sisters of Charity–Halifax, for generously allowing me access to their archives; Sisters Gabriela Villela and Catherine McGowan for providing thoughtful oral interviews; Sister Villela for sharing her detailed memoire, "In Response to a Call: Sisters of Charity (Halifax) First Latin American Mission to Peru 1968–1974 (2001); and Mary Flynn, archivist.

NOTES

1 Teaching, the primary apostolate of the Sisters of Charity in 1968, engaged 62 per cent of all professed sisters, while nursing and para-medical work, social service, and clerical work in schools and hospitals engaged 7 per cent, 4 per cent, and 2 per cent of all sisters, respectively. "Report to 12 General Chapter: 1968–72" (1972), Sisters of Charity–Halifax Archives, file 1-4-9, 53–62; 65–9. Even as the largest English-speaking congregation of women religious in Canada, the sisters were too few in number to accept the many new requests each year for their sisters to run schools, especially during the postwar baby boom in both Canada and the United States.
2 See, for example, Bridges (2008, 46), Depaepe and Smeyers (2008, 379–89), and Tröhler (2009, 3, 32).
3 The bishop of Antigonish referred to the "hydra of anti-Catholic bigotry" of the 1850s and 1860s in Nova Scotia but agreed it had diminished by the turn of the century (McGowan 1992, 16). However, Orange Lodges remained popular in the Maritimes well after the Second World War.
4 The Sisters of Charity–New York came to Halifax in 1849, and an independent branch, the Sisters of Charity–Halifax, was founded in 1856. Regarding Roman Catholic schooling, see Fay (2002, 97–9).

5 As one of the council's final decrees, it implicitly recognized earlier decrees that referred to the preferential option for the poor, such as *Dignitatis Humanae: Decree on the Right of the Person and of Communities to Social and Civil Freedom in Matters Religious* (1965).
6 See, for example, Gutiérrez (1973).
7 *Ad Gentes* (1965, 40): "Whether they would not be able to extend their activity for the expansion of the Kingdom of God among the nations; whether they could possibly leave certain ministries to others so that they themselves could expend their forces for the missions."
8 This response was affirmed in principle in the chapter of renewal preparations: that the congregation would "continue and strengthen our initial response to the mandate of Vatican II to work with the peoples of underdeveloped and developing nations" ("Statement on Missionary Activity" n.d., 35).
9 Archbishop James Skinner to Archbishop Hayes, 2 March 1967 (forwarded by Hayes to Mother Maria Gertrude, 21 March 1967), Sisters of Charity–Halifax Archives, Z2A-1, 3.
10 "Scarboro Missions: History," http://www.scarboromissions.ca/about-us/history.
11 The Halifax missionary tour team visited MacKinnon's grave early in 1967 (Villela 2001, 21).
12 Sister Gabriele Villela, email to Heidi MacDonald, 26 August 2017.
13 The sisters were Sisters Zelma LeBlanc, Gabriela Villela, Catherine Conroy, and Agnes Burroughs; the priests were Fathers Louis Cassie and Kevin McPherson. "The Sisters of Charity in Peru" n.d., 3–4.
14 For an example of Canadian sisters' encounter with violence in Latin America, see Smyth (2017, 163–4) regarding the Sisters of St Joseph of Toronto.
15 Haiti was the only Latin American country to receive more Canadian missionaries (Goudreault 1983, 372).
16 Oral interview with Sister Gabriela Villela, Sisters of Charity–Halifax, Edmonton, 13 January 2013, 5–8. (In possession of the author.)
17 Soon, literacy classes held in people's homes were added to the home management classes.
18 Annals, Bani Mission, Sisters of Charity–Halifax Archives.
19 Once the sisters arrived, they met with President Belaguer again on 4 September 1970, and he assured them of his cooperation. Annals, Bani Mission, Sisters of Charity–Halifax Archives, and McKenna (1998, 187).
20 The sisters who initially went to Bani were Sisters Rita MacDonald, Catherine McGowan, and Sheila Ann Nylan. McKenna (1998 187).
21 Oral interview, Sister Catherine McGowan, Halifax, 20 December 2012, 1–2. (In possession of the author.)
22 McGowan interview, 9.

23 McGowan acknowledged the women were looking for an income alternative to prostitution. *Sisters of Charity–Halifax in the Dominican Republic* (2011, 3).
24 McGowan interview, 15.
25 McGowan interview, 20.

REFERENCES

Alexander, Anne. 1997. *The Antigonish Movement: Moses Coady and Adult Education Today*. Toronto: Thompson Educational Publishing.

Baum, Gregory. 2011. "Vatican Council II: A Turning Point in the Church's History." In *Vatican II and Canada*, edited by Michael Attridge, Catherine E. Clifford, and Gilles Routhier, 360–77. Ottawa: University of Ottawa Press.

Bevans, Stephen, and Jeffrey Gros. 2009. *Evangelization and Religious Freedom: Ad Gentes, Dignitatis Humanae*. Mahwah, NJ: Paulist Press.

Bridges, David. 2008. "Educationalization: On the Appropriateness of Asking Educational Institutions to Solve Social and Economic Problems." *Educational Theory* 58 (4): 461–74. https://doi.org/10.1111/j.1741-5446.2008.00300.x

Bruno-Jofré, Rosa. 2019. *Beyond the Possible: From Ultramontanism to Eco-spirituality, the Sisters of Our Lady of Missions (RNDM) in Canada, a Teaching Congregation*. Toronto: University of Toronto Press.

Bruno-Jofré, Rosa, and Ana Jofre. 2015. "Reading the Lived Experience of Vatican II – Words and Images: The Canadian Province of the Sisters of Our Lady of Missions in Peru." *Historical Studies* 81 (1): 31–51.

Canadian Religious Conference. 1975. "Statistics of the Religious Congregations of Canada." Canadian Religious Conference Archives, Montreal.

"Chapter Communications and Explorations for Renewal." n.d. [ca. 1967]. Sisters of Charity–Halifax Archives, file 1-3-5.

"Culture at the Service of Faith." 1968. *Scarboro Missions Magazine* (March): 30.

Depaepe, Marc, and Paul Smeyers. 2008. "Educationalization as an Ongoing Modernization Process." *Educational Theory* 58 (4): 379–89. https://doi.org/10.1111/j.1741-5446.2008.00295.x

Diocese of Charlottetown. 2006. *You Walked with Us Awhile*. Charlottetown: Diocese of Charlottetown.

Ecclesiae *Sanctae II*. 1966. Apostolic letter. 6 August. http://www.vatican.va/holy_father/paul_vi/motu_proprio/documents/hf_p-vi_motu-proprio_19660806_ecclesiae-sanctae_en.html.

Fay, T. 2001. *A History of Canadian Catholics: Gallicanism, Romanism, and Catholicism*. Montreal and Kingston: McGill-Queen's University Press.

Garneau, James F. 2001. "The First Inter-American Episcopal Conference, November 2–4, 1959: Canada and the United States Called to the Rescue of Latin America." *Catholic Historical Review* 87 (4): 662–87. https://doi.org/10.1353/cat.2001.0153

Goudreault, Henri. 1983. "Les missionnaires canadiens à l'étranger au XXe siècle." *SCEC Sessions d'étude* 50(1): 361–80.

Gutiérrez, Gustavo. (1968) 1973. *A Theology of Liberation: History, Politics, and Salvation*. Translated and edited by Sister Caridad Inda and John Eagleson. New York: Maryknoll.

Higman, B.W. 2011. *Concise History of the Caribbean*. New York: Cambridge University Press.

Hogg, W. Richey. 1967. "Some Background Considerations for *Ad Gentes*." *International Review of Mission* 56 (223): 281–90. https://doi.org/10.1111/j.1758-6631.1967.tb03011.x.

Klaiber, Jeffrey. 2009. "The Catholic Church, Moral Education, and Citizenship in Latin America." *Journal of Moral Education* 38 (4): 407–20. https://doi.org/10.1080/03057240903321899.

Klaren, Peter Flindell. 2000. *Peru: Society and Nationhood in the Andes*. New York: Oxford University Press.

Labaree, David F. 2008. "The Winning Ways of a Losing Strategy: Educationalizing Social Problems in the United States." *Educational Theory* 58 (4): 447–60. https://doi.org/10.1111/j.1741-5446.2008.00299.x.

Lernoux, Penny. 1989. *People of God: The Struggle for World Catholicism*. New York: Viking.

– 1991. *Cry of the People: The Struggle for Human Rights in Latin America – The Catholic Church in Conflict with US Policy*. New York: Penguin.

MacKinnon, J.B. 2005. *Dead Man in Paradise: Unraveling a Murder from a Time of Revolution*. Vancouver: Douglas and McIntyre.

McGowan, Mark. 1992. "Rethinking Catholic-Protestant Relations in Canada: The Episcopal Reports of 1900–1901." *CCHA Historical Studies* 59: 11–32.

McKenna, Olga. 1998. *Charity Alive: Sisters of Charity of Saint Vincent de Paul, Halifax, 1950–1980*. Boston: University Press of America.

"Orientation Program." 1968. *Scarboro Missions Magazine* (March): 18

Paul VI. 1965a. *Ad Gentes* (Decree on the Mission Activity of the Church). Proclaimed 7 December. http://www.vatican.va/archive/hist_councils/ii_vatican_council/documents/vat-ii_decree_19651207_ad-gentes_en.html.

Paul VI. 1965b. *Perfectae Caritatis* (Decree on the Adaptation and Renewal of Religious Life). Proclaimed 28 October. http://www.vatican.va/archive/hist_councils/ii_vatican_council/documents/vat-ii_decree_19651028_perfectae-caritatis_en.html.

Paul VI. 1967. *Populorum Progressio* (On the Development of Peoples). Proclaimed 26 March. http://w2.vatican.va/content/paul-vi/en/encyclicals/documents/hf_p-vi_enc_26031967_populorum.html.

Randall, Stephen J., and Graeme S. Mount. 1998. *The Caribbean Basin: An International History*. New York: Routledge.

Reid, Michael. 2007. *Forgotten Continent: The Battle for Latin America's Soul.* New Haven, CT: Yale University Press.
Roberts, Hayden. 1982. *Culture and Education: A Study of Alberta and Quebec.* Edmonton: University of Alberta Press.
Scarboro Fathers. 1968. "There Is No Substitute for Competency." Scarboro Fathers Archives.
"Scarboro Pre-mission Training." 1968. *Scarboro Missions Magazine* (January): 16–21.
Sheahan, John. 1999. *Searching for a Better Society: The Peruvian Economy from 1950.* University Park: Pennsylvania State University Press.
Sisters of Charity–Halifax in the Dominican Republic, 1970–2010. 2011. Halifax: Sisters of Charity.
"The Sisters of Charity in Peru: Background of the Establishment of the Mission." n.d. Sisters of Charity–Halifax Archives, Z2A-6, 3.
Skidmore, Thomas E., Peter H. Smith, and James N. Green. 2014. *Modern Latin America*, 8th ed. Oxford: Oxford University Press.
Smyth, Elizabeth M. 2017. "From Serving in the Mission at Home to Serving in Latin America: The Post–Vatican II Experience of Canadian Women Religious." In *Catholic Education in the Wake of Vatican II, 1962–1965*, edited by Rosa Bruno-Jofré and Jon Igelmo Zaldívar, 158–69. Toronto: University of Toronto Press.
"The Spanish Language Course." 1968. *Scarboro Missions Magazine* (March): 20–1.
"Statement on Missionary Activity." n.d. *Guidelines for Renewal, 1968.* Sisters of Charity–Halifax Archives, file 1-3-36.
Tröhler, Daniel. 2009. "The Educationalization of the Modern World: Progress, Passion, and the Protestant Promise of Education." In *Educational Research: The Educationalization of Social Problems*, edited by P. Smeyers and M. Depaepe, 31–46. Dordrecht, NL: Springer. https://doi.org/10.1007/978-1-4020-9724-93.
Villela, Gabriela, SCH. 2001. "In Response to a Call: Sisters of Charity (Halifax) First Latin American Mission to Peru." 2001. Sisters of Charity–Halifax Archives.

7 The Educationalization Process and the Roman Catholic Church in North America during the Long Nineteenth Century

JOSEPH STAFFORD

This chapter examines the process of educationalization of faith and social concerns within the Catholic Church in North America during the long nineteenth century, a period that, in the context of church history, extends from the French Revolution to the end of the pontificate of Pius XII in 1958 (O'Malley 2008, 4), a period in which political power became centralized in the papacy and bishops became accustomed to obeying papal encyclicals. This centralization was an essential aspect of the educationalization process. The term "educationalization" is understood as "the general concept to identify the overall orientation or trend towards thinking about education as the focal point for addressing or solving larger human problems" (Depaepe and Smeyers 2008, 379). The educationalization process within the Catholic Church during the long nineteenth century also had deep roots in its own history (see the discussion in chapter 3 by Rosa Bruno-Jofré in this volume). Educationalization was closely linked to confessionalization, even as there was a preoccupation to develop political and economic skills among students. One of the traditional purposes of Catholic education since the time of Augustine has been the "formation of individuals who will be good citizens" (Arthur 2009, 233). Another traditional principle of Catholic education has been to promote the "common good," as the church understood it.[1] For the church, educationalization was international in scope and focused on countering what it considered to be the "errors" of the modern world. The church therefore used education to actualize its own purposes and agenda.

Two 1870 encyclicals of Pius IX were critical to this educationalization process: *Dei Filius*, on the apostolic constitution on faith, which clarified the church's position on the relationship between faith and reason; and *Paster Aeternus*, which proclaimed the pope's infallibility in matters of faith and morality. These encyclicals greatly influenced Leo XIII, during whose pontificate (1878–1903) the nineteenth-century process of educationalization began to take shape, especially with his encyclicals *Aeterni Patris* (On the Restoration of Christian Philosophy) and *Rerum Novarum* (On Capital and Labour). In *Aeterni Patris*, Leo proposed that the philosophy of Thomas Aquinas, who articulated what the pope believed to be the perennial and objective truths of Christianity, was the best antidote to the modern intellectual and philosophical "errors" of modernity. Faith and reason, as the church understood them, were both critical components of Aquinas's philosophy. Aquinas also emphasized the importance of leading a virtuous life and explained how it could be achieved through the church. Such teachings were the first stage of the educationalization process, though which individuals came to possess the "truth" and learn how to lead a virtuous life. In *Rerum Novarum*, Leo articulated the second stage in this process, emphasizing how education could help improve the troubled relationship between employers and employees, a relationship central to the promotion of the common good. This encyclical had an evangelical dimension, in that Leo argued that conversion to Christian values was necessary in order to solve the social, economic, and moral problems of Europe, North America, and, indeed, the world. This conversion would occur through the actions of lay Catholics, who were called to bear witness to their faith. By the end of the pontificate of Leo XIII, then, the essential nature of the educationalization process was in place: Catholics, educated in neo-Thomism, would convert others to Catholicism, thereby solving the problems plaguing modern society.[2] After Leo's pontificate, the educationalization process became more formalized under the leadership of the papacy. Pope Pius X imposed a strict neo-Thomism on Catholic schools and, despite a growing pluralism within neo-Thomism, insisted on a strict interpretation of Aquinas's philosophy. Objective truth was what the teaching body of the church, the magisterium, decided it was. Furthermore, Pius X and Pius XI both promoted the second stage of educationalization, placing a multitude of Catholic charitable organizations under the supervision of an umbrella organization called Catholic Action to ensure that lay Catholics were faithful to church doctrine in their conversion efforts.

In North America, the educationalization process was facilitated by the dominant culture within Catholic communities. Most Catholics in North America shared a set of values and a world perception that some scholars have called the "Catholic mind," reflecting what Bernard Lonergan described as a classicist culture in which the larger community, not individuals themselves, determined meaning and value. The individual assimilated this meaning and value, and learned from great intellectuals of the past (Rymarz 2010, 754). Within this culture, most North American Catholics shared a sense of certainty concerning their faith, and, by the early 1920s, most Catholics accepted the magisterium's strict form of neo-Thomism, which was taught in most Catholic high schools and universities. Possessing the "truth" and understanding the Thomistic ethics of virtue, many Catholics became active members of the different organizations under Catholic Action that rapidly spread across North America beginning in the 1930s.[3] Catholic values and meaning were thus integrated into a shared vision that Catholics pursued in their education and in the practical work of Catholic Action: to renew society through conversion to Catholicism. This shared vision was the goal. The degree to which the church achieved this goal is difficult to measure, since it is unclear how many Catholics actually shared in this vision and participated in conversion efforts. The church did, however, achieve considerable success in imposing its educational agenda on the schools, where the local hierarchy was compliant and closely supervised education in its respective jurisdictions. Yet imposition did not necessarily mean that North American Catholics were "educationalized" – that they truly understood or accepted what they had been taught. The rapidity with which traditional Catholic education was rejected after Vatican II raises serious doubts about Catholic understanding of their own faith.

The Centralized Papacy and the Pontificate of Leo XIII

The gradual centralization of power within the papacy was a critical factor in the educationalization process of the church. It is key to understanding why Pope Leo XIII issued his encyclical *Aeterni Patris*, why he believed it was his responsibility to assume a leadership role in education, and why he expected obedience from Catholic educators and scholars. This process began with the Gregorian reforms of the eleventh century, lagged somewhat in the late Middle Ages, but accelerated during the 1800–1950 period (O'Malley 2008, 31). Gradually, papal authority increased at the expense of the various ecumenical councils convened over the centuries. At these councils, major church decisions were made with the bishops, and secular political leaders played an important role.[4] By the time of the First Vatican Council in 1869, however, the pope had assumed a position of authority over the bishops, and the laity no longer participated (27). During the nineteenth century, the papal bureaucracy, the Curia, also became more powerful, especially the Suprema Congregatio – the Holy Office. The decisions of various congregations had to be approved by the Holy Office, whose presiding cardinal was second only to the pope in terms of authority. Increasingly, the pope encouraged the congregations to announce their own judgments on a variety of issues, and, by the end of the nineteenth century, the pope and the congregations of the Curia made all of the important decisions. The power had shifted from the bishops to the pope in an increasingly monarchized papacy (Hennesey 1978, S191).

The papal circular letters, the encyclicals, had become a major teaching tool and an instrument of papal authority. Pius VI (1775–99) had issued only two encyclicals, Pius IX (1846–78) thirty-eight, and Leo XIII seventy-five (O'Malley 2008, 55–6). In these encyclicals, the popes acted as teachers, explaining at great length theological and doctrinal issues. The encyclicals were also "authoritative doctrinal pronouncements" (55). The power of the papacy was reflected in the style of discourse adopted in the encyclicals, in the congregational statements, and in canon law – a style dominated by words of authority, intimidation, threat, condemnation, and punishment.[5] These "power-words" indicated how the church operated, particularly from the latter half of the nineteenth century until Vatican II (45). By then, most Catholics had become accustomed to the predominant role of the papacy in almost every aspect of their religious life, looking to Rome "for answers to all questions" (56).

Thus, by the second half of the nineteenth century, the papacy itself controlled the educationalization policy of the church and had identified what it considered to be the major threat to its teachings: modernity. According to the church, modern Europe had "erred," particularly in terms of cultural and intellectual development. One of the major "errors" involved the relationship between faith and reason. Many European intellectuals accepted the Enlightenment concept of rationalism, which understood reason as an "independent, self-grounding, disembodied form of thought – systematically divorced from Christian revelation in its operations" (McCool 2000, 178). Pope Pius IX in his encyclical *Dei Filius* responded to these "errors" by articulating the church's position on the relationship between faith and reason. Faith was an "operative habit inhering in the intellect," and thus natural reason could prove the existence of God and the "reasonableness of the act of faith" (McCool 1989a, 7) God could also be known by faith through God's revelation because the "divine mysteries" were, by their very nature, beyond complete understanding and accepted on faith (Cummings 2007, 104). *Dei Filius* argued, then, that natural reason and revelation co-existed in harmony, since God was the source of both (Mettepenningen 2010, 19). What is critical here is not whether the church was correct in its understanding of human reason, but that it was convinced that it was correct. Hence it maintained that objective truth could be discovered within the context of its interpretation and authority – an authority declared infallible in terms of morality and faith with the encyclical *Paster Aeternus*. The church therefore insisted that the magisterium would determine this objective "truth" and thus rejected a subjective understanding of this truth.

This understanding of faith and reason was central to the church's educationalization process. Leo XIII, who benefited from the "enhanced authority and mystique" bestowed upon the papacy by *Paster Aeternus* (Daly 1980, 9), believed that the philosophy of Thomas Aquinas embodied this understanding and indeed the entire intellectual tradition of the church. He further believed that this philosophy, if taught to Catholics, would serve as an "antidote" to the modern errors of rationalism and subjectivity – errors that had penetrated Catholic thought in what Leo termed as "a plague of perverse opinions" (Leo XIII 1879, 28). In *Aeterni Patris*, Leo contended that that the Greek philosophers and the fathers of the church had conceived "sound doctrines" of genius. Medieval scholars then collected "the fertile and copious harvest of doctrines, scattered in the large volumes of the holy fathers, and Thomas, who had "inherited the intellect of them all," organized them into a coherent philosophy (Pereira 2002, 153–4). It was this philosophy that neo-Thomism inherited. The neo-Thomists contended that no significant change had occurred in Christian theology and philosophy since the days of the church fathers. Thus, religious "truths" were immutable and had "crystallized into assertions in Scripture and in doctrines of tradition" that theologians then supported through deductive reasoning (Daly 1980, 19). Neo-Thomists also contended that immanence and subjectivity played no part in the search for the truth and the establishment of doctrine. Emphasized instead was the role of the intellect and the will. The first stage in the educationalization process, then, was to insist that Catholic schools teach neo-Thomism – that is, the objective religious truth, as the church understood it.

Aeterni Patris was an integral component of Leo XIII's overall effort at social renewal and conversion, the second stage in the educational process. Indeed, the document was intended to chart the "grand design of philosophical renewal" that would lead to social and political renewal (Hennesey 1978, S195). In it, Leo claimed that "domestic and civil society ... which ... is exposed to great danger from this plague of perverse opinions, would certainly enjoy a far more peaceful and secure existence if a more wholesome doctrine were taught in the universities and high schools – one more in conformity with the teachings of the Church, such as is contained in the works of Thomas

Aquinas" (Leo XIII 1879, 28). In his other encyclicals and teaching letters, Leo almost always discussed or referenced Aquinas in the context socio-political problems (Royal 2015, 39). His most famous encyclical, *Rerum Novarum*, published in 1891, stood in the tradition of Aquinas's social ethics (McCool 2000, 174). Central to this ethics was the need to live a virtuous life, which was possible only by properly forming the intellect and the will. Aquinas identified seven virtues, which became central to Catholic moral tradition. These were the four natural virtues of prudence, justice, fortitude, and temperance, and the three supernatural virtues that exceeded human natural capacities and thus could be obtained only through the sacraments of the church: faith, hope, and charity (Marshall 2014, 43–8). Aquinas defined a virtue as a "quality or habit of the soul" that was an integral part of human nature. Virtue ethics was "a learned and applied life of virtue," a moral lifestyle that involved a daily effort at practising virtue (49). In his encyclical, Leo therefore emphasized that every citizen had to contribute to the common good and that, since the goal of society is "to make men better, the chief good that society can possess is virtue" (Leo XIII 1891, 34). For this goal to be achieved, workers needed to share in "the benefits which they create" through their labour. Otherwise, it would be impossible for them to engage in "virtuous action" if their main goal remained obtaining the essentials of life (34). It was therefore a matter of natural justice that workers receive a fair wage; if not, they are "made victim of force and injustice" (45). It was also the role of the church to influence "the mind and the heart so that all may willingly yield themselves to be formed and guided by the commandments of God" (26). Leo insisted that "human society" could be saved only by a "return to Christian life and Christian institutions," arguing that society was "perishing" because it had strayed from its foundational Christian principles (27). Conversion was therefore needed, and "all those who are concerned in the matter should be of one mind and according to their ability act together" (31). He also called on Catholics to form associations for the common good, in particular to promote "concerted action, and for practical work." In these associations, religious instruction needed to be given the "foremost place" so that their members would be warned and strengthened with special care against wrong principles and false teaching (57). These practical associations could play an "incalculable service" by inviting "the returning wanderers" back to the church, "a haven where they may securely find repose" (61).

Examined together, the two encyclicals *Aeterni Patris* and *Rerum Novarum* laid the foundation for the church's educationalization process that lasted until Vatican II: Catholics, educated in neo-Thomism, were called on to renew society in face of the "errors" of modernism and to return it to its Christian principles through their participation in various Catholic associations striving for the common good.

The Imposition of Strict Neo-Thomism

The church's insistence that Catholics adhere to its educationalization program was clear when it adopted draconian measures to ensure obedience during the modernist crisis that began in the 1890s and continued into the 1920s. Despite *Aeterni Patris*, many modernists within the church raised serious questions about the neo-Thomist understanding of Aquinas and the nature of doctrine and tradition. The "modernists," a vague term applied to anyone who criticized the neo-Thomism sanctioned by the magisterium, used a historical-critical method to criticize some of the fundamental positions of neo-Thomism, contending that doctrine was not immutable but was open to change as new content and new interpretations emerged as a result of historical study (Daly 1980, 5, 19). The modernists were also critical of an overly intellectual neo-Thomist philosophy that neglected the personal, subjective component of religious experience. These modernist ideas presented a major challenge to the church's strict interpretation of neo-Thomism and to its entire educationalization process.

The church's reaction was extreme. During the pontificate of Pius X, the church adopted a reactionary approach to any ideas or actions that it deemed modernist. In 1907, Pius X published his encyclical *Pascendi* (On the Doctrine of the Modernists), condemning modernism in the church (Royal 2015, 44). The overall result of this encyclical was "unbridled carnage" among critics of neo-Thomism, many of whom were forbidden to publish or to teach (Mettepenningen 2010, 25). This encyclical was followed in 1910 by another draconian measure, an anti-modernist oath for priests, which remained in place until 1967. It declared that church dogma was immutable, that faith was not connected to any sentiment of the heart, and that the historical-critical method could not be used to discover religious truth (Royal 2015, 126–7). The magisterium thus remained in control of the church's educational process and silenced many of its critics.

Even after the modernist crisis had passed, the church insisted that strict neo-Thomism be taught in Catholic schools. This is evident from Daly's analysis of the manuals used in seminaries for future priests, many of whom would assume positions in secondary and postsecondary education. The official magisterium neo-Thomism – also known as the Thomism of the strict observance or strict neo-Thomism – permeated the manuals (Daly 1980, 19). Pius XI's 1929 encyclical, *Divini Illius Magistri* (On Christian Education), the most important papal statement on education until Vatican II, also reflected this strict neo-Thomism and "set the agenda" for Catholic education for the next fifty years (Kelty 1999, 11). The encyclical emphasized that Christ "conferred infallibility" on the pope, "commanding" the church to teach His doctrine, and declared that Christ had entrusted the church to "keep whole and inviolate the deposit confided to her ... in accordance with revealed doctrine." This "deposit" was immutable (Pius XI 1929, 16). Even after a certain degree of pluralism developed within neo-Thomism, and with more theologians questioning its essential tenets, the church insisted that Catholic schools adhere to its strict interpretation.[6] Only with the Second Vatican Council did the church abandon strict neo-Thomism as its official philosophy and thus as an integral part of its educationalization process.

The Development of Catholic Action

After Leo issued *Rerum*, the church remained very much involved in promoting the social renewal component of the educationalization process in the form of a return to Christian virtues enunciated by Thomas Aquinas. In 1905, Pius X published the encyclical *Il Fermo Proposito* (On Catholic Action in Italy), defining Catholic Action as an "extremely vast" field of action that does not "exclude anything ... which pertains to the divine mission of the Church" (Pius X 1905, 3). Even though the encyclical was addressed to the Italian bishops, Pius made it clear that he was also encouraging Catholic Action activities throughout the world (2). He emphasized the authority of Rome, expecting that "our words will be heard in a spirit of docility and obeyed by all" (2).[7] Catholics involved in Catholic Action were to be properly educated in neo-Thomism, so that they were "sound Catholics, firm in faith, solidly instructed in religious matters, truly submissive to the Church" (11). Although other popes also concerned themselves with Catholic Action, it was Pius XI who provided the impetus for the proliferation of Catholic Action groups throughout the world, in charity organizations, in the marketplace, and in the establishment of Catholic journals and newspapers (O'Malley 2008, 81). He mentioned Catholic Action in almost all of his speeches and documents, earning the unofficial title of the "Catholic Action Pope" (Gleason 1987, 141). During his pontificate, Catholic Action emerged as a "visible organization" as Pius clarified its relationship with Rome. In his first encyclical, *Ubi Arcano Dei Consilio* (On the Peace of Christ in the Kingdom of Christ), Pius clearly connected its activities to social renewal, to "spreading far and wide the kingdom of Christ" as Catholics "participate in the works of the apostolate" (Pius XI 1922, 53, 58). In his encyclical *Non Abbiamo Bisogno* (Catholic Action in Italy), he defined Catholic Action as the "collaboration of the laity in the hierarchical apostolate," clearly placing it under the authority of the church (Pius XI, 1931, 5). His successor, Pius XII, established the Central Office of Catholic Action under the supervision of the secretary of the Cardinals Commission, which communicated with the bishops. Thus, Catholic Action was not an autonomous organization but an umbrella organization of various groups that were expected to obey their local bishops and to adhere to the official teachings of the church.

The Educationalization Process in North America: Strict Neo-Thomism

In Catholic communities in North America, educationalization was facilitated by what one of the leading theologians of the twentieth century, Bernard Lonergan, referred to as "classicist" culture. Catholic belief permeated the entire culture, which did not understand itself as one culture among many, but as "the only culture any right-minded and cultivated person would name as culture" (Rymarz 2010, 754). Essential to this culture was a deeply embedded respect for antiquity – in particular the Greco-Roman classical era – an antiquity that had been assimilated into Christian culture (Lonergan 1974, 160). In terms of education, the different academic disciplines were infused with Catholic theology and philosophy, while remaining distinct disciplines (McCool 1989a, 29–30). Catholic thought therefore permeated the entire educational system and shaped the individual's self-identity and perception of reality. Catholics were predisposed to accepting church teachings and to following church traditions to such an extent that the term "Catholic mind" was commonly used to express the collective Catholic world view. As Gerald B. Phelan commented in his 1953 address to the Catholic Education Conference in Toronto, "To the Catholic mind, the whole tradition of Western thought and culture is impregnated with the teaching of Jesus Christ and His Church. The Catholic feels at home in it and revels in its triumphs."[8] Another leading scholar, Bishop Emmett Carter, noted that North American Catholics strictly adhered to "even the minutiae of Church discipline," adding that "probably nowhere in the world is the observance of Church customs and laws as strict as in the strongly Catholic areas of North America" (Carter 1961, 1).[9]

Most North American Catholics readily accepted the church's educationalization process, especially after the fiftieth anniversary of *Aeterni*

Patris in 1929 stimulated an intense interest in neo-Thomism. A number of North American colleges and universities strengthened their departments of philosophy with an increased emphasis on this school of thought. During the same year, a leading neo-Thomist, Etienne Gilson, established the Pontifical Institute of Medieval Studies in Toronto, which in its early years focused mainly on philosophy (Flahiff 1949, 251–2). The various religious orders, particularly through their philosophical journals, such as the Jesuit *Modern Schoolman*, played a critical role in promoting neo-Thomism, so much so that, according to G.A. McCool, the neo-Thomist movement in North America would not have become "the powerful movement which it became after 1930" without "the expertise, the resources, and support of the religious orders" (1988, 193). The overall result was that strict neo-Thomism had a powerful and lasting influence on Catholic higher education in North America. (186–7).[10] Philip Gleason's article "In Search of Unity: American Catholic Thought, 1920–1960" chronicles the influence of neo-Thomism in Catholic education in the United States, the goal of which became "integral wholeness." The major role for educators was a practical one of "bringing home to the faithful the full realization of what this unity meant to them personally" (1979, 190–1).

Even as late as 1960, the "Thomistic establishment reigned" in the vast majority of American colleges and universities, where an "explicitly Catholic point of view" was evident in the teaching of most secular subjects. Furthermore, in theology classes, students were unlikely to study the works of outstanding European Catholic scholars who were questioning neo-Thomism (Hitchcock and O'Brien 1985, 177–8). Exuding supreme confidence in their beliefs, the leading proponents of strict neo-Thomism remained self-assured in any debate with scholars who questioned strict neo-Thomism, as it was "obvious" that there was only one truth about God – St Thomas's philosophy was "not just one theology among others; it was an exposition of the mind of God" (Gleason 1979, 203). Jesuit institutions in particular emphasized the "union of classical humanism and scholastic philosophy" that characterized neo-Thomism (McCool 1987, 134). The extent to which strict neo-Thomism permeated postsecondary Catholic education is epitomized by George Bull's 1933 essay "The Function of the Catholic Graduate School," wherein he argues that there is a "distinctive Catholic life of the mind" (364), that contemplation, not research, is needed, since "wisdom had been achieved" (368), and that "the frame within which all man's thinking is to be done, has been set" (367). Neo-Thomism, the inheritor of the immutable truths from the classical, apostolic, and patristic eras, provided this frame, this "communal life of the mind"

(368). According to Bull, "every Catholic has and must have a sense of a finished Revelation," which is "part of the furniture of the mind over which we never fall." This "same assumption" holds true in the "realm of the humanities," where classical literature mirrors "the permanent and ultimate values of human nature," for Christianity only "purified" them without fundamentally altering them (377).

Strict neo-Thomism also characterized Catholic secondary education in North America, as is evident from an analysis of the policies of the Archdiocese of Toronto. It is clear that the magisterium controlled the educationalization process at the secondary level. In 1935, the Sacred Congregation of the Council issued a decree called "The Better Care and Promotion of Catechetical Education," expressing serious concern about what it considered to be the deplorable state of religious education. Citing several canon laws to justify its call for improvement, the council emphasized the critical importance of effective teacher training and of treating religious instruction as the most significant subject offered in Catholic schools (Sacred Congregation of the Council 1935, 12). The church demanded complete obedience and emphasized the power of local religious authorities to enforce the decree and to "inflict on the obstinate and the negligent the ecclesiastical penalties prescribed," including those involving suspension of duties and excommunication (7).[11] In order to highlight the importance of religious instruction, the council called for the institution of a Diocesan Catechetical Office, which would "control the entire catechetical instruction in the diocese" (10). One of the major functions of this office was to ensure that in all parishes, schools, and colleges "Christian doctrine be taught by properly prepared teachers according to the traditional form of the Church" (10). The council also called for the establishment of a Catechetical Day in order to celebrate Christian doctrine, and provided specific instructions as to how to organize the day (11). Bishops were ordered to complete a detailed questionnaire every five years concerning the "state of the diocese entrusted to them" (13).

In 1941, the Archdiocese of Toronto obediently completed the questionnaire, reporting that a Catechetical Office existed, known as the Office of Religious Instruction, and that every year the Catechetical Day was celebrated, following the precise instructions from Rome.[12] The archdiocese also decided to have religion exams at the end of each year of high school in order to enhance the importance of religion education at the secondary level.[13] The Grade 12 exam was given special status. In 1944, for example, the graduation exercises for all those who passed the diocesan religion exam were held at St Michael's Cathedral on Catechetical Day.[14] The evidence therefore indicates that, in the

Archdiocese of Toronto, the high school religion curriculum adhered to strict neo-Thomism, with the archdiocese strictly following the ordinances from Rome concerning secondary education.

An analysis of the mandated textbooks of the 1940s and 1950s provides further evidence of this adherence. For example, the 1940s textbook *Religion: Doctrine and Practise* emphasized one of the major tenets of strict neo-Thomism, that there had been no change in the "deposit of faith" – that is, the "sum of revealed doctrines" – since the death of the last apostle, and that St Thomas Aquinas had inherited this deposit (Cassilly 1934, 350). Furthermore, "no new revelation has been proposed by the Church" and "whenever there is a question of settling or defining a disputed point of faith, the Church always decides according to the teaching of tradition" (351). The textbook was organized by a series of questions, which were then followed by answers. One such question dealt with two new, controversial doctrines, papal infallibility and the Immaculate Conception of Mary. The students were asked whether or not the church defines new doctrines, and then were provided with the answer: The church "does not define new doctrines, but ... from time to time it gives more explicit knowledge and exposition of what was revealed to the Apostles" (350). Another question was "Do the doctrines of the Church change?" The answer: "No, the doctrines of the church do not change" (350). In the 1950s, the mandated textbooks were in *The Quest for Happiness* series, widely used throughout English Canada, according to the archdiocese.[15] *The Quest for Happiness* reflected the self-assured, confident neo-Thomist perspective, and expected students to accept church teachings and doctrines without question. In the Grade 12 textbook, *The Eternal Commencement*, the authors declare that "the only proof needed by a Catholic that the Blessed Virgin was preserved from original sin ... is the official, infallible definition of the doctrine of the Immaculate Conception by Pope Pius IX, on December 8, 1854" (Elwell 1951, 30). The authors also claimed that the Gospels were "reliable authentic historical documents" and that historical biblical criticism reflects "outdated" ideas (494–5). Near the end of the textbook, the authors warn students not to bother arguing with anyone who still holds such ideas and emphasized the "guaranteed certainty" to be found in Gospels written by eyewitnesses who were willing to die for their faith (494–5). Strict neo-Thomism is also reflected in another popular textbook used in the 1950s, although it was originally published in 1881 and contains a letter of praise from Pope Leo XIII. *Bible History* adopts a literal interpretation of the Bible and question-answer method of instruction (Gilmour 1894).[16] In the 1956–7 program of Christian Doctrine Studies of the Archdiocese of Toronto,

Bible History was the mandatory text for the senior elementary grades, preparing them for the high school *Quest for Happiness* series.[17]

The impact of strict neo-Thomism and the adherence to the ordinances of Rome was also reflected in professional development for teachers, which fell under the jurisdiction of the inspector for Catholic separate schools of the archdiocese, John M. Bennett. His overall responsibility was the "supervision and visitation of all classes" to ensure that the policies of the Ontario Ministry of Education and the Archdiocese of Toronto were upheld (Bennett 1954). This supervision included ensuring that teachers were properly prepared to teach church doctrine. In a lengthy paper distributed at a catechetical conference for teachers in 1953, Bennett explained the church's position on faith and reason, emphasizing that "faith is greater than reason," and the need to remain on the offensive against "atheism and materialism" with the "sword of the spirit" by implementing the weapons of "prayer, work (teaching), and sacrifice" (1953, 1). Teachers were entrusted with the "task of imparting supernatural truth" and strengthening the will of the students through "encouragement, reprimands, reminders" and "inspiration" in order to "have children seek the Grace of God" by praying, attending Mass, and availing themselves of the sacraments (2). Bennett also emphasized the importance of developing a "Catholic mind," asking teachers, "Can we work the truths of faith so deeply into the minds and hearts of our youth by means of activities in Christian study in early youth that they will be men and women of Christian principles throughout life?" (4). After referring to the efforts of the Catholic University of America to accomplish this task by issuing the "Faith and Freedom Basic Readers" and a curriculum guide, "Guiding Growth in Christian Social Living," Bennett stressed that it was a "difficult task to carry the cross and only definite principles and the Grace of God will help us ... as teachers to endeavour to develop a Catholic mind to wish to do this" (4). He then provided a list of classroom activities that could help to facilitate the deepening of the "truths of faith" in the minds of youth. When discussing the overall curriculum of a Catholic school, Bennett emphasized that there was a "Catholic culture to impart," and he highlighted different academic disciplines that needed to be integrated with Catholic theology and philosophy – for example, Catholic poetry, Catholic music, and Catholic literature.

Catholic Action in North America

Bennett emphasized a key aspect of the church's educationalization process: the integration of the different disciplines, bound together by a strict neo-Thomism, into a curriculum that would cultivate a "Catholic mind." This integration was also critical to Catholic Action: a leading American scholar, John Courtney Murray SJ, emphasized that once individuals possessed the "splendid organic wholeness" of the Catholic faith, they also possessed a "tightly integrated system of motives" to inspire them to moral action under the direction of the church (Gleason 1987, 149). In North America, the major aim of Catholic Action was to promote this "organic wholeness," first among Catholics, who would then convert the entire society to this Catholic vision (28). Catholic Action promoted "practical tasks" that would further the integrated Catholic vision throughout North American society (141). To accomplish this significant stage in the educationalization program, Catholic Action became more of an organized movement, following Pius XI's instructions. The United States and Canada established central offices to supervise and coordinate Catholic Action activities. By the mid-1930s the General Assembly of Bishops of Canada had formed two committees, one for doctrine and the other for social action, that were responsible for keeping the church hierarchy informed of activities in these two areas.[18] Throughout Canada, specific days were declared "parochial days of Catholic Action," when parishes convened "diocesan congresses" at which selected Catholic Action activities were discussed and studied. In the United States, the National Catholic Welfare Conference was responsible for supervising Catholic Action, and in 1937 the Department of Lay Organizations was established to promote social-welfare initiatives among the laity. It also sponsored a series of conferences to educate priests in Catholic social teachings in order to prepare them to provide the necessary leadership for these initiatives (Zotti 1990, 390–1).[19] Thus, by the late 1930s, Catholic Action had emerged as a major instrument of the church's educationalization process, initiating a wide range of activities throughout North America.

Prominent among these activities were various opportunities for lay peeople to learn more about both doctrine and social renewal. In May 1939, a three-week School of Catholic Action was held in Chicago, at which lay Catholics were told that, as members of Christ's mystical body, they were called "to socialize souls, so that hearts and minds may unite in the Mystical Body of Christ" (Zotti 1990, 395).[20] Catholic Action Summer School sessions were offered, such as in 1951 in Cumberland, Ontario, where any lay individual could register for a three-week course with the purpose of restoring "the world in Christ." After learning about the spiritual foundations of Catholic Action, participants studied the topic of the "mystical body of Christ in action."[21] In October 1951, the World Congress of the Lay Apostolate was held, focusing on various subjects such as doctrinal foundations and the Christian social order, with the overall of aim of organizing a "world plan and the opportunity of common action according to this plan."[22] Throughout North America, study groups were established under episcopal direction, adhering to the belief that practical action must be based on Catholic truth and not life experience (Zotti 1990, 391). These groups used a social inquiry method, briefly described as "see, judge, act" (Hurley 1997, 30). Catholic Action was also involved in the international catechetical renewal, biblical study, and liturgical reform movements, serving as a way to reach the ordinary Catholic (194, 260).

Several specialized Catholic Action groups were also formed in order to realize Pius XI's goal that "workers must be the apostles of the workers, farmers the apostles to farmers, students the apostles of students" (Zotti 1990, 388). One of the most significant groups was the Young Christian Workers, which aimed at promoting workers' right to live in a just society and at developing leaders who, as members of Christ's mystical body, were dedicated to reforming society (387). Two other groups that developed in the United States were the Young Christian Students and the Christian Family Movement, which was very active among married couples in parishes across North America (Power, Brock, et al. 2008, 215). The group Pax Romana, which was influential among university students, established a North American Commission in Toronto in 1951. One of its major goals was for students to "place their intellect at the service of God," according to a leading neo-Thomist, Etienne Gilson.[23] Pax Romana was to give students "a sound character," enabling them to make "practical judgments" in terms of improving society.[24] Such specialized Catholic Action groups played a critical role in the church's educationalization process by contributing to an integrated Catholic culture, by teaching neo-Thomist doctrine, and by engaging in apostolic action. In the words of Father Louis Pultz at the University of Notre Dame, a major leader in the Young Christian Workers movement, "We will not convert others by preaching or by telling others about our religion; we will do it by our service" (Zotti 1990, 395–6).

Conclusion

The Catholic educationalization process in North America was facilitated by the church's dominant classicist culture wherein the church itself decided an individual's sense of value and meaning. The evidence indicates that strict neo-Thomism was adopted in most North American Catholic secondary schools, particularly where the local church hierarchy remained obedient to Rome and closely supervised education within its jurisdiction.[25] In addition, many Catholics became involved in various

Catholic Action activities, accepting the two stages of the educationalization process: a neo-Thomist education and a conversion effort based in social renewal. The two strands were intimately connected. Armed, through their education, with the "truth," Catholics could then convert others to Catholicism and encourage lapsed Catholics to return to the church. Everything about a person's education and daily life was integrated in a Catholic vision of social renewal, which by the 1940s became identified with the Mystical Body of Christ. The various Catholic Action groups promoted this integral Catholic culture among its lay members. Most ordinary Catholics shared the self-assured confidence of neo-Thomist scholars. In the 1940s and 1950s, most Catholics were proud to belong to the "one true Church" (McNamara 1991, 17). During the baby boom years, at least before 1955, most young Catholics were even proud of the church's position on birth control, since it was identified with an "unyielding defence of Christian morals" and was therefore accepted as "a kind of tribal marker – a proud if onerous badge of Catholic identity" (Tentler 2004, 9). Novelists and essayists portrayed a "Catholicism of clear and clean definition," and most ordinary Catholics did not question the authority of the church and its representatives, the priests, brothers, and sisters. Questions were not needed, only devotion (McNamara 1991, 18, 29).

Despite these signs of success, it is nonetheless difficult to determine the extent to which the church was successful in its educationalization process. The evidence does indicate that it was successful in imposing its educational agenda on the schools as long as Catholic educators dutifully obeyed magisterium ordinances. Yet it is an open question as to how many Catholics actually embraced the vision of social renewal and conversion. It is also difficult to ascertain the extent to which Catholic students understood the strict neo-Thomism that they were taught. What needs to be studied further is the relationship between the educationalization process of the church and the dominant classicist Catholic culture that facilitated it. After the Second World War, this culture began to be undermined as Catholics, a minority in a predominantly Protestant North America, gradually assimilated into the mainstream culture (Gleason 1987, 31–2). Moreover, a fundamental change after Vatican II was the shattering of the Catholic classicist culture that had sustained the "Catholic mind." As this culture declined, so too did the sense of certainty that most Catholics had that the fundamental precepts of the faith were the "truth" (188–9). This culture was replaced by an empiricist culture, one in which individuals determined meaning and value for themselves – a culture that, in the non-Catholic world, had gradually developed since the beginning of the seventeenth century (Lonergan 1974, 159–60). As this classicist Catholic culture collapsed, so too did the existing educationalization process of the church. The rapidity with which strict neo-Thomism was abandoned in Catholic schools after Vatican II raises serious doubts concerning the extent to which it had actually been understood, given the traditional teaching methods of rote memorization. Indeed, a common complaint from students was that they did not "know why we believe it, or why we do this or that. It's the law and we have to."[26] Soon after Vatican II, Catholics students no longer were inclined to obey such a "law." The search then began for an educationalization process suitable to contemporary Catholic life – a search that continues today.

NOTES

1 This tradition was upheld during the long nineteenth century, which is evident in the definitive statement on Catholic education prior to the Second Vatican Council – Pope Pius XI's 1929 encyclical, *Divini Illius Magistri* (On Christian Education). The "common good," however, was understood in terms of the church's own concept of the proper moral social order, in which the church itself determined the exact nature of the common good. In the 1965 Vatican II educational statement, the *Declaration on Christian Education*, the traditional importance of the common good continued to be emphasized (Pohlschneider 1969, 13–15 and Flannery 1998, 727).
2 The term "neo-Thomist" is somewhat contentious. At times "neo-scholasticism" and "neo-Thomism" are used interchangeably (Gleason 1987, 146–9). Furthermore, some scholars use the term neo-Thomist to refer only to the period 1870–1920, whereas others use the term more broadly and also include the period 1920–60. According to Fr J. Grange, curator of the Gilson Collection at the Pontifical Institute of Medieval Studies, Etienne Gilson, usually identified as a neo-Thomist, considered himself a Thomist, since he focused on the actual works of Thomas Aquinas and not on later commentaries (email to author, 23 May 2017). In this chapter, the term "neo-Thomist" will be used in the broader sense for the sake of consistency.
3 I contend here that this neo-Thomist classicist culture constituted the dominant Catholic culture prior to Vatican II. This argument relies on recent studies in cultural dominance that contend that, in any given society, a specific culture dominates largely because it serves the interests of the "elites" or "governing powers," which use various strategies, including education, to protect and sustain this culture. These studies include Miedema (2005), McKay (1992), Massolin (2001), Palmer (2009), Williams (1980), and Curtis (1988). As Williams argues (1980, 38), the dominant culture establishes a hegemony – that is, a "central, effective, and dominant system of meanings and values, which are not merely abstract but which are organized and lived."

4 There were twenty ecumenical councils before Vatican II; the pope was not even present at the first eight (O'Malley 2008, 27).
5 In the late fourth century, the church was granted the power to issue its own laws, which became known as canon laws. One of the results of the Gregorian reform movement was the first major codification of all the canon laws (Cantor 1993, 62, 312–13).
6 The distinct forms of neo-Thomism became identified with specific intellectuals: the strict neo-Thomism of Reginald Garrigou-Lagrange; the historical neo-Thomism of Etienne Gilson; the transcendental neo-Thomism of Joseph Marechal; and the intuitive neo-Thomism of Jacques Maritain (McCool 1987, 138.) The church gradually relaxed its imposition as long as the essential tenets of neo-Thomism were upheld. In his 1950 encyclical *Humani generis*, Pius XII allowed the "free discussion of experts" as long as "things of faith and morals are not directly related" (Pereira 2002, 167). Neo-Thomism, however, remained the official philosophy of the church.
7 Pius also explained why he had hesitated to offer words of encouragement earlier, citing the "undisciplined tendencies" of some Catholic Action groups that were not acting for the "common good," as the church understood it.
8 Archives of the Roman Catholic Archdiocese of Toronto (hereafter ARCAT), EDS002.315. Phelan was an associate of Etienne Gilson, with whom he helped establish the Pontifical Institute of Medieval Studies in Toronto.
9 This is not to argue that all Catholics "strictly adhered" to church discipline, but it is to argue that neo-Thomistic classicism was the dominant Catholic culture prior to Vatican II, and that most Catholics did their best to obey church laws. In post–Second World War North American society, after years of economic depression and war, most people longed to return to "normalcy," to what they considered a normal life – a longing that reinforced this dominance. Religious practice was considered integral to this "normalcy," and not only for Catholics, since in the postwar years the major Protestant denominations experienced a religious revival, especially in the expanding suburbs (Miedema 2005, 34–5). An excellent example of how most Catholics tried to adhere to church laws involved the ban on the use of contraceptives, certainly one of the most challenging church "disciplines." According to L.W. Tentler, in *Catholics and Contraception: An American History*, during the late 1940s most Catholics obeyed this ban, but this was during the early baby boom years, when having several children was considered "normal." By the mid-1950s, the situation changed, with more Catholics finding it difficult to follow this particular teaching. In a 1955 poll, 30 per cent of American Catholic women admitted that they had used contraceptives, and many of them felt ashamed for doing so (Tentler 2004, 9–10). Poll data also indicated that "large numbers of Catholics" disagreed with the church's teaching, even as they continued to obey it (ibid., 199). The evidence suggests that most Catholics tried to obey

this teaching, and, if they failed to do so, they did not participate in the sacraments, in accordance with church law. For example, several sociological studies found that "married thirty-somethings" stayed away from the sacraments in "significantly larger numbers" than other Catholics, and it was "widely assumed" that they were using contraceptives (ibid.).

10 It is important to note that not all neo-Thomists were strict observant. Strict neo-Thomists, however, were the most dominant group and shaped the overall character of Catholic education. For example, the strict neo-Thomist W. Farrell's four-volume *Companion to the Summa* was widely used in Catholic universities (Gleason 1987, 148).

11 In this instance, the decree refers to canons 1330, 1331, and 1332, all of which deal with punishment.

12 Questionnaire on the Teaching of Christian Doctrine, the Archdiocese of Toronto Office of Religious Instruction (1941), ARCAT, GSO25.65 (b).

13 Ibid., 12.

14 Report on "Diocesan Catechetical Activities" for 1944–5, ARCAT, EDSC04.66.

15 In response to a 1957 request from the Sacred Congregation of the Council concerning the textbooks used in the archdiocese, Monsignor J.P. Fulton, Chancelor of the Archidiocese of Toronto, stated that the *Quest for Happiness* series was the mandated high school textbook in his archdiocese and that it was widely used throughout English Canada. ARCAT, MGDS59.07A and MGDS5907B.

16 This was the textbook used in Trenton, Ontario, when Father Brian Price, archivist for the Archdiocese of Kingston, was in Grade 9.

17 "Program of Christian Doctrine Studies," ARCAT.

18 Interview with Cardinal Villeneuve of Quebec, in the National Catholic Welfare Conference News Service release for the week of 6 November 1933, p. 33.

19 Pope Pius XI's encyclical *Divini Redemptoris* (On Atheistic Communism) was the impetus for the increase in Catholic Action activities in North America, as Pius called upon Catholics to undertake study circles, lecture courses, conferences, and other activities in order to promote the Catholic solution to existing social problems (Zotti 1990, 390).

20 The church was understood increasingly as the mystical body of Christ (Mettepenningen 2010, 27–8), especially after Pope Pius XII's 1943 encyclical *Mystici Corporis Christi* was issued. This concept meshed nicely with Catholic classicism, the "Catholic mind," and the social vision of Catholic Action.

21 *Canadian Register*, June 1951 https://digital.catholicregister.org.

22 *Canadian Register*, 14 April 1951.

23 *Canadian Register*, 3 March 1951.

24 *Canadian Register*, 16 February 1952.

25 There were no doubt notable exceptions. See chapter 3 by Rosa Bruno-Jofré in this volume.
26 The 1968 Sub-commission on Christian Education Focusing on Youth, London Diocese Synod, Archives of the Diocese of London, Bishop E.G. Carter Papers, box 25, file 28.

REFERENCES

Arthur, James. 2009. "Secularisation, Secularism, and Catholic Education: Understanding the Challenges." *International Studies in Catholic Education* 1 (2): 228–39. https://doi.org/10.1080/19422530903138226.

Bennett, J.M. 1953. "Teaching of Religion." Pepared for the Catechetical Conference for Kingston. October. In Archives of the Sisters of Providence (Kingston, ON), 13B2, 304.5, 1.

– 1954. "Duties of Inspectors." Report by the inspector for Division XVIII, Metropolitan Catholic Separate Schools of Greater Toronto. January. In Archives of the Roman Catholic Archdiocese of Toronto, EDSCO4.38 c.

Bull, George. 1933. "The Function of the Catholic Graduate School" *Thought* 13 (3): 364–80. https://doi.org/10.5840/thought193813343.

Cantor, Norman F. 1993. *The Civilization of the Middle Ages*. New York: Harper Collins.

Carter, Emmett. 1961. *The Modern Challenge to Religious Education*. New York: Palmer Publisher.

Cassilly, Francis B., SJ. 1934. *Religion: Doctrine and Practice*. Chicago: Loyola University Press.

Cummings, Owen. 2007. *Prophets, Guardians, and Saints: Shapers of Modern Catholic History*. New York: Paulist Press.

Curtis, Bruce. 1988. *Building the Educational State: Canada West, 1836–1871*. London, ON: Althouse Press.

Daly, Gabriel. 1980. *Transcendence and Immanence: A Study in Catholic Modernism and Integralism*. Oxford: Clarendon Press.

Depaepe, Marc, and Paul Smeyers 2008. "Educationalization as an Ongoing Modernization Process." *Educational Theory* 58 (4): 379–89. https://doi.org/10.1111/j.1741-5446.2008.00295.x.

Elwell, Clarence. 1951. *Our Quest for Happiness*. Book 1. *Our Goal and Our Guides*. Chicago: Mentzer, Bush, and Company.

Flahiff, G.B. 1949. "The Pontifical Institute of Mediaeval Studies at Toronto." *Speculum* 24 (2): 251–5. https://doi.org/10.2307/2848565.

Flannery, Austin. 1998. *Vatican Council II: The Conciliar and Post Conciliar Documents*. Vol. 1. New York: Costello Publishing Company.

Gilmour, Richard. 1894. *Bible History*. New York: Benziger Brothers.
Gleason, Philip. 1979. "In Search of Unity: American Catholic Thought, 1920–1960." *Catholic Historical Review* 65 (2): 185–205. http://www.jstor.org/stable/25020551.
– 1987. *Keeping the Faith: American Catholicism Past and Present*. Notre Dame, IN: University of Notre Dame Press.
Hennesey, James. 1978. "Leo XIII's Thomistic Revival: A Political and Philosophical Event." *Journal of Religion* 58: S185–S197. https://doi.org/10.1086/jr.58.41575990.
Hitchcock, J., and D.J. O'Brien. 1985. "How Has American Catholic Intellectual Life Changed over the Past Thirty Years?" *US Catholic Historian* 4 (2): 176–87. http://www.jstor.org/stable/25153726.
Hurley, Robert J. 1997. *Hermeneutics and Catechesis: Biblical Interpretation in the Come to the Father Catechetical Series*. Lanham, MD: University Press of America.
Kelty, Brian J. 1999. "Toward a Theology of Catholic Education." *Religious Education* 94 (1): 6–23. https://doi.org/10.1080/0034408990940102.
Leo XIII. 1879. *Aeterni Patris* (On the Restoration of Christian Philosophy). Papal Encyclicals Online. www.papalencyclicals.net.
– 1891. *Rerum Novarum* (On Capital and Labour). Papal Encyclicals Online. www.papalencyclicals.net.
Lonergan, Bernard. 1974. "The Future of Christianity." In *A Second Collection: Papers by Bernard J.F. Lonergan, SJ*, edited by William F.J. Ryan, SJ, and Bernard J. Tyrrell, SJ, 127–40. London: Darton, Longman and Todd.
Marshall, Taylor R. 2014. *Thomas Aquinas in 50 Pages: A Layman's Quick Guide to Thomism*. Irving, TX: Saint John Press.
Massolin, Philip. 2001. *Canadian Intellectuals, the Tory Tradition, and the Challenge of Modernity, 1939–1970*. Toronto: University of Toronto Press.
McCool, Gerald A. 1978. "Twentieth-Century Scholasticism." *Journal of Religion* 58: S198–S221.
– 1987. "Neo-Thomism and the Tradition of St Thomas." *Thought* 62 (2) 131–46. https://doi.org/10.5840/thought198762223.
– 1988. "The Tradition of Saint Thomas in North America: At 50 Years." *Modern Schoolman* 65 (3): 185–206. https://doi.org/10.5840/schoolman198865328.
– 1989a. *Nineteenth-Scholasticism: The Search for a Unitary Method*. New York: Fordham University Press.
– 1989b. "Spirituality and Philosophy: The Ideal of the Catholic Mind." *Sacred Heart Review* 10 (1): 1–18. http://digitalcommons.sacredheart.edu/shureview/vol10/iss1/3.
– 2000. "From Leo XIII to John Paul II: Continuity and Development." *International Philosophical Quarterly* 40 (2): 173–83. https://doi.org/10.5840/ipq20004021.

McKay, Ian. 1992. *The Challenge of Modernity: A Reader on Post-Confederation Canada*. Toronto: McGraw-Hill Ryerson.

McNamara, Patrick. 1991. *Conscience First, Tradition Second: A Study of Young American Catholics*. New York: State University of New York Press.

Mettepenningen, Jürgen. 2010. *Nouvelle Theologie – New Theology: Inheritor of Modernism, Precursor of Vatican II*. London: T. and T. Clark International.

Miedema, Gary R. 2005. *For Canada's Sake: Public Religion, Centennial Celebrations, and the Re-making of Canada in the 1960s*. Montreal and Kingston: McGill-Queen's University Press.

O'Malley, J.W. 2008. *What Happened at Vatican II*. Cambridge, MA: Belknap Press of Harvard University Press.

Palmer, Bryan D. 2009. *Canada's 1960s: The Ironies of Identity in a Rebellious Era*. Toronto: University of Toronto Press.

Pereira, Jose. 2002. "Thomism and the Magisterium: From *Aeterni Patris* to *Veritatis Splendor*." *Logos: A Journal of Catholic Thought and Culture* 5 (3): 147–83. https://doi.org/10.1353/log.2002.0043.

Pius X. 1905. *Il Fermo Proposito* (On Catholic Action in Italy). Papal Encyclicals Online. www.papalencyclicals.net.

Pius XI. 1922. *Ubi Arcano Dei Consilio* (On the Peace of Christ in His Kingdom). Papal Encyclicals Online. www.papalencyclicals.net.

– 1929. *Divini Illius Magistri* (On Christian Education). Papal Encyclicals Online. www.papalencyclicals.net.

– 1931. *Non Abbiano Bisogna* (Catholic Action in Italy). Papal Encyclicals Online. www.papalencyclicals.net.

Pohlschneider, Johannes. 1969. "Declaration on Christian Education." In *Commentary on the Documents of Vatican II*, edited by Herbert Vorgrimler, 1–48. Montreal: Palm Publishers.

Power, Michael, Daniel J. Brock, et al. 2008. *Gather Up the Fragments: A History of the Diocese of London*. London, ON: Diocese of London.

Royal, Robert. 2015. *A Deeper Vision: The Catholic Intellectual Tradition in the Twentieth Century*. San Francisco: Ignatius Press.

Rymarz, Richard. 2010. "Conversion and the New Evangelization: A Perspective from Lonergan." *Heythrop Journal* 51 (5): 754–67. https://doi.org/10.1111/j.1468-2265.2009.00545.x.

Sacred Congregation of the Council. 1935. "Decree on the Better Care and Promotion of Catechetical Education." National Center of the Confraternity of Christian Doctrine, Washington, DC. In the Archives of the Roman Catholic Archdiocese of Toronto, MGSO25.65 a.

Tarnas, Richard. 1991. *Passion of the Western Mind: Understanding the Ideas That Have Shaped Our World*. New York: Ballantine Books.

Tentler, Leslie Woodstock. 2004. *Catholics and Contraception: An American History*. Ithaca, NY: Cornell University Press.

Tröhler, Daniel. 2013. *Pestalozzi and the Educationalization of the World*. New York: Palgrave Macmillan.
– 2016. "Educationalization of Social Problems and the Educationalization of the Modern World." In *Encyclopedia of Educational Philosophy and Theory*, edited by Michael A. Peters, 1–10. Singapore: Springer. https://doi.org/10.1007/978-981-287-532-7_8-1.
Williams, Raymond. 1980. *Problems in Materialism and Culture: Selected Essays*. New York: Verso.
Woods, Thomas E. 2005. *How the Catholic Church Built Western Civilization*. Washington, DC: Regnery Publishing.
Zotti, M. 1990. "The Young Christian Workers." *US Catholic Historian* 9(4): 387–400. http://www.jstor.org/stable/25153925.

8 Educationalization in the Spanish Second Republic and the Expulsion of the Jesuits from Spain

JON IGELMO ZALDÍVAR

This chapter examines how study of the restoration of the Bourbon monarchy (1876–1931) and the Second Republic (1931–6) reveals specific elements of discourse continuity in the history of education in Spain. This continuity has considerable bearing on the concept of "educationalization." In this chapter, I pay particular attention to the suppression of the Society of Jesus by the first republican government. My interest here is to observe how strategic Jesuit institutions for internal training and scientific research in Spain, such as the three maximum colleges located in Oña (Burgos), Granada, and Barcelona, were first seized by the authorities of the Second Republic and then replaced by institutions that, from the point of view of educationalization, provided continuity to the same disposition of discourse. This analysis begins with as precise a definition as possible of the idea of educationalization, which is key to this article. Here I take David Labaree as a reference:

> The educationalization of society integrates society among a set of common experiences, processes, and curricular languages. It stabilizes and legitimizes a social structure of inequality that otherwise may drive us into open conflict. It stabilizes and legitimizes government by providing an institution that can be assigned difficult social problems and that can be blamed when these problems are not solved. It provides orderly and credible processes for people to live their lives, by giving employers grounds for selecting a workforce, workers a mechanism for pursuing jobs, and families a mechanism for passing on privilege and seeking social opportunity, even if the rhetorical rationales for these processes (human capital, individual merit) lack credibility. Most of all, it gives us a mechanism for expressing serious concern about social problems without actually doing anything effective to solve those problems. (2008, 459)

The theoretical framework throughout this chapter integrates the concepts of "habitus," "capital," and "field." These three concepts are categories of analysis put forward by Pierre Bourdieu to help explain a particular practice at a specific time in history. The practice under study in this chapter, as I mentioned, relates to the authorities of the Second Republic replacing the teaching activity headed by the Society of Jesus in Spain. Although the new progressive authorities presented that activity to the citizens as a break from the old structures anchored in traditionalism, it nevertheless offers a historical perspective on elements of discourse continuity that can be analysed. Bourdieu's three concepts are of great use here in studying these elements of continuity inserted into the practice of replacing the Jesuit institutions.

In this section, I schematically present the elements that belong to these three notions. To Bourdieu, the three are expressed as follows: [(habitus) (capital) + field = practice] (Asimai and Koustorakis 2014, 122). In the present context, the "field" relates to the ideas of social reform, faith in progress, and interest in politics that became prevalent in the political, economic, and social debate in Spain in the late nineteenth century. "Capital" refers to the cumulative effort made by the main agents in the same field. Noteworthy here are two main protagonists that had a great amount of capital accumulated by February 1932: the Catholic Church and, more specifically, the Society of Jesus, on the side of orthodoxy, and the regenerationalist intellectuals on the side of heterodoxy, also represented by major institutional networks such as the Free Teaching Institute, the Reformist Party, and the *Agrupación al Servicio de la República*, a political movement founded in early 1931. Both held a privileged social position in the relational field that afforded them a "top-down" view of the social, political, and cultural problems of the day. "Habitus" – that is, the common disposition that generates understanding of what individuals in a society can reasonably expect – explains the institutional replacement and is the embodied disposition of educationalization.

Identifying educationalization with Bourdieu's concept of habitus entails considering that the agents who take part in a given conflict while also having their own personal back story – that is, their own ideas associated with a milieu – are also "the product of a collective history, and the categories of thought, of understanding, the schemata of perception, values systems, etc., are the product of incorporating social structures" (Bourdieu and Chartier 2011, 70). To Bourdieu, habitus and field are both relational. Moreover, although different actors may explicitly occupy different spaces within the same field, habitus becomes the element of continuity that leads individuals who act in the same field to perceive the social word around them in very similar ways and to react in relatively analogous ways.

The Expulsion of the Jesuits, January 1932

The Society of Jesus had more than 3,000 members in Spain at the start of the Second Republic in the spring of 1931 (Verdoy 1995). At that time, Jesuits managed a noteworthy number of educational institutions, including sixteen training centres, of which five were apostolic schools or minor seminaries, seven novices or juniorates, three philosophy and theology schools, and one a house of tertianship. They also managed eighteen secondary schools and one business school, three universities, two houses for spiritual exercises, a writers' house, and the Ebro Observatory (Revuelta González 2004, 344). There were 6,798 students and 532 teachers (116 secular and 416 Jesuits) in their secondary schools in 1929–30 (Compañía de Jésus en España 1931, 94). The Jesuits were also involved in proselytizing and disseminating science carried out in the many journals published by Spanish Jesuits, such as *Razón y Fe, Sal Terrae, Estudios Eclesiásticos, Ibérica, Mensajero del Corazón de Jesús*, and *Hechos y Dichos*.

The importance of the numbers involved in the work of the Jesuits in the five provinces that made up their presence in Spain in 1931 was closely linked to the Society of Jesus's progressive growth during the Restoration. At the end of the nineteenth century, Spanish society had faced a process of re-Christianization that led to an increase in the numbers of regular clergy. As Fernando García de Cortázar notes, "After the first few years of the Restoration, the regular priests in Spain numbered 2000 at most, but doubled that by the turn of the century" (García de Cortázar 1981, 227). Indeed, according to García de Cortázar's data, by 1902 there were 10,630 regular priests and 40,030 nuns (227–8) in the country. Liberal and progressive Spaniards observed such growth with mistrust. From their point of view, the re-Christianization process was a step backwards in the modernization of Spain.

For their part, at the start of Alphonse XII's reign, with the last Carlist War (1872–6) drawing to a close, Spanish Jesuits regardedthe country's political changes with mistrust. Their main objection was that they considered the new regime an "expression of liberalism condemned by the Pontiffs" (Revuelta González 1991, 43). By the end of the nineteenth century, the position of the Society of Jesus had shifted from outright rejection of the state institutions to one of abstentionism, and, in the early twentieth century, to more "compromising attitudes of possibilities" (ibid.). That stance was articulated under the thesis of the "lesser evil" by the Jesuits on the pages of *Razón y Fe*, and was backed by Pope Pius X in 1906 (Montero 1993, 177). As Manuel Revuelta González notes:

> The Society of Jesus entered the 20th century well equipped with institutions and well secured in personnel. Their rate of growth was not so intense but still progressed. Institutional interrelations were maintained as a basic support for activities that held their course. New additions in the early 20th century were more qualitative than quantitative; they were more complements to what already existed, new approaches and new accents on habitual works. These variations and new aspects were demanded by the changing times, which were creating new needs, and spurred on by anti-clerical attacks. (2004, 323)

The above helps explain why the proclamation of the Second Republic was not good news for the Jesuits. As Enara García Martínez notes, "the Jesuits had plenty of reasons to be afraid: after having notably supported the Primo de Rivera dictatorship (1923–30), the fall of that regime logically brought them terrible consequences" (2007, 99). The events in May 1931 in Madrid and other major cities in Spain, particularly in the south, only confirmed their fears. In the capital city, convents and monasteries were put to the torch, and although no lives were claimed among the Jesuits, there was significant material damage to their buildings and installations in Madrid and in the south and east of Spain. This outbreak of anticlerical violence led the order's leaders to advocate dispersing some of the communities situated in the areas where the attacks had been the most virulent. Consequently, Jesuits in cities such as Madrid, Malaga, Cadiz, and Gijon moved to the north, especially to the Basque Country, where there was less of a threat.

On 9 December 1931, the Constituent Courts of the Second Republic ratified the new constitution. Article 26 of the final text dealt a severe blow to the Jesuits: "Any religious orders whose statutes impose, in addition to the three canon vows, vows of special obedience to any authority other than the legitimate authority of the State are hereby dissolved. Their possessions shall be nationalized and put to use for charity and educational purposes." The following month, on 23 January, Alcalá Zamora as president of the republic signed the Order to Dissolve the Society of Jesus. By means of this decree, Jesuit priests and novices were given ten days to disband their communities within Spanish territory; their possessions would become property of the state, to be put to charity and educational uses (Consejo Editorial de Razón y Fe 1932, 537–9). With this decree, according to Manuel Revuelta González, the Jesuits underwent "the most serious dissolution in contemporary history ... In 1931 [the Society of Jesus] was a full, mature institution, perfectly organized and equipped in endeavours of social, educational and cultural influence. It was arguably the most dynamic and strongest institution in the Spanish Catholic Church" (2004, 343).

Regarding the immediate dismantling of the institutions managed by the Society of Jesus in Spain in early 1932, a document published in 1938 by the Gregorian University in Rome points out:

> All our houses were taken over by the government. The only exceptions were our fathers at the Ebro Observatory, [who acted] as civil servants, because the government could find no way of replacing them. They and the nuns who were nurses were even expelled from the Leper Sanitorium of Fontilles; in exchange for removing religion from this charitable work that proved such a credit to it, they [the government] showed no remorse at handing the ill over to impiety with all its consequences, even death, which took vengeance on them from then on. Also left were the professors and coadjutor brothers at the Seminary of Comillas, which the government did not seize on account of being the property of the Holy See. ("La Compañía de Jesús en España" 1939, 10)

The following list, organized by province, indicates the training houses and their destination in exile:

- Province of Aragón: novices to Gozzano, Italy; juniors to Avigliana and to St Croce, both in Italy; theologians and philosophers mainly to Aalbeek, Germany,, with a few to India and Argentina; tertiaries to Tournai, Belgium; the provincial to Perpignan, France
- Bética Province: novices to Fayt, Belgium; juniors first to Tronshiennes, and then to Wittouck, both in Belgium; theologians and philosophers to Marneffe, Belgium; the provincial to Gibraltar
- Province of Castille: novices, juniors, and tertiaries to Tournai, Belgium; philosophers and theologians to Marneffe, Belgium; the provincial to Hendaya, France
- Province of León: tertiaries to Portugal; novices to Tournai, Belgium; juniors to Arlon, Belgium; philosophers (second and third year) and theologians to Marneffe, Belgium; philosophers (first year) to La Barde, France, and then to Meerbeek-lez-Ninove, Belgium; the provincial to St Jean de Luz, France
- Province of Toledo: novices to Diglette, Belgium; juniors to Eegenhoven, Germany, and then to Chevetogne, Belgium; philosophers and theologians to Marneffe, Belgium; the provincial to St Jean de Luz, France ("La Compañía de Jesús en España" 1939, 10)

The Process of Replacing Institutions: The Case of the Maximum Colleges

For the Society of Jesus, the discourse disposition of educationalization can be found in their own origins as a Catholic order born in the context of the Counter-Reformation. One of the first Jesuits, Pedro de Ribadeneira, wrote a letter to Phillip II, King of Spain, explaining the feeling of commitment within the order of St Ignatius of Loyola and its network of colleges and the confidence that were making a good impression in the main Catholic cities. As de Ribadeneira argued, "All the well-being of Christianity and of the whole world depends on the proper education of youth" (quoted in O'Malley 1993, 209). What the Society of Jesus was discovering and fostering even back in the sixteenth century was the chance of bettering social status by means of education (211).

At the time when the authorities of the Second Republic ordered the Spanish Jesuits to disband, there were three maximum colleges in the country exclusively for Jesuits: in Oña, Granada, and Barcelona. While the institutional nature of these colleges was reflected in their housing the Faculties of Philosophy and Theology, where future Jesuits carried out their studies in accordance with the *Ratio Studiorum*, they also were sources of dynamic pastoral activity that included the promotion of Marian sodalities, rural missions, night schools, and grammar schools for young lay people. To a certain extent, the maximum colleges were institutional mechanisms with a pastoral Catholic orientation that were responsible for initiating key elements in educationalization. The following section analyses the replacement process undergone by the three maximum colleges when their facilities were seized by the authorities of the Second Republic in early 1932.

The Maximum College of Granada

The Maximum College of Granada began its teaching activities in 1894 in a monumental neo-Mudejar-style building on a rise a few yards from the charterhouse of Granada. Its purpose was to continue the formation work begun at the Monastery of St Geronimo in Murcia. From the start, the facilities were used to carry out the Society of Jesus's internal training programs for novices, juniors, and philosophers, and, after some time, theologians as well. As Revuelta González stated, this was "the great Maximum College of the Province of Toledo, the mother house of that province in the late nineteenth century and of Andalusia when it was formed in 1924" (1991, 843).

According to an anonymous document in the Historic Archives of the Society of Jesus at the Vatican, the Granada college began to feel threatened shortly after proclamation of the Second Republic. The events that began in Madrid on 10 May 1931, when churches and convents were set on fire, had repercussions in Granada, where the Catholic daily paper *La Gaceta del Sur* and the pro-monarchy paper *El Noticiero Granadino* were attacked. Attempts were made to set fire to the Marian college, the Augustinian monastery, and the convent of the Nuns of Realejo, and arsonists succeeded in burning down the Capuchin monastery in Granada. Consequently, in the afternoon of 12 May, "nearly the entire Community" of Jesuits in Grenada "dispersed, distributed in groups of two or three, fleeing to friends' houses, who had been warned and made ready ahead of time" ("Relación de las cosas" 1932, 1). That same night, the residence and church of the Jesuits in Granada were attacked. The college was also attacked: A mob "wanted to scale up to our College, but did not get past the lower doorway in the farmhouse; the riffraff came in with candles and ornaments they had stolen from the churches sacked in the city" (ibid.). In the end, the college building was guarded by the Civil Guard and soldiers from the Regiment of Artillery. After these events, all the students of philosophy and theology went to the maximum college in Oña, where the political situation was calmer. When the dissolution order was declared in January 1932,

> from the moment we found out, on that morning of the 24th of January, we could only finish up what needed to be done for the dispersion of the Community ... A few days later, when the time was up, as per their criteria, the Governor sent over his Police Commissioner, Mr. Cristino Jalón, and two police officers, to serve us the order to leave and to seal all the doors except those to the Observatory and its offices, so that it would continue operating, until the inventory could be drawn up as planned. (Ibid., 2)

The country estate known as Cercado Alto de Cartuja, where the maximum college was located until February 1932, was taken over by the government of the Second Republic and immediately handed over to the Ministry of Public Instruction. Fernando de los Ríos, a socialist minister in the first Republican government presided over by Niceto Alcalá Zamora and an alumnus of the Instituto Libre de Enseñanza (ILE, the Free Teaching Institute), took charge of the process of transferring the confiscated facilities to the University of Granada. A project in 1933 led by the rector of the University of Granada contained a plan to use the building to house the Faculty of Letters and Law and the Faculty of Sciences, as well as a student residence college and its sports fields. The plan's high cost (nearly one million pesetas), along with the political instabilities that toppled a succession of governments during the Second Republic and the tedious bureaucracy involved, kept it from being carried out. After General Franco's coup d'état in July 1936, the tortuous project of enlarging the University of Granada campus using the seized Jesuit facilities ended.

The Maximum College of San Ignacio in Barcelona

In 1892, a Jesuit college was founded in the Barcelona neighbourhood of Sarriá. In 1915, the Maximum College of Tortosa was moved to the Jesuits' new facilities in Barcelona. From that date on, "the College of Sarriá became the Society of Jesus's most important scientific centre in Spain until its dissolution in 1932" (1991, 998). The official name for this educational facility became the Maximum College of San Ignacio. It featured spaces for training of great renown, such as the Sarriá Chemistry Institute, the Biological Laboratory, the Museum of History, and the Museum of Antiques (Bosch Giral et al. 2010, 84–5). Furthermore, in 1925 under the leadership of Father Ferrán M. Palmés, the maximum college in Sarriá became home to the prestigious Laboratory of Experimental Psychology, and in 1927 to the Psycho-Pedagogy Research Office, which was the first to be founded in Spain (Peralta Serrano 1994, 463).

On Sunday, 24 January, hardly a day after the decree was signed to dissolve the Society of Jesus, Father Antonio Upegui wrote from the maximum college in Sarriá:

> At 10 pm last night, the Ministry of Justice notified the journalists of the decree, who spread it immediately. By midnight everyone had heard about it. And so many questions! What could we take with us? What could we not? The decree stated that the State expropriated all the Society's possessions, and that all the societies, banks and private citizens that held in their power anything belonging to the Jesuits had to declare them, under severe penalties. What to do? Everything in this one single building, where more than 800 people live, so many things, a month wouldn't be enough to get them all out. (Upegui 1932, 1)

On 5 February, the newspaper *ABC* reported on what happened at the college in Sarriá: "When the civil governor received the journalists this morning, he told them about the seizure of the four buildings owned by the Jesuit fathers ... Left in charge of said buildings were the rector of the University and the School Board" (*ABC*, 5 February 1932, 28).

The paper noted that the confiscation had led to open rifts on the school board, and the resignation of a Mr Pellicena, a city councillor. By the end of 1932, the republican authorities began to make use of the seized properties. On 7 November, the *Gaseta Municipal de Barcelona* published the constitution of three new school groups that were housed in buildings seized from the Society of Jesus in the municipality of Barcelona.[1] The testimony of Emilio Valls Puig, an alumnus of one of these school groups, is of great interest, since it pinpoints the supplanting of Ignacian pedagogy by a school model founded on republican ideals:

> It was not a purely rationalist school like the Escuela Moderna had been, founded in the early 20th century by Francesc Ferrer i Guárdia, who was shot by a firing squad for that reason in Montjuic after the Week of Tragedy. Nevertheless, the pedagogy used at the Sarriá School Group was most likely influenced by the Ferrer experience. Catholic teaching had been replaced by a free moral and human emancipation and a constant development of civic values. The practice followed the old saying, "There are no rights without duties and no duties without rights" ... Although the course subjects making up the basic curriculum never went beyond the ones officially known at all public and private schools, they still had a very different look and feel. We younger students couldn't understand it at first ... The purpose of the school was for the students to manage themselves. That result could be achieved only by having a group of teachers who were professionally competent but who also had the eminently democratic vocation of making us conscientious citizens of the Republic. (Valls Puig 2005, 142–3)

The Maximum College of Oña

In 1880, the Society of Jesus set up a maximum college at the Monastery of Oña, in the north of Burgos Province. By the end of the century, as Revuelta González notes, "the largest Jesuit community in Spain lived far from the madding crowd, in the ancient Benedictine abbey of Oña (1991, 1162). In January 1932, in addition to the community that constituted the Maximum College of Oña, there were also many students of philosophy and theology from Toledo, Andalusia, Portugal, and Colombia enrolled at the institution. Several months earlier, all the philosophy students from Toledo and Andalusia had left their buildings and gone to the houses in the north of Spain. The situation in the small town of Oña in the winter of 1931–2 was dire for the large community that lived in the buildings of the Monastery of San Salvador.

Added to the hardships of the harsh winter in the mountains north of Burgos was a terrible fire in one of the college buildings during the night of 8 January 1932.

The testimony of Father Huidobro shows how the republican authorities seized the building from the Society of Jesus. The news regarding the dissolution of the order was brought on 24 January 1932 by the captain of the Civil Guard, who travelled from Burgos to Oña in the morning to convey the order. The Jesuits were given ten days to abandon their facilities. As Father Huidobro described, "The consultants spent many long hours in meetings with the Rector. He decided that of the 338 of us at home, 200 would leave directly for Marneffe [Belgium] and the rest, born in the Basque Country provinces, would split up and go back to their family homes" (1932, 1).

Along with organizing the Belgian exile of teachers and students in the months prior to the January 1932 order to dissolve, the other main concern of the Jesuits who remained at the college in Oña was that of saving as many objects of value as possible, especially books.

> On the night of October 14, 1931, the best books were locked inside a small room in the Observatory tower, at the entrance to an attic ... Many other books were subsequently put underground, at great effort, in the large spaces between the vaulting of the Refectory and the floor of the Library. These hiding places were not deemed safe so, in December and January, up in the attics, buried under black dust, we spent many hours burying those wretched books. So many flights up and down, eager yet weary, day and night, through the cloisters or up among the roof beams in the attic, when our legs refused to hold up the mortal weight of the body let alone the heavy, heavy reams of paper! (Huidobro 1932, 3)

In early February, the not very invasive action of the government came to an end. From then on, according to Father Huidobro's testimony, it became clear to the Jesuits that "life in the town of Oña revolved around our case" (6). In fact, among the more republican-leaning townspeople, seeing trucks driving off day after day, loaded with objects from the maximum college, the idea spread that by law, "all of it was theirs as spoils of victory" and "the plunder was pouring through their fingers" (6). Consequently, on 2 February at half past three o'clock, the Civil Guard prohibited any more material from being removed from the centre. Governor Solsola himself, escorted by Cavalry Guards from Briviesca, notified the Father Minister of the maximum college in person of the order. At the same time, the governor repeatedly expressed his deep sadness in that regard: "Father, [I regret] that it was given to me to do this!" (6)

On 4 August 1933, the Second Republic passed a law against vagrancy, known as the Slacker's Law. The law did not penalize crimes but, rather, tried to prevent their being committed in the future. It included measures for removing, controlling, and detaining those who were deemed supposedly dangerous until it could be determined that they were no longer a threat. The idea was to influence convicts' habits in order to rehabilitate them and turn them into useful individuals integrated into society by means of work. The Slacker's Law was quite unprecedented in the history of Spain with respect to the faith it put in education as a means for social reinstatement. Article 6 of the law included work establishments and farming colonies for habitual vagrants, ruffians, and pimps, those who justify illicit trade, to those who exploit forbidden games and gambling, those who show an inclination to crime, and dangerous criminals of repeated offences (*La Gaceta de Madrid*, 5 August 1933, 875). After 1933, the facilities of the Jesuits' maximum college in Oña were turned into a "farming colony for vagrants and crooks."

Educationalization as an Element of Historical Continuity between the Restoration and the Republic

By studying the seizure of the Society of Jesus's holdings, including the facilities of the three maximum colleges and their replacement with other educational institutions, a line of continuity can be found based on the discourse dispositions of the political regimes of the Bourbon Restoration and the Second Republic. In this case, continuity is not focused so much on any painstaking conceptual search, but on the level of disposition or habitus of educationalization in its "top-down" logic. Educationalization is configured in a shared matrix of perceptions, appraisals, and actions. The habitus both gathers the historicity of the agents interacting in a particular field and also "pre-shapes future practices, orienting them to reproduce the same structure" (Capdevielle 2011, 35).

This shared matrix is not incompatible with the sharp differences within Spanish society at the start of the 1930s and is reflected in the dispute between Catholics and anticlericals. Two political figures, Gil Robles and Manuel Azaña, can be used to help illuminate the spectrum defined by these nearly opposite political positions. Gil Robles defended the role of the Catholic Church using modernizing positions in the 1920s, both in the National Catholic Agrarian Confederation as well as in the Popular Social Party. He actively collaborated with the Primo de Rivera dictatorship and in 1931 took part in founding the Catholic National Action Party (which later became the Popular Action Party), whose purpose was to uphold the Catholic religion, religious education, the rights of the church and of property, and the centrality of the family once the Second Republic was declared.

In contrast, as an intellectual and political figure, Azaña represented the position held by republicanism and anticlericalism in the later years of the Bourbon Restoration and the early years of the Second Republic. Few intellectuals in the decade before the proclamation of the Second Republic developed such a markedly educationalizing discourse as Azaña. In a well-known speech in Parliament on 13 October 1931, and published the next day in the newspaper *El Sol*, he observed that "Spain is no longer Catholic." Similarly, Azaña, who was the first president of the Second Republic, is the creator of two concepts that are imbued with a clearly elitist educationalizing tone, namely, the "educator state" and the "teaching republic." As Fernández Soria points out, lurking in these concepts is "the influence of Krausian institutionalism in particular and regenerationalism in general" (2011, 89).

By analysing educationalization in Spain during the first three decades in the twentieth century as a transversal axis running the ideological gamut from conservative Catholicism to republican anticlericalism, one can trace the consistency in the discourse with respect to the replacement of Jesuit institutions in 1932. That discourse led the authorities of the Second Republic to plan to use those same facilities to house even more ambitious educational projects than the Jesuits' own, for the purpose of recasting the foundations of republican citizenship by means of education. To do so, they took on several projects: a higher education institution at the Maximum College of Granada; a primary school on the premises of the Maximum College of Barcelona; and a farm colony for vagrants and criminals on the premises of the Maximum College of Oña, aimed at social reinstatement by means for education in farm work.

According to the thesis of this chapter, this replacement was made possible by continuity in the disposition of educationalizing discourse. This continuity provides clear evidence of the institutional space taken over by education during the first three decades of the twentieth century in Spain. Although this space was relatively small in much of the nineteenth century, it took only a few decades to become a core of political and social debate. Its centrality largely explains the interest the civil republican authorities had in late 1931 and early 1932 in immediately replacing the teaching institutions of the Society of Jesus.

At this point, it is worth turning to the words of David Labaree to delve further in the disposition of educationalization as set in the middle of social and political debates in Spain in the early twentieth century. From Labaree's perspective,

We assign formal responsibility to education for solving our most pressing social problems in light of our highest social ideals, with the tacit understanding that by educationalizing these problem-solving efforts we are seeking a solution that is more formal than substantive. We are saying that we are willing to accept what education can produce – new programs, new curricula, new institutions, new degrees, new education opportunities – in place of solutions that might make real changes in the ways in which we distribute social power, wealth, and honor. (2008, 448)

In the specific case of early twentieth-century Spanish society and culture, the educationalizing habitus arose from three main ideals with a strong transversal component that delimited the space of Bourdieu's notion of field: social reform, faith in progress, and interest in politics. On the basis of these ideals, education became the means to solve the most pressing problems, but always on a more formal, discursive level.

With respect to the first ideal, the 1891 papal encyclical *Rerum Novarum* and the regenerationalist movement of the early twentieth century are two expressions of social reform that, although self-defined as mutually antagonistic, are found in the same discursive field. The encyclical attempted to provide a reformist answer to the problems of industrial society. As Agustín Escolano notes, one consequence of the encyclical was "a peculiar type of regenerationalism with its pedagogic repercussions" (2002, 251). In fact, "the ideals of this Catholic regenerationalism were compatible with a renewalist stances in education" (ibid.). For their part, on the side of the anticlerical regenerationalist movement, the education system and rural milieu became the two primary mainstays on which to base the highest ideals of reform. The work of Joaquín Costa, a major regenerationalist leader after the Spanish-American War of 1898, is especially relevant, particularly for some of his renown quotes: "The school and the pantry, the panty and the school: there are no better keys to open the way to Spanish regeneration" (1916, 215).

Likewise, trust in progress is an ideal that appears in the discursive field analysed here. The more conservative positions in the political spectrum in the first decade of the twentieth century held an optimistic conception of progress on a moral basis that, in turn, became "a harmonious vision of the relationship between capital and work as complementary factors necessarily bound to get along and to accord with their respective interests" (Montero 1999, 481). The conservative Catholic politician Eduardo Sanz y Escartín's book, *El Estado y la reforma social* (The State and Social Reform), published in 1893, does much to explain how the notion of progress was integrated into Catholic thought. Thus, faith in progress is successively raised as a banner for regenerationalism, reformism, and republicanism in Spain from 1898 to 1931. Nevertheless, in this case, it was not a harmonious vision of the labour/capital relationships that prompted faith in progress; rather, it was grounded in an acknowledgment of the dichotomy of exploiters and the exploited, in the anti-war movement, and in a rejection of inequality and as an alternative to the Catholic Church.

Finally, with respect to the third ideal, interest in politics, in the first few decades of the twentieth century, Catholic Action was the platform that best represented the interest politics sparked among the Catholic base and specific sectors of the church hierarchy. With an evident influence for Jacques Maritain's Christian democracy, "Catholic Action's hallmark was apoliticalism, even though in their training program, civic education and formation in the values of the Church's social doctrine involved a pre-political or para-political form of education" (Montero 2007, 170). In the case of Spain, the foundation of the Popular Socialist Party (PSP) in 1922, which was struck down shortly thereafter by the Primo de Rivera dictatorship, was a clear indication of the interest some of the organized sectors of civil Catholic society had in participating in politics. Years later, at least in its origin and prior to the fascist turn taken by some of its more renowned figures in the 1930s, the Spanish Confederation of Autonomous took up the PSP's banner in a decided attempt to consolidate a social, democratic, decentralizing Catholic party.

Similarly, the interest in politics brought about by republicanism has no precedent in the history of Spain. The main reflection of this interest can be seen in the results of the first elections held in the Second Republic on 28 June 1931. A large number of parties that identified with republican ideals won seats in Parliament, and the seven parties that won the greatest number of seats were identified with the progressive ideals of the new republic: the Partido Socialista Obrero Español (the Socialist Worker's Party), the Partido Republicano Radical (the Radical Republican Party), the Partido Republicano Radical Socalista (the Radical Socialist Republican Party), the Esquerra Republicana de Catalunya (the Republican Left Party of Catalonia), Acción Republicana (Republican Action), the Derecha Liberal Republicana (the Republican Liberal Right), and the Partido Republicano Democrático Federal (the Federal Democratic Republican Party).

Conclusion

Depaepe and Smeyers (2008) have noted that, instead of trying to adapt society to fit the people, educationalization processes try to get the people to adapt to particular models of society. This has led to "the domestication of thinking and not emancipation" (383). If we use this lens to analyse the contents of the 1891 encyclical *Rerum Novarum* or the writings of some of the regenerationalist intellectuals, the pieces fit. The encyclical points out that it is the church's task to influence spirits and bend wills so that they let themselves be ruled and governed by the teachings of divine precepts. Equally clear are the words of the regenerationalist Joaquín Costa, when he stated that it is the job of state education to provide "men useful to the State, and we would not see so many slackers, runts and vagabonds as we do, who are more burdens than boons" (1916, 215). Following this logic, as this chapter has analysed, in the end it defines the continuity in the process of replacing the Jesuits' maximum colleges with republican education institutions in 1932. That continuity can be analysed on the basis of elements in the disposition of educationalization understood as "habitus." That disposition was fundamentally elitist in its "top-down" logic.

From the perspective of history, it is interesting to note that this replacement process of the spaces of the church's educational institutions had very few precedents in the processes in which church lands were seized and sold in the nineteenth century and replaced by the "educator state." Likewise, there is no indication of any processes to replace Jesuit buildings when the revolution was proclaimed in 1868. And, with respect the last quarter of the twentieth century, with the regime change from Franco's dictatorship to a democratic monarchy reinforced by the Constitution of 1978, it is nearly impossible to find records of any processes of the state's taking over church educational institutions. One need only look today at the majestic buildings of the diocesan seminaries that held great importance in the 1940s and 1950s after the Spanish Civil War: by the 1980s and 1990s, in the midst of an accelerated process to secularize Spanish society and while the technocratic educationalization of the masses was taking form, most of the buildings were abandoned or converted into state-run luxury hotels to meet the demands of the mass tourism that began to invade life in the provincial capital cities of Spain.

NOTES

1 Regarding the specific case of the building that a few short months earlier had become home to the College of San Ignacio, the following can be said:

> There are 1,300 children currently enrolled. The kindergarten classes are co-educational, mixing boys and girls. All other classes are for boys.

Of all the students, there are 300 from the Sarriá neighbourhood, and the rest are boys from District V who were not going to school and came from unwholesome places, but are now enjoying the wholesome life of that group. These 1,000 boys also enjoy free transportation to Sarriá on the streetcars, as long as they wear the blue bracelet with the city crest, provided by the Commission of Culture. These 1,000 boys eat lunch at the school canteen, and, as in the other groups, all their school material is free. The teaching and organization of work makes this group a veritable open-air school. Great importance is given to physical education. A wide variety of sports are played in accordance with the boys' age: Basque pelota, tennis, basketball, football, swimming. In addition, there are teams that undertake farming practices. The teaching in this group is complete: it covers all the primary school grades. (Gaseta Municipal de Barcleona 1932, 1042)

REFERENCES

Asimai, Anna, and Gerasimos Koustorakis. 2014. "Habitus: An Attempt at a Thorough Analysis of a Controversial Concept in Pierre Bourdieu's Theory of Practice." *Social Sciences*, 3 (4): 121–31. doi: 10.11648/j.ss.20140304.13.

Bosch Giral, Pedro, Juan F. García de la Banda, Joaquín Pérez Pariente, Manoel Toural Quiroga. 2010. *Los protagonistas de la química en España: Los orígenes de la catálisis*. Madrid: Consejo Superior de Investigaciones Científicas.

Bourdieu, Pierre, and Roger Chartier. 2011. *El sociólogo y el historiador*. Madrid: Abada Editores.

Capdevielle, Julieta. 2011. "El concepto de habitus: 'con Bourdieu y contra Bourdieu.'" *Anduli: Revista Andaluza de Ciencia Sociales* 10: 31–45.

Compañía de Jesús en España. 1931. *Los Jesuitas en España: Sus obras actuales*. 2nd ed. Madrid: n.p.

"La Compañía de Jesús en España, 1931–1938." 1939. Issued by the Pontifica Universidad Gregoriana. Archivum Romanum Societatis Iesu, Nouva Compagnia, "ExAssistentia Hispanica," Folder: I Epistolae (Assistentiae) 1015 (12) (1931–3).

Consejo Editorial de Razón y Fe. 1932. "Documentos sobre la disolución de la Compañía de Jesús." *Razón y Fe* 423 (March/April): 537–9.

Costa, J. 1916. *Maestro, Escuela y Patria*. Madrid: Biblioteca Costa.

Depaepe, Marc, and Paul Smeyers. 2008. "Educationalization as an Ongoing Modernization Process." *Educational Theory* 58 (49): 379–89. https://doi.org/10.1111/j.1741-5446.2008.00295.x.

Escolano Benito, Agustín. 2002. "La educación en la España de la Restauración y la Segunda República." In *Historia de la educación (Edad Contemporánea)*, edited by Alejandro Tiana Ferrer et al., 233–54. Madrid: UNED.

Fernández Soria, Juan M. 2011. "Manuel Azaña y el estado educador en la Constitución Española de 1931." *Cuestiones Pedagógicas* 21: 85–119.
García de Cortázar, Fernando. 1981. "La renovación de los efectivos eclesiásticos en la España de la Restauración." In *Universitas, Theologia, Ecclesia (I)*, edited by José María Lera, 223–48. Bilbao: Universidad de Deusto y Ediciones Mensajero.
García Martínez, Enara. 2007. *Los Jesuitas en la Guerra Civil (1936–1939)*. Bilbao: Universidad de Deusto-Instituto Ignacio de Loyola.
Gaseta Municipal de Barcelona. 1932. "L'obra constructuva de l'Ajuntament: Nous Grups Escolars." *Gaseta Municipal de Barcelona* 19 (44): 1033–48.
Huidobro, Fernando. 1932. "Desde Oña a Marneffe." ARSI Inventario dei documenti inviati alla Curia Generalizia, Parte IIa, Nuova Compagnia (1814). 1009 Hipania 1932 1. Dissolutio Societatis. Document 5.
Labaree, David F. 2008. "The Winning Ways of a Losing Strategy: Educationalizing Social Problems in the United States." *Educational Theory* 58 (4): 447–60. https://doi.org/10.1111/j.1741-5446.2008.00299.x.
Montero, Feliciano. 1993. *El movimiento Católico en la España del siglo XX: Entre el integrismo y el posibilismo*. Madrid: Eudema.
– 1999. "La crítica católica de la economía clásica y el primer catolicismo social (Sobre el impacto de 'Rerum novarum' y la aportación de los católicos españoles al reformismo social)." In *Economía y economistas españoles*. Vol. 5. *Las críticas a la economía clásica*, edited by Enrique Fuentes Quintana, 451–93. Madrid: Galaxia Gutenberg-Círculo de Lectores.
– 2007. "Del movimiento católico a la Acción Católica: Continuidad y cambio, 1900–1930." In *La secularización conflictiva. España (1898–1931)*, edited by Julio De la Cueva Merino and Feliciano Montero, 169–213. Madrid: Biblioteca Nueva.
O'Malley, John W. 1993. *The First Jesuits*. Cambridge, MA: Harvard University Press.
Paton, H.J. 2013. *Kant's Metaphysic of Experience: Commmentary on the First Half of the Kritic Der Reinen Vernunft*. London: Routledge.
Peralta Serrano, A. 1994. "El padre Ferran Ma Palmés y el laboratorio de Psicología Experimental del Colegio Máximo San Ignacio de Sarriá de Barcelona." *Revista de Historia de la Psicología* 15 (3/4): 461–75.
"Relación de las cosas ocurridad en el Colegio Máximo de Granada desde la proclamación de la República. Abril 1931." 1932. Archivum Romanum Societatis Iesu, Inventario dei documenti inviati alla Curia Generalizia, Parte IIa, Nouva Compagnia (1814), 1009 Hipania 1932, "1. Dissolutio Societatis." Document 11.
Revuelta González, Manuel. 1991. *La Compañía de Jesús en la España contemporánea:*. Vol. 2. *Expansión en tiempo recios (1884–1906)*. Madrid: Sal Terra-Mensajero-Universidad Pontificia de Comillas.
– 2004. "Estabilidad y progreso de la Compañía durante la restauración Alfonsina (1875–1931)." In *Los Jesuitas en España y en el mundo hispánico*, edited by Teófanes

Egido, Javier Burrieza, and Manuel Revuelta González, 313–42. Madrid: Marcial Pons.

Upegui, A. 1932. "Relación de los sucesos ocurridos en Sarriá en la disolución de la Compañía." Archivum Romanum Societatis Iesu, Inventario dei documenti inviati alla Curia Generalizia, Parte IIa, Nouva Compagnia (1814), 1009 Hipania 1932 "1. Dissolutio Societatis." Document 154.

Valls Puig, Emilio. 2005. *Los hijos de la República*. Lleida, ES: Editorial Milenio.

Verdoy, Alfredo. 1995. *Los bienes de los Jesuitas: Disolución e incautación de la Compañía de Jesús durante la Segunda República*. Madrid: Trotta.

9 Waldorf Education and the Educationalization of Spirituality in the Plural Context in Late Twentieth-Century Spain

PATRICIA QUIROGA UCEDA

Waldorf pedagogy can be found today in contexts displaying a wide range of religious traditions. Schools using this pedagogical model base their teaching on the esoteric movement of anthroposophy, conceived by Rudolf Steiner in Germany in 1913. The theoretical approach behind anthroposophy is based on a viewpoint on human beings and a notion of spirituality weaned on different elements such as theosophy and Christianity. The synthesis of different religious traditions along with a noteworthy perspective regarding human nature helped make the pedagogical conception of anthroposophy-based schools become permeable in very different spaces. Consequently, Waldorf schools can be found in diverse parts of the world, including China andAfrica. In Israel, an initiative started nearly thirty years ago, *Tamrat el Zeitoun* (Fruit of the Olive Tree), has Muslim, Christian, and Druze children sharing the same classroom. That school constitutes a paradoxical case of how Waldorf pedagogy has been integrated into an Arab community.

Practically from the start, growth of the Waldorf pedagogy movement has been constant. Currently there are 1,150 schools in sixty-four countries (Freunde der Erziehungskunst Rudolf Steiners 2018). This expansion process is also occurring in Spain: the first school, El Jardín de Infancia Micael, was founded in Madrid in 1979, and there are now twenty-eight schools dotting the nation (Asociación de Centros Educativos Waldorf-Steiner de España 2018). Interest in this esoterically based model of education is relatively recent in Spain, where religious debate has historically been polarized between Catholicism and secularism (mainly anti-Catholic), although other religious ideas have had a minor presence. The same may be said of esoteric movements. For example, the few associations linked with movements such as theosophy hardly extended beyond Madrid and Barcelona: in 1913, the Theosophical Society had 155 members; by 1922 the number had more than doubled but was still small, at 377 (Louzao 2008, 515), and it peaked at 469 members in 1934 (Penalva 2013, 120). On the pedagogical level, the Fraternidad Internacional de la Educación founded the Escola Teosófica Damón de Vallcarca in 1927 in the city of Barcelona, which remained open for ten years.

The topic covered in this chapter is the way in which the reception of Waldorf education in Spain at the end of the Franco dictatorship and its subsequent creation of schools in the transition to democracy responded to an educationalizing logic of spirituality. In order to study the changes in religious matters in Spain, I have taken up the two paradigms used in recent decades to analyse the transformations underway in religious matters in terms of modernity: secularization and plurality. I have approached these paradigms by taking as a reference point their two most representative authors. Charles Taylor is a Canadian philosopher whose work *A Secular Age* (2007) has taken on great relevance in the development of the paradigm of secularization. The main thrust of Taylor's philosophy is that modernity has led to a loss of religiousness and a decline in religions. In contrast, the paradigm of plurality is represented by its main exponent, the American sociologist Peter L. Berger, whose *The Many Altars of Modernity* (2014) stated that, far from secularization, the contemporary world is characterized by a veritable explosion of fervent religiousness.

Berger and Taylor thus join the rich debate that other authors have been keeping alive. For example, Hugh McLeod, in *Secularization in Western Europe, 1814–1914* (2000), explores the different dimensions underlying the concept of secularization. He takes countries such as France, England, and Germany as reference points in examining the processes of secularization that took place between 1814 and 1914, showing the complexity and differences that existed among them, due in part to the predominant religious traditions in each context. Another author who has delved into this subject is Callum G. Brown, who, with works such as *The Death of Christian Britain: Understanding Secularization, 1800–2000* (2001), aims to study the secularization process of Christianity in Great Britain that took root in the eighteenth and nineteenth centuries. In his recent book *Becoming Atheist: Humanism and the Secular West* (2017), Brown makes a large-scale analysis of the phenomenon of atheism as part of the cultural shift in the West in the 1960s and the profound distancing from faith that took place especially as of the 1990s. Lastly, this brief synthesis also highlights the work of Pippa Norris and Ronal Inglehard, whose *Sacred and Secular: Religion and Politics Worldwide* (2004) developed and supported the thesis that religious beliefs are closely related to the degree of existential and job security felt by different groups of people. They point out that people in precarious circumstances tend to place greater importance on religious values.

The research questions articulated in this work can be broken into two categories: 1) What presence has Catholicism had in Spain since the nineteenth century in the area of education, and what spaces have there been for other religious manifestations? Can any trend toward secularization be found in the second half of the twentieth century? 2) What paradigm helps us understand the interest in and reception of Waldorf pedagogy in Spain in the 1960s and its subsequent spread in the transition period to democracy and the years following the transition? To what extent can Waldorf pedagogy be understood as a teaching model that sought to educationalize spirituality? To answer these questions, this chapter has been structured into three parts. The first part analyses Charles Taylor's secularization paradigms and Peter Berger's paradigm of religious pluralism in reference to the specific case of education in Spain. Thereafter, I examine each paradigm to help answer the initial questions posed above. The second part looks at the way in which the secularization paradigm explains the process undergone in the Catholic religion in terms of its presence in the Spanish education system. Finally, the last section analyses how Waldorf pedagogy became a teaching model that conformed to certain spiritual and educational aspirations of a minority group of Spaniards during and after the transition to democracy. In line with Berger's thesis, this plural context made it possible to receive esoteric spiritual ideas and implement their educational institutions.

Taylor's Paradigm of Secularization and Berger's Paradigm of Pluralism

Recent decades have seen heated debate regarding the study of transformations in religious matters since the start of modernity. As noted above, this chapter examines the paradigms of secularization and pluralism through the works of two of their most representative authors, Charles Taylor and Peter L. Berger, respectively. This first section therefore looks at the main theses held by each author. Their paradigms differ greatly on some points but may be seen as having complementary elements on others. The ultimate purpose of my analysis is to place the coordinates in which education in Spain has found itself immersed and, specifically, the reception of Waldorf pedagogy as a function of the parameters provided by the two paradigms.

In his extensive *A Secular Age*, Taylor identifies different ways of understanding secularization. The first refers to the transformations that have occurred in the religious world since modernity. Taylor states that, "whereas the political organization of all pre-modern societies was in some way connected to, based on, guaranteed by some faith in, or adherence to God, or some notion of ultimate reality, the modern western State is free from this connection" (2007, 1). In other words, the public space has been emptied of the religious dimension it had sustained prior to modernity. "In these earlier societies, religion was 'everywhere,' was interwoven with anything else, and in no sense constituted a separate 'sphere' on its own" (2). In this way, in Taylor's view, modernity has brought a decline in the numbers of believers, "the falling off of religious belief and practice, in people turning away from God, and no longer going to Church" (2). Berger does not consider Taylor's assertion to be true. The American sociologist asserts that the main error in the theory of secularization is to assume that modernity necessarily leads to the decline of religion (2014, 51). Thus, while Taylor argues that modernity has brought about a profound decrease in religious beliefs, to Berger the predominant feature of modernity is the existence of plural forms of conceiving and living religiousness.

Nevertheless, despite the profound differences between the two authors, they hold a number of points in common. For one, secularization theory matches up with pluralism in regard to the "conditions of belief." According to Taylor, "the shift to secularity in this sense consists, among other things, of a move from a society where belief in God is unchallenged and indeed, unproblematic, to one in which it is understood to be one option among others" (2007, 3). Along this line of argument, Berger points out that "modernization leads to a huge transformation in the human condition from fate to choice" (2014, 5). In other words, human beings are not destined to take on and practise the religion of the community where they are born and live. Rather, in contrast to that past tradition, individuals have a new capability of choosing among existing religious options, or opting not to believe in or practise any religion or to live without concern to matters of a spiritual nature. Thus,

> Individuals constantly find themselves clashing with people who do *not* take for granted what used to be traditionally held as true in their community. Nowadays they must reflect on the cognitive and normative assumptions of their tradition, and they must choose accordingly. Any chosen religion, at no matter what level of intellectual complexity, is different from a religion that is taken for granted. It may not be less fervent, nor might it force a change in its propositional doctrines. What varies is not so much the *what* but the *how* of religious belief (Berger 2005, 11; emphasis in original).

Said another way, Taylor and Berger coincide on the idea that people today generally have the freedom to choose whatever belief or religion to follow and practise, whereas that opportunity to choose did not exist, or was less prevalent, in pre-modern times. To Taylor, "secularity consists of new conditions of belief; it consists of a new shape to the experience which prompts to and is defined by belief; is a new context in which all search and questioning about the moral and spiritual must proceed" (2007, 20).

Taylor and Berger diverge on how human conscience has integrated the new secular or plural discourses. In Taylor's view, secularization has replaced religious discourse with secular discourse, thereby creating a gap in the different spheres of activity. According to Taylor, "as we function within various spheres of activity – economic, political, cultural, educational, professional, recreational – the norms and principles we follow, the deliberations we engage in, generally don't refer us to God or to any religious beliefs; the considerations we act on are internal to the 'rationality' of each sphere" (2007, 2). Berger is found at the opposite end of this viewpoint and notes that it is rather the other way around: "the secular discourse inserts itself into the turbulent world of religious pluralism" (2014, 53). Thus, he deems that the secularization paradigm overstates the consistency of human conscience, since, for most people, secularity and religion are not mutually contradictory, and "the ability to handle different discourses ... is an essential trait of a modern person" (53).

The question of the consistency of human conscience helps us understand where Catholic and anti-Catholic discourses fit in the context of Spain. Indeed, consistency has been one of the dominant keys regarding religion. As the following section will show, the Catholic versus anti-Catholic logic has proved dominant in Spain, aside from minorities professing a religion different from Catholicism. This logic of consistency was present from the nineteenth century to the last decade of the Franco dictatorship, at which point a significant portion of society still considered itself Catholic, and another sector, which grew in numbers at the end of the dictatorship, distanced itself from church dogma by taking a more secular stance.

The last decade of the Franco dictatorship was a time in which processes of secularization overlapped with an incipient plural scenario. It was a time in which society's aspirations for freedom were keenly felt, and alternative forms of spirituality began to be explored, among which was anthroposophy. In Berger's words, "religious freedom, for obvious reasons, intensifies the pluralistic trend" (2014, 45). Religious freedom was ultimately guaranteed in the Spanish Constitution of 1978, when, to borrow another concept from Berger, a "plausibility structure" emerged – that is, "a social context in which any cognitive or normative definition of reality is plausible" (31). In the case of Spain, one of the possibilities this new structure brought about was that of adopting a plural religious identity, a possibility that continues today.

The Secularization Process in Education in Spain

The importance of school as a space where the state's ideology is transmitted is well known. Berger has stated it thusly: "Not surprisingly, for a long time the schools have been the principal battlefields in boundary disputes between secular and religious discourses" (2014, 75). Indeed, schools have historically been privileged spaces where the dominant political ideology reached all citizens and impregnated the future generations. As is evident from the chapters in this volume, schools have historically constituted privileged spaces for inculcating a particular faith. In the context of Spain, the Catholic religion has been the predominant religion. Nevertheless, during the past two hundred years, it has not remained unaffected by the secularization processes Taylor qualifies as "the falling off of religious belief and practice, in people turning away from God, and no longer going to Church" (2007, 2). This section therefore looks into the presence of Catholicism in the Spanish education system, which has undergone a process of secularization.

As education historian Antonio Viñao points out, Spain is country where "the prevailing model, traditionally in effect in primary education, has been that in which the Catholic religion has been a compulsory subject to the exclusion of any other religion" (2014, 19). Similarly, in the words of the education sociologist Carlos Lerena, in the nineteenth century, the principle dominated the field of education in Spanish society "is not the principle of compulsory education, but the principle of compulsory church" (2005, 336). Catholicism has been the only religion associated with the Spanish state, and therefore it played a major role in the field of education. This predominance of Catholicism in the history of Spain was occasionally curtailed by a secularization trend that coexisted with Catholicism – periods Pérez-Agote (2007, 66) has called "waves of secularization," as a metaphor for a secularization process as a force that, much like a wave in the sea, breaks upon the national scene and later withdraws into the background.

The complex phenomenon of secularization, as noted by Redondo and Vergara, points to a *revision* of the role and the intervention of the Catholic Church, especially of the "hierarchical" church, in worldly matters. This revision is usually made by the state in the name of civil society. It implies that the two main players in the process are the church and the state and that the process is shaped by the borders of their respective spheres of action, their mutual relations, and the particularity of their respective missions. Thus, the so-called secularization process consisted of giving civil society a set of activities and functions that, until then, had been carried out by the church, either on its own or in cooperation with civil institutions (Redondo and Vergara 1994, 68–9). This new assignment of functions is found in the different waves of secularization.

The first wave took place in the late nineteenth and early twentieth centuries. According to Pérez-Agote, this was when "major secularizing forces were at work, represented by politicians and intellectuals belonging to the modern era. Freedom of thought grew among some of the modern urban elite while industrialization of some areas ushered in the development of socialist, communist and anarchist ideas among the working classes in the city and countryside alike ... Given the lack of any internal secularization in the religion itself, secularization is carried out against religion and against the Church (i.e., anti-clericism)" (2007, 68). The secularizing spirit made its first appearance in Spain in the Constitution of 1812. However, the return of King Ferdinand VII and his absolutist monarchy caused the constitution to be annulled. The next attempt at secularization took place shortly thereafter during the Three Liberal Years (1820–3). At that time, Ferdinand VII was obliged to swear to uphold the Constitution of 1812, and the general regulation on public schooling was passed in 1821. This regulation, which was the first attempt at giving education a consistent meaning and organic structure (Redondo and Vergara 1994, 69), "was strict in establishing full secularization of teaching" (Puelles 2010, 126). However, it lasted only short three years.

The instability in education as a result of a succession of decrees and plans over the subsequent decades was the reason for drafting the first law on education, the Moyano Law of 1857 (the Law on Public Instruction). In religious matters, this law, which remained in force until 1970, developed the agreements reached in the Concordat of 1851 with the Holy See, thereby giving the church a leading role in education. Article 2 of the condordat made it mandatory for all public and private education to conform to Catholic doctrine, and recognized the right of the ecclesiastical hierarchy to check up on and enforce compliance. Both of these aspects were included in articles 295 and 296 of the 1857 Law on Public Instruction. Teachers were obliged to instruct students in "Christian doctrine and notions of Sacred History" (Viñao 2014, 21).

Indeed, the Moyano Law established a framework such that what was taught in school was subordinate to Catholic doctrine.

For the rest of the nineteenth century and the early part of the twentieth, there were a few attempts made in Spain to reduce the presence of the church in the state and in education, although their scope was very limited. In fact, as Viñao (2014, 19) notes, there are only three exceptions to this scenario monopolized by the Catholic Church. These exceptions, dating back to 1870, 1876, and the Second Spanish Republic (1931–6), differed in their impact and duration, and two of the three made exclusive reference to teaching religion at school. The first came about as a result of the freedom of public and private worship and of teaching granted in articles 21 and 24, respectively, of the Constitution of 1870. An order from 14 September 1870 addressed to the presidents of the provincial juntas for primary teaching in some of the provinces of Andalucía authorized waiving the teaching of the Catholic religion to children of any families of "evangelical worship" who had requested that they not be taught "any positive religion" at all. That order was repealed five years later. The second exception came about as a result of the Constitution of 1876, which once again made Catholicism the state religion (art. 11) while also declaring freedom of private worship. It was not until 1913 that a royal decree was passed to regulate the compulsory nature of teaching Catholic religion except to "the children of parents who wish otherwise because of belonging to a religion other than Catholic" (art. 2) (Viñao 2014, 21–3).

The third and most effect exception was the one adopted by the Second Republic in 1931. The decree of 6 May 1931 made studying the Catholic religion voluntary, at the express request of parents. The subsequent declaration of the non-confessional state in article 3 of the Constitution of 1931 and of the secularism of schools (art. 48) provided the basis for the order of 12 January 1932, which banished religious worship and teaching at school and forbade "any sign that implied religion" (Viñao 2014, 21–4). The secularization of the state and of education as carried out by the government of the Second Republic brought about one of the most relevant decisions made in that regard: the dissolution of the Society of Jesus, with its long history in education (see the discussion in chapter 8 in this volume), and the prohibition of all existing religious orders from teaching. This decision stripped the church of the right to teach, thus stepping from a confessional state to absolute laicism (Puelles 2010, 263–5).

During the Spanish Civil War, education was made into an instrument for ideology (Puelles 2010, 279) that was wielded by both the National Front and the Republicans. With victory of the former, the

Franco dictatorship began. As Viñao (2014) notes, one of the bastions of the new government's politics was the defence of the Catholic Church in its Spanish nationalist, ultraconservative version, and the persecution, repression, or social ostracism of anyone who opposed or did not belong to it. The result became known as "national Catholicism" and, in the field of teaching, as national-Catholic education (Gervilla 1990). In terms of the state's relations with the Vatican, an agreement was signed in 1941 reinstating the first four articles of the Concordat of 1851 proclaiming the Catholic confession of the Spanish state and consequently the conformity of all teaching with the doctrine of the Catholic Church. The consequences of this new political and legislative framework profoundly affected the status and position of the Catholic religion as a school subject. Not only did it become compulsory, to the exclusion of any other, and evaluable, and on academic par with other subjects, it also took place at every level and in every modality of education. At the same time, its weight and influence in the curriculum increased as religious activities and practices were added, especially in primary school (Viñao 2014, 31–2).

Although, at the normative level, national Catholicism was the framework in place throughout the entire Franco period (1936–75), the 1970s initiated what Pérez-Agote has labelled "the second wave of secularization." This wave began with the economic development of Spain in the 1960s, especially as regards mass consumption. Pérez-Agote uses the term "a more secularized secularization" to describe not so much a new contrary or belligerent view of religion and the Catholic Church but, rather, a more passive, uninterested attitude toward them. The decline of the ties that individuals maintained with the Catholic Church did not mean an equal drop in the belief in God or in religiousness (2007, 68).

It was in this context of secularization and a dwindling interest in Catholicism in the 1970s that the New Age movement began to gain followers of modern esotericism worldwide. As a general rule, its participants shared the hope for a new age of love and light that would be attained by personal transformation and healing. All of this helped nurture the uneasiness a group of people developed toward anthroposophy. One reason is that, in national-Catholic Spain, this emerging configuration came as a veritable breath of fresh air, given the intense discrimination against other religions and spiritual heterodoxies. In the words of Antonio Malagón, one of the participants in the clandestine group of anthroposophy and a subsequent co-founder of the first Waldorf project, "The Church could not accept anything from the Christology present in anthroposophy. It acted in inquisitional manner. Vigilance was overwhelming. In fact, society constantly felt it was being spied on from both fronts: the Franco regime and the Church, despite both being on the same side."[1] Moreover, any concession in allowing new belief systems was viewed as an attack against the confessional state and the survival of Catholic unity, as was made clear by the difficulties encountered by the Protestant community (Moreno 2001, 353). It is true that one of the consequences of the renewal process in the Catholic Church brought on by Vatican II was the 1967 Law on Religious Freedom in Spain.[2] This law, however, proved insufficient: it was restrictive and directed only at non-Catholics, since it developed only tolerance without adding religious freedom (358). Yet, it had an important political effect in that it made it look as if the regime was modernizing and adapting itself to the Vatican Council, despite Catholicism's remaining at the forefront in political, social, and cultural life (ibid.). In this political and religious climate, it was impossible to develop the anthroposophy publicly, given its strong esoteric underpinnings, and the people interested in Steiner's philosophy had to look for underground or clandestine means of pursuing it.

As a function of all the above, "the logic of consistency" noted by Berger was clearly predominant in Spain up through the last decade of the Franco regime. That logic strove for both Catholic and secular consistency, but with the former outweighing the latter. Nevertheless, as the Franco regime wore on, a secularization process took place in Spain along with a distancing from Catholicism: in this regards, Taylor's secularization paradigm best explains the process underway in Spanish society practically up to dictator Francisco Franco's death in 1975. As of that date, a transition process to democracy began that reformed the denomination of the state as non-confessional. The Constitution of 1978 granted freedom of worship, and, progressively, the laws on education were reworked to fit this new, more secular context. Thus, the secularization process regarding the state religion at the end of the Franco dictatorship and the subsequent protection of religious freedom helped open Spain up to new ideas and thus to religious plurality.

The Reception in Spain of Waldorf Education and Its Aim to Educationalize Spirituality

The thesis of this chapter is that Waldorf education in Spain was a model of teaching that fit in with the spiritual and educational aspirations of a minority of Spaniards at the end of the Franco dictatorship. The reception of this teaching model and its subsequent initiatives took place during the transition toward a plural social and educational model, or, in Berger's terms, when a "structure of plausibility" is configured, which in the case of Spain occurred during and after the democratic transition period. That structure of plausibility had begun to take form in the last few years of the Franco regime, at a time when both the structures and the hardline discourse of the regime were weakening. In the 1960s, alongside the climate of repression, new spaces began opening that sparked hope in at least parts of society for greater openings and for exploring or participating in those spaces. Nevertheless, under Franco, people interested in anthroposophy and Waldorf pedagogy could read, think over, and discuss Steiner's esoteric philosophy only if they met clandestinely.

Anthroposophy embodied a kind of quest that made it appealing in times of ideological repression. One of the characteristic features Berger points out in the paradigm of religious pluralism is that the individual undergoes a major process of subjectivation: "The modern mantra is 'I want to find out who I am.' ... All life becomes an interminable process of redefining who the individual is in the context of the seemingly endless possibilities presented by modernity" (2014, 5). In that regard, anthroposophy contained important elements for personal development, starting with conquering spirituality by meditative work in four bodies: the physical, the esoteric, the astral, and the self. Furthermore, study of and interest in anthroposophy also took place in informal ways that had little to do with religious institutions. Rather, it became a way of developing spirituality that liberated individuals by distancing them from religious institutions (8).

People interested in anthroposophy in Spain took up Steiner's postulates indicating that human beings are able to know the spiritual world and perceive it on their own, without the need for intermediaries. Steiner's epistemological considerations repeatedly showed the ability humans had of developing a mental activity that would give them access to the spiritual world. In this regard, the Christian Community, which is the anthroposophic application of Christianity, was conceived as a place to make a group effort at carrying out that individual search for Christ. Steiner noted that this would be a "temporary" meeting space, since it should disappear when people no longer need it after they themselves have attained a high, autonomous level of spiritual development.

Such theses are in line with the thinking of Gilles Lipovetsky, whose "à la carte religions" have emerged in these "hyper-modern" times:

> The West has many movements that fit in with the liberal culture of the individual in charge of his own fate. Proof thereof can be found in the many "à la carte religions," i.e., groups and networks that combine the spiritual traditions of East and West, and use religious tradition as a means for

subjective fulfilment of their practitioners. Here there is no conflict with individualist modernity, since tradition has been left to the criteria of the individuals, jury-rigged and put into play for purposes of self-realization and integration into the community. The hyper-modern era does not do away with traditions of a sacred nature; rather, it simply restructures them by individualizing, disseminating, and emotionalizing the beliefs and practices. This current trend is giving rise to an increase in unregulated religions and post-traditional identities. (2006, 98–9)

In this way, and along the line noted by Berger regarding the proliferation of ways of understanding and experiencing religions in a context characterized by plurality, Lipovetsky explains how these eclectic religious beliefs flourish:

Here ... we should be aware of seeing new spiritualties as a residual phenomenon, regression or pre-modern archaism. In fact, it is from within the hyper-modern cosmos that the religious domain is reproduced, in so far as the hyper-modern generates insecurity, the loss of fixed guidelines, the disappearance of secular utopias, and an individualist disintegration of the social bond. In the uncertain, chaotic, atomized universe of modernity, new needs for unity and meaning, for security and a sense of belonging, arise: this is a new opportunity for religions. (99)

As a spiritual philosophy, what is interesting about anthroposophy is its difficulty in being studied in terms of Berger's consistency. Anthroposophy is known to sustain a version of history and human development deeply rooted in Christianity while also combining those elements with esoteric ones of a mainly theosophical basis (Quiroga 2015). As regards its Christian component, it is important to note that, in the Spanish context, anthroposophy meant a kind of continuity with traditional Catholic values. The fact that it was not a radical break may have enhanced its appeal among those who wanted to renew their Catholic religious convictions and led to rejection from those who sought completely alternative currents devoid of any Christian underpinnings.

Particularly significant is the case of four nuns who forsook their habits and convents to lead a lay life while participating in and disseminating anthroposophy and Waldorf education. A personal crisis with religious life brought the four nuns to learn about anthroposophy. Two of them had already left the convent, and, as a last chance before giving up their habits, the other two chose to bring anthroposophy into their life in the convent in order to renew their faith. When that possibility was turned down, they left the convent in 1977 and took up anthroposophy.

In the case of one of the nuns, her career as a teacher led her to take part in Waldorf pedagogy. According to her statement, "in anthroposophy I found what is primal to Christianity." For another, "It was a path to evolution. In the Catholic Church everything was static: heaven, hell, purgatory, mass, communion and confession." A third nun recalled that, "When I first heard of reincarnation and karma, I found it logical." In contrast, for a fourth nun, "The whole reincarnation idea put my teeth on edge. I loved the pedagogy and Christology but couldn't take some of the other things they said. I heard them talk of Christ, and was fine. Everything else ... made me uneasy."[3] Thus, anthroposophy proved attractive in its connections to Christianity and because its main postulates converged on a model of education. At the same time, the esoteric component of anthroposophy was perceived as a different way of understanding spirituality: more modern, with a more experiential and subjective component. Furthermore, the language encompassing it, rife with Steiner's own concepts (e.g., the Consciousness Soul, the etheric body, seven-year cycles, and so on) made it tremendously appealing in the New Age messages in the late years of the Franco dictatorship and the early years of the transition to democracy.

The Constitution of 1978 featured two key rights necessary for the development of Waldorf education in Spain: article 16, protecting religious and ideological freedom, and article 27, on the right to education, academic freedom, and university autonomy. From then on, the state was no longer confessional, and therefore the Catholic Church no longer had an ideological monopoly on education. These changes provided a favourable legal framework for the founding of Waldorf schools. And so, the first Waldorf project in Spain was inaugurated in Madrid in 1979: the Micael Kindergarten. It was followed by a set of initiatives of an anthroposophic bent. This new situation contrasted sharply with the days of national Catholicism, when Waldorf schools and their esoteric underpinnings were quite unacceptable: it was in the new democratic context that religious heterodoxies found a setting that made them possible. The years 1979–82 were considered the "foundational triennial" of anthroposophy in Spain (Malagón 2007: 33). During those years, summer courses on anthroposophy were held and initiatives were undertaken such as the above-mentioned kindergarten, the Rudolf Steiner Publishers, the Anthroposophic Society of Spain, a vocational centre for the disabled, the Rafael Workshop of Sociotherapy, and the Biodynamic Agriculture Association for the Canary Islands. Clearly, it was a time in which the foundations of this movement began to be laid.

And yet, in what way did Waldorf pedagogy constitute an attempt at educationalizing spirituality? This question can perhaps best be answered by looking at a 2008 article by David Bridges, in which he points out:

> Educational institutions accept some responsibility for resolving social and economic problems out of a mixture of ambition, enlightened self-interest, and an appetite for government funding. I believe, however, that many have been drawn into education out of an honest conviction that they can thereby contribute in some general or more specific way social benefit, perhaps even help to build a better world ... There is a connection between education and some kind of search for individual and social improvement. We cannot really conceive of education without reference to some selection of human qualities we want to cultivate and of the kind of social world we expect or perhaps want our pupils to occupy. (466)

In other words, for Bridges, the concept of educationalization, and the very work of educational institutions themselves through their daily contact with the new generations, implies an intention for bettering society. This *leitmotif* brimming with idealism becomes materialized in daily practice in the selection of particular qualities meant to be cultivated and developed in children. Waldorf pedagogy, especially in terms of its reception and implementation in Spain, contained these aspirations for three reasons. First, education was by no means immune to the upheavals in the process of political change underway in Spain during the transition to democracy. The intent was that schools would gradually reflect the changes in the nation, particularly in becoming more democratic spaces with more active pedagogical methods. The movements for pedagogical renewal that had begun in the 1970s advanced greatly at this time and questioned many of the practices that had been implemented.

Second, in Waldorf education, in relation to the "selection of the human qualities" to foster in the school children (Bridges 2008, 466), a pedagogical project was designed that would largely do away with the teaching practices habitually used in Spanish classrooms, thereby making teachers and parents alike believe in its uniqueness and worth. For example, to Heidi Bieler, one of the first Waldorf teachers, "This kindergarten could not be compared to any other. Firstly because of where it was located: fields and pine trees all around. At first we had no sandbox, no swing sets. We refurbished an old chicken coop. It was simply countryside, and in the background, some train tracks. The kids were enthralled watching the trains go by. The atmosphere at the kindergarten, with the countryside and old trees, the poppies and the tall grass ... it was unheard of in Spain. It was like a dream for

Spain."[4] And for the mother of one of the students, "At a time when Spain was still very grey, we came across a school where the classrooms were bursting with color" and "the children baked bread and painted with wonderful watercolours."[5]

Third, for the first participants in this pedagogy, the development of Waldorf education meant that Spain was joining with the international education mainstream. With Waldorf pedagogy came experimentation with a different concept of spirituality, one whose esoteric basis hinted at an education reform that would move beyond the old Catholic/non-Catholic dichotomy. Moreover, anthroposophy also had an application in other fields of knowledge, and had already an established presence in Europe, the United States and Canada. For the small group in Madrid, anthroposophy offered an appealing message that lived up to their expectations of opening up to the world.

All in all, it is important to note that Waldorf pedagogy constituted then, and constitutes today, a minority movement in pedagogy, and, thus, the processes of educationalizing spirituality must be regarded in the scope of its own dimensions. As schools forming part of an esoteric movement, they look for their space in a type of teaching that the state cannot provide – a marginal position these schools seek out because of the curricular independence it provides.

Conclusion

This chapter has used paradigms on secularization from Taylor and plurality from Berger to analyse the changes in matters of religious education in Spain. While the secularization paradigm helps understand the process of decline felt by the Catholic religion in society and in the school curriculum through the end of the Franco dictatorship, the paradigm of plurality began to emerge in the last decade of the regime, when some sectors of the population sought out alternative forms of spirituality other than Catholicism.

Spain was a predominantly Catholic country up until the final years of the Franco regime, and education was strongly influenced and even managed by the church. As Viñao (2014) has pointed out, since the eighteenth century there have only been three exceptions in Spain in regard to questioning the Catholic monopoly. Two of them were aimed at restricting the teaching of religion at school by means of rules and regulations that proved very short-lived, and the third, of greater depth, happened at the time of the Second Spanish Republic, when a decided effort was made to secularize both the state and education. What is interesting in the case of Spain is the polarization between the sectors that defended

Catholicism and those that called for a secular, chiefly anti-Catholic model. The latter made themselves more visible at the end of the Franco period, when, as Taylor puts it, believing in God became one of many options. Many people gave up their Catholic beliefs in a noticeable trend toward secularization in the late twentieth century.

Nevertheless, the paradigm that best explains the reception of anthroposophy and the creation of schools based on Waldorf education is that of plurality developed by Berger. In fact, as of the second wave of secularization, some minority groups have sought out other ways of understanding spirituality. With the Constitution of 1979, Spain had a structure of plausibility that fostered its development, since it guaranteed religious freedom and the freedom to open new schools. As an esoteric philosophy with a Christian base, anthroposophy was attractive because of the new concepts it brought to a population weary of Catholicism without its being excessively strange, since it contained messages and people that were part of Christianity. Even so, what is interesting about this pedagogical model was that it represented a manner of educationalizing spirituality in an increasingly secular and plural context.

The educationalization of spirituality found in Waldorf pedagogy, as Bridges points out, also brought an intention of improving society and the world by means of its daily contact with the younger generations for three main reasons. First, in the context of pedagogical renewal underway in Spain during the transition to democracy, Waldorf pedagogy found a niche as an alternative model of teaching. Second, the pedagogical project that these schools contained was unique and appealing for teachers and families alike. And, finally for the founders and receivers of this pedagogy, having the chance to create Waldorf schools meant contributing to the development of Spain and bringing it up to date, on par with other countries in Europe and around the world that already had a firm background in this pedagogy.

NOTES

1 Antonio Malagón, interview with the author, 21 January 2014, Madrid.
2 This law was not the result of any penchant for tolerance by the Franco regime but, rather, was a tactic by the sectors in the Catholic Church after the Second Vatican Council's *Dignitatis humanae* declaration, which began in 1962 and concluded in 1965. The Vatican declaration stated that people have the right to religious freedom and this right must be recognized in the constitutional order of society (López 2000, 225).

3 Author's interviews with anonymous sources, 21 February 2016.
4 Heidi Bieler, interview with the author, 21 January 2014.
5 Rosario Sanz, interview with the author, 16 January 2014.

REFERENCES

Asociación de Centros Educativos Waldorf-Steiner de España. 2018. "Centros educativos Waldorf." *Revista Waldorf-Steiner Educación*, Año XII, no. 28, 3–6. Retrieved from http://colegioswaldorf.org/28.pdf.
Berger, P.L. 2005. "Pluralismo global y religion." *Estudios públicos* 98: 5–18.
– 2014. *The Many Altars of Modernity: Toward a Paradigm for Religion in a Pluralistic Age*. Boston: De Gruyter.
Bridges, D. 2008. "Educationalization: On the Appropriateness of Asking Educational Institutions to Solve Social and Economic Problems." *Educational Theory* 58 (4): 461–74. https://doi.org/10.1111/j.1741-5446.2008.00300.x.
Brown, C.G. 2001. *The Death of Christian Britain: Understanding Secularization, 1800–2000*. London: Routledge.
– 2017. *Becoming Atheist: Humanism and the Secular West*. London: Bloomsbury.
Freunde der Erziehungskunst Rudolf Steiners. 2018. *Waldorf Worldwide List*. Accessed 5 December 2018. https://www.freunde-waldorf.de/fileadmin/user_upload/images/Waldorf_World_List/Waldorf_World_List.pdf.
Gervilla, E. 1990. *La escuela del nacional-catolicismo: Ideología y educación religiosa*. Granada, ES: Impredisur.
Lerena, C. 2005. *Reprimir y liberar: Crítica sociológica de la educación y la cultura contemporáneas*. Madrid: Akal.
Lipovetsky, G. 2006. *Los tiempos hipermodernos*. Barcelona: Anagrama.
López, M. 2000. "Problemas que afronta la ley de libertad religiosa de España y soluciones que ofrece para los mismos." *Anales de Derecho, Universidad de Murcia* 18: 223–42.
Louzao, J. 2008. "Los idealistas de la fraternidad universal: Una aproximación a la historia del movimiento teosófico español (1890–1939)." *Historia Contemporánea* 37: 501–29.
Malagón, A. 2007. "La pedagogía Waldorf en España." *Revista Waldorf-Steiner Educación* 6 (2): 32–4.
McLeod, H. 2000. *Secularization in Western Europe, 1814–1914*. Basingstoke: Macmillan.
Moreno, M. 2001. "El miedo a la libertad religiosa: Autoridades franquistas, católicos y protestantes ante la Ley de 28 de junio de 1967." *Anales de historia contemporánea* 17: 351–63.
Norris, P., and R. Inglehard. 2004. *Sacred and Secular: Religion and Politics Worldwide*. New York: Cambridge University Press.

Penalva, V. 2013. "El orientalismo en la cultura española en el primer tercio del siglo XX: La Sociedad Teosófica Española (1988–1940)." PhD diss., Universitat Autónoma de Barcelona.

Pérez-Agote, A. 2007. "El proceso de secularización en la sociedad española." *Revista CIDOB* 77: 65–82.

Puelles, M. 2010. *Educación e ideología en la España contemporánea*. Madrid: Tecnos.

Quiroga, P. 2015. "La recepción de la pedagogía Waldorf en España." PhD diss., Universidad Complutense de Madrid.

Redondo, E. and Vergara, J. 1994. "La Iglesia y la educación, en Delgado." Ed. B. Criado. In *Historia de la educación en España y América*, vol. 3, 67–109. Madrid: Morata.

Taylor, C. 2007. *A Secular Age*. Cambridge, MA: Belknap Press of Harvard University Press.

Viñao, A. 2014. *Religión en las aulas: Una materia controvertida*. Madrid: Morata.

PART III

Educationalization and the Right to Education/Schooling

leaving aligned vaults © Alan R. Wilkinson

10 Educationalization, Schooling, and the Right to Education

FELICITAS ACOSTA

Since the nineteenth century, education has been central to states' agendas. The twentieth century witnessed one of the greatest cultural transformations ever – mass schooling in the form of educational systems. While the implementation of that transformation across the globe has been far from uniform, international discourses on education came together to instil the idea of the right to education and the expansion of schooling as means of access to that right.

Indeed, article 26 of the International Declaration of Human Rights adopted by the United Nations General Assembly on 10 December 1948 states that all persons have the right to education. Since then, a number of agreements, conventions, covenants, and declarations have proposed definitions of exactly what the right to education means, as well as its scope. The International Covenant of Economic, Social, and Cultural Rights (ICESCR) adopted by the UN in 1966 establishes the right of persons to receive a period of mandatory education free of charge (initially conceived for primary education but to be eventually gradually extended to secondary education). Article 13 of the covenant specifies the state's obligation to guarantee that right in the framework of the notion of liberty in teaching – that is, the right of parents or legal guardians to choose for their children or wards schools or other educational institutions that meet the minimal standards laid down by the state.

Similarly, the Committee of Economic, Social, and Cultural Rights, created in the framework of the United Nations Economic and Social Council in 1985 to monitor the progress of the ICESCR, described the right to education as epitomizing the indivisibility and interdependence of all human rights. Attempts to enshrine the right to education include Article 1 of the World Declaration on Education for All (Jomtien, Thailand, 1990); paragraph 1 of article 29 of the Convention on the Rights of the Child; part 1 of paragraph 33 and part 2 of paragraph 80 of the Vienna Declaration and Programme of Action; and paragraph 2 of the Plan of Action for the United Nations Decade for Human Rights Education. More recently, in May 2015, the United Nations Educational, Scientific and Cultural Organization (UNESCO), the United Nations International Children's Emergency Fund (UNICEF), the United Nations Development Program (UNDP), the United Nations High Commissioner for Refugees (UNHCR), the United Nations Population Fund (UNFPA), the United Nations Entity for Gender Equality and the Empowerment of Women (UN-Women), and the World Bank organized another meeting of the World Education Forum, in Incheon, Korea, in order to establish a roadmap for global education until 2030 (López 2015). The course laid out by that map consists of goals or indicators for progress in schooling.

I argue in this chapter that, in contemporary societies, education and schooling are considered one and the same, and that educational systems are the material manifestation of the process of educationalization. The origins of that process lay in the eighteenth century, when a new set of social problems in the wake of the dissolution of the feudal world – mainly the problem of subjective and collective destructuralization – turned education into the new technology of moral and social regulation. The educationalization of social problems advanced over the course of the nineteenth century with the spread of schooling and, in the twentieth, with the consolidation of educational systems that culminated with the right to education explicitly formulated in terms of schooling – that is, the right to schooling. I argue that, while mass schooling does constitute a fundamental advance in access to lettered culture, it also has limitations. A more equitable distribution of knowledges requires re-examining schooling as a privileged form in the process of educationalization.

On the basis of an analysis of the equivalence between education and schooling, and from a perspective of the internationalization of schooling, this chapter is structured in two parts. The first attempts to separate the notions of schooling and education. By re-examining the historical process that led to that equivalence, we can discern which educational problems schooling solves and which it does not. Returning to the right to education, the question would be, then, what it means to formulate the right to education in terms of the right to schooling. The second part of this chapter addresses the situation in Latin America in relation to the expansion of schooling, in particular, the scope and limits of that project. It discusses the weakness of educational reforms arising from the failure to take into account the effects of schooling on the real promotion of the right to education.

Is Schooling Education? The Right to Education as Right to Schooling

> For some time now, I have found myself working in the complex, dynamic, and contradictory set of national and international networks and organisms that deals with the governance of education. Some of the questions that arise from time to time in the intricacies of those networks never cease to startle me. I would like to mention three specifically. The first is shortsightedness regarding the contemporary challenge of providing quality education to all. The second is disdain for history as a tool for leveraging future change. The third is the lack of awareness of or reflection on processes for the construction of mechanisms, as opposed to institutional structures, for the international governance of education, and its growing division into differentiated networks that, despite a world more and more interdependent, are themselves less and less interdependent. (Braslavsky 2005, 269)

To grapple with the right to education and its relationship to schooling means to turn it into an object of analysis. The passage cited above is useful to that end, specifically in relation to:

- a historical understanding of processes by which discourses and practices are passed on – that is, how they constitute a legacy that gives shape to school institutions (Acosta 2014; Tröhler and Lenz 2015);
- a systemic understanding of the dynamics through which school practices are structured – in particular, processes of systematization and segmentation (Mueller, Ringer, and Simon 1992; Schriewer and Harney 1992; Viñao 2002; Acosta 2011; 2014); and
- the internationalization of education – more specifically, the relationship between global tendencies and national practices in the context of the expansion of schooling (Schriewer 2002, 2010).

Building a framework to analyse schooling rests on a number of suppositions. It is based on the thesis of the internationalization of ideas and models in the configuration of educational systems in general. The concept of "internationalization," as developed by Schriewer (2002; 2010), refers to the process of transnational migration, expansion, and reception, a process constructed historically according to a range of logics of appropriation determined by deep cultural structures (Caruso and Tenorth 2011). At the same time, internationalization assumes the global expansion of transnationally standardized educational models and the persistence of various networks of socio-cultural interconnection (Schriewer 2010).

The following processes of internationalization are the basis for this analysis of the configuration of the educational system:

- the triumph, in the late nineteenth century, of a schooling culture based on the variables of nationalization, simultaneity, and graduated schools;
- the shaping of educational institutions and systems that revolved around systematization and segmentation (Mueller, Ringer, and Simon, 1992); and
- the configuration of the secondary school as an institution with a distinct role in the process of educational segmentation (Steedman 1992).

Thist is the framework for the historical overview of the relationship between educationalization, mass schooling, and the right to education that I will offer in the coming pages.

As stated above, education has occupied a key place in the agenda of states since the nineteenth century. In the twentieth, international discourses on education came together to formulate the notion of the right to education and the expansion of schooling as means of access to that right. The figure of an educating state is tied to the process by which educational systems, as technology for the expansion of schooling, took shape. Indeed, it could be said that that global expansion has become the basic concept underlying schooling, a myth as well as a guide to legitimize institutions and states as they operated in education. At stake in the arrangement of those institutions and states, both at present and in the past, are systematic and institutional questions as well as a whole set of actors and agents engaged in developing a vision and a plan of action.

It would seem, then, that educational systems are the result of state action. But that's not the whole story, since educational systems are complex structures where a whole range of agents act and interact on different planes, from the formulation of educational principles that can be seen as global in scope to making decisions regarding daily life at particular schools.

The expansion of schooling and its connection to the state can be analysed from two perspectives. On a political-judicial level, the origin of an educating state and the expansion of schooling at a national scale lay in the French Revolution, although previous experiences took place in reformed areas of Germany and in Switzerland.[1] As Clérico (2009) points out, it was not until the French Revolution in 1789, and the subsequent configuration of the classical liberal state in the late eighteenth century, that individuals were seen as having private and public rights under rule of law in a state of and by citizens. Notwithstanding these roots, the welfare state is what ushered in the notion on a large scale that all men and women have a right to universal education free of charge, with mandatory levels defined by each state in a system organized around articulated levels. Education then became a fundamental human right, a benefit that required active state intervention to ensure that all the individuals in a given country had effective access to it.[2] But it is through schooling that states guarantee the right to education, which means that the right to education is, in fact, the right to schooling.

From the perspective of the expansion of schooling, understanding the process whereby education and schooling became equivalent requires analysing three passages: the passage from the discourse of education to the discourse of schooling in the late eighteenth century; the passage from a school based on rudimentary institutional arrangements to the modern school in the nineteenth century; and the passage from a school system to an educational system in the mid-twentieth century (Acosta 2014).[3]

Those passages, analysed below, show an increasing process of educationalization (Tröhler 2013; Tröhler, Popkewitz, and Labaree 2011) – that is, the deployment of mass schooling as a means to address social problems, such as the consolidation of nation states and capitalism. The formation of citizens, as a new way of self-regulation and of social governance, became the cornerstone of the schooling agenda or, in the words of Popkewitz (2009), the new moral issue (2009).

The Passage from the Discourse of Education to the Discourse of Schooling

An analysis of the three passages mentioned above reveals increasing state intervention in the regulation of educational practices. The emergence of an educating state is tied to the passage from the discourse of education to the discourse of schooling. The end of the eighteenth century witnessed growing educationalization of new social problems, many of them bound to the consolidation of the liberal state and to capitalist modes of production (Tröhler 2013; Tröhler, Popkewitz, and Labaree 2011). It was at that moment that states delved into the task of regulating educational practices.

How did that shift occur? The Enlightenment idea of the social contract positioned the state in the role of educator: its responsibilities included making citizens aware of their rights and obligations to ensure passage from the state of nature to civil society. The state was the agent that defined "man" in terms of his educability; man needs the state in order to rid himself of unjust governments (and of subjugation) and to be able to obtain respect for his rights, based on the principle of reason.

"All men are born free and equal" was the first link in a chain of ideas that culminated in the creation of the figure of the fully autonomous citizen – that is, the individual unhindered by subjugation. Education was defined as the means to that autonomy, or, as Kant would put it, – to the use of reason and free will to choose worthy ends. More than provide education per se, the state had to ensure the existence of a citizenry understood as autonomous and not subjugated. The Enlightenment, then, constructed a new object of intervention ("man" as future citizen); a new educational actor (the state as guarantor of an individual's rights and, therefore, as responsible for making those rights, and corresponding obligations, known to all); and a new educational object ("man," who becomes man through education and therefore does not need religious practices to develop a moral sense but, rather, can do so by mastering reason/understanding). While the Enlightenment placed the actors involved in education – that is, the state and the population as citizens – at the centre of education, its discourse was not strictly scholastic. Some Enlightenment thinkers (Kant, for instance) argued that schools take charge of education, but others – Rousseau and Locke – did not.[4]

It was on the basis of those objects and actors that the French revolutionaries of 1789 designed the first policies in which the national state was responsible for schooling. The nineteenth century then witnessed a shift as discourse on education turned into discourse on the need to open schools – that is, the need for schooling. The question is why it came to be believed that this new form of regulation could be enacted by creating or expanding school systems (Tröhler, Popkewitz, and Labaree, 2011).

Both the French Revolution and the Industrial Revolution turned the problem of educational practices as means to ensure moral regulation into a problem of social regulation. The key to that transformation was scale, which, crucially, was thought to be universal in times of revolution and industrialization – that is, when "universal" meant both simultaneous and homogeneous. Multiple educational practices existed, but the one privileged was the one most experienced in the expansion of scale (precedents for that expansion included Martin Luther and educational legislation in seventeenth-century Germany and in other reformist states[5]) and in simultaneous organization (precedents in simultaneous organization included John Amos Comenius's theoretical proposals in his *Didactica Magna* and in the Christian schools created in France during the second half of the seventeenth century[6]). This shift was manifested in a second passage, the passage from *rudimentary* institutional arrangements to mandatory elementary school.

The Passage from a School Based on Rudimentary Institutional Arrangements to the Modern School

By the early nineteenth century, there was widespread consensus on the ability of schools to distribute knowledge on a mass scale. It was necessary, however, to turn the existing institutions into universal, simultaneous, and homogeneous educating technologies. The state intervened in that process by means of regulations that would distribute to individuals, on the one hand, a set of knowledge necessary to operating in the new social order and would ensure the regulation of the social whole, on the other, in the face of revolutionary processes.

The triumph of the modern school as hegemonic educational form was possible only with state intervention. The state was an agent that, by means of laws on mandatory education, could require parents or guardians to give their children or wards over to schools in exchange for the knowledge needed to perform certain social functions. In relation to education, the state became, then, an all-encompassing figure that acted through an institution that aspired to the same vastness.

On how that process ensued in the West and the place the state occupied in it, Green (1994) underscores the differences in both the timeframes and modalities adopted by each country as it implemented a widespread model of schooling. He distinguishes three different arrangements within a global model embraced by Western nations, a model characterized by a publicly funded system with an administrative bureaucracy for the regulation of schools and by increasingly structured educational institutions and agents. Those three arrangements are:

- the Germanic states, France, the Netherlands, and Switzerland, which established rudimentary modern educational systems in around 1830;
- the northern states in the United States, which, on the basis of a decentralized model, set up a rudimentary modern educational system between 1830 and the beginning of Civil War; and
- Great Britain, southern Europe, and the southern states in Latin America, which set up rudimentary modern educational systems between the end of the nineteenth century and the beginning of the twentieth.

Regardless of differences in timeframe, the expansion of schooling, in all cases, depended on assigning the state a key role in the process of systematization or what could be called state systematization of schooling. In this sense, following Tröhler, Popkewitz, and Labaree (2011), schooling is understood as a set of institutional and cultural practices associated with the assembly of the society through the construction of a particular subject: the future citizen. It can be linked to the global phenomenon of national developments toward society and school modelling as a result of the intersection between the emergence of schooling and the formation of the nation state. From the perspective of internationalization, this wider process is bound to other processes such as state educational systems as essential to the ability of republics to survive, the growth of republics throughout the world over the nineteenth and twentieth centuries, and the mass expansion of schooling around the world in those centuries. This list would indicate that the combination of republicanism and education was a worldwide success.

Tröhler, Popkewitz, and Labaree (2011) also argue that, during the eighteenth century, this coordinated action of the state and the school became necessary insofar as social problems were educationalized, and education was increasingly seen as the answer to any social problem. The association of the republic as the political form, reformed Protestantism, and education seems to have been the formula for global success and the engine for development. In other words, even though, in its origins, the notion of the citizen was not directly tied to the constitution of liberal democracies, by the end of the nineteenth century and the beginning of the twentieth, those two were inseparable – and constituted the terms in which the discussion around schooling took place. Looking to Tröhler's notion of languages of education (2013), we might think of a "language of schooling" as based on a supposed relationship between schooling and democracy. Indeed, Popkewitz (2009) points out that, starting in the early twentieth century, educational reforms were implemented as part of the ideal of democracy.

The Passage from a Network of Schools to Educational Systems: A Language of Schooling

The passage from a system of schools to an educational system occurred between the end of the nineteenth and beginning of the twentieth centuries, although states began intervening in education in the mid-nineteenth century, specifically by regulating, via different means, post-elementary or post-primary instruction. The educational system took shape as the state began to forge multiple relationships between different forms of schooling and scholastic institutions and to define their functions. The concept of systematization as applied to education is important to understanding the process that took place in the very late nineteenth and early twentieth centuries: a vaguely defined group of diverse schools was gradually turned into a highly structured and carefully delimited system of educational institutions with interrelated functions. The limits of different types of educational institutions were established, and the contents of curricula and the requirements of graduates specified. The functional relationships between the different parts of what was taking shape as a school system were worked out.

The processes of systematization and segmentation so clearly laid out by Mueller, Ringer, and Simon (1992) encapsulated the different ways of coordinating an expanding school system and a *process of social reordering* that entailed, among other things, increasing demand for more education. That transformation did not culminate until the mid-twentieth century with the expansion of secondary schools. Although these schools were initially in response to a social demand, they were later embraced by the state – a process that ultimately led to a structure built around different educational levels (Viñao 2002).

This passage actually entailed a change in scene that took place in two distinct moments. The first moment, the change itself, was bound to the emergence of the welfare state, with which the educating state reached its maximum potential. With the expansion of social rights (education chief among them) and the demand for qualified human resources in a process of re-industrialization, the state embraced the project of expanding secondary education (until 1940, no more than 10 per cent of the age-appropriate population attended secondary schools in even the most advanced countries). The second moment is tied to the ultimate configuration of educational systems, now in a context of steady expansion of secondary instruction and reforms that, starting in the 1960s, were devised to tackle this new scale – a problem that entailed not only the creation of new institutions but also modifying existing institutional models in order to handle new students. It was in that context that, in 1966, the right to education was sanctioned by the ICESCR. Indeed, as pointed out by Tröhler and Lenz (2015), the launching of the Sputnik in 1957 gave way to a continuous cycle of educational reforms under the gaze of international organizations such as UNESCO and the World Bank. These passages show not only how schooling came to be equated with education but also how the cycles of the expansion of schooling are, it would seem, what determined the scope of the right to education.

In sum, this section examined the historical process by which schooling became the privileged means to address the problem of the distribution of new knowledge. It was necessary, in a new scene and on a larger scale, to constitute a universal, simultaneous, and homogeneous school network that formed the basis for educational systems by means of processes of systematization and segmentation. The effects of this change on the expansion of schooling are patent: an authentic cultural revolution that gradually brought the population into a new system for the configuration of subjectivity and social regulation. The limits and contradictions of educational systems are implicit in the fact that school experience arises in the tension between simultaneity and homogenization, and a school career in the tension between propaedeutics (systematization) and inter-institutional diversification according to social background (segmentation). In the following section, I will analyse educational systems in Latin America in relation to the processes described above.

The Expansion of the Right to School in Latin America: Scope and Limitations

Educational systems in Latin America have always operated at a pace different from that of their counterparts in European countries. The origin of many of these differences seems to lie in how the region took part in the Enlightenment's emancipation project and in the consolidation of the modern state. The following pages present a brief historical overview and description of the present state of Latin American educational systems in relation to the expansion of schooling.

The Configuration of Educational Systems in Latin America

As Ossenbach has pointed out (1997), after emancipation from the metropolis, public education in Latin America was handled at the municipal level. It was not until post-independence wars came to an end that central states began to take charge of primary schools according to the notion of common education where the state defined itself as the educating state. Educational systems in Latin America contributed to both the forming of the nation through a process of social and cultural homogenization and to the emergence and development of the middle classes.

Puigrós (1994) sums up the main characteristics of the intersections between the modern educational system and Latin American societies:

- the introduction of the French model of a centralized state-run schooling system during the second half of the nineteenth century

- the production of multiple combinations at the juncture between the centralized education system and the particular cultural, political, and educational features of local communities
- the shaping of citizenry according to a single mould (homogenization), with varying degrees of success: modern education's goal of homogenizing society using public schooling was not met.

Puigrós sorts Latin American countries into five groups, according to the historical context for the development of their educational systems:

- Argentina, Uruguay, Chile (albeit to a lesser extent): small Indigenous populations in the nineteenth century coupled with a mass influx of European immigrants; a broad segment of the population participated in education; socio-economic differences greater than cultural ones
- Bolivia, Ecuador, Guatemala, and Peru: large Indigenous populations; the large peasant and mining classes did not take part in the educational system due to a weak and monolingual state; failure to impose cultural unity across the nation
- Mexico: early development of a school system that grew in conjunction with state hegemony; the system's instruction entailed the subordination or outright elimination of peasant and working-class cultures
- Brazil: later development of the school system (not until 1930); difficulty providing widespread access until the 1990s; a number of different cultural matrices
- Cuba and Nicaragua under the Sandinistas: an educational transformation that included all social sectors in the modern school system; pedagogical and cultural centralization (high-quality, if authoritarian, instruction characteristic of the modern educational model). The process in Nicaragua was curtailed.

Regarding the project of homogenization that gave rise to national integration as the distinctive matrix of modern educational systems, two main traits distinguish the configurations of those systems in Latin America from their European counterparts. The first is the precarious connection, until the 1950s if not later, between the configuration of the educational system and economic development. The second is a striking disparity within the Latin American region in the degree of consolidation and expansion of educational systems, with important differences in the quality of educational supply between elite and popular schools. The first of these traits tended to diminish, starting in the fifties, thanks to developmentalist economic policies, which facilitated the consolidation and expansion of educational systems in some Latin American countries. The second trait persisted, as many clusters of the population continued not to have access, or to have significantly less access, to schooling.

Regional differences were also marked by educational configurations of a hybrid nature that took shape with the expansion of educational systems. In the countries of the Southern Cone, where the system modernized earlier, primary school education organized and expanded relatively quickly. The early development of secondary schooling was characterized by rapid expansion in volume and a significant pre-university bent. While these countries experienced their first major educational expansion in the mid-twentieth century, that expansion – unlike its European counterparts – was effected by a middle-level educational system with little capacity for structural change. In other words, the secondary school's institutional model proved resistant to change, and, unlike in Europe or the United States, there was no comprehensive reform (Acosta 2013).

The second significant expansion took place in the late eighties. It was partly an attempt to respond to the criticism – formulated by some in the seventies – that educational practices had ceased to be meaningful, due to the weakening of the state's role in the provision of schooling. That criticism also addressed the apparent inability of pedagogical theories to provide the actors in the educational system with guidance (Braslavsky 1999). In some countries in Latin America, the late eighties also witnessed a process of economic and social disintegration that required changes in policies in all areas and spheres of schooling.

The Expansion of Educational Systems in Latin America: Scope and Limitations

To different degrees, due to ongoing educational segmentation and the neoliberal policies of the nineties, primary education had, by 2000, reached most of the population. At present, the transition between primary and secondary levels of education is fluid. In the vast majority of the countries in the region, the rate of transition from primary to high school is high, with an average regional rate of 93.5 per cent. The focus of the debate shifted, then, to the need for increasing investment (table 10.1) so as to guarantee the need for schooling expansion.

According to UNESCO (2012), the gross rate of schooling has increased over the course of the past three decades. In 1985, it stood at 50.2 per cent; by 1997, it had reached 62.2 per cent; and in 2010 it had climbed to 72.2 per cent. Following SITEAL (2010), the countries in the

Table 10.1 Percentage of GDP invested in education by country in Latin America (2003–2013)

Country	Year	%	Year	%	Trend
Argentina	2005	3.5	2012	5.1	+1.6
Bolivia	2003	6.4	2012	6.4	No change
Brazil	2005	4.5	2012	6.3	+1.8
Chile	2005	3.2	2012	4.6	+1.4
Colombia	2005	4.0	2013	4.9	+0.9
Ecuador	2001	0.98	2012	4.2	+3.22
Paraguay	2004	3.4	2012	5.0	+1.6
Peru	2005	2.9	2013	3.3	+0.4
Uruguay	2005	2.7	2011	4.4	+1.7
Venezuela	2006	3.7	n/d	n/d	n/d

Source: World Bank and SIPI data.

region can be grouped into five categories with respect to the expansion of the educational systems:

- Countries with high rates of enrolment in primary and secondary school: Argentina, Chile, and Peru. The problem for these countries is the dropout rate in the final years of secondary school.
- Countries with high rates of enrolment in primary school and mid-level rates of enrolment in secondary school: Bolivia, Brazil, Colombia, Costa Rica, Ecuador, Mexico, and Panama. The problem for these countries is late access to secondary education and high dropout rates.
- Countries with high rates of enrolment in primary school and low rates of enrolment in secondary school: Paraguay and Uruguay. The problem is falling behind in primary school and dropping out before secondary school is started.
- Countries with mid-levels of enrolment in primary school and in secondary school: the Dominican Republic and El Salvador. The problem is falling behind at all levels.
- Countries with mid-levels of enrolment in primary school and low levels of enrolment in secondary school: Honduras, Guatemala, and Nicaragua. The problem is that primary education in these countries is not universal and access to and completion of secondary school extremely limited (only one-quarter of the population between the ages of twenty and twenty-two has finished secondary school).

Regional heterogeneity is evident in other educational indicators as well. The percentage of children who receive some schooling ranges from 72 to 97 per cent (SITEAL 2010), and the percentage who attend secondary school fluctuates tremendously within countries according to socio-economic level. The regional average for secondary school attendance ranges from 93.6 per cent among a country's wealthiest children to 78.9 per cent among its poorest. The countries where the gap between the rich and the poor is the smallest are Venezuela, the Dominican Republic, Chile, and Colombia, with gaps of around 5 per cent. Guatemala and Honduras, meanwhile, are at the other extreme, with gaps of over thirty percentage points (UNESCO 2012).

Lastly, and in keeping with the aforementioned limited capacity for structural change that lay at the origin of the creation of mid-level schooling, relatively extensive access to education does not seem to have altered the internal selection processes at the foundational matrix of the educational system. After the age of thirteen, the proportion of students who drop out of school increases steadily. Generally speaking, those who drop out at that age do so before they have finished primary school or, if they have finished primary school, they have not done so on schedule. After the age of thirteen, dropping out and repeating years become so widespread that almost half of adolescents between the ages of seventeen and eighteen (the age when, theoretically, secondary school should be completed in most Latin American countries) are not in school. Only 32 per cent of all young people between the ages of seventeen and eighteen have completed middle school (SITEAL 2010).

Another relevant indicator is repetition rate, which brings with it a change in the course of students' school careers (see tables 10.3 and 10.4). With a regional average of 5.9 per cent, this rate did not drop in the

Table 10.2 Net rate of secondary schooling by country in Latin America (2005–2013)

Country	Year	Rate	Trend
Argentina	2005/2013	82.06/85.00	+ 2.94
Bolivia	2005/2011	69.77/73.98	+ 4.21
Brazil	2004/2011	74.98/76.60	+ 1.62
Ecuador	2006/2011	66.35/79.17	+ 12.82
Paraguay	2006/2013	59.18/72.35	+ 13.17
Peru	2005/2012	67.68/79.78	+ 12.10
Uruguay	2005/2013	75.54/77.37	+ 1.83
Venezuela	2005/2011	70.05/76.03	+ 5.98

Source: SITEAL 2010.

Table 10.3 Percentage of students age 12 to 14 who have repeated years in secondary school by country in Latin America (2004–2013)

Country	Year	%	Year	%	Trend
Argentina	2005	13.99	2013	12.80	−1.19
Bolivia	2005	26.70	2011	24.38	−2.32
Brazil	2004	11.54	2011	4.99	−6.55
Chile	2006	14.98	2011	13.06	−1.92
Colombia	2005	31.36	2010	25.67	−5.69
Ecuador	2006	18.17	2011	11.31	−6.86
Paraguay	2006	29.98	2013	23.23	−6.75
Peru	2007	18.37	2012	24.31	+5.94
Uruguay	2005	16.09	2013	13.59	−2.50
Venezuela	2005	26.74	2011	12.99	−13.75

Source: SITEAL 2010.

Table 10.4 Percentage of students age 15 to 17 who have repeated years in secondary school by country in Latin America (2004–2013)

Country	Year	%	Year	%
Argentina	2005	21.63	2013	30.09
Bolivia	2005	21.52	2011	22.71
Brazil	2004	21.70	2011	13.37
Chile	2006	9.54	2011	7.95
Colombia	2005	47.71	2010	37.80
Ecuador	2006	26.50	2011	16.60
Paraguay	2006	9.35	2013	21.12
Peru	2007	26.76	2012	24.31
Uruguay	2005	24.50	2013	27.46
Venezuela	2005	38.51	2011	22.35

Source: SITEAL 2010.

last decade. Failure rates are coupled with a high and sustained dropout rate in secondary school. In the eighteen countries with comparable data, the average dropout rate in secondary school diminished by slightly more than two percentage points from 2000, when it stood at 17.8 per cent, to 15.5 per cent, the rate in 2010. In other words, each year, one of six students drops out of secondary school in Latin America and the Caribbean. The exception is Bolivia, where the dropout rate plummeted from 41 per cent to 12 per cent over the past decade).

A comparison of the situation of these groups of countries between the time the region's educational systems were configured and the present reveals significant changes, particularly in those countries where that configuration was late and non-inclusive. The comparison of these groups of countries at these two moments attests to a triple challenge facing the region. First is the challenge of solving historical problems related to access and coverage, infrastructure, and the professionalization of teachers pursuant to the first great expansion. The second is the ability to effectively include all school-age children and to enable them to complete their school careers, a problem that dates back to the second great expansion and that could be linked to the institutional model.[7] The third challenge is the provision of quality knowledge and the achievement of an equitable social distribution of quality learning that enables the development of human resources with skills relevant to the contemporary world, a problem particularly pressing in these times.

The historical and contemporary heterogeneity of educational systems in Latin America may well be one of the reasons why those systems have failed to formulate major agreements or common goals that would have a clear impact on the educational policy agenda. The Organization of American States's so-called Education Goals for 2021 call for basic and upper-level secondary school enrolment and completion rates from 40 to 90 per cent.

This section has attempted to shed light on the relationship between the process by which educational systems took shape in Latin America and the cycles of the expansion of schooling. It shows uneven development, which current programs to keep students in school attempt to offset. Yet those alternatives require and generate conditions: they require physical and human resources and they generate the demand to innovate traditional schooling. If those conditions are not met, programs of this sort might become meaningless and even aggravate the segmentation in the existing system for the distribution of knowledge, which – as explained above – rests on the dynamic of systematization of the educational system (the articulation of the system) and on its segmentation (differences in schooling based on social inequality).

Synthesis and Conclusions

> We share the determination to construct quality education for all, where quality education is understood as the set of personal and collective experiences that enable people to develop as individuals and to contribute to the development of their local communities and of humanity. But we

also believe that quality education for all will not be possible on the basis of the educational and pedagogical practices of early modern educational systems. It is hard to believe that educational systems and a pedagogy that contributed so successfully to stratifying societies could contribute to assembling a horizontal network or what could be called the utopia of the creative circle. It seems more likely that they would contribute to stratifying humanity in a different way, on a scale now global rather than national. (Braslavsky 2005, 270)

This chapter has attempted to question the discourse of the right to education from a perspective of the internationalization of schooling. Our vision takes into account the historical and international processes by which central discourses and practices circulate to configure educational systems. We envisioned this process as the materialization of a greater process, mainly the educationalization of social problems. The formulation of the right to education as the right to schooling is a clear manifestation of the triumph of educationalization under the guise of schooling.

Countries characterized by rich cultural diversity – like the ones in Latin America – require the development of alternative modalities in the expansion of schooling. Modern educational systems are, after all, recent inventions whose origin lies in western Europe. The key to their success was the ability to design a device – the school – capable of delivering mass literacy. But the school and schooling both require and generate conditions.

The right to education is a key element because it means that the state must ensure the existence of the educational supply and that this supply must meet certain minimal requirements (availability, accessibility, adequateness, adaptability; Scioscioli 2014). When understood as right to schooling, the right to education means scale, but it also implies that any educational supply is constructed *on the basis of* or *in tension with* the forms of schooling. That does not mean denying that right or those forms; it means, simply, that policies oriented to the expansion of education, like the ones being enacted in Latin America, should be re-examined from this perspective.

ACKNOWLEDGMENTS

We acknowledge the comments provided by the participants at the symposium where this paper was originally presented as well as those of discussant of this paper, Dr Cristian Cox.

NOTES

1 I agree with Tröhler that the conditions for the shift toward the educationalization of the world can be traced to the time period before the second half of the eighteenth century – that is, before the French Revolution – in particular in Protestant circles, which later influenced the Enlightment and the revolutionaries. See his chapter in the present volume.
2 Any human right implies a set of positive or negative services that the state must fulfil. If the state does not fulfil its obligations, protection mechanisms must be established to demand the fulfilment of these obligations. This constitutes the principle of recoverableness, which gives place to protection, allowing the holder of the right to claim against the breach of the state obligation (Clérico 2010).
3 A fourth passage, related to an educationalized world under the guise of internationally assessed education systems, could well serve to describe the present-day situation of schooling. In this paper, I will not refer to this fourth passage, as my historical argument deploys around the process of configuration and expansion of school systems.
4 Differences among these three intellectuals regarding schooling are remarkable. Kant, in *Pedagogía* (On Education) ([1803] 1991) believed that public education, as opposed to private domestic education, would be most advantageous: "Public education seems to be more profitable, in general, than the private one, not only from the point of view of skill, but also for what is refers to as the character of the citizen. It is very frequent that domestic education not only does not correct the lacks of the family but increases them." He asked, "How long should education be?" His response: "Up to the epoch in which the same Nature has decided that man should behave for himself, when the sexual instinct develops in him; when he could manage to be a father and must educate; approximately up to sixteen years. Past this time, it is still possible to use the resources of culture and apply a disguised discipline, but not a regular education" (32, 42; my translation).

John Locke (1631–1704) considered in his *Some Thoughts Concerning Education* ([1693] 1986) that the gentry could learn nothing but bad habits at schools:

> For, as for that boldness and spirit which lads get amongst their playfellows at school, it has ordinarily such a mixture of rudeness and ill-turn'd confidence, that those misbecoming and disingenuous ways of shifting in the world must be unlearnt, and all the tincture wash'd out again, to make way for better principles, and such manners as make a truly worthy man. He that considers how diametrically opposite the skill of living well, and managing, as a man should do, his affairs in the world, is to that mal-pertness, tricking, or violence learnt amongst schoolboys, will think the faults of a privater education infinitely to

be preferr'd to such improvements, and will take care to preserve his child's innocence and modesty at home, as being nearer of kin, and more in the way of those qualities which make an useful and able man. (33)

Jean-Jacques Rousseau (1712–1778) in *Emile, or on Education* ([1762] 1997b) disregarded not only educational institutions – "I do not consider public institutions, those laughable establishments called schools" (4; my translation) – but also the possibility of educating the child outside nature: "In slavery the civil man is born, lives and dies; when born, they sew him in a wrapper; when he dies, they fix him inside a coffin; and while he has human figure, our institutions chain him" (6; my translation). The fact that Rousseau has been highly regarded for *Emile*, rather than for his suggestions with respect to creating national education systems in *Considerations on the Government of Poland* ([1762] 1997a), might indicate this tension between education and schooling during the Enlightenment. On this paradoxical issue in Rousseau, see Soëtard (1994).
5 Indeed, it is possible to find in the reformer Martin Luther one of the first discourses related to the need of extending schools for peasants, inviting the princes to get involved in this task. This invitation was later turned into the first systematic state educational programs in Europe. See Lutero ([1523] 2006).
6 Comenius was considered the creator of modern pedagogy. A Protestant pastor himself, during the seventeenth century he was invited by philanthropists and rulers to develop his ideas on pansophian schools under the ideal of giving whole knowledge to all men. This ideal would be achieved by simultaneous teaching. See Comenio ([1632] 1986).

The Brothers of the Christian Schools were a religious community created by Jean Baptiste de La Salle (1651–1719) in France. La Salle funded a network of free schools for poor children in the main cities of France, competing with other charitable institutions. La Salle adopted the simultaneous model and combined it with disciplining strategies, applying it toward the regulation of voices and bodies in the schoolroom. See La Salle ([1720] 2012).
7 It should be noted that policies of educational inclusion developed during the last decade attempted to break the historical problems of educational segmentation.

REFERENCES

Acosta, F. 2011. "Escuela secundaria y sistemas educativos modernos: Análisis histórico comparado de la dinámica de configuración y expansión en países centrales y en la Argentina." *Revista HISTEDBR* 11 (42): 3–15. https://doi.org/10.20396/rho.v11i42.8639863.

– 2013. *Trabajo analítico (multi país) sobre experiencias de cambio en la escuela secundaria con foco en políticas destinadas a la reinserción y permanencia de los jóvenes en la escuela en América Latina (Cono Sur)*. Informe de consultoría para OEI/EUROsoCIAL.
– 2014."Entre procesos globales y usos locales: Análisis de categorías recientes de la historia de la educación para el estudio de la escuela secundaria en la Argentina." *Revista Espacio, Tiempo y Educación* 1 (2): 23–37. https://doi.org/10.14516/ete.2014.001.002.001.
Braslavsky, C. (1999). *Rehaciendo escuelas: hacia un nuevo paradigma en la educación latinoamericana*. Buenos Aires: Santillana.
– 2005. "La historia de la educación y el desafío contemporáneo de una educación de calidad." In *Pedagogía y Educación ante el siglo XXI*, edited by J. Ruiz Berrio, 269–86. Madrid: Universidad Complutense de Madrid.
Caruso, M., and H. Tenorth. 2011. "Introducción: Conceptualizar e historizar la internacionalización y la globalización en el campo educativo." In *Internacionalización: Políticas educativas y reflexión pedagógica en un medio global*, edited by M. Caruso and H. Tenorh, 13–35. Buenos Aires: Granica.
Clérico, L. 2009. *El examen de proporcionalidad en el derecho constitucional*. Buenos Aires: EUDEBA.
Comenio [Comenius], J.A. (1632) 1986. *Didáctica Magna*. Madrid: Akal.
Green, A. 1990. *Education and State Formation: The Rise of Education Systems in England, France, and the USA*. London: Macmillan.
Kant, E. (1803) 1991. *Pedagogía*. Madrid: Akal.
La Salle, J.B. (1720) 2012. *Guía de las escuelas dividida en tres partes*. Madrid: Biblioteca Nueva.
Locke, J. (1693). "Thoughts Concerning Education." https://thefederalistpapers.org/wp-content/uploads/2012/12/John-Locke-Thoughts-Concerning-Education.pdf.
López, N. 2015. *Las leyes generales de educación en América Latina: El derecho como proyecto político*. Rio de Janeiro: Iniciativa Campaña Latinoamericana por el Derecho a la Educación.
Lutero [Luther], M. (1523) 2006. "A los magistrados de todas las ciudades alemanas, para que construyan y mantengan escuelas cristianas." In *Lutero obras*, edited by T. Egido. Salamanca, ES: Ediciones Sígueme Salamanca.
Mueller, D., F. Ringer, and B. Simon, eds. 1992. *El desarrollo del sistema educativo modern: Cambio estructural y reproducción social 1870–1920*. Madrid: Ministerio de Trabajo y Seguridad.
Ossenbach, G. 1997. "Las transformaciones del Estado y la Educación Pública en América Latina en los siglos XIX y XX." In *Escuela, historia y poder: Miradas desde América Latina*, edited by A. Martínez Boom and M. Narodowski, 121–48. Buenos Aires: Ediciones Novedades Educativas.
Popkewitz, T.S. 2009. *El cosmopolitismo y la era de la reforma escolar*. Madrid: Morata.

Puigróss, A. 1994. *Imaginación y crisis en la educación latinoamericana*. Buenos Aires: Aique.
Rousseau, J.-J. (1762) 1997a. *Consideraciones sobre el gobierno de Polonia*. Madrid: Tecnos.
– (1762) 1997b. *Emilio o de la Educación*. Mexico City: Editorial Porrúa.
Schriewer, J. 2002. "Educación comparada: Un gran programa ante nuevos desafíos." In *Formación del discurso en la educación comparada*, edited by J. Schriewer, 13–40. Barcelona: Pomares-Corredor.
– 2010. "Comparación y explicación entre causalidad y complejidad." In *La comparación en las ciencias sociales e históricas: Un debate interdisciplinar*, edited by J. Schriewer and H. Kaelbe, 17–62. Barcelona: Octaedro/ICE-UB.
Schriewer, J., and K. Harney. 1992. "Los sistemas de educación y su comparabilidad: comentarios metodológicos y alternativas teóricas." In *El desarrollo del sistema educativo moderno: cambio estructural y reproducción social 1870–1920*, edited by D. Mueller, F. Ringer, and B. Simon, 283–300. Madrid: Servicio de Publicaciones.
Scioscioli, S. 2014. "El derecho a la educación como derecho fundamental y sus alcances en el derecho internacional de los derechos humanos." *Journal of Supranational Policies of Education* 2: 6–24. https://doi.org/10.15366/jospoe.
SITEAL. 2010. *Metas educativas 2021: Desafíos y oportunidades*. http://www.siteal.iipe-oei.org/informe/227/informe-2008.
Soëtard, M. 1994. "Jean-Jacques Rousseau." *Perspectivas* 24 (3/4): 435–48.
Steedman, H. 1992. "Instituciones determinantes: Las endowed grammar schools y la sistematización de la educación secundaria inglesa." In *El desarrollo del sistema educativo moderno: Cambio estructural y reproducción social 1870–1920*, edited by D. Mueller, F. Ringer, and B. Simon, 161–94. Madrid: Ministerio de Trabajo y Seguridad.
Tröhler, D. 2013. *Los lenguajes de la educación: Los legados protestantes en la pedagogización del mundo, las identidades nacionales y las aspiraciones globales*. Barcelona: Octaedro.
Tröhler, D., and T. Lenz. 2015. "Trayectoria del desarrollo de la escuela moderna: Entre lo nacional y lo global: Introducción." In *Trayectorias del desarrollo de los sistemas educativos modernos: Entre lo nacional y lo global*, edited by D. Tröhler and T. Lenz, 11–19. Barcelona: Octaedro.
Tröhler, D., T.S. Popkewitz, and D. Labaree. 2011. *Schooling and the Making of Citizens in the Long Nineteenth Century: Comparative Visions*. New York: Routledge.
UNESCO. 2012. *Situación Educativa de América Latina y el Caribe: Hacia una educación para todos 2015*. UNESCO. http://www.orealc.cl/.
Viñao, A. 2002. *Sistemas educativos, culturas escolares y reformas*. Madrid: Morata.

PART IV

Educationalization and Democratic Spaces in the Digital Era

time records movement © Alan R. Wilkinson

11 Educationalization as Technologization

WILLIAM F. PINAR

Modernity depends on education, or so it would seem from Daniel Tröhler's panoramic history of those terms, summarized in the concept of "educationalization."[1] Tröhler chronicles how the concept expanded over time, incorporating the "educationalization of social problems" and, now, "the world" (2016, 3). The educationalization of the world, he emphasizes, is "not limited to solving social problems" but is also "connected to the process of modernization itself, brought about by the modern sciences and the ideas of freedom" (7). These three concepts converge in our time in "technologization," another expansive term, which incorporates product development and the "creative destruction" of culture it encourages, including shifts in subjectivity, politics, and schooling.[2]

The Canadian educator George Grant (1918–1988), who saw these shifts coming, decried them while providing historical contextualization. He saw science as the secularization of Christianity, with its religious-like faith in progress, which was to be achieved through a solely material form of incarnation: technological development.[3] Nowhere is that eschatology resounding louder than in education, wherein the promise of technology has expanded to promise progress in what was once accepted as the human condition. "The design of educational technologies by learning scientists," Williamson (2013, 81) notes, "has been described as a method for 'designing people' through 'engineering' particular forms of learning, actions, and dispositions."[4] Fuelled first by the Cold War[5] and the space race, and now especially by the lure of profits,[6] educationalization has expanded from applications of science in tools, including conceptual tools, into a STEM state of mind.[7]

Like the scientific ambition to produce nomological laws, technology promises to predict – indeed, produce – outcomes. Such predictions can generate collateral damage, Grant knew. "The desire to overcome chance," he observed, "from which modern techniques came forth and which is realized in any technique, involves always the reduction of the different to the same" (Davis and Roper 2009, 87). Yet (paradoxically it might seem) modernity "requires revolution in its primary sense of again and again and again. And recurrence," Grant continued, "is expressed as a mechanical recurrence" (ibid.). Mechanical reproducibility – so associated with Walter Benjamin – intensifies the demand for what is not exactly the same. This is "what is so dear to modernity," Mary Ann Doane (2002, 100) points out: "the possibility of the new, novelty, the continual difference and variation that constitutes the sensory basis of the modern."[8] Not only the sensory basis, I suggest, but also modernity's state of mind turns on the promise of "the new."

The "new" conception of the student – now no longer a human subject or a person, with the subjective coherence and continuity those terms imply[9] – is a variable element of "big data," information for manipulation so that learning can be assured, learning as quantified outcomes – that is, outcomes that mask what is in fact being learned: subjection to technology. Teachers and textbooks are replaced by curriculum online; school buildings disappear as students stare at screens anywhere they like (or are forced to be). Demoted to entrepreneurs in the "gig" economy, teachers become self-employed monitors of technological learning. Community comes to connote association of the same, not the inclusion of difference. Fused with the screens at which s/he stares, the human subject conforms to patterns of interaction permitted by the software that operates these screens. Diversity disappears as everyone becomes a technician, no longer a public servant but now a domestic one.

Privatization

Privatization is well underway in the United States, as Silicon Valley worms its way into the nation's public schools. A recent review by Natasha Singer – on the front page of the *New York Times* – provides a glimpse. In San Francisco's public schools, Marc Benioff, the chief executive of Salesforce, is offering middle school principals $100,000 "innovation grants" to encourage them to act like start-up entrepreneurs (not professional educators). In Maryland, Texas, Virginia, and other states, Netflix's chief, Reed Hastings, is promoting a math-teaching program in which Netflix-like algorithms determine which lessons students see. In more than a hundred schools nationwide, Mark Zuckerberg, Facebook's chief, is promoting software that supposedly positions children to direct their own learning, repositioning teachers as facilitators and, perhaps, mentors. Singer (2017, A1) concludes: "Technology giants have begun remaking the very nature of schooling on a vast scale ... Through their philanthropy, they are influencing the subjects that schools teach, the classroom tools that teachers choose and fundamental approaches to learning." There have been, Singer observes, "few checks and balances" (A14). A professor of public policy at the University of Michigan – Megan Tompkins-Stange – told the *Times* that tech executives and their companies "have the power to change policy, but no corresponding check on that power. It does subvert the democratic process" (ibid.).

All the hype may not help children learn the school subjects, but, in any case, US tech companies want to revise those subjects. Financed with more than $60 million from Silicon Valley companies, Code.org, a major non-profit group, intends to persuade every public school in the United States to emphasize computer science in the curriculum. Together with Microsoft and other partners, Code.org has lobbied across the country, pressuring states to rewrite education laws and require the funding of computer science courses. Code.org has persuaded more than 120 school districts to introduce such curriculum and has trained more than 57,000 teachers. Code.org's free coding programs, called Hour of Code, have enrolled more than 100 million students worldwide.

Unlike earlier philanthropic gifts to education, these "gifts" are entirely self-promoting. To ensure success, Singer reports, tech executives are tackling "every step of the education supply chain by financing campaigns to alter policy, building learning apps to advance their aims and subsidizing teacher training" (2017, A14). This "end-to-end" influence represents an "almost monopolistic approach [to] education reform," observed Larry Cuban, professor emeritus of education at Stanford University. "That is starkly different from earlier generations of philanthropists" (quoted in ibid.). These efforts complement – indeed are aggressively in the service of – a larger Silicon Valley campaign to sell computers and software to US schools, a market projected to reach $21 billion by 2020 (ibid.).

Place

If only technologization proceeds fast and far enough, advocates believe, students will learn whatever we teach them. Social problems will be solved; the economy will soar. Secular salvation is assured, if only we tithe technology. Grant ([1965] 2005, 52) emphasized that such a "universal" and "egalitarian" society would indeed represent the teleology of "historical striving."[10] Such a society – "a very tough, tight, twilight society," he lamented (Davis and Roper 2005, 597) – would be installed via "modern science," by enabling the "conquest of nature," especially human nature (Grant [1965] 2005, 52).[11] Where is the epicentre of this accelerating event? It is "particularly" in the United States, Grant argued, that "scientists concern themselves with the control of heredity, the human mind, and society" (ibid.). Yet Tröhler shows that "educationalization" is not confined to the United States: it is now worldwide.[12]

Modernity comes in multiple forms.[13] In the United States, Grant argued, individualism, capitalism, and technology fused with the nation's faith in its divinely inspired exceptionality, producing a volatile, at times, explosive, mix of economics, politics, and culture. Canada's destiny was to be different from the United States, Grant reminded us. Canada was intended to be a society more "ordered" and "caring," decidedly "less violent" (Emberley [1994] 2005, lxxx). Technology enforces its own intentionality, however, one that incorporates the manifest destinies of nations and their inhabitants through its totalizing tendencies. Therein lie the progressive dreams and apocalyptic nightmares of modernity: universality as conformity, equality as "sameness" (lxxxi). Efficiency, technology's "driving principle," Emberley concludes, effaces "local differences, particular loyalties, and credible resistances" (lxxxii). Whether nations, or cultures or classes within nations or across borders, "differences" are what disappear in modernity. Consumers replace citizens;[14] the economy replaces culture.[15]

Grant acknowledged the achievements of modernity[16], but, he added, "as soon as that is said, facts about our age must also be remembered: the increasing outbreaks of impersonal ferocity, the banality of existence in technological societies, the pursuit of expansion as an end in itself" (Grant [1965] 2005, 92). Modernity means the concentration of economic powers in multinational entities, corporations that enforce "creativity" as the "bottom line" assures homogeneity.[17] Such is the "fate," Grant warns, of "any particularity" in the technological era (Grant [1970] 2005, lxxii). Canada, he announced, "has ceased to be a nation" ([1965] 2005, 85).

Pain

The nation and the shared memory of its peoples disappear, but the state – in service to the economy – remains. Affluence, we are told unceasingly, depends on ongoing technological advancement, and that advancement, Grant noted, "develops within a state capitalist framework" (1969, 74). He worried that the "wealthy" of Canada would abandon their "nationalism" should it conflict with their "economic" interests" (Grant [1965] 2005, 14). The wealthy are not the only culpable ones: Grant allowed that "many" North Americans know no "ideology" but one: "affluence" (1969, 74).

The ideology of affluence reproduces itself not only through the promise of profit and pleasure but also through its corollaries: pain and deprivation. It is, Grant advised (1969, 141), "only" by attuning ourselves to "deprival" that we can "live critically" in the "dynamo." That "dynamo" is not only the constant change technology stimulates, but also its concomitants, among them manufactured fears that reactionary politicians propagate. I am thinking of the US presidential administrations of George W. Bush and Donald J. Trump, but the phenomenon in that country is long-standing (Hofstadter [1965] 1996).

With the selection of Betsy DeVos as US secretary of education, the manufactured school crisis now is to be "solved" by consumer choice, as DeVos pressures for public funding of private schools (Berliner and Biddle 1995; Green 2017),[18] a sector in which she and her family have significant financial investments (Cohen 2017, A1; Fink, Eder, and Goldstein 2017, A1). After studying the impact of DeVos's political lobbying in Michigan, David E. Kirkland, an education professor at New York University, warned that she will "badly hurt public education" by removing resources from public schools (quoted in Huetteman and Alcindor 2017, A20).[19] "Her extensive conflicts of interest and record of diverting money away from vulnerable students and into the pockets of the rich make DeVos completely unfit for the position," Kirkland said (ibid.).

"People have sometimes taken National Socialism in Germany as an aberration," George Grant appreciated, "and it certainly was in detail, but as a way of thought it was also something more universal" (Cayley 1995, 149–50).[20] When ideology (for Grant, it is a "surrogate" religion) triumphs, idols – the state, race, the nation – replace icons (Davis and Roper 2009, 185).[21] Ideologues destroy "common sense and moderation," he knew, "the two great protectors of the health of the public realm" (ibid.). Grant cautioned: "English-speaking people are well advised to remember the German experience. The Germans were the first to build universities in which 'objective' science and scholarship was exalted above all questions of the good" (ibid.).[22] Instead of the eternal – Grant was a progressive Christian Platonist[23] – we are left with "only the moving image, and our experience as listeners and as readers, and indeed as living human beings," and that "is grounded in temporal sequence" (464). The ignorant past is superseded by the technological future, fuelled by science and mathematics, implemented by engineering.

Practicality

A STEM state of mind institutionalizes ignorance. "The fact [is] that our ruling classes have become technicized," Grant lamented, "and our universities have largely excluded from the curriculum the serious study of the most important questions" (Davis and Roper 2009, 185–6). Grant worried that "the reading of the morning newspaper has taken the place of the morning prayer" (ibid., 181), a ritual replaced today by staring at social media. Grant's point remains: "At the beginning of the day when we need to pay attention to what is necessary to our good we turn that attention to reading about public events, not to the eternal" (ibid.). One can only hope that public (and private) events can provide portals to eternal topics.[24]

Grant saw that modernity's demand for nomological knowledge was not confined to the social sciences, imperfect copies of natural science as they are. Philosophy – specifically its Anglo-American versions in which logic, not experience, governs – and the humanities more generally have become dominated by modernity's demand for "objectivity."[25] The concept of "research" began to replace the more traditional notion of "scholarship," Grant noticed (1986, 37), the latter concept implying that the scholar's undertaking was a calling not a contract job. In contrast to the researcher – with that concept's expectation of new discoveries and solutions to social problems – the scholar sought truth. Demands for methodological uniformity – limiting the search to what was observable and, often, measurable – undermined as it quantified that aspiration. As the sacred calling of study fell silent, the name remained, as if on a tombstone. In research, there are objects to be investigated, outcomes to be reported. In the humanities, Grant pointed out, that "object" became "the past" (ibid.).

One point of a cosmopolitan curriculum is not to reduce the past to the polemics of the present.[26] For Grant, the danger seemed in the opposite direction: objectivity froze the fluidity of the past by conceiving it scientifically, as if someone here and now could, spectator-like, apprehend the dynamics of then and there. For Grant, it was the distinctiveness of the past that could communicate its present significance. When the past became an "object," however, its meaning was muted. Both the dead and the living became entombed in the temporally empty present.

Instead of the past speaking to us in the present, research requires, Grant complained, that its protocols provide us with practical information, techniques that equip us to profit from what we learn. The intensifying emphasis on vocationalism commands students and faculty alike to accent the practical point of what is studied. Not only in the

United States have university students "flooded into computer science courses," training to take "coveted jobs" at companies like Apple, Google, and Microsoft, perhaps even starting their own companies that could become worth millions (Bidgood and Merrill 2017, A1).[27]

With the prospect of profit, questions of meaning and significance become secondary, sometimes even suspicious. In January 2016, for instance, the governor of the state of Kentucky, Matt Bevin, asserted that students majoring in French literature should not receive state funding for their college education. A 2016 Republican presidential candidate, Senator Marco Rubio of Florida, called for more welders and fewer philosophers. Governor Rick Scott of Florida criticized anthropologists, and Governor Patrick McCrory of North Carolina belittled gender studies (Cohen 2016, B1, B3).

Grant would not have been surprised, as universities had in his lifetime devolved into "corporations for organizing the technical society" (Davis and Roper 2009, 156), declining to educate the public toward truth but instead "teaching young people techniques by which they can do things in the world" (Grant [1959] 1966, 38). Absent, he observed, is "concern in our educational system with seeing that our young people think deeply about the purposes for which these techniques should be used" (ibid.). Today, cognitive science threatens to reduce education to neurology and pharmacology.[28]

Rationalizing questionable behaviour as an acceptable means to whatever ends "freedom" allows, Grant alleged, amounted to "personal power combined with social engineering" (Grant [1959] 1966, 87). Constant craving in search of satiation, such "activism" casts its counter-disciplines – Grant lists daydreaming, sensuality, art, prayer, theoretical science, and philosophy – as "leisure," endeavours that do not "directly" produce measurable outcomes (ibid.).[29] "Non-manipulative" and with "joy" and "adoration" as their "ends" – not "power" and "control" – these evidently antiquated disciplines had become entirely optional. "Our practicality has made us uninterested in systematic thought," Grant ruefully observed. A "common moral language is seldom systematized" (ibid., 88)

A common faith was among John Dewey's ([1934] 1962) projects, but Grant only complains about the American philosopher. "Pragmatism has had such a pervasive influence in our schools," Grant thought, "because it ... was implicit in our way of life" (Grant [1959] 1966, 89).[30] While there are also Canadian versions of US progressivism (Tomkins 1986, 106; Christou 2012), the referent for Grant's use of "our" seems the United States, as the "spirit" of democracy, pioneering, and science converged in educational theory the Puritans[31] and later immigrants devised to produce what Grant summarizes as "egalitarian technologism" (Grant [1959] 1966, 84).[32] Determined to find freedom in the land they took from Indigenous peoples, colonists were willing to destroy not only what was there but also what they had brought from Europe, indeed anything that "limited" a presumably "open society" (85).[33] "In the field of education," Grant concluded, "the decisive victory of the technical over the older studies has allowed .... success to consist of purely technical skills: engineering, commerce, etc." (ibid.).[34]

Confirming and updating Grant's analysis, LaCapra (2004, 203–4) points out that the university is now managed like a "corporation," that it has devolved into a "complement of private-sector business enterprises," with "knowledge" reduced to "information," wherein "information technology is dominant." This trend is evident from "the primacy of the 'hard' sciences to the restructuring and 'digitalization' of the library," where substantial funds are devoted to "continual technical 'upgrades' of systems that far exceed (or even counter) the needs of those who use libraries most, the humanists." Once the core disciplines of the university, the humanities are no longer stems but ornaments.

Conclusion

Educationalization as technologization secularizes the salvational structure of Western culture, promising solutions to social and well as psychic problems, every problem now ultimately an economic one. Such technologization recodes students – and teachers – as, in Williamson's words, "inner-focused individuals whose own self-responsibility, competence, and well-being – their deep inner soul, interior life, and habits of mind – have been fused to the political objective of economic innovation" (2013, 83). Teachers must personify a "total pedagogy," downloading into their students and themselves "a continuous disposition to be trained" (96). The curriculum is no longer an ongoing ethical question – what knowledge is of most worth? – but whatever software designers deem saleable, "learning activities" now redesigned as "consumer goods" (97).

Can reactivation of the past[35] – not only of lost good but of nightmares under threat of being forgotten – encourage non-coincidence with what is to enable educational experience of the present as well as intimations of that to which one might become attuned, to what Grant termed "the Good"? Recall that Grant thought that "only" by attuning ourselves to "deprival" that we can "live critically" in the "dynamo" (1969, 141). Deprival drives efforts at not only physical but also psychic and spiritual survival – no knee-jerk reactivity but prolonged study in the service of subjective reconstruction (Ruitenberg 2017). What Grant is advising,

O'Donovan notes (1984, 104), is most fundamentally *"to think* our deprival." For Grant, she explains, *"recollecting* the good and *thinking* our deprival are one" (129). Such reactivation might provide passage to the past, "becoming historical"[36] in this temporally empty moment of (de)vice, stuck in the screens at which we stare. For George Grant, educationalization requires not technologization but spiritualization.

NOTES

1 Tröhler (2016, 4) starts in France in the court of King Louis XIV at Versailles, where occurred the "quarrel of the Ancients and the Moderns." He ends with educational interventions of the OECD and World Bank (8).
2 Few theorize these shifts as chillingly as Ben Williamson (2013). "In the projects that constitute the curriculum of the future," he summarizes, "new identities are being sculpted and 'prototyped'" (103). As passages I will quote will make clear, concern for the child or for the citizen is replaced by commands for profit-making "creativity."
3 Grant finds that the very idea of time as history derives from the Bible, telling David Cayley (1995, 117):

> Here were these people chosen by God and [they] went into the wilderness, and then into exile, and are going to come back to Jerusalem – God as a great and immediate purpose for these people. Then Christianity comes into [being] and says that this purpose has been realized in Christ. I think this is the origin of the idea in the West, though the word history is Greek. The modern West seems to me to be taking this biblical vision and secularizing it – that is, eliminating God from it. So history, as Rousseau formulates it, becomes the idea that man comes to be by accident, but then it is his purpose to realize a rational society here on earth. That rational society is scientific society, technologically structured.

4 Forgotten, Grant observed, is that "the central truth of Western ethical teaching has been that no human being should be treated simply as a means – but also as an end" (Davis and Roper 2005, 128).
5 "The U.S. educationalized the Cold War by passing National Defense Education Act," Tröhler (2016, 2) asserts. Such "educationalization" accomplished the deflection of political responsibility for the Sputnik event. America's schoolteachers – not the military or scientific establishment – were to blame. Eisenhower associated national defence with education, initiating what would become the scapegoating of US teachers and an intensifying politicization of so-called educational reform.

6 This is hardly the first time that profits have been the motivation, as Tröhler (2016, 4) suggests that the second transformation in the perception of history and development had to do with "the relation of money to politics, which changed at the end of the seventeenth century at first in England."
7 The "technologizing of thought," as Grant phrased the matter (Davis and Roper 2005, 614). The grammar of capitalism, technology can be "transmitted to the inner life of individuals through a kind of rhythmic patterning" (not unlike economic values, as Marshall McLuhan noted (Stamps 1995, 112)).
8 Here Doane is discussing the concept of scandal in the work of Charles Sanders Peirce.
9 For a history, see Martin and Barresi (2006).
10 "Grant also sees the establishment of the universal and homogeneous state in theological terms," Sibley (2006, 102) notes, "recognizing that it necessitated the de-divinization of the 'Other' that is God."
11 "We see," Grant complained, "that freedom has only brought us enslavement by science. And enslavement by scientists is surely even more dangerous than enslavement by prelates" (Davis 2002, 31). Why might he say that? Science led to "modern medicine," Grant acknowledged, but it also threatens "modern nuclear war" (Davis and Roper 2009, 539). Now global warming threatens the biosphere.
12 See Spring 2012 for an overview of the situation in the United States; for China, see Qian 2015.
13 "There is no such thing as modernity in general," Herf (1984, 1) concludes from his study of the Weimar Republic: "There are only national societies, each of which becomes modern in its own fashion."
14 "Democratic citizenship," Grant asserted, "is not a notion compatible with technological empires" (Christian and Grant 1998, 85).
15 In this revelation, Grant was not alone. Pier Paolo Pasolini believed that consumer capitalism meant "cultural genocide" (Mariniello 1994, 115, 125).
16 "While in the past it was natural necessity that enslaved human beings," Athanasiadis (2001, 124) observes, "today it is technological necessity."
17 "Affective labour and creativity in the digital economy displace faceless bureaucracies with a caring and sharing capitalism, or business with personality," Williamson (2013, 50) writes. "In this 'creativity explosion' business culture values creativity over routine, and education seeks to promote in children the creativity required for nonlinear thinking and generating new ideas."
18 As they have so often in the United States, capitalism and Christianity (at least conservative versions of it) merge. At a 2001 gathering of conservative Christian philanthropists, Betsy DeVos singled out education reform as a way to "advance God's kingdom" (Stewart 2016, A31). In an

interview, she and her husband, Richard DeVos, Jr, said that school choice would lead to "greater kingdom gain."

19 As one of the architects of Detroit's unregulated charter school system, DeVos is implicated in what "even charter advocates acknowledge is the biggest school reform disaster in the country" (Harris 2016, A21).

20 That "something," Grant suggested, was a "lower form of society even than contractarian capitalism" (Cayley 1995, 150).

21 Re "surrogate" religion, see Davis and Roper (2009, 185). Grant admired Eastern Christianity's embrace of mysticism and rationality, evident in the role of icons in worship. "The Western church fundamentally chose Aristotle; the Eastern church fundamentally chose Plato," Grant told Cayley (1995, 77), adding: "As far as my own thought goes, I have fundamentally chosen Plato." In July 1988 – in conversation with William Christian two months before his death – Grant reaffirmed his allegiance: "I'm on the Eastern Church's side, because it's essentially Platonic against the Aristotelian" (Davis and Roper 2009, 743).

22 Grant reflected: "The Germans [now] have the great advantage over us of already having faced the political incarnation of the triumph of the will" (Christian and Grant 1998, 149).

23 "Grant was raised a progressive," Davis (2006, 63) reminds us, "and became a Christian Platonist." I am suggesting that he remained a progressive while espousing Christianity and Platonism, embracing the latter due to his sense of what was at stake historically and, more specifically, politically. A "critical historical understanding," Angus (2006, 358) appreciates, "underlies Grant's non-progressive and anti-technological Christianity."

24 For example, the curriculum could be organized (in part) as allegories of the present: after the 2010 mid-term elections in the United States, studying the Weimar Republic seemed to me a suitable concept of US curriculum design.

25 Grant tells Cayley (1995, 164) that even "studies of literature are more and more technological." On another occasion Grant names Northrop Frye as complicitous (see Davis and Roper 2009, 987).

26 In April 2016, Princeton University announced that it would keep US president Woodrow Wilson's name on its school of public and international affairs and a residential college despite calls to expunge his name from those institutions due to his support of racial segregation (Anderson 2016, A5). Absent abrasive reminders, will not the past be bleached from the present? Of course, Confederate monuments are more than abrasive; they have become testimonies to white supremacy and neo-Nazism in the United States and must be moved to museums.

27 The "exploding interest in these courses," Bidgood and Merrill (2017, A1) report, has resulted in sky-rocketing rates of high-tech plagiarism. "There's a lot of discussion about it, both inside a department as well as

across the field," admitted Randy H. Katz, a professor in the electrical engineering and computer science department at the University of California, Berkeley; Katz discovered that 100 of his roughly 700 students had violated the course policy on collaborating or copying code.

28 The so-called learning sciences, Taubman (2009, 160) points out, have "provided the switch point or transfer points that allowed the discourses and practices associated with the business world to enter education." One example is the rapid rise in use of medications for "learning" problems, a development that has prompted criticism that pharmaceutical firms, pursuing profits in an $11 billion international market for ADHD drugs alone, are driving the global increase in diagnoses. In 2007, for instance, countries outside the United States accounted for only 17 per cent of the world use of Ritalin; by 2012, that number had grown to 34 per cent (Ellison 2015, D6).

29 In the curriculum of the future, Williamson (2013, 52) sees everything incorporated into the economic: "The merging of play and work has resulted in 'playbor,' a neologism that accurately captures the ways in which the affective elements of play have now been emerged into the value-making tasks of the economy." As a result, "commercial activities may now shape the structure of the school day, influence the content of the school curriculum, and determine whether children have access to a variety of technologies" (53).

30 Kinzel (2009, 11) points out that "Grant did not treat pragmatism as a philosophy in its own right but only with reference to a particular historical situation."

31 Among the references one might consult is McKnight 2003.

32 Quoting Grant, O'Donovan (1984, 46) comments, "American 'egalitarian technologism' is the extreme historical development of Calvinist Puritanism with its 'theology of revelation' that discouraged contemplation and exalted Christian freedom in its practical expression."

33 Open to exploit others economically, of course, fraying any moral fabric the colonists might have brought with them.

34 "Technological society requires an enormous number of highly specialized people," Grant tells Cayley (1995, 163), "and the multiversity is to a very great extent a product of that, is it not? It produces all kinds of specialists to serve the technological society."

35 For Grant, Christian (1990, 194–5) clarifies, recollection is not psychoanalytic (as it is for me, hence the term "reactivation"), but Platonic, recalling the ancient myth that "all souls, before they were embodied, had knowledge of the eternal and transcendent reality, but just prior to embodiment they were washed in the river Lethe, or Forgetfulness. The knowledge which they enjoy in this world, then, is the consequence of recollecting what has once been known and then subsequently forgotten." For Grant,

O'Donovan (1984, 73) acknowledges, "the restoration of past thought [w]as a theoretical possibility." It exists, after all, in the present, still.

36 "Becoming historical," Toews (2008, 438) explains (discussing Kierkegaard and Marx), "involved a historical reconstruction of the current forms of self-identification ... as a specific product of human practices in time. The goal was to experience the self that was simply given as a self that was historically particular and contingent." As particular and contingent, the self was not only determined by circumstances but was capable of changing them, in the present context through renegotiation and repair.

REFERENCES

Anderson, Nick. 2016. "Princeton Keeps Wilson's Name on 2 Institutions." *Washington Post*, 5 April, A5.

Angus, Ian. 2006. "Socrates' Joke." In *Athens and Jerusalem: George Grant's Theology, Philosophy, and Politics*, edited by Ian Angus, Ron Dart, and Randy Peg Peters, 341–68. Toronto: University of Toronto Press.

Athanasiadis, Harris. 2001. *George Grant and Theology of the Cross: The Christian Foundations of His Thought*. Toronto: University of Toronto Press.

Berliner, David C., and Bruce J. Biddle. 1995. *The Manufactured Crisis: Myths, Fraud, and the Attack on America's Public Schools*. Cambridge, MA: Perseus.

Bidgood, Jess, and Jeremy B. Merrill. 2017. "A College Scourge of Plagiarized Language, This Time in Code." *New York Times*, 30 May, A1, A13.

Cayley, David. 1995. *George Grant in Conversation*. Toronto: House of Anansi Press.

Christian, William. 1990. "The Magic of Art." In *By Loving Our Own: George Grant and the Legacy of Lament for a Nation*, edited by Peter C. Emberley, 189–202. Ottawa: Carleton University Press.

Christian, William, and Sheila Grant, eds. 1998. *The George Grant Reader*. Toronto: University of Toronto Press.

Christou, Theodore Michael. 2012. *Progressive Education: Revisioning and Reframing Ontario's Public Schools, 1919–1942*. Toronto: University of Toronto Press.

Cohen, Patricia. 2016. "A Rising Call to Foster STEM Fields, and Decrease Liberal Arts Funding." *New York Times*, 22 February, B1, B3.

Cohen, Patricia. 2017. "New Optimism in Education's Profit Industry." *New York Times*, 21 February, A1, A18.

Davis, Arthur, ed. 2002. *Collected Works of George Grant*. Vol. 2. *1951–1959*. Toronto: University of Toronto Press.

– 2006. "Did George Grant Change His Politics?" In *Athens and Jerusalem: George Grant's Theology, Philosophy, and Politics*, edited by Ian Angus, Ron Dart, and Randy Peg Peters, 62–79. Toronto: University of Toronto Press.

Davis, Arthur, and Henry Roper, eds. 2005. *Collected Works of George Grant*. Vol. 3. *1960–1969*. Toronto: University of Toronto Press.

– 2009. *Collected Works of George Grant*. Vol. 4. *1970–1988*. Toronto: University of Toronto Press.

Dewey, John. (1934) 1962. *A Common Faith*. New Haven, CT: Yale University Press.

Doane, Mary Ann. 2002. *The Emergence of Cinematic Time: Modernity, Contingency, the Archive*. Cambridge, MA: Harvard University Press.

Ellison, Katherine. 2015. "A.D.H.D. Rises, But Support Lags." *New York Times*, 10 November, D6.

Emberley, Peter C. (1994) 2005. Foreword to the Carleton Library Edition of *Lament for a Nation* by George Grant, lxxviii–lxxxv. Montreal and Kingston: McGill-Queen's University Press.

Fink, Sheryl, Steve Eder, and Matthew Goldstein. 2017, "Weak Support for Treatment Tied to DeVos." *New York Times*, 31 January, A1, A21.

Grant, George. (1959) 1966. *Philosophy in the Mass Age*. Toronto: Copp Clark.

– (1965) 2005. *Lament for a Nation*. 40th anniversary ed. Montreal and Kingston: McGill-Queen's University Press.

– 1969. *Technology and Empire*. Toronto: Anansi.

– (1970) 2005. "Introduction." *Lament for a Nation*, Carleton Library Edition, lxix–lxxvi. Montreal and Kingston: McGill-Queen's University Press.

– 1986. *Technology and Justice*. Toronto: Anansi.

Green, Erica L. 2017. "Saying Money Isn't the Answer, DeVos Calls for More School Choice." *New York Times*, 30 March, A16.

Harris, Douglas N. 2016. "The Wrong Way to Fix Schools." *New York Times*, 28 November, A21.

Herf, Jeffrey. 1984. *Reactionary Modernism: Technology, Culture, and Politics in Weimar and the Third Reich*. Cambridge: Cambridge University Press.

Hofstadter, Richard. (1965) 1996. *The Paranoid Style in American Politics and Other Essays*. Cambridge, MA: Harvard University Press.

Huetteman, Emmarie, and Yamiche Alcindor. 2017. "DeVos Confirmed for Education by Pence's Vote." *New York Times*, 8 February, A1, A20.

Kingsley, Patrick. 2017. "With Thousands Purged, Chaotic Turkey Struggles to Fill Void." *New York Times*, 13 April, A1, A7.

Kinzel, Till. 2009. "Metaphysics, Politics, and Philosophy: George Grant's Response to Pragmatism." *Cultura: International Journal of Philosophy of Culture and Axiology* 6 (1): 7–21. https://doi.org/10.5840/cultura20096115.

LaCapra, Dominick. 2004. *History in Transit: Experience, Identity, Critical Theory*. Ithaca, NY: Cornell University Press.

Mariniello, Silvestra. 1994. "Toward a Materialist Linguistics: Pasolini's Theory of Language." In *Pier Paolo Pasolini: Contemporary Perspectives*, edited by Patrick Rumble and Bart Testa, 106–26. Toronto: University of Toronto Press.

Martin, Raymond, and John Barresi. 2006. *The Rise and Fall of Soul and Self: An Intellectual History of Personal Identity*. New York: Columbia University Press.

McKnight, E. Douglas. 2003. *Schooling, the Puritan Imperative, and the Molding of an American National Identity: Education's "Errand into the Wilderness."* Mahwah, NJ: Lawrence Erlbaum.

O'Donovan, Joan. 1984. *George Grant and the Twilight of Justice*. Toronto: University of Toronto Press.

Qian, Xuyang. 2015. "Technologizing Teachers Development?" In *Autobiography and Teacher Development in China: Subjectivity and Culture in Curriculum Reform*, edited by Zhang Hua and William F. Pinar, 163–78. New York: Palgrave Macmillan.

Ruitenberg, Claudia W., ed. 2017. *Reconceptualizing Study in Educational Discourse and Practice*. New York: Routledge.

Sibley, Robert C. 2006. "Grant, Hegel, and the 'Impossibility of Canada.'" In *Athens and Jerusalem: George Grant's Theology, Philosophy, and Politics*, edited by Ian Angus, Ron Dart, and Randy Peg Peters, 93–107. Toronto: University of Toronto Press.

Singer, Natasha. 2017. "Tech Billionaires Reinvent Schools, with Students as Beta Testers." *New York Times*, 7 June, A1, A14.

Spring, Joel. 2012. *Education Networks: Power, Wealth, Cyberspace, and the Digital Mind*. New York: Routledge.

Stamps, Judith. 1995. *Unthinking Modernity: Innis, McLuhan, and the Frankfurt School*. Montreal and Kingston: McGill-Queen's University Press.

Stewart, Katherine. 2016. "DeVos and God's Plan for Schools." *New York Times*, 13 December, A12, A31.

Taubman, Peter M. 2009. *Teaching by Numbers: Deconstructing the Discourse of Standards and Accountability in Education*. New York: Routledge.

Toews, John. 2008. *Becoming Historical: Cultural Reformation and Public Memory in Early Nineteenth-Century Berlin*. New York: Cambridge University Press.

Tomkins, George S. 1986. *A Common Countenance: Stability and Change in the Canadian Curriculum*. Scarborough, ON: Prentice-Hall.

Tröhler, Daniel. 2016. "Educationalization of Social Problems and the Educationalization of the Modern World." In *Encyclopedia of Educational Philosophy and Theory*, edited by Michael A. Peters, 1–10. Singapore: Springer.

Williamson, Ben. 2013. *The Future of the Curriculum: School Knowledge in the Digital Age*. Cambridge, MA: MIT Press.

12 Countering Patterns of Educationalization: Creating Digital Tools for Critical Evidence-Based Thinking

ANA JOFRE

> You have not discovered a potion for remembering, but for reminding; you provide your students with the appearance of wisdom, not with its reality. Your invention will enable them to hear many things without being properly taught, and they will imagine that they have come to know much while for the most part they will know nothing. And they will be difficult to get along with, since they will merely appear to be wise instead of really being so.
> – Socrates on the forgetfulness that comes with writing, from Plato, *Phaedrus*

This chapter appears within the context of a collection on educationalization, a concept that describes the modern trend that places social issues of various sorts under the domain of education. Daniel Tröhler posits that educationalization emerged as a feature of modernity. As a response to the excesses of capitalism, educationalization reconciles the republican ideal of the selfless citizen (a modern notion) with the anarchic forces and avarice of modern industrial capitalism by using the educational system to instil pupils with the values and principles needed for good citizenry. Contemporary critics of educationalization, such as David Labaree, have pointed out the inefficacy of this approach, noting that the social problems educationalization aims to fix remain unresolved while the pressure on the educational system to address these problems is, at the very least, unabated (Labaree 2008).

I am coming from a perspective shared with Josh Cole, who has contributed an account and analysis of the Antigonish movement in Nova Scotia to this volume. This chapter shares his interests in education beyond regular schooling (including adult education, also known as andragogy), in "education that is not an educationalization," and in "schools with no walls" that blur the distinction between "school" and "society." While the concept of educationalization was built by and large with institutions of learning in mind, andragogy can address causes of social concern through grassroots movements, through discourse in the public sphere. I share the notion, theorized by Jürgen Habermas, that learning does not stop after an arbitrary age when formal education is no longer enforced by society, and that, instead, it is "not-learning" that is un-natural (Habermas 1975). The andragogy at Antigonish exemplified a hierarchy-free grassroots learning community driven by a shared conception of the common good. This is not an isolated example: there were grassroots experiences in Latin America with a similar counter-discourse, with the best-known examples being the Movement of Basic Education (Movimento de Educação de Base) in Brazil (see, for example, Adriance 1985) and the methodology developed by Paulo Freire in those grassroots literacy projects (Freire 2000). While Antigonish was facilitated by the twentieth-century technology of public radio, here I explore ways in which digital technology can facilitate learning within the public sphere in the twenty-first century. Digital technology, the internet in particular, offers the promise of a wider audience for public education campaigns and more opportunities to build learning communities. In this chapter, I contribute to the question of how to use digital technology for pedagogy, with a particular interest in andragogy and learning in the public sphere.

I am particularly interested in creating tools that support and stimulate critical evidence-based thinking, with a specific focus on understanding data. While questions of open access to data have been widely debated throughout academia in recent years (Laakso et al. 2011), these discussions have not sufficiently addressed how to make data meaningfully accessible to the general public. Knowing how to interpret data amounts to understanding how to weigh evidence. Therefore, in an approach to education that counters educationalization, citizen education must include learning to interpret, understand, and critique data. In our information age, the average citizen faces a deluge of data on a daily basis. While digital technology can be blamed for this information overload, my approach is to instead ask: how can we use our digital tools to help citizens sift through and make meaning of this deluge of data?

The advent of every major new technology seems to bring scepticism about how it will impact education. The famous quote by Socrates about the technology of writing, reproduced above, can be easily placed within today's discussions about digital technology and the internet. The world wide web, in particular, has an unprecedented ability to disseminate information, but there are doubts about the extent to which the information turns into knowledge. On the one hand, the world wide web increases the public's access to continuing education; on the other, this type of accessibility often does not extend beyond a simple exposure to information. Simply exposing the public to information is not enough to make it accessible. Information can be presented in unintelligible ways, such as when it is dispersed across many sites, or in open data repositories; it can be presented in misleading ways, such as in the cases of deceptive visualizations (Pandey et al. 2015; "Misleading Data Visualization Examples" 2015) or in the recent phenomena of fake news (Allcott and Gentzkow 2017); or it can simply fail to engage the learner, such as in the case of many massive open online courses (MOOC) whose dropout rates are high ("Dropout Rates of Massive Open Online Courses" 2017) and whose enrolment tends to favour those who already have access to higher education (Hansen and Reich 2015). To achieve real accessibility, the public must also be given the tools by which to engage with, understand, and make meaning of the information.

I address here ways in which such accessibility can be accomplished, and provide examples from my art and design practice that aim to achieve this goal. In particular, I focus on data visualization techniques, with attention to interactivity, specifically an interactivity that allows the user to see the data from multiple perspectives. Interactive data visualizations can communicate data in an accessible manner, because visualizations tap into the brain's pre-attentive processing powers to elucidate trends and patterns in the phenomena that the data represent. Cognition and analysis may be strengthened even more through embodied interaction with data, and so I also consider ways in which to integrate tactile experiences into data exploration. The use of tactile three-dimensional objects could facilitate understanding of abstract concepts, augment user engagement, and foster collaboration. I also consider the importance of creating software that is not proprietary and amenable to modifications, allowing users to tailor it to their needs.

I present here two examples of my work, whose aim is to increase accessibility to and understanding of information. In one example, I examine the entire *Time* magazine corpus and consider how to communicate the insights that such an archive can provide about American cultural history. Using computer vision techniques, our team extracted and analysed images from the corpus to present another layer of accessibility to the public, one that reveals historical trends and provides understandings that cannot be achieved by browsing through individual issues. In another example, our team created software that allows users to explore a data visualization by manipulating graspable table-top objects. The objective of the software is to provide users with alternative ways to interact with data.

Data Visualization as a Means for Data Accessibility

Graphical representation, or visualization, is recognized as an effective means for communicating data, particularly complex data, since visualization leverages our perceptual cognition (Ware 2012). Representing data by visual means allows viewers to find patterns that may be obfuscated by non-visual means. Therefore, various authors argue that data visualization represents a key opportunity for citizen education with data, thereby promoting civic engagement (Zambrano and Engelhardt 2008; Lewis 2013; Bohman 2015).

Public visualizations have been proposed and used to help citizens better understand urban issues, with promising results (Moere and Hill 2012), and a recent study found that visualization interfaces situated in public spaces led to sustained behavioural changes, increased discourse, augmented awareness of locally relevant topics, and meaningful participation with government. Public displays of data may increase dialogue or collaboration – arguably an indication of informed civic engagement.

However, while visualizations are excellent communicators of data, the full democratization of data requires that citizens have the ability to manipulate and explore data sets independently, because a single visualization may show only one facet of the data. To examine the data from multiple perspectives and, in some contexts, to input their own data, citizens need to be able to examine the data set independently, either through the interactive affordances of the visualization or by constructing their own visualizations from a data set. Raw data files, particularly when available in open (non-proprietary) formats, require tools to read and manipulate them. The development of tools to interactively manipulate data is therefore an important part of the movement toward data democratization (Jofre, Szigeti, and Diamond 2016).

One important initiative toward the democratization of data is the non-profit venture Gapminder (Rosling 2008). At gapminder.org, visitors can access a repository of data on the health and wealth of every nation in the world over several years. (The data include over 400 socio-economic indicators, such as GDP per capita, life expectancy, unemployment rates, energy consumption, and education.) Visitors can either download the data or view it using Gapminder World, which is Gapminder's proprietary online visualization software. The software allows users to create an animated visualization that interactively explores relationships between two or three different measures, by country and by year. This tool has been successfully used in public health education initiatives (Rosling and Zhang 2011) and also as a classroom tool to teach students geography (Keller 2012) and statistics (Le 2013).

One key feature of successful data visualizations such as Gapminder is their highly interactive nature: users can choose the data they want to look as well as how they want to look at them. Interactivity forces users to take an active role in the visualization and mitigates the passivity of on-screen displays.

Beyond Data: Using Visualization for Cultural Studies

Archives of periodical publications are a treasure trove of cultural history: reading a magazine from decades past can provide tremendous insight into the cultural context of the time. This notion has inspired me to work with collections of magazines in my art and design practice, to give viewers a bird's-eye view of how things have changed over time and to help them reflect on their own cultural history. Here I will talk about my work with *Time* magazine as an example of how the intersection of art, design, and digital technology can render a cultural product into insightful visualizations about our cultural and socio-political history. With an interdisciplinary approach, and in collaboration with colleagues in the humanities and computer science, we apply methodologies, such as data mining, computer vision analysis, and visualization, to expose patterns that hint at the cultural history contained within the corpus.

We chose *Time* magazine because it is a culturally significant and ubiquitous publication, and we believe much can be learned from these archives about how Americans perceived politics and culture throughout the twentieth and early twenty-first centuries. We theorize *Time* magazine as both a record of American cultural history and an active participant in it. Therefore, an analysis of this cultural product could enrich our understandings of the past hundred years.

Our approach is to provide users with a bird's-eye view of the entire corpus to give the viewer an overview of the trends and patterns within this particular cultural product. The work is centred on the analysis of the magazine's images. We believe that looking at magazine images offers an important complement to studies focusing solely on textual content, and computer vision analysis along with data visualization can provide insights and new meanings to those exploring the corpus.

The focal point of our investigation is on the faces contained within *Time* and how their characteristics have changed over time. We focus on the face because, arguably, faces constitute the most pertinent images in *Time*: most of the iconic images that appear in the magazine are photographs (or illustrations) of influential people, and a significant portion of advertisements feature images of human faces. Our analysis seeks trends and patterns in the representations of faces throughout the corpus, and endeavours to fit such patterns of representation within the larger historical, political, and cultural context of the publication in which they appear. Some of the specific research questions we ask are: What can a visual analysis of all of the faces in *Time* tell us about the intersections of race, gender, and class since 1923? How has the "face" of *Time*, and perhaps of the United States, changed over the years? How do faces in advertising differ from faces in news articles?

The main goal of this project is to create visualizations that convey a visual critical history of gender and race representations from this particular media outlet, and that provide an alternative perspective of the archive.

Strategy and Related Work

We approach this work with Ben Shneiderman's visual information-seeking mantra, "overview first, zoom and filter, then details on demand" (Shneiderman 1996; 2008). We focus on creating insightful overviews that can serve as starting points for exploration. A useful overview of a large data set must have a carefully thought-out arrangement (Shneiderman 2008; Hornbæk and Hertzum 2011), and so an important consideration in our presentation will be how the data are sorted. Another sense-making feature of a meaningful overview is aggregation. To visually clarify a large data set, data are aggregated (Elmqvist and Fekete 2010), either by using the data's inherent hierarchical order (for example, making nested categories not visible at the highest level overview) or by grouping the data and describing the group by its statistical features.

Our methodology is strongly inspired by the technique of direct visualization (Crockett 2016), which makes use of the images in their original visible format. This technique has been used extensively by Lev Manovich and is featured in various projects, including the visualization of *Time* magazine covers (softwarestudies.com 2009), of Instagram images ("Phototrails: Visualizing 2.3 M Instagram Photos from 13 Global Cities" 2016), of selfies ("Selfiecity" 2016), and of other cultural products ranging from Manga (Manovich 2016b) to Mondrian and Rothko paintings (Manovich 2016a).

We also draw inspiration from recent work at the Yale library, which provides historical insights through computational analysis of images and text in the *Vogue* magazine corpus ("Robots Reading Vogue" 2016). Of particular interest is the work on image analysis, such as the visualizations of *Vogue*'s colour palette over time ("Robots Reading Vogue: Colormetric Space" 2017), and the ongoing work on facial analysis ("What's in Vogue?" 2016; Rushmeier et al. 2015). While our project uses similar techniques to penetrate *Time* magazine, the work we propose here will incorporate a layer of interpretation and contextualization to the visualizations of the corpus.

Preliminary Results

In our preliminary work, we used algorithms from Python's OpenCV library ("OpenCV" 2017; Heinisuo n.d.) to extract images of faces from the corpus,[1] and we have attempted to find meaningful patterns in the images by computational analysis of the RGB pixel values. We sort and position the images in various ways according to these values, and we calculate a mean of the images using these values. We also formed composite faces over a year, and over a decade, to gain a rudimentary, yet informative, impression of how features average out. From a visualization theory perspective, the key ideas we are working with are sorting and aggregating.

All visualizations created for this project are being designed for a web browser platform, following our theme of accessibility. Our latest results are posted as they are produced and can be viewed on our project page.[2] Putting things on the web makes them most accessible, and interactivity is key for engagement. Furthermore, it is important to include ways for the user to access details on demand about a particular photo, such as the date, the issue, the context (e.g., whether the image is from a news article or an advertisement), and other metadata.

SORTING

Sorting data by visual features is a very effective way to communicate patterns and convey ideas. We sort the images by year to bring attention to temporal changes in the features we are analysing. In one overview visualization that we created in our preliminary work, the images were arranged on a grid, where each column represents one year, and the background colour of each column, over which the images are placed, is the colour representation of the average RGB pixel value for each year. Along the vertical direction, the images are sorted by their RGB value so that the darkest image is on top. There are a few interesting things that immediately become apparent upon viewing this overview, and we are working to tie these observations to historical trends or events. The first thing is the abrupt increase in the use of colour in the mid-1980s. The second thing is the abrupt change in colour tone of the faces in the first decade of the twenty-first century from pinkish to brown. A third observation is that the images get lighter in the late 1920s and into the Depression, then become darker again after the Depression.

We are also experimenting with using computer vision methods for sorting the images into visually similar groupings with unsupervised machine learning algorithms ("YaleDHLab/Pix-Plot" 2018).

AGGREGATION

While a sorted big-picture view of the corpus helps elucidate temporal patterns and trends, this view disconnects the viewer from the richness in the images. We therefore also consider how an aggregate of these images can be represented. Aggregation is particularly interesting because it brings up productive questions about data processing. In what ways do the data become clearer or more obscured as they are aggregated? Filtering and aggregation are helpful to explore large data sets, but what information is lost in the process? What is gained? We remain cognizant of these questions as we aggregate and filter the data.

One of the ways in which we aggregated our data was to construct composites of all faces within each year, and within each decade. Interestingly, we found that some of the patterns discovered on the sorted overview were still represented in the aggregated composite images, whether aggregated by year or by decade. For example, even when aggregating by decade, the same pattern in colour persists. The persistence of such key features is promising because being able to accurately and clearly convey results of a large data set with fewer images can allow users to have a more intimate experience with the data. Allowing users to focus on one image at a time can encourage qualitative observations and lead to tangential insights.

These preliminary results are the first steps toward developing methods to create alternative perspectives of periodical archives by extracting, decontextualizing, and recontexualizing their images. All our visualization results are and will be fully accessible on the web.

Three-Dimensional Affordances

While the web provides an accessible visualization platform for two-dimensional computer screen interaction, I am also curious about exploring other modalities for interacting with data. In particular, I believe cognition and analysis may be strengthened through embodied or tangible interaction with data. Tangible interaction, or interactions with graspable three-dimensional objects, while thinking through data may also foster collaboration, which contributes to pleasurable user experiences and augments problem-solving abilities.

Here I present work that I led at the Visual Analytics Lab at OCAD University in Toronto, where we developed a tool for interrogating data sets using graspable three-dimensional objects (tangibles). I start by reviewing an extensive body of research suggesting that tangibles foreground opportunities for collaboration and engagement. The rationale for our design work is based on the premise that the physical manifestation of data, and the manipulation of data through interaction with graspable objects, supports collaborative behaviour and may lead to an improved understanding of any particular data set.

Why 3D?

A well-designed tool is one that optimizes human performance by leveraging innate human abilities (Jofre, Szigeti, and Diamond 2016). For example, a pair of scissors is designed to fit into a human hand and to make optimal use of its natural motion. So it should be expected that, as we optimize our digital tools, they will increasingly engage our sense of touch and three-dimensional space (Sharlin et al. 2004). For example, touch screens take advantage of our intuitive gestures and allow us to apply our sense of touch to the task (Wigdor and Wixon 2011; Weiyuan Liu 2010). Eventually, with the development of ubiquitous computing and the internet of things (Olson, Nolin, and Nelhans 2015), we will be able to use everyday objects to interact with data and natural gestures to formulate operations. In addition to ease of use, handling and interacting with physical objects has been shown to benefit learning (Chapman 1988).

Tangible Interfaces

Tangible user interfaces (TUI) are broadly defined as graspable 3D physical objects with which to interact with digital information. Research in TUI for learning applications has found that they support learning by augmenting student engagement with tasks, and by fostering collaborative problem-solving. For example, in one study (Shaer and Hornecker 2010) engagement with digital learning tools was significantly increased when children were allowed to use their everyday physical play objects to interact with the digital information. Another study (Schneider, Jermann, et al. 2011) found that learners using a tangible interface worked on puzzles much more collaboratively than those using a multi-touchscreen, and the collaboration in turn improved their learning outcomes.

Tangibles and Collaboration

I am particularly interested in the role that tangible interfaces play in encouraging collaboration for at least two reasons. One, the ability to work collaboratively is essential for meaningful public participation in a democracy. Two, there is an empirical correlation between collaborative problem-solving and improved learning outcomes (Schneider, Jermann, et al. 2011).

The enhancement of collaborative behaviour may be a key differentiator between tangible and screen-based interfaces (Hornecker and Buur 2006; Lee et al. 2012). A study using eye-tracking devices found that participants working in small groups on a problem-solving task experienced more moments of joint visual attention when working with graspable movable objects on a tabletop than when working with a screen-based interface (Schneider, Sharma, et al. 2015).

Interestingly, the eye-tracking study by Schnieder, Sharma, et al. (2015) that measured increased joint visual attention with the use of tangibles also suggested that there was a correlation between joint visual attention and learning outcomes. Previous empirical studies have shown that using tangible interfaces usually results in better task performance of the group, but using them did not always affect the learning outcomes of the individuals (Do-Lenh et al. 2010). Other studies (Kim and Maher 2008) have shown that the collaboration fostered by TUI may improve creative outcomes in group work: groups using TUI performed multiple cognitive actions in a shorter time, made more unexpected discoveries of spatial design features, and exhibited more problem-solving behaviours.

DataBlocks: A Tangible Interface for Interactive Data Query

The body of literature reviewed above suggests that TUI's ability to engage people, to help process abstract concepts, and to foster collaboration could make these interfaces useful for citizen data exploration. Interestingly, while the use of tangible interfaces has been extensively explored in gaming applications (not discussed here) and in pedagogical applications (discussed above), there has been comparatively little work done in using tangible interfaces for data query. Here I present a project that I led at OCAD University, where we created a system for interacting with data using hand-held graspable tabletop objects (Jofre et al. 2016, 2015; "DataBlocks Visualizations" 2017). In this project, we take advantage of the benefits that tangible data representations bring, and combine these with graphical representations in a highly interactive environment.

12.1 A schematic drawing of users interacting with our software (Jofre et al. 2016, 2015; Jofre, Szigeti, and Diamond 2016).

One of the first tangible data query systems was designed to interactively convey historical information at a tourist site, using blocks that can be positioned to form a query (Camarata et al. 2002). The idea of rearranging objects to create data queries was later used in Stackables (Klum et al. 2012) and in Cubequery (Langner, Augsburg, and Dachselt 2014), whose cubes include a small display screen for the output.

In contrast to these systems, the system we developed at OCAD University, which we named DataBlocks, does not require any specialized hardware, a feature we believe to support the idea of data democratization. Our system requires only standard equipment: a computer, a webcam, and a projector.

In DataBlocks, users create queries by placing and arranging clearly demarcated objects (that are handheld in size) onto a common tabletop, and the results of the query are displayed onto an overhead screen placed at one end of the table. The visualizations that appear on the screen respond to the configuration of the objects on the table.

The objects are tracked by means of a camera placed discretely beneath a transparent tabletop. The bottom of each object is labelled with a fiducial marker, and the camera placed below the table captures the image of the fiducial markers in real time. The fiducial markers are read using open-source reacTIVision software (Kaltenbrunner and Bencina 2007). The reacTIVision software outputs the position of the markers, if they are in the field of view of the camera, and this information is input into DataBlocks, our software, which constructs the visualizations from a (user-provided) database, filtered by the user's query.

DataBlocks works on a browser to interpret the markers and to create the visualizations. We chose to build a browser-based system because it is a universal platform on which visualizations can be easily shared. Our software is web-based and we use the TUIO.js library (Kaltenbrunner et al. 2005; "Tuio.js by fe9lix" n.d., "fe9lix/Tuio.js" n.d.) to push the messages from the reacTIVision (Kaltenbrunner and Bencina 2007) tracker onto the browser, and to create responsive events out of changes in token presence, position, and rotation.

We are designing DataBlocks such that it can be adapted to any data set, as the system allows users to provide their own formatted data. We have demonstrated it for constructing visualizations of demographic data (Jofre et al. 2016, 2015); we have demonstrated that we can connect DataBlocks to function with Tableau, a popular data visualization tool; and we have even demonstrated that we can use DataBlocks for browsing through our collection of *Time* magazines (Jofre 2017).

DataBlocks is designed such that it can be individually customized by users, and is geared toward makers. Users can create their own representational objects that are used to explore their own data, and the fiducial markers, which are tracked by the camera, can be printed and glued onto the bottom of the objects. Our software is written in JavaScript, which allows users to easily see the source code, and it is constructed using open-source software and an open-source library. I believe that software that is transparent and allows for individualized user modifications can be truly democratizing, in contrast to proprietary, closed-source software – such as those provided by companies like Microsoft – which force users to conform to prescribed methods. Open source and transparency allow users to participate in the creation of their own tools. Furthermore, the internet is rife with open-source communities that support learners in meeting new programming challenges.

Democratization of data not only requires that active citizens be able to create and share their own visualizations, but it also requires a venue for discussion. While data analytics is typically performed individually, DataBlocks encourages data exploration to be a group/team activity with the tabletop interface.

Results from our pilot studies of test users support our assertion that our tangible interactive tool for data query encourages communication and collaborative data exploration, which is consistent with the literature on tangible interfaces. We organized participants into small groups of two to four, and gave them problems to solve using the data. Participants exhibited collaborative behaviour, and, in subsequent surveys, they reported positive feelings toward their teammates and about their interaction as a group.

In addition to encouraging collaboration, the playful nature of the tangible interaction could lead to a greater degree of engagement. Preliminary observations of users are promising – test subjects seem eager to handle the objects, and they take on a playful disposition when interacting with the system. Turning data query into a pleasurable experience can encourage people to spend more time exploring data, which, in the information age, is essential to being an educated and engaged citizen.

Conclusions

My view of digital technology is an optimistic one. Although I am cognizant of the potential pitfalls of using it for educational intervention, which are similar to the concerns Socrates had about the technology of writing (namely, that it can encourage superficial thinking), I don't believe that the technology itself, the tool, needs to be coupled to any specific outcome. William Pinar's contribution to this collection very pertinently critiques the technocratization of education, which, as he points out, is reducing education to indoctrination into the capitalist market economy. It is my hope, however, that Pinar's well-described characterization of technocratization in education is a shift in values that is occurring in parallel to, but that is not necessarily dependent on, the development of digital technology learning tools. It is my hope that the development of digital learning tools can help augment human cognition without necessarily placing them in service of the capitalist economy. Pinar also aptly critiques the intervention of capitalist market interests into educational goals, taking sharp aim at the tech industry. Indeed, as he points out, the move to make computer science central to elementary and secondary curricula is happening in parallel to a boom in the tech industry, which stands to gain from increased sales of devices and software. But to counter this, giving people the tools to process information, to code, and to develop their own software puts power back into the community's hands. In Antigonish, the tool of radio broadcasting was used for grassroots public interests that promoted the common good.

Like those involved in the Antigonish movement, I'm interested in an andragogy and pedagogy where learners participate in tailoring their own educational materials, and I'm interested in the use of technology to facilitate communication. Visual displays of information have the power to convey data in a meaningful manner, and interactivity allows users to engage with the data and view them from multiple perspectives. Furthermore, the use of customizable open-source software allows users to participate in the creation of their own learning tools.

In this chapter, I reviewed two recent projects. One is a digital public humanities project, in its beginning stages, in which visualization is used to convey underlying meanings carried in cultural products, such as periodical publications. The other is a tangible user interface for data visualization, made up of graspable tabletop objects.

Digital technology allows us to extract and expose insights from large cultural archives, such as *Time* magazine, which has been in print since 1923. I have presented here a digital humanities project in which images of faces are extracted from *Time* with the goal of revealing trends in race and gender representations. This is also a public humanities project, as the insights and visualizations will be made publicly available through the internet. Engaged citizens must have the means by which to understand their own cultural history, and this project is aimed at supporting such understanding.

Extending digital technologies to three-dimensional spaces can enhance user engagement and collaboration. With this intention, I led the creation of DataBlocks software, a tangible user interface for data exploration, in which users form queries by manipulating hand-held blocks on a tabletop. The software is open-source and highly customizable, which adds a deeper level of interactivity for users: the ability to modify the tool to their own needs.

My art and design practice considers the use of digital technology for public pedagogy, as I am interested in creating tools for critical, reflective, evidence-based learning in the public sphere. As information created through our civilization continues to accumulate, it is imperative to build tools to help people make sense of it and engage with it. The internet has allowed for unprecedented access to information, which can seem chaotic and overwhelming. However, digital tools for exploring the information offer our best hope for interpreting the information.

ACKNOWLEDGMENTS

DataBlocks was created at the Visual Analytics Lab at OCAD University, Toronto, directed and funded by Dr Sara Diamond. Research assistants Stephen Keller and Lan-Xi Dong participated in the creation of DataBlocks. The *Time* magazine project is being done in collaboration with Dr Kathleen Brennan and Dr Vincent Berardi. The *Time* magazine project followed from work that I initiated with Dr Brennan and Dr Berardi during the Culture Analytics Long Program at the Institute for Pure and Applied Mathematics (IPAM) at UCLA in Los Angeles, California.

NOTES

1 This rough first run extracted only about 23 per cent of the face images. A later attempt at extraction, using an algorithm trained on *Time* magazine, was able to extract more than 95 per cent of the faces in the archive.
2 Available at http://magazineproject.org/TIME/.

REFERENCES

Adriance, Madeleine. 1985. "Opting for the Poor: A Social-Historical Analysis of the Changing Brazilian Catholic Church." *Sociology of Religion* 46 (2): 131–46. https://doi.org/10.2307/3711056.

Allcott, Hunt, and Matthew Gentzkow. 2017. "Social Media and Fake News in the 2016 Election." Working Paper 23089. National Bureau of Economic Research (US). https://doi.org/10.3386/w23089.

Bohman, Samuel. 2015. "Data Visualization: An Untapped Potential for Political Participation and Civic Engagement." In *Electronic Government and the Information Systems Perspective*, edited by Andrea Kö and Enrico Francesconi, 302–15. New York: Springer International Publishing. https://doi.org/10.1007/978-3-319-22389-6_22.

Camarata, Ken, Ellen Yi-Luen Do, Brian R. Johnson, and Mark D. Gross. 2002. "Navigational Blocks: Navigating Information Space with Tangible Media." In *Proceedings of the 7th International Conference on Intelligent User Interfaces*, 31–8. IUI '02. New York: ACM. https://doi.org/10.1145/502716.502725.

Chapman, Michael. 1988. *Constructive Evolution: Origins and Development of Piaget's Thought*. Cambridge: Cambridge University Press. https://books.google.ca/books?hl=en&lr=&id=7WgCnXmdX1MC&oi=fnd&pg=PR7&dq=Origins+and+Development+of+Piaget%27s+thoughts&ots=jJrALSuHbr&sig=0dftyPoKgBBRjQB50p12dnVt_UM.

Crockett, Damon. 2016. "Direct Visualization Techniques for the Analysis of Image Data: The Slice Histogram and the Growing Entourage Plot." *International Journal for Digital Art History* No. 2. https://doi.org/10.11588/dah.2016.2.33529.

"DataBlocks Visualizations." 2017. Accessed 16 July. http://datablocks.org/.

Do-Lenh, Son, Patrick Jermann, Sébastien Cuendet, Guillaume Zufferey, and Pierre Dillenbourg. 2010. "Task Performance vs. Learning Outcomes: A Study of a Tangible User Interface in the Classroom." In *Sustaining TEL: From Innovation to Learning and Practice*, edited by Martin Wolpers, Paul A. Kirschner, Maren Scheffel, Stefanie Lindstaedt, and Vania Dimitrova, 78–92. Berlin: Springer. http://link.springer.com/chapter/10.1007/978-3-642-16020-2_6.

"Dropout Rates of Massive Open Online Courses: Behavioural Patterns – WRAP. Warwick Research Archive Portal." 2017. Accessed 16 July. http://wrap.warwick.ac.uk/65543/.

Elmqvist, N., and J. Fekete. 2010. "Hierarchical Aggregation for Information Visualization: Overview, Techniques, and Design Guidelines." *IEEE Transactions on Visualization and Computer Graphics* 16 (3): 439–54. https://doi.org/10.1109/TVCG.2009.84.

"fe9lix/Tuio.js. 2016. GitHub. Accessed 12 September. https://github.com/fe9lix/Tuio.js.

Freire, Paulo. 2000. *Pedagogy of the Oppressed*. London: Bloomsbury Publishing.

Habermas, Jürgen. 1975. *Communication and the Evolution of Society*. Boston: Beacon Press.

Hansen, John D., and Justin Reich. 2015. "Democratizing Education? Examining Access and Usage Patterns in Massive Open Online Courses." *Science* 350 (6265): 1245–48. https://doi.org/10.1126/science.aab3782.

Heinisuo, Olli-Pekka. n.d. Opencv-Python: Wrapper Package for OpenCV Python Bindings. Version 3.3.0.10. MacOS, Operating System. C++, Python. https://github.com/skvark/opencv-python.

Hornbæk, Kasper, and Morten Hertzum. 2011. "The Notion of Overview in Information Visualization." *International Journal of Human-Computer Studies* 69 (7/8): 509–25. https://doi.org/10.1016/j.ijhcs.2011.02.007.

Hornecker, Eva, and Jacob Buur. 2006. "Getting a Grip on Tangible Interaction: A Framework on Physical Space and Social Interaction." In *Proceedings of the SIGCHI Conference on Human Factors in Computing Systems*, 437–46. CHI '06. New York: ACM. https://doi.org/10.1145/1124772.1124838.

Jofre, Ana. 2017. "DataBlocks: A Tangible Interface for Data Visualization." Paper presented at Festival Internacional de la Imagen, Manizales, Columbia, 11–18 June, 2017. http://festivaldelaimagen.com/portfolio-item/datablocks-a-tangible-interface-for-data-visualization/.

Jofre, Ana, Steve Szigeti, and Sara Diamond. 2016. "Citizen Engagement through Tangible Data Representation." *Foro de Educación* 14 (20): 305–25. https://doi.org/10.14516/fde.2016.014.020.015.

Jofre, Ana, Steve Szigeti, Stephen Tiefenbach Keller, Lan-Xi Dong, David Czarnowski, Frederico Tomé, and Sara Diamond. 2015. "A Tangible User Interface for Interactive Data Visualization." In *Proceedings of the 25th Annual International Conference on Computer Science and Software Engineering*, 244–7. CASCON '15. Riverton, NJ: IBM. http://dl.acm.org/citation.cfm?id=2886444.2886484.

Jofre, Ana, Steve Szigeti, Stephen Tiefenbach-Keller, Lan-Xi Dong, and Sara Diamond. 2016. "Manipulating Tabletop Objects to Interactively Query a Database." In *Proceedings of the 2016 CHI Conference Extended Abstracts on Human Factors in Computing Systems*, 3695–8. CHI EA '16. New York: ACM. https://doi.org/10.1145/2851581.2890260.

Kaltenbrunner, Martin, and Ross Bencina. 2007. "reacTIVision: A Computer-vision Framework for Table-Based Tangible Interaction." In *Proceedings of the 1st International Conference on Tangible and Embedded Interaction*, 69–74. TEI '07. New York: ACM. https://doi.org/10.1145/1226969.1226983.

Kaltenbrunner, Martin, Till Bovermann, Ross Bencina, and Enrico Costanza. 2005. "TUIO: A Protocol for Table-Top Tangible User Interfaces." In Proceedings of the 6th International Workshop on Gesture in Human-Computer Interaction and Simulation, 1–5. https://www.researchgate.net/profile/Martin_Kaltenbrunner/publication/225075863_TUIO_A_Protocol_for_Table-Top_Tangible_User_Interfaces/links/55adfa4708ae98e661a4510d.pdf.

Keller, Kenneth H. 2012. "Gapminder: An AP Human Geography Lab Assignment." *Geography Teacher* 9 (2): 60–3. https://doi.org/10.1080/19338341.2012.679893.

Kim, Mi Jeong, and Mary Lou Maher. 2008. "The Impact of Tangible User Interfaces on Spatial Cognition during Collaborative Design." *Design Studies* 29 (3): 222–53. https://doi.org/10.1016/j.destud.2007.12.006.

Klum, Stefanie, Petra Isenberg, Ricardo Langner, Jean-Daniel Fekete, and Raimund Dachselt. 2012. "Stackables: Combining Tangibles for Faceted Browsing." In *Proceedings of the International Working Conference on Advanced Visual Interfaces*, 241–8. AVI '12. New York: ACM. https://doi.org/10.1145/2254556.2254600.

Laakso, Mikael, Patrik Welling, Helena Bukvova, Linus Nyman, Bo-Christer Björk, and Turid Hedlund. 2011. "The Development of Open Access Journal Publishing from 1993 to 2009." *Plos One* 6 (6): e20961. https://doi.org/10.1371/journal.pone.0020961.

Labaree, David F. 2008. "The Winning Ways of a Losing Strategy: Educationalizing Social Problems in the United States." *Educational Theory* 58 (4): 447–60. https://doi.org/10.1111/j.1741-5446.2008.00299.x.

Langner, Ricardo, Anton Augsburg, and Raimund Dachselt. 2014. "CubeQuery: Tangible Interface for Creating and Manipulating Database Queries." *In Proceedings of the Ninth ACM International Conference on Interactive Tabletops and Surfaces*, 423–6. ITS '14. New York: ACM. https://doi.org/10.1145/2669485.2669526.

Le, Dai-Trang. 2013. "Bringing Data to Life into an Introductory Statistics Course with Gapminder." *Teaching Statistics* 35 (3): 114–22. https://doi.org/10.1111/test.12015.

Lee, Bongshin, P. Isenberg, N.H. Riche, and S. Carpendale. 2012. "Beyond Mouse and Keyboard: Expanding Design Considerations for Information Visualization Interactions." *IEEE Transactions on Visualization and Computer Graphics* 18 (12): 2689–98. https://doi.org/10.1109/TVCG.2012.204.

Lewis, Jaymee. 2013. "Empowering Communities through Data Democratization." In APHA. https://apha.confex.com/apha/141am/webprogramadapt/Paper287274.html.

Manovich, Lev. 2016a. "Mondrian vs Rothko: Footprints and Evolution in Style Space." Accessed 30 December. http://lab.softwarestudies.com/2011/06/mondrian-vs-rothko-footprints-and.html.

– 2016b. "One Million Manga Pages." Accessed 30 December. http://lab.softwarestudies.com/2010/11/one-million-manga-pages.html.

"Misleading Data Visualization Examples." 2015. BI Blog / Data Visualization and Analytics Blog / Datapine (blog). 2 December. http://www.datapine.com/blog/misleading-data-visualization-examples/.

Moere, Andrew Vande, and Dan Hill. 2012. "Designing for the Situated and Public Visualization of Urban Data." *Journal of Urban Technology* 19 (2): 25–46. https://doi.org/10.1080/10630732.2012.698065.

Nasrine Olson, Jan Michael Nolin, and Gustaf Nelhans. 2015. "Semantic Web, Ubiquitous Computing, or Internet of Things? A Macro-Analysis of Scholarly Publications." *Journal of Documentation* 71 (5): 884–916. https://doi.org/10.1108/jd-03-2013-0033.

"OpenCV." 2017. Accessed 5 January. http://opencv.org/.

Pandey, Anshul Vikram, Katharina Rall, Margaret L. Satterthwaite, Oded Nov, and Enrico Bertini. 2015. "How Deceptive Are Deceptive Visualizations? An Empirical Analysis of Common Distortion Techniques." In *Proceedings of the 33rd Annual ACM Conference on Human Factors in Computing Systems*, 1469–78. CHI '15. New York: ACM. https://doi.org/10.1145/2702123.2702608.

"Phototrails: Visualizing 2.3 M Instagram Photos from 13 Global Cities." 2016. Accessed 30 December. http://lab.culturalanalytics.info/2016/04/phototrails-visualizing-23-m-instagram.html.

"Robots Reading Vogue." 2016. Accessed 8 November. http://dh.library.yale.edu/projects/vogue/.

"Robots Reading Vogue: Colormetric Space." 2017. Accessed 5 January. http://dh.library.yale.edu/projects/vogue/colormetricspace/.

Rosling, Hans. 2008. "Gapminder: World." http://www.gapminder.org/world.

Rosling, Hans, and Zhongxing Zhang. 2011. "Health Advocacy with Gapminder Animated Statistics." *Journal of Epidemiology and Global Health* 1 (1): 11–14. https://doi.org/10.1016/j.jegh.2011.07.001.

Rushmeier, Holly, Ruggero Pintus, Ying Yang, Christiana Wong, and David Li. 2015. "Examples of Challenges and Opportunities in Visual Analysis in the Digital Humanities." Proc. SPIE 9394, Human Vision and Electronic Imaging XX, 939414. https://doi.org/10.1117/12.2083342.

Schneider, B., P. Jermann, G. Zufferey, and P. Dillenbourg. 2011. "Benefits of a Tangible Interface for Collaborative Learning and Interaction." *IEEE Transactions on Learning Technologies* 4 (3): 222–32. https://doi.org/10.1109/TLT.2010.36.

Schneider, Bertrand, K. Sharma, S. Cuendet, G. Zufferey, P. Dillenbourg, and A.D. Pea. 2015. "3D Tangibles Facilitate Joint Visual Attention in Dyads." In *International Conference on Computer Supported Collaborative Learning (CSCL)*, 158–65. http://blog.bertrandschneider.com/wp-content/uploads/2012/01/9.MC-0182-paper-edit1-LD.pdf.

"Selfiecity." 2016. Selfiecity. Accessed 30 December. http://selfiecity.net/.

Shaer, Orit, and Eva Hornecker. 2010. "Tangible User Interfaces: Past, Present, and Future Directions." *Foundations and Trends Human-Computer Interactions* 3 (1/2): 1–137. https://doi.org/10.1561/1100000026.

Sharlin, Ehud, Benjamin Watson, Yoshifumi Kitamura, Fumio Kishino, and Yuichi Itoh. 2004. "On Tangible User Interfaces, Humans, and Spatiality." *Personal Ubiquitous Computers* 8 (5): 338–46. https://doi.org/10.1007/s00779-004-0296-5.

Shneiderman, B. 1996. "The Eyes Have It: A Task by Data Type Taxonomy for Information Visualizations." In *IEEE Symposium on Visual Languages, 1996. Proceedings*, 336–43. https://doi.org/10.1109/VL.1996.545307.

– 2008. "Extreme Visualization: Squeezing a Billion Records into a Million Pixels." In *Proceedings of the 2008 ACM SIGMOD International Conference on Management of Data*, 3–12. SIGMOD '08. New York: ACM. https://doi.org/10.1145/1376616.1376618.

softwarestudies.com. 2009. *Timeline: 4535 Time Magazine Covers, 1923–2009*. Photo. https://www.flickr.com/photos/culturevis/3951496507/.

"Tuio.js by fe9lix." 2016. Accessed 12 September. http://protium-labs.co/Tuio.js/.

Ware, Colin. 2012. *Information Visualization: Perception for Design*. Waltham, MA: Elsevier.

Weiyuan Liu. 2010. "Natural User Interface-Next Mainstream Product User Interface." *2010 IEEE 11th International Conference on Computer-Aided Industrial Design & Conceptual Design* 1 (1): 203–5. https://doi.org/10.1109/CAIDCD.2010.5681374.

"What's in Vogue? Tracing the Evolution of Fashion and Culture in the Media." 2016. Yale News. Accessed 8 November. http://news.yale.edu/2014/09/05/what-s-vogue-tracing-evolution-fashion-and-culture-media.

Wigdor, Daniel, and Dennis Wixon. 2011. *Brave NUI World: Designing Natural User Interfaces for Touch and Gesture*. Burlington, MA: Elsevier.

"YaleDHLab/Pix-Plot." 2018. GitHub. Accessed 31 August. https://github.com/YaleDHLab/pix-plot.

Zambrano, Raul Niño, and Yuri Engelhardt. 2008. "Diagrams for the Masses: Raising Public Awareness – From Neurath to Gapminder and Google Earth." In *Diagrammatic Representation and Inference,* 282–92. Springer. http://link.springer.com/chapter/10.1007/978-3-540-87730-1_26.

PART V

Educationalization as a Tool of Colonization and Its Counter-Dimension in Indigenous Educational Agendas: Limits and Possibilities

brackets create space © Alan R. Wilkinson

13 Educationalization in Canada: The Use of Native Teacher Education as a Tool of Decoloniality

BONITA UZORUO

Educationalization is commonly referred to as the inclination by governments to look to educational institutions to solve perceived social and moral problems (Bridges 2008). Daniel Tröhler and Rosa Bruno-Jofré in their respective chapters in this volume provide important historical perspectives on the origins and use of educationalization in the Protestant and Catholic church. In his chapter, Tröhler suggests that the educationalization of the world as a Western way of interpreting and interacting with the world and its (perceived) challenges and problems, is a Protestant phenomenon arising from competing Protestant religions. Bruno-Jofré, in her chapter, does not dispute the origins of educationalization, but refers to the uses of education by the Catholic Church from early modernity to the long 1960s. She contends that educationalization processes were mediated by the official doctrine of the Catholic Church and also by emerging contextual, theological, and social configurations, as well as by individual agency (free will).

In their elaborated explanation of the term, Depaepe and Smeyers (2008) describe educationalization as the process of assigning to educational institutions the responsibility for solving particular issues that arise from social inequalities (related to class, race, and gender) and social responsibilities (the authors mention reducing traffic deaths, obesity, teenage sex, and environmental destruction). The authors also acknowledge that the phenomenon of educationalization has received more attention in Europe – and, I would add, the United States – than in Canada. In this chapter, I draw on two examples of educationalization from a Canadian perspective. The first is the use of education by the Canadian government as a brutal tool for assimilating First Nations children during the state's nation-building era, beginning in 1867, with the creation of Canada, and continuing through to the 1960s. The second is the use of teacher education by First Nations to address and overcome the negative social and economic impacts from more than a century of government control.

In the first part of this chapter I trace the Canadian government's agenda to target for extermination First Nations culture, language, and way of life with the implementation and imposition of segregated federal residential schools from 1867 to the late 1950s and again during the 1960s as further assimilation agendas were prioritized within provincial school integration. I then turn to the socio-political climate of the late 1960s and early 1970s that not only enabled First Nations to regain control of their education but also stimulated a vision for a Native-value education that could help to narrow the social, political, economic, and educational gap between First Nations and the rest of Canada.

The development of early Native teacher education programs (NTEPs) in western Canada during the 1970s to the 1980s is examined in the second part of this chapter, where I explore the collaborative efforts of First Nations communities and postsecondary institutions to actualize the goals for First Nations education as stated in the National Indian Brotherhood's seminal policy *Indian Control of Indian Education* (1972). Here I pay close attention to the creation of the Brandon University Northern Teacher Education Program (BUNTEP) during the mid-1970s in the province of Manitoba and reflect on the use of Native teacher education as a tool of decoloniality.

A Note on Terminology

Over the years Indigenous people in Canada have been identified by the government in a number of ways. In this chapter, I use the term "Native," a common term of reference until the late 1980s, when it was replaced by "Aboriginal" – an all-encompassing term used to include status and non-status Indians, Metis, and Inuit. The term "First Nations," references both status and non-status Indians.

The Native teacher education programs discussed in this chapter reflected combined funding agreements between the federal and provincial governments. These early programs were accessible to all First Nations; however, the type of funding a student received was based on whether they identified as a status or non-status Indian.

Residential School Education

The Confederation of Canada in 1867, accelerated colonization efforts, particularly in the North and West, where European settlement was significantly sparser than in the eastern regions of the new country. The new federal government perceived the Native presence, especially in western Canada, as a significant obstacle to Canada's nation-building efforts. To make way for the influx of settlers and to capitalize on the region's natural resources, the federal government became increasingly motivated to solve its "Indian problem" and acquire Native lands. The creation of the Indian Act in 1876 helped to provide the legal grounds for the federal government to assume control over all matters pertaining to First Nations people. This marked the beginning of a long-standing convoluted paternalistic relationship between the Canadian government and the First Nations people in Canada.

Under the newly enacted Indian policy and through the manipulation of the signed Treaties, the federal government moved to confine First Nations to reserves, outlaw their cultural and spiritual practices, and execute or jail any Aboriginal leaders who opposed the government's control (Truth and Reconciliation Commission 2015, 166). In addition to its policies prompting political, economic, and social control, the Canadian government began an education campaign that would seek to systematically exterminate First Nations culture and fully assimilate First Nations peoples into the new Canadian society. As had been the case in the East, missionaries in the West had already established themselves and implemented an agenda that aimed to "civilize" First Nations people through schooling (Milloy 1999, 53). It is not surprising, then, that the federal government chose to form an alliance with the various religious institutions, such as the Roman Catholics, Anglicans, and Presbyterians, to deliver residential school education with the intention of producing good Christian girls and boys (Cardinal 1999, 44).

In the territory that was to become the province of Manitoba, missionaries, such as Methodists beginning in the 1840s, Oblates in 1845, and Grey Nuns in the 1850s, had established both day and boarding schools, which offered First Nations children formal religious education (Miller 1996). After Confederation, missionaries were granted permission to continue their Christianizing and "civilizing" agendas on the prairies within federal residential schools. According to Fuchs, "The package deal that accompanied literacy included continuing efforts to 'civilize the natives'... Children were removed – sometimes forcibly – long distances from their home, the use of Indian languages by children was forbidden under threat of corporal punishment, student were boarded out to white families during vacation times, and native religions were suppressed" (1970, 55).

From 1870 until 1952, Roman Catholic, Anglican, Presbyterian, and Methodist churches helped to establish residential schools throughout

Canada's West, which sought to imbue First Nations with the characteristics associated with civilization and industry (Milloy 1999, 13). As noted by Fuchs, this saw the forceful removal of First Nations children from their homes and their placement in isolated residential schools where they were kept until the age of sixteen. These schools were often located far from the students' home reserves, allowing very little, if any, communication with parents. Moreover, First Nations children were commonly denied the right to speak their language, told their cultural beliefs were sinful, and forced to forget traditional teachings and learn industrial trades and agriculture (Truth and Reconciliation Commission 2012).

In chapter 15 in this volume, Sol Serrano and Macarena Ponce de León examine the establishment of missionary schools for Indigenous peoples in Chile from 1881 to the 1930s. The authors argue that the wave of Protestant and Catholic missionaries of the nineteenth century went hand-in-hand with European colonial expansion and played an important role in imposing dominant (Western) culture on Indigenous peoples. From that chapter, it is clear that the official state educational policies of Chile and Canada shared a similar agenda on the cultural extermination of the Native peoples. However, there are noteworthy differences between the two countries in the role that the missionaries played. In the case of Canada, the government founded a national residential school system that enlisted the help of various church missionaries. According to the Truth and Reconciliation Commission (TRC), a commission established to document the impact of the residential school system in Canada, the government provided the churches with incentives to compete with one another in recruitment campaigns and to enrol the maximum allowable number of students, even if they were in poor health or suffering from infectious disease (Truth and Reconciliation Commission 2012, 16). Missionaries were encouraged not only to fill their schools to capacity but also to follow the government's educational directives toward assimilation. In contrast, while Capuchin friars from Bavaria established missionary schools on Mapuche lands, Serrano and Ponce de Leon emphasize that the friars rejected the state's official policy of cultural extermination and often incorporated elements of Mapuche culture and language within the schools.

The Move to Provincial School Integration

The federal government's control of First Nations education for almost a century had an overwhelmingly negative impact on First Nations children, their families, and communities. Following the end of the

Second World War, the government initiated a Special Joint Committee of the Senate and the House of Commons (SJC) to hear concerns on the condition of Natives living on reserves (Miller 1996). After the SJC published its official report in 1948, documenting the bleak conditions facing First Nations people, the federal government moved to adopt an educational policy that favoured integration, which, according to Frideres (1974), was a radical departure from its earlier policy of isolation. Under the new integration framework, First Nations students would be schooled alongside non-Native children in provincial or territorial schools.

Several years after the government embarked on its plan for provincial school education, the failure of the nation's residential school system was exposed to the public in the 1967 Hawthorn Report. Not surprisingly, the authors of the Hawthorn Report supported the federal government's new integration policy, as evidenced in the following statement:

> The new ideology favours progressive integration of the Indians within the entire Canadian family from sea to sea. Since the various Indian groups across Canada occupy widely differing economic and social positions, the time required for the process of acculturation and integration will vary considerably from one group to the next. The ultimate aim is as follows: that the Indians be considered on the same footing as the other citizens of the country and that they enjoy the same services and the same standard of living. With this aim in view, the governments will encourage greater participation by the Indians in the management of their own affairs until they are able to assume full responsibility. School integration, which allows Indian children to attend the same schools as non-Indians is being encouraged as the principal means of achieving complete social integration. The new policy tends then to encourage as much as possible the attendance at joint schools by Indian children. Curricula are also being planned on an integration basis. (Hawthorn 1967, 41)

Indian Control of Indian Education

The federal government's *Statement of the Government of Canada on Indian Policy, 1969,* commonly referred to as the White Paper, called for the elimination of "special privileges" for First Nations by dismantling the Indian Act (Indian Affairs and Northern Development 1969). The government expected that the elimination the Indian Act would result in the total assimilation of First Nations into Canadian society. It would also mean that the control of social services, including education, for First Nations would be tranfered from the federal government to the provinces. In fact, prior to the release of the White Paper, the federal government had already begun the process of creating comprehensive capital and tuition agreements with provincial governments without the involvement of First Nations (Abele, Dittburner, and Graham 2000, 4). For example, in 1964 the federal government had initiated the process of forming an agreement with the province of Manitoba, to establish a uniform tuition fee for First Nations students paid for by the Indian Affairs Branch of the federal government (Frideres 1974, 34).

First Nations vehemently opposed the White Paper, seeing it as yet another attempt by the federal government to erase their distinct rights and status in Canada (St Denis 2007, 1075). Additionally, the attempt to transfer control of First Nations education to the provinces provoked a serious reflection among First Nations leaders on who should be controlling such education. As Cardinal (1977) states, "It struck us, if the federal government wasn't going to control Indian education, then the control should be given to the Indians, not passed on to the provincial governments which lacked even the heritage of trusteeship held by Ottawa. Essentially, in 1968 our concept of Indian education system was that it should be separate from the existing provincial system, geared much more directly to meeting the needs of our communities" (196).

The idea that First Nations self-determination could be achieved through education was first conceptualized in 1970, beginning with the Indian Association of Alberta's (IAA) Red Paper and later in several provincial policy papers such as the Manitoba Indian Brotherhood's (MIB) *Wahbung: Our Tomorrows* (1971). Underlying all such papers was the idea that education was key to improving the political, economic, and social conditions of First Nations people. Thus, by the time the recently formed National Indian Brotherhood (NIB) released its paper *Indian Control of Indian Education* (ICIE) in 1972, the foundation for change had already been laid. ICIE strongly advocated for the improvement of First Nations people through an education system based on Indian values. ICIE was accepted in principle and, after approval by the executive council of the NIB, was presented to the minister of Indian Affairs, Jean Chrétien (Cardinal 1999, 57).

Native Teacher Education Programs in Western Canada

Since the 1970s, there has been considerable effort to remove the barriers imposed by the vastness of Canadian geography in order to meet the educational needs of those living in sparsely populated areas (Wagner 1988). Prior to the 1970s, postsecondary participation rates for First Nations were very low. Statistics from 1967–8 show that only 156 Native people were enrolled in universities across Canada and that, of those enrolled, only 6 per cent actually graduated, while about 17 per cent voluntarily withdrew (Frideres 1974, 47). By the early 1970s, the number of First Nations students attending university programs had doubled, but completion rates were still quite low, due to factors such as a lack of accommodation for Native languages, little recognition of cultural differences, and Native students' experiencing discrimination (ibid.).

The statistics were even bleaker for Native teachers. Prior to the 1970s, very few First Nations teachers taught in Canada. In 1965, only 7 per cent of teachers hired by the Department of Indian Affairs (DIA) were of First Nations ancestry; by 1970, this figure had increased only slightly, to 10 per cent (ibid.). In that same year, within the province of Manitoba, which had one of the largest Aboriginal populations in Canada, only twelve of 12,000 teachers were Aboriginal (McAlpine 2001, 108). Moreover, a 1971 report by the Manitoba Indian Brotherhood (MIB) estimated that there were only seven federally employed First Nations teachers within the province (Manitoba Indian Brotherhood 1971). Given these statistics, it is not surprising that both the MIB and the NIB strongly believed that any improvements to First Nations education would depend greatly on increasing the number of First Nations teachers. The NIB recommended that:

> The Federal Government must take the initiative in providing opportunities for Indian people to train as teachers and counsellors. Efforts in this direction require experimental approaches and flexible structures to accommodate the native person who has talent and interest, but lacks minimum academic qualifications. Provincial/territorial involvement is also needed in this venture to introduce special teacher and counselor training programs, which will allow native people to advance their academic standing at the same time as they are receiving professional training. (National Indian Brotherhood 1972, 18)

First Nations leaders and parents believed that Native teachers would be in better positions to assess and respond to the learning needs of Native students, due to similarities in the cultural backgrounds of the teacher and the student; would serve as role models to motivate Native students to achieve greater educational success; and would remain in their home communities and become part of the local educational process (Barnhardt 1977, 88–9).

One way of addressing this need was through the creation of more Native teacher education programs. These programs, which emerged in the late 1960s and early 1970s, were designed as specialized university programs for students of First Nations ancestry and were based on a three-fold rationale: the need to address the lack of Native teachers; the need to improve the quality of education for Native children, who were not having their needs met by the existing educational system; and the need for an alternative program to train Native teachers in a supportive environment that addressed their personal, educational, and cultural needs (Bouvier 1984). The following is a brief outline of the NTEPs that emerged between 1970 and 1975 in western Canada (not including the province of Manitoba, which I will detail in a later section).

British Columbia

In the province of British Columbia, the transfer of a federally operated reserve day school at Mount Currie to the local Indian band in 1973 prompted the establishment of the British Columbia Mount Currie three-year teacher-training program, which was a cooperative arrangement with Simon Fraser University (Clarke and MacKenzie 1980). Then, in 1974, the Native Indian Teacher Education Program (NITEP) was established through the University of British Columbia (UBC). The NITEP model offered a two-year degree-granting program that blended an on-campus component at UBC and a community-based program that worked in partnership with local community campuses and First Nations communities (Eastmure 2011, 44).

Alberta

The University of Calgary began offering Native teacher education programs in 1974, through the establishment of an Outreach Teacher Education Program (OREP) on three of the province of Alberta's Indian reserves. The Maskwachees Cultural College on the Hobbema reserve was run entirely by a Native board and was funded through the Department of Indian Affairs and Northern Development (DIAND) (Clarke and MacKenzie 1980, 23). Native students enrolled in the OREP program completed its first three years at the Hobbema site and then attended the main campus in Calgary for their final year (Moore-Eyman 1977 4).

In 1975, under the direction the University of Alberta, a similar outreach program, known as the Morningstar Project, emerged. It provided the first two years of a bachelor of education degree at the First

Nations – controlled Blue Quills School near St Paul, Alberta (Clarke and MacKenzie 1980, 23). Upon successful completion of the blended three-year on- and off-campus program, candidates received an interim teacher certification.

Saskatchewan

Two Aboriginal teacher education programs emerged in the province of Saskatchewan through the University of Saskatchewan and the University of Regina. The Indian Teacher Education Program (ITEP) began at the University of Saskatchewan in 1972. ITEP was developed with the support of the Federation of Saskatchewan Indians through the Indian Cultural College and was initially a two-and-a-half year program leading to teacher certification but later became a four-year bachelor of education program for elementary and secondary education (Eastmure 2011).

In 1977, the Northern Teacher Education Program (NORTEP) was created in partnership with the Northern School Board, the University of Regina, and the University of Saskatchewan (Eastmure 2011). The Northern School Board offered school-based training opportunities for First Nations teacher aides and Native language instructors. At the time of its creation, NORTEP was structured as a school-based program, with students spending half their time in their home communities under guidance of a classroom teacher and half the year in LaRonge completing university credited courses (ibid.).

Native Teacher Education in Manitoba and the Creation of the Brandon University Northern Teacher Education Program

In 1971, a two-year teacher certification program called the Indian and Métis Project for Action in Careers through Teacher Education (IMPACTE) was created for First Nations students by Brandon University, in partnership with northern communities, the provincial government, and rural school boards (Robertson and Loughton 1976). Coinciding with the launch of IMPACTE was the Program for the Education of Native Teachers (PENT), which allowed First Nations students to work for pay within schools and complete teacher education courses over the summers. In 1974, the University of Brandon took over the administration of IMPACTE, and a third teacher education program was developed in Winnipeg, known as the Winnipeg Centre Project. All three programs laid the foundation for the creation of the Brandon University Northern Teacher Education Program (BUNTEP) in 1975

(Robertson and Loughton 1976). In January of that year, Brandon University announced that, to increase the number of certified teachers of Native origin in rural northern Manitoba, it had extended its services in the northern region of the province.

The motivation for BUNTEP came from a number of individuals, including Abe Bergen of the Frontier School Division, Sylvia Haslem of the federal Department of Indian Affairs, Verna Kirkness, a Native educator from Norway House, Jack Deinas, Jack Laughten, and Don Robertson of IMPACTE, all of whom were concerned about the lack of postsecondary education opportunities for the predomintly First Nations population in the northern regions of the province (von Stein 1984, 154). In the summer of 1974, Brandon University co-sponsored and supervised the Northern Education Summer Project with IMPACTE, which served as a pilot project for extending teacher education in the province's remote northern communities (Robertson and Loughton 1976). At the end of this pilot project and through a series of agreements, IMPACTE was absorbed into BUNTEP and its centres in The Pas and Camperville were transferred. During BUNTEP's first year of operation, the Camperville centre continued to be administered by IMPACTE, although it was funded through BUNTEP; at the same time, the centre in The Pas continued to follow the IMPACTE model of relocating students to The Pas more than recruiting students from within that community (Robertson and Loughton 1976). By January 1975, with the addition of three more centres, at Nelson House, Cross Lake, and Island Lake, BUNTEP reached an enrolment of fifty-two students (ibid.).

BUNTEP was designed to be a four-year bachelor of education program with both streams for prospective elementary and junior high school teachers. The elementary stream consisted of sixty credit hours in arts, science, music, and physical education; eighteen credit hour in a minor subject; and an additional sixty credit hours of education courses (More 1981). The junior high school stream involved seventy-two credit hours in arts, science, physical education, and music; eighteen credit hours in a selected minor; and forty-eight credit hours in education courses. Both streams required students to complete a field-based practicum of twenty-three weeks (ibid.).

The BUNTEP Model

Several key features contributed to the uniqueness of BUNTEP. The first was its strategy of recruiting students from within participating communities, thereby bringing teacher education programs to northern residents. In addition, the community-based model incorporated local involvement; the program's unique field- based student teaching experience was completed entirely within the participating community; and, finally, a unique combination of permanent and visiting teaching staff facilitated the program (Robertson and Loughton 1976).

In 1969 and 1970, Brandon University was experiencing only limited success in providing Native students with on-campus teacher education. Issues associated with recruiting Native students from remote rural areas and relocating them to the urban setting of Brandon became major obstacles, because many potential students were older than most university students and were often married with dependent children (von Stein 1984, 151). It became clear that a new approach to Native teacher education was needed, and a community-based model was proposed as a way to allow Native students to remain in their communities to complete the postsecondary program. BUNTEP expanded the off-campus, community-based teacher education model that was first established by IMPACTE.

In an effort to support a community-based program, BUNTEP strategically recruited northern Native students from the communities that were involved in the program. It also gave consideration to the number of spaces within the local band schools that were available for students seeking to complete their practicum (Robertson and Loughton 1976, 7). This recruitment strategy helped to bring postsecondary opportunities to northern communities and to their members who otherwise would not have been able to access a university education.

Data from BUNTEP's first year of implementation show that the typical student was Native, female, and between the age of 23 to 25, and had dependent children had a 10th grade education. In terms of their work history, BUNTEP students tended to be employed as teachers' aides or clerical workers, or they had worked intermittently in other jobs (Robertson and Loughton 1976, 7).

A core feature of the BUNTEP program was that it was delivered as a community-based program in remote northern communities of Manitoba. Its success relied on community cooperation, and local involvement was encouraged, especially in the planning and development phase. Communities saw the program as a means to change the schooling environment of their children (Taylor, Crago, and McAlpine 2001, 49). Accordingly, members of the community sought to attract candidates who would help preserve and pass on traditional knowledge, as well as prepare children to be successful members of the community. In 1976, key recommendations were made for BUNTEP to enhance the regular program with culturally relevant content and materials that would better reflect the community and the children in local schools (Robertson and Loughton 1976, 48).

Field-based student teaching experience was a core feature of many on-campus teacher education programs, and BUNTEP students were expected to complete their extended field-based practicums (Robertson and Loughton 1976, 36). However, the BUNTEP program was unique in that both classroom learning and student teaching experiences were conducted entirely within the students' own rural communities.

The centre coordinators and the visiting professors were fundamental to the facilitation of BUNTEP. Each BUNTEP centre had a permanent coordinator; visiting professors would attend the centre only for the duration of their courses, which was generally a few months at a time. Centre coordinators were also professors: they taught core courses in addition to being directly involved in program policy and acting as community liaisons between the university, community members, and students (Robertson and Loughton 1976, 14). The primary role of the visiting professor was to deliver courses and adapt them to the unique needs of the BUNTEP program.

Native Teacher Education as a Tool of Decoloniality

Tuck and Yang (2012) describe the process of decolonization as the repatriation of Indigenous land and life. When the NIB released *Indian Control of Indian Education* in 1972, it sparked a movement by First Nations people to reclaim sovereignty over their affairs by way of education. The NIB articulated a position on education that reflected the shared aspirations and goals of First Nations people across Canada. Education was believed to be the key to improving the social and economic situation of First Nations people. Additionally, assuming the rights to control education was seen by First Nations as a way to reclaim culture, language, and identity that had been stripped away through a century of federal government control. In 1972, the NIB clearly articulated a desire by the people to reclaim education in the following profound statement:

> Unless a child learns about the forces which shaped him: the history of his people, their values and customs, their language, he will never really know himself for his potential as a human being. The Indian child who learns about his heritage will be proud of it. The lessons he learns in school, his whole school experience, should reinforce and contribute to the image he has of himself as an Indian.

The present school system is culturally alien to native students. Where the Indian contribution is not entirely ignored it is often cast in an unfavourable light. School curricula in federal and provincial schools should recognize Indian culture, values, customs and the Indian contribution to Canadian development. Courses in Indian history and culture should promote pride in the Indian child and respect in the non-Indian student.

A curriculum is not an archaic, inert vehicle for transmitting knowledge. It is a precise instrument, which can and should be shaped to exact specifications for a particular purpose. It can be changed and it can be improved. Using curriculum as a means to achieve their educational goals, Indian parents want to develop a program which will maintain balance and relevancy between academic/skill subjects and Indian cultural subjects. (National Indian Brotherhood 1972, 9)

The Native teacher education programs that were established in the early 1970s were developed with the goal of producing Native teachers who would assist in the revitalization of Native languages and cultures and who would cultivate positive developments in the instruction and curriculum of Native education. This marked a fundamental shift that saw education change from a tool used by the federal government to colonize/assimilate First Nations people, to one that was driven by First Nations people to create opportunities for change, which is now synonymous with decoloniality.

According to Battiste (2013, 66), to effect reform, educators need to make conscious decisions to nurture Indigenous knowledge, dignity, identity, and integrity by making direct change in school philosophy, pedagogy, and practice. Native teacher education programs that initially sought to fill the need to quickly train and certify Native teachers through hands-on classroom training have, over the past forty years, enabled Native teachers to help reclaim Indigenous self-determrnation, culture, language, and identity.

Conclusion

The latter part of this chapter has presented a fairly optimistic view of educationalization as employed by First Nations to address a host of social conditions. Effectively, First Nations were trying to use (re)education to solve (mis)education. The federal government's acceptance of *Indian Control of Indian Education* was a surprise departure from previous decades of authoritarian control. Perhaps the government's acquiescence stemmed from the cumulative effect of the growing number of commissioned reports that exposed its failures to adequately oversee Aboriginal affairs, or perhaps the government simply saw this as an opportunity to offload the tangled mess it had created. Quite possibly, a combination of these two factors persuaded Canada to officially accept ICIE into policy in 1973. Regardless, First Nations education was catapulted to the forefront of provincial educational policies, and First Nations organizations, governments, and educational institutions all began to eagerly strategize on ways to resolve the issues and conditions that First Nations peoples were facing.

The education of Native teachers was one measure that was adopted to help solve the pressing issues First Nations people faced. The swiftness with which this measure was accepted can be seen in the number of Native teacher education programs that emerged throughout western Canada in the years following the publication of ICIE and, as I have demonstrated, in the rapid development and expansion of BUNTEP in the province of Manitoba.

REFERENCES

Abele, Frances, Carolyn Dittburner, and Katherine A. Graham. 2000. "Towards a Shared Understanding in the Policy Discussion about Aboriginal Education." In *Aboriginal Education: Fulfilling the Promise*, edited by Marlene Brant Castellano, Lynne Davis, and Louis Lahache, 3–24. Vancouver: UBC Press.

Bouvier, Rita. E. 1984. "Specialized Training in the Saskatchewan Urban Native Teacher Education Program: A Case Study." Master's thesis, University of Saskatchewan.

Barnhardt, Ray. 1977. "Field-Based Education for Alaskan Native Teachers." In *Cross-Cultural Issues in Alaskan Education*. Vol. 1, edited by Rya Barnhardt et al., 87–100. Fairbanks, AK: Centre for Northern Educational Research, University of Alaska.

Battiste, Marie. 2013. *Decolonizing Education: Nourishing the Learning Spirit*. Saskatoon, SK: Purich Publishing.

Bridges, David. 2008. "Educationalization: On the Appropriateness of Asking Educational Institutions to Solve Social and Economic Problems." *Educational Theory* 58 (4): 461–74.

Cardinal, Harold. 1977. *The Rebirth of Canada's Indians*. Edmonton, AB: Hurtig Publishers.

– 1999. *The Unjust Society: The Tragedy of Canada's Indians*. Vancouver: Douglas and McIntyre.

Clarke, Sandra, and Marguerite MacKenzie. 1980. "Indian Teacher Training Programs: An Overview and Evaluation." In *Papers of the 11th Algonquian Conference*, edited by William Cowan, 19–32. Ottawa: Carleton University.

Depeape, Marc, and Paul Smeyers. 2008. "Educationalization as an Ongoing Modernization Process." *Educational Theory* 58 (4): 379–89. https://doi.org/10.1111/j.1741-5446.2008.00295.x.

Eastmure, Lori Patterson. 2011. "Honouring the Past, Touching the Future: Twenty-Two Years of Aboriginal Teacher Education in the Yukon." *Northern Review* 34 (Fall): 35–60.

Frideres, J.S. 1974. *Canada's Indians: Contemporary Conflicts*. Scarborough, ON: Prentice-Hall.

Fuchs, Estelle. 1970. "Time to Redeem an Old Promise." *Saturday Review*, 24 January, 54–7.

Hawthorn, Harry, ed. 1967. *A Survey of the Contemporary Indians of Canada: Economic, Political, Educational Needs and Policies*. 2 vols. Ottawa: Queen's Printer Press.

Indian Affairs and Northern Development. 1969. *Statement of the Government of Canada on Indian Policy, 1969*. Ottawa: Queen's Printer.

Indian Association of Alberta. 1970. *Citizens Plus*. Edmonton, AB: Author.

Manitoba Indian Brotherhood. 1971. *Wahbung: Our Tomorrows*. Winnipeg, MB: Author.

Manitoba Information Services Branch. 1978. "BUNTEP to Expand in the North." *News Service*. Retrieved from http://news.gov.mb.ca/news/archives/1979/07/1979-07-06'buntep'_to_expand_in_north_manitoba.pdf.

McAlpine, L. 2001. "Teacher Training for the New Wilderness: Quantum Leaps." In *Aboriginal Education in Canada: A Study in Decolonisation*, edited by K.P. Binda and S. Calliou, 105–19. Mississauga, ON: Canadian Educators' Press.

Miller, J.R. 1996. *Shingwauk's Vision: A History of Native Residential Schools*. Toronto: University of Toronto Press.

Milloy, John S. 1999. *A National Crime: The Canadian Government and the Residential School System, 1879 to 1986*. Winnipeg: University of Manitoba Press.

Moore-Eyman, E. 1977. *Native Education and University Planning*. Report to the Vice-President (Academic). Calgary, AB: University of Calgary

More, Arthur J. 1981. "Native Teacher Education: A Survey of Native Indian and Inuit Teacher Education Projects in Canada." Faculty of Education, University of British Columbia. Retrieved from ERIC database (ED249029). https://files.eric.ed.gov/fulltext/ED249029.pdf.

National Indian Brotherhood. 1972. *Indian Control of Indian Education*. Policy Paper presented to the Minister of Indian Affairs and Northern Development. Ottawa: National Indian Brotherhood.

Robertson, D.A. and A.J. Loughton. 1976. *BUNTEP: The Profile of a Teacher Education Project*. Brandon, MB: Brandon University. Retrieved from ERIC database (ED138425). https://files.eric.ed.gov/fulltext/ED138425.pdf.

St Denis, Verna. 2007. "Aboriginal Education and Anti-Racist Education: Building Alliances across Culture and Racial Identity." *Canadian Journal of Education* 30 (4): 1068–92.

Taylor, Donald, Martha Crago, and Lynn McAlpine. 2001. "Toward Full Empowerment in Native Education: Unanticipated Challenges." *Canadian Journal of Native Studies* 21 (1): 45–56.
Truth and Reconciliation Commission of Canada. 2012. *They Came for the Children*. Ottawa: Truth and Reconciliation Commision of Canada.
– 2015. *Canada's Residential Schools: The History, Part 2, 1939–2000*. Vol. 1. Montreal and Kingston: McGill-Queen's University Press.
Tuck, Eve, and Wayne K. Yang. 2012. "Decolonization Is Not a Metaphor." *Decolonization: Indigeneity, Education, and Society* 1 (1): 1–40.
von Stein, Joachium. 1984. "Providing University Courses and Programs to People Living in Northern Communities in Alberta, Saskatchewan, and Manitoba: Three Case Studies." PhD diss., University of Manitoba.
Wagner, R. 1988. "University Accommodation of Distance Education in Canada." *Journal of Distance Eduation* 3 (1): 25–38.

14 Indigeneity and Educationalization

CHRIS BEEMAN

In this chapter, I follow David Labaree's analysis, which holds that educationalization is a formalist process, with schools being the vehicle for its enactment. In this process, societal aspirations are permitted to be expressed, with the expectation, not that education will solve the problems, but rather that it will *fail* to solve the problems, as indeed has been the case historically (2008). If this analysis holds, then the endeavour to educate First Nations, Metis, and Inuit (FNMI) students may be understood as an extreme case of the convenient segregation of a "problem" to a sphere in which it is unable to be solved, and is known to be unable to be solved, while it appears that an attempt is being made to solve it. With this in mind, educationalization can be seen as one aspect of colonization. If this is the case, though, then a corollary to this may also emerge: because, to a lesser extent, the effects of educationalization apply to many students, then a kind of colonization may be posited to occur, though to a lesser extent and in a different way, with non-Indigenous students as well. As I will discuss below, this may be the case if the colonization that occurs is ontological in nature. In effect, many may be colonized by being forced to be part of schools that, while denying in their form the intimate interaction with the more-than-human that is mother earth – *jujum dakim*[1] – also claim to be solving the social problems that they contribute to creating.

The first part of this chapter examines Labaree's and others' work to situate the idea of educationalization. The second part attempts to use these analyses to understand some broad historical experiences around education for First Nations, Metis, and Inuit youth in Canada, with specific reference to sections of the Truth and Reconciliation Commission's calls for action. The third part aims to give an ontological explanation for why this particular social "problem" is unable to be solved through education. Indeed, I suggest that the "problem" is not

Indigenous education; the "problem" – at least for the modern global West – is Indigeneity/Authochthony[2] itself, because, considered ontologically, and from the viewpoint of certain Knowledge Keepers, it may be a being state that is incompatible with that of the modern, global West (Beeman 2006). I also look at the relevance of the case of Indigenous educationalization that I raise here for Labaree's theory, with specific reference to notions of colonization. It might be that the experience of education from an Indigenous point of view can contribute more generally to understanding the breadth of the educationalizing effect of public schools.[3]

On Labaree's Thesis: Addressing the Apparent Paradox between What Education Says It Is Doing and What It Is Doing

In his chapter in the present volume, Daniel Tröhler traces some of the historical origins of the term "educationalization," going back to Sunday school classes in the early half of the nineteenth century through driver education classes and Sputnik-era changes in American education after 1957. But he suggests that the roots of these changes were to be found far earlier in shifting cosmologies around the beginning of the eighteenth century, when a linear conception of life and time replaced a repeated, circular one. Conceiving of history as linear made changing direction theoretically possible, and, with the possibility of change, came the perceived need to improve. While it might be reasonable to challenge how much of today's meaning of the term relates to the earlier phases Tröhler mentions, this is a useful idea that provides some understanding of how current liberal democracies came to conceive of education, especially state-sponsored education, as a locus for the modification of attitudes, ideas, and skills of individual students, in consciously shaping students to meet the needs of the state.

Depaepe and Smeyers's (2008) description of educationalization encompasses much of the usual current meaning of the term:

> As an institution, the school is, among other things, held accountable for solving social inequalities (related to class, race, and gender); for reducing traffic deaths, obesity, teenage sex, and environmental destruction; and for enhancing public health, economic productivity, citizenship ... Pushing these kind[s] of "social" responsibilities on schools is a process that has been under way for a long time and coincides with the role of education in the formation of the modern nation-state. (379)

To this list, and specifically suited to an American context, David Labaree adds even more things the project of education is responsible for, including economic development and crime reduction (2008, 447). But the point behind the ever-growing list is the same: the institution of education has come to serve neoliberal interests of the state in shaping minds, careers, attitudes, and life choices. While Labaree limits his particular analysis, especially some aspects of it that note the way in which political systems intersect with educational ones, to the United States of America, the similarity to a Canadian context is starkly apparent.

Educationalization is the "downloading" of social problems to the process of schooling. When a social problem emerges, educative practices are expected to solve it. A part of Labaree's thesis is that at the heart of educationalization in the United States is a paradox: that while educational processes have been happy to take on countless social problems, from gender equity, to race and class issues, to public health concerns, they have been remarkably unsuccessful in the long term at solving them. How to explain this apparent paradox is central to understanding what educationalization is about.

Labaree's argument moves a step beyond what might be called "initial educationalizing theory." This is a little like reaching a point at which we realize that we no longer need be surprised at the latest outrageous thing the current United States president has said. A president such as Trump is predictably mercurial, so to be surprised by his latest act ought, after quick reflection, to be unsurprising. Similarly, when it comes to the project of colonization, that schools in their educationalizing function would serve to maintain the status quo is unsurprising: to do otherwise would be to defeat a central aspect of their purpose. What is perhaps most remarkable is the persistence of the perceived veracity of the claims educational systems make, (not unlike Trump's, to his constituency) through language and ideology, around the capacity of schools to be societally shaping forces.

Labaree's major contribution is that this is all to be expected: that failure is a necessary fulfilment of the language used to describe the attempt to change what actually must be addressed in other ways if an attempt at change is to be successful. Labaree suggests the following: the segmentation of social fields of play and the concomitant failure to resolve orphaned issues are natural outcomes of a broader failure to seek out deep reasons for social and ecological ills. The appropriate response to these ills would be broad structural change, superseding the personal responsibility and transformation expected of individual students in an educationalizing model.

While Labaree is careful to limit his comments to an American context, it in large part still applies to a Canadian one. In Labaree's argument, aspects of American culture and society that lead to the educationalization of social problems include: individualism, professional interest, and political interest. While Canada is less focused on *life, liberty, and the pursuit of happiness*, and rather more on *peace, order, and good governance*, it shares many of the qualities of a liberal democracy with the United States. And, while the pattern is more nuanced in Canada, the need to protect individual rights over social good is at the heart of liberal democracy.

With Labaree, I think the substance of the idea of educationalization has changed. It has changed from just being the attempt to address or solve social problems through education (Depaepe and Smeyers 2008). Now it is the *feigned* attempt to solve social problems through education, in the interest of protecting individual freedoms over public good. Labaree (2008) writes:

> One way of thinking about this is that education may not be doing what we ask, but it is doing what we want. We want an institution that will pursue our social goals in a way that is in line with the individualism at the heart of the liberal ideal, aiming to solve social problems by seeking to change the hearts, minds, and capacities of individual students. Another way of putting this is that we want an institution through which we can express our social goals without violating the principle of individual choice that lies at the center of the social structure, even if this comes at the cost of failing to achieve these goals. (448)

Thus, the process of education has to appear to do a poor job of solving what it claims it wants to do to satisfy its actual function, which is not to solve the problems it has been tasked with at all. That is the function of educationalization – to appear to be doing what it is not doing. To introduce a parallel case that will later be examined in more detail, if these same words were said to an informed Indigenous person in North America (and, for that matter, in the rest of the world) about the purpose of government in general, or perhaps the purpose of government in negotiating treaties, it is unlikely they would be surprised. So, perhaps there is no paradox in Labaree's observation of what educationalization does: Its purpose is not to do and it does not do. A paradox would occur only if the system that is truly intended to do such and such a thing, and is designed to do so, does not do it. As Labaree puts it:

> In this sense, then, we can understand the whole grand educational enterprise as an exercise in formalism. We assign formal responsibility to education for solving our most pressing social problems in light of our highest social ideals, with the tacit understanding that by educationalizing

these problem-solving efforts we are seeking a solution that is more formal than substantive. We are saying that we are willing to accept what education can produce – new programs, new curricula, new institutions, new degrees, new educational opportunities – in place of solutions that might make real changes in the ways in which we distribute social power, wealth, and honor. (448)

Thus, the current tendency in liberal democracies to make individual citizens, rather than responsible governments, the vehicle for solving broad social problems is emphasized. And with this perspective, education comes to be viewed as a natural site for the formation of individuals who are able to make these changes. As Labaree writes, "American individualism tends to reduce social problems to individual problems, locating the root cause of everything from poverty and illness to criminality and racism in the capacities and motives of individuals. If these are the primary roots of social problems, then education is the natural solution, because its central focus is on changing the capacities and motives of individual students" (450).

The purpose of examining Labaree's analysis is to see how well his notion of educationalization may apply to the experience of First Nations, Metis, and Inuit peoples in Canada. I hope that, by doing so, these experiences may in turn reflect on, enrich, and contribute to a modification of Labaree's theory.

How the Probable Failure of Reconciliation in Education May Still Carry Hope

In this part, I attempt to apply Labaree's understanding of educationalization to the historical experiences of First Nations, Metis and Inuit students in Canada. The limitations of space preclude an in-depth analysis; what I propose to do here is to make reference to some broad historical understandings of the residential school project and to look at the recently published Truth and Reconciliation Commission (TRC) report (2015), which includes several education-specific calls to action.

Labaree's concept of educationalizing, noted above, as applied to the subject of reconciliation, helps us understand the overall process of colonization. Many of the Elders[4] with whom I have spoken during the past 15 years have noted at least one of the following faults with the historical actions of the federal government: an inability to adhere to specific parts of treaty agreements, an inability to honour and adhere to the spirit of treaty agreements, and an inability to meet the needs of Aboriginal peoples in adapting to new governing climates and contexts. In other words, they have all noticed the stark failure of governing bodies, at their levels, to not do what they said they would do. In particular, this tendency plays out in education.

In *Shingwauk's Vision* (1996), J.R. Miller recounts the long histories of Turtle Island residential schools, beginning in about 1620, systematized in the late 1800s, and not terminated until the last decade of the twentieth century (39). These schools were not about learning; they were about unlearning a culture (103). As Duncan Campbell Scott, enactor, if not originator, of Canada's policy of assimilation and head of the Department of Indian Affairs from 1913 to 1932 said, "The happiest future for the Indian race is absorption into the general population, and this is the object and policy of our government" (Cook and Lindau, 2000, 239).

Almost everything about these schools differed from the previous lived experience of the students. For example, the well-established principle of non-interference with a young person's path, of individual autonomy (Miller 1996, 35), that is common to many FNMI cultures was antithetical to the unstated presuppositions that undergirded the process of attending a residential school: the complete relinquishment of self in the face of correction by representatives of the church and state. Thus, before an educative act ever occurred, before "content" was ever introduced in the classroom, cultural practices were transgressed. Even now, in education in the modern global West, the role of students includes submitting to the educative will of a teacher, who is recognized as being better equipped to guide their learning. Historically, this was unfamiliar to FNMI students: a teacher was always someone personally known and trusted, and what was learned followed the natural inclinations and proclivities of students (Miller 1996).

More broadly, many provincial curricula (motivated perhaps more by concerns over "success rates" of FNMI students than a sincere wish to understand difference) have characterized differences in teaching and learning modes by opposing non-Aboriginal and Aboriginal styles. Thus, they emphasize teaching through land- and place-based versus classroom-based models; working with local Knowledge Keepers as alternatives to formal authority; valuing community-generated versus centralized knowledge; generating authentic experiences versus abstract knowledge; and considering individualized formative assessment versus comparative, summative assessment (Alberta Education 2005). While useful as a preliminary description of differences that may alert teachers to just how great the divide may be between historical practices of education among FNMI peoples and even modern and "enlightened" schools, the utility of such dualism is limited. What works may be more diverse and less reliant on centralized standards and directives than is normally accepted in the culture of the global modern West.

However, in this chapter I do want to explore and make use of one kind of teaching that has been deeply significant in long-term work with Elders of my acquaintance: stories. The intentional use of nuanced stories, which are able to be understood in many ways, is perhaps one of the most significant modes of teaching that emerges from FNMI contexts. A story might explain some facts about trapping, or the character of certain animals, such as the curiosity of deer people, for example. But the same story might contain ethical guidance for the listeners about how human people ought to behave around animal people. And it might also have a particular moral that the Elder telling the story might wish to direct to one particular listener (Miller 1996, 32).

The value of stories in my own work with Elders of the Teme Augama Anishinaabe cannot be overstated. Take Alex Mathias's story of the cow moose as she is teaching a lesson to her own offspring. Alex says:

> In the spring of the year after the calf is born –
> if the mother knows that she will give birth again –
> well, she cannot take care of two so
> she finds a time when both she and the calf are browsing
> near a creek or something
> and when there is some distraction
> she walks off up the creek
> hiding her scent with the water
> so that her calf cannot find her.
> That way, she is free to give birth
> and to take care of the new calf. (Alex Mathias, personal communication)

Layers upon layers: The cow moose is giving a final lesson to her calf that she may use with her own calf; she is giving a final lesson on something like attention and diversion that may enhance the calf's ability to survive; Alex is telling me a story about natural things that come from his own experience; this story is evidence of the kind of knowing that cannot easily be found through Western research – it has to be learned through experience – so there is a story there too. And perhaps Alex is giving me a story about our ultimate parting, when he moves on.

Stories figure prominently in the teaching of a course in Indigenous studies in a Faculty of Education because, through story, so much happens at one time. These stories, by their presence and nature, question perceived efficacies of the mechanistic sort of outcomes-based teaching design currently so popular in postsecondary institutions across

North America. A parallel might be made to permaculture in the growing of food: the synergy of mutually beneficial crops increases yields and builds soil health in ways that the meagre human understanding of nitrogen, phosphorus, and potassium, meted out to individual crops, simply cannot fathom. In permaculture, growth and ecosystem health are understood to be more complex than human knowing can understand. So, less interference is better. The same could be said for how stories feature in Indigenous understandings of learning and human development. Like a permaculture farmer, whose goal is to interfere as little as possible with the naturally occurring systems already present in a healthy ecosystem, the teacher ought only to, with the gentlest delicacy, nudge growth in a direction that might be a good one. Stories provide a way for this to happen. Preserving the integrity of the spirit of the learner is absolutely central. And attendance to all aspects of being, including emotion, the physical body, mind, and spirit, is necessary in educative practice. Stories as pedagogical practice answer all of these needs.

Keith Basso's epic *Wisdom Sits in Places* (1996) relates the value of stories in teaching moral lessons, in this case with prominent features in a landscape, in ways that do not diminish the spirit of the learner. The lesson is quite literally *out there* – that is, the lessons are contained in the spaces that become place (Tuan 1977) through the stories told about them. And learners can put themselves *in there* in the ways that they wish to. No one else need know how the learner places themselves in the story, or in which character, or, for that matter, where in the now-dwelt place (Heidegger 2008, Ingold 2000, Clarke and Mcphie 2014). Similarly, the skilled teller of the tale cannot be resented in the way a teacher who demands a certain outcome can. In the case Basso relates, a young man guilty of romantic impropriety is gently, teasingly, and humorously guided on a riding trail by two older riders who tell the tale of that particular place and the moral lessons it holds. The young man is never ostracized or shamed directly, but he can choose to understand the story in ways that might cause him to note these feelings in himself. Rather, the act of telling the well-known story that is linked to this part of the land is an act of acceptance of him by the storytellers. And, I would argue, the place itself may have some agency here. It is not just that the human people have imbued it with a certain power according to the stories they tell; it is also that the place suggested those stories in the first place (Clarke and Mcphie 2014).

Perhaps what is most notable in Miller's account of early Indigenous education is the gentleness with which the spirit of young learners was historically treated. That affect could influence knowledge – as though the two could ever have been separated – is clearly understood. And it stands in stark contrast to Miller's description of residential schools, which sought to force assimilation through destroying culture, community, and connections with the more-than-human world. Accounts of survivors of residential schools are detailed in the Truth and Reconciliation Commision report (2015). Retelling such stories is not within the parameters of this chapter. What I would like to do, though, is to pose some questions on educationalization to the report. One of my concerns is that a trivialized version of "Indigenizing" in postsecondary and public curricula may reify a notion of Indigeneity and may contribute to further undermining the FNMI people.

Notes on the Report of the Truth and Reconciliation Commission

Within the section on education, there are seven calls to action (6–12) in the Truth and Reconciliation Commision report (Truth and Reconciliation Commision of Canada 2015, 321). Several of these deal with socio-economic conditions surrounding, but not within education, so would not properly be categorized as educationalizing. These include, for example, a call to publish annual reports documenting and comparing the income attainment of Aboriginal and non-Aboriginal peoples (Call 9). In other words, the report recognizes influences such as income that affect the ability of Aboriginal students to succeed in schools. These calls to action might well lead to the kind of broad, societal change that Labaree (2008) correctly notes *ought* to occur outside schools.

However, one of the calls to action (10) requires the federal government to work with Aboriginal people to draft new legislation about the education of Aboriginal people. This call has seven subsections to it. It reads:

We call on the federal government to draft new Aboriginal education legislation with the full participation and informed consent of Aboriginal peoples. The new legislation would include a commitment to sufficient funding and would incorporate the following principles:

i   Providing sufficient funding to close identified educational achievement gaps within one generation.
ii Improving education attainment levels and success rates.
iii Developing culturally appropriate curricula.
iv Protecting the right to Aboriginal languages, including the teaching of Aboriginal languages as credit courses.
v   Enabling parental and community responsibility, control, and accountability, similar to what parents enjoy in public school systems.
vi Enabling parents to fully participate in the education of their children.

vii Respecting and honouring Treaty relationships. (Truth and Reconciliation Commision of Canada 2015, 320–1)

All of these principles might be thought of as ensuring respect for the difference of Aboriginal peoples, and ensuring an opportunity of equality in educational practices. Several of the principles address structural issues, such as ensuring adequate funding from all levels of government and respecting treaty relationships. Yet looking at this from the perspective of educationalization, the calls for action may also do something else: they may succeed in implicating Indigenous parents, culture, and of course, students, within a system that is designed, paraphrasing Bridges's view (quoted in Labaree 2008), both to do too much and to not do it well. In other words, despite the good intentions of all participants in the TRC, particularly the survivors of the abusive form of education that was the residential schooling system, the efforts to change the education system might be leading only to a more subtle form of what is ultimately the same process of colonization. This time, though, those who largely direct the process may be FNMI people themselves. Will this change mean that survivors will correctly discern and act upon both the beneficial and compromising aspects of structural forces, such as standardized tests, or will they simply be implicated more deeply in their own oppression?

More than this, it appears that calls for action in the field of education might possibly lead (it would appear unintentionally) not to actual Indigenous control of education (following Eber Hampton's (1993) notion of Indigenous education, *sui generis*) but to collaboration in a project that is inherently colonizing. After all, it is the colonizers who ultimately still run the show, and it is in the interests of the colonizers (under significant legal pressure) that this policy of educationalization, in the form of the TRC report's calls for action around education, be enacted. This appears to be a reasonable inference from Labaree's work: educationalization's end effect is to appear to be making the changes that the culture collectively would like to think they could make, stating the ideals that the culture as a whole might like to attain, while not actually changing anything (448).

As is evidenced by the call to action from Truth and Reconciliation Commission report noted above, however, what is different about educationalization as it applies to Indigenous peoples is that it is the *structures* around education that are being manipulated to solve the problem. As Depaepe and Smeyers (2008) and Labaree (2008) describe it, normally it is what is *taught* in schools, rather than the *structure* of schooling, that is educationalized. There is evidently some fluidity between subject material and structures, as Labaree notes, but the modification of educational structures is a key element in the proposed changes to education that the TRC report calls for. The implications of this are difficult to predict. It can be argued, as above, that, following the overall pattern of educationalization, if the structures around education are addressed in ways recommended by the report, then the educationalizing effect of these apparent attempts to change the structures around education will be to fail, and thus to necessarily implicate Indigenous people in their own oppression. It is possible, though, that this process may also be liberatory, although, as Hampton (1993), Coulthard (2014), and many others have noted, there is little evidence that cooperation with the various levels of government in Canada will lead to liberation.

Even if it is allowed that the changing of structures around education *could*, with effect, be used counter to overall patterns of colonization, a more serious philosophical objection remains: the first sub-point of Call 10 is "to provide sufficient funding to close identified achievement gaps within one generation." While the term "one generation" has resonance with the Indigenous idea of *seven generations*, the achievement gaps that are mentioned are according to the standards of modern Western culture and designed for its own (comparative and neoliberal-oriented) purpose. Certainly, on the face of it, ensuring that FNMI students succeed is schools appears to be a good thing. The TRC report was authored by Murray Sinclair, a very thoughtful writer of a significant document, yet this call to action appears to presuppose the desirability of accepting the sort of standards of achievement that have historically been used to control FNMI peoples, and that are designed by the modern global West to train skilled workers, whose real job may be to create profit. Standards of this kind are necessary in a competitive, neoliberal-inspired economy of the kind we have in Canada. And of course, this is not said to undermine the need for better access to good jobs for FNMI people. But, while work is important, meaningful work in an economy that is considered by many to be inherently exploitative is rare. Thus, if standards that are ultimately designed to simply train willing workers are followed, then the likelihood that this in itself would lead to reconciliation appears low.

Further, this call for action wants to *close those gaps*. If ontological difference were not at issue, this might appear to be a lofty aim. But considered from an ontological perspective (roughly, *state of being*, described below), this is deeply troubling, for at least some of the affected FNMI students. It is not implausible that the closing of these gaps might be an exact fit for the loss of an ontologically interconnected way of being with the world – in other words, a weakening of the *ontos* Indigeneity within FNMI peoples today.

Following Depaepe and Smeyers's commentary (2008) on Erich Ribolits and Johannes Zuber: "Educationalization does not lead to emancipation but to the subjection of the spirit. Instead of adapting the society to people, the process of educationalization (which constitutes the logical response to globalization and modernization in our own time) leads to the adaptation of the people to the neoconservative society. The result is, therefore, the domestication of thinking and not emancipation" (383). I would suggest adding to this that the result is not only domestication of thinking, but of *being*. Even looking at simply the act of educating, it surprises me that the first two points in Call 10 are to do with funding and improving success rates. While it is true, in subsequent points such as (iii), "Developing culturally appropriate curricula," that much ontologically sensitive learning could occur, this and other points seem to only vaguely hint at any significant changes to education. The overall project of the global, modern West, which is that education in its usually accepted form needs to happen, and in its happening, needs to try to attempt to solve social problems that it is not equipped to solve, seems to be accepted by the report.

Still, following Labaree's thesis, while the purpose of putting social issues in the dossier of education is precisely for them not to be solved, at least the good that may come out of this is that the issues are tagged as ones that, even if not immediately solvable, are at least identified as significant. And, it could be argued that this may be a good thing for Indigenous peoples. However, Indigenous scholars and Elders alike have rightly pointed out that, without the need for any contribution in this vein from educationalization, we are already at a place where little is being done and it is known not to be done (Coulthard 2014) Depending upon which treaty territory is in view, the patient waiting has been going on for several centuries. The issues are already immediately visible as necessary and pressing.

In the next section, I would like to make the case that what is most painfully missing from the attempts in public curriculum documents and the Truth and Reconciliation Commission report is an understanding of just how different the *ontos* of Indigeneity is from that of *homo mobilis*. The only way for reconciliation to truly occur is not just a change of heart – that phrase is too easily stated and too easy to be made trite. It is an experience of the *ontos* of Indigeneity. And because these two systems may be incommensurable, the outlook for communication between them remains bleak.

Indigeneity/Autochthony and Ontological Incommensurability

Please recall Daniel Tröhler's helpful chapter, which addresses some of the intellectual changes that made the ground fertile for the new project of education. These changes had to do with the replacing of a cyclical notion of time with a linear one. Linearity made possible the notion of progress, and education could serve to ensure progress. The process of educationalization would overtake education itself, as the notion of progress came to be the individual's responsibility to make change in his or her own life, as opposed to large-scale alteration of social structures – at least, as Labaree argues, in the United States. Thus, it was natural, in concurrent processes of colonization, that the project of education would be infused by the interests of the state and that the inevitable problems with those colonized would be educationalized.

There are at least two contemporary aspects to this model that live on. The first is that the description of what had been done to FNMI peoples would become part of the curriculum: a later educationalizing though school *content* of what is now a "social problem." Part of my job where I teach in Manitoba is working with undergraduate students who will become teachers to face (I hope in a more liberatory way than a simple *prima facie* introduction would give) the structurally racist nature of this culture and to develop strategies to teach in this context. The second is the *form* of education that this educationalizing initiative began, as it has applied directly to FNMI peoples, over time. It would be employed first, with physical force in residential schools (Truth and Reconciliation Commission of Canada 2015) and later, following the argument of Depaepe, "physical compulsion (which was also accompanied by psychological pressure) had to give way to a more psychological 'treatment' of the child. Brutalizing elements of physical violence were 'professionally' converted into a 'disembodied' educational intervention that tended to intensify emotional manipulation" (381). While this quotation was not made in reference to FNMI peoples in Canada, it might easily apply in this context. As I noted in earlier work (Beeman 2017), one explanation for the brutality of residential schools is the failure to recognize the difference of Indigenous students as possibly ontologically, and not simply culturally based. Thus, residential schools and the attempt through them to educationalize the "problem" of Indigeneity can be considered a failed attempt at ontological reconfiguration. By this I mean that Indigeneity/Autochthony may be considered not merely culturally, but ontologically – that is to say, as a particular way of being in the world, a lived relationship with place such that the well-being of the more-than-human and human participants are considered and enacted in each moment of interaction (Beeman 2006; 2017). Such a being state may be incommensurable and thus invisible to that of *homo mobilis*, the being state of the global modern West.

If this is true, it is something that will not fit, even within the dismal landscape of Labaree's theory: there is no place to begin to address something that cannot be either known or imagined to exist by the dominant *ontos*[5] of *homo mobilis*. So, when it comes to Labaree's observation that what is educationalized may still be useful, because this allows the culture to identify what it would like to address, even if it does not address it successfully or appropriately in schools, we are still at an impasse. The only thing the *ontos* of *homo mobilis* may be capable of comprehending in this context is something that is discretely knowable – such as a student identifying as Dakota or Teme Augama Anshinaabe or Swampy Cree. These are markers of categorization, in the *ontos* of *homo mobilis*; they are only peripherally linked to the ontological condition of Indigeneity.

The impasse seems resolute. Yet the work of new materialists (Barad 2007; Bennett 2009; Coole and Frost 2010, Gough 2016, Mcphie and Clarke 2015) is bringing attention to the idea that the world might have agency in ways that the global modern West conveniently denies. A dualist Cartesian world view both prioritizes human knowing and separates (in a Spinozan description) mind from matter. A more-than-human world in which other beings and the world itself have agency is part of many First Nations' cosmology. As Ingold (2000) and Clarke and Mcphie (2014), and others note, in a Spinozan world view, separate (or individual) human identity may give way to a view of the world in which undifferentiated mind/matter may be considered nexuses with attributes of humanness or treeness or rockiness or smoothness. Nodes of interaction in the mind/matter substrate provide slight differences in character and give another view of what apparent thingness could be constituted, without giving way to a necessary Cartesian dualism.

In other words, to use Barad's apt onto-epistemological insight (2007), by being in the world in a distinctly other way, other kinds of knowing become possible. So, there might appear to be hope in bridging *ontos*. Hope would be dashed is if members of *homo mobilis* continue to believe that, by simply thinking, a bridge can be built between otherwise incommensurable *ontos*. What makes commensurability possible at all would then be lived understanding emerging from enacting a different ontological position. And this both takes time and is inherently unattractive to *homo mobilis*'s predilection for abstraction.

Gadamer's (2004) differentiation between *Erlebnis* and *Erfahrung* might also help in this project. Both terms may be translated by the English "experience." But *Erlebnis* refers to the kind of limited experience that is already fully knowable because it is already part of us. In the hermeneutic process, the going out of oneself to meet the other (the *travelling* element of the root of *Erfahrung*) involves gaining increasing awareness of one's own pre-judgments/forehaving as part of an attempt to move outwards to meet what is attempting to be known. I like this as a metaphor for what it might be like to try to meet the *ontos* of Indigeneity hermeneutically. Yet Gadamer describes an intellectual process, and the metaphor may not extend to an ontological one.

Yet, I do not think that the ontological journey of *Erfahrung* can be made in the same way. Good intentions and consciousness of presuppositions, with a sincere attempt to understand what is outside of oneself, are laudable intellectual and emotional processes. But they cannot bridge the immense gap that is not just world view (again, this would entail merely intellectualizable difference) but another (and possibly incommensurable) *ontos*.

Take, for example, the idea that the more-than-human world may operate with agency. Except for the earlier insights of Barad (2007) and of a very few current theorist such as Clarke and Mcphie (2014), and of course many living FNMI Elders and countless Indigenous people throughout time, considering that the more-than-human world operates with agency quite apart from human interpretation is an immense step away from the inflated importance and centrality of the human that has characterized so much discourse in the modern West. But, of course, Indigenous people have always known this – or at least they have known it *ab originalis*.

If it is the case that the world is actually a being force that, while certainly existing in relationship to the humans who are a part of it, also has its own being, which (if it could be imagined to have agency in human terms) sometimes just does not give a hoot, it behooves us humans *to just be still and listen up awhile*, because the overall wellbeing of the ecosystem may be in part dependent upon our doing so. But listening is not such an easy thing to do. This is one of the reasons why First Nations ceremony has always acknowledged and given importance to the more-than-human world, sometimes through words, sometimes through the invocation of animal and other persons.

Consider the words of Alex Mathias, when speaking about altered ways of knowing a spirit place. When the usual concept of self in the modern global West gives way to another identity that conjoins and is not differentiatable from places, then other ways of knowing may occur. Alex describes the kind of knowing made possible through interaction with Cheeskon Abikon thus:

> people getting answers
> maybe not by hearing voices
> but in their mind
> the answers coming to them (Beeman 2006)

The way that Alex is describing is a truly different way of understanding the world that may not permit communication between ontological positions. If this is the case, then there would appear little that can be done to bridge the intellectualizable gap in response to the educationalizing of education for FNMI students: the only visible route would be an ontological one.

Remaining Questions

I close with some questions. I am working with the idea that, in the dance of colonization/decolonization, we must be aware of reciprocal interaction – that is, what is the *colonized*, the apparent "recipient" of the "colonizing act," doing to the *colonizer*? By extension, then, we ought to be thinking what Indigeneity is doing to educationalization. Is there something in this relationship in which more "give" than "take" is at play? If Indigeneity/Autochthony consists in a being state that is incommensurable with that of *homo mobilis*, and this is what accounts for the "failure" of some FNMI students in schools, could this be viewed as a kind of resistance against the otherwise successful (in its planned failure) educationalizing influence in the modern global West?

If I am right about Indigeneity/Autochthony as a different *ontos*, and thus that the *homo mobilis*–infused practice of education cannot therefore penetrate it, then perhaps the concomitant is also so: that Indigeneity is incapable of being "schooled" in precisely the way the designers of assimilation-based practices like residential schools wanted to make it. And this is why, with respect to the project of education, I have claimed elsewhere (Beeman 2017) that there is an incommensurability between the mode of being of *homo mobilis* and that of Indigeneity/Autochthony.

Yet this situation is not without hope: what it speaks to in Labaree's theory is that there are some things – such as the claims educationalization makes about what it will do through the process of education – that cannot be known for what they are. They are only the symbols of what a culture would, in an ideal world, address under the (useful) formalized structure of educationalization. After all, this is one of the hopes that Labaree's theory holds for the formalist nature of educationalization: that while problems of the kind dumped into the project of education could not be solved, they could at least be identified as notes to the culture as a whole that these areas need work.

What, then, may educationalization speak to colonization? So many of the aspects of educationalization identified by Labaree and Depaepe and Smeyers are direct parallels with colonization. So, which is it? If educationalization is, as it were, a broader and less direct form of colonization, then what – and, more precisely, who – is being colonized? Public education extends to almost all citizens. Colonization usually refers to a powerful colonial country's domination of other people. But what might it be for a state to "colonize" its own citizens? And what might the resistance of the position of Indigeneity/Autochthony bring to an understanding of broader colonial resistance of all citizens to the state?

NOTES

1 This is a transliteration of the phrase Alex Mathias used to describe *mother earth* in the Teme Augama Anishinabemowin dialect. Etymologically, it relates to the idea of a giver of milk. Thus, land is understood, even in the name given to it, to be a provider of sustenance.
2 The terms "Indigeneity" and "Autochthony" are used roughly interchangeably. As this chapter later notes, they are intended to suggest an ontological (roughly "being related") state, and hence are not simply descriptors of ethnicity. My use of these terms has changed substantially, as in Canada, the term "Aboriginal" was used in academic writing until about 2015. Now the term "Indigenous "is preferred. However, in earlier writings, I had used the term "Indigeneity" to refer to a praticular being state. Please see note 3 below. Also, please see Beeman 2017, for a fuller discussion.
3 The meanings and uses of the terms "Indigenous/Indigeneity" and "Aboriginal/Aboriginality" are undergoing rapid shifts. When the Truth and Reconciliation Committee, chaired by Murray Sinclair, made its report in 2015, the term "Aboriginal" was still in use to broadly refer to First Nations, Metis, and Inuit peoples in Canada. The report reflects this terminology. In the intervening years years, the term "Indigenous," which had hitherto in Canada been used more to refer to First Peoples in international contexts, has taken its place. As will become clear, in this chapter, because some of the resources I consulted still use the term "Aboriginal," I will use that term when referring to ethnic heritage and when discussing that body of work. I will sometimes use the term "Indigenous" in this way, but will also suggest the term "Autochthonous" to describe a position of ontological

difference, as an ontological bridge between ethnicities, shared between FNMI and non-FNMI people.
4 The term "Elder" is also undergoing revision as this chapter goes to press. Currently, the term "Knowledge Keeper" or "Knowledge Holder" is coming to be preferred. Different Elders/Knowledge Keepers prefer to be described differently. Because those I work with normally use the term Elder, I will do so in this chapter.
5 I use *ontos-*, separated from its usual partner *-logos*, to point to the predominantly "being related" difference proposed here.

REFERENCES

Alberta Education. 2005. *Our Words, Our Ways: Teaching First Nations, Metis, and Inuit Learners*. Edmonton: Alberta Ministry of Education.
Barad, K. 2007. *Meeting the Universe Halfway: Quantum Physics and the Entanglement of Matter and Meaning*. Durham, NC: Duke University Press.
Basso, Keith, 1996. *Wisdom Sits in Places: Landscape and Language among the Western Apache*. Albequeque: University of New Mexico Press.
Beeman, C. 2006. "Another Way of Knowing and Being." PhD diss., Queen's University, Kingston, ON.
– 2017. "Indigenous Education as Failed Ontological Reconfiguration." In *Catholic Education in the Wake of Vatican II*, edited by Rosa Bruno-Jofré and Jon Igelmo Zaldívar. Toronto: University of Toronto Press.
Bennett, J. 2009. *Vibrant Matter: A Political Ecology of Things*. Durham, NC: Duke University Press.
Clarke, D.A.G., and J. Mcphie. 2014. "Becoming Animate in Education: Immanent Materiality and Outdoor Learning for Sustainability." *Journal of Adventure Education and Outdoor Learning* 14 (3): 198–216. https://doi.org/10.1080/14729679.2014.919866.
Cook, Curtis, and Juan Lindau. 2000. *Aboriginal Rights and Self-Government: The Canadian and Mexican Experience in North American Perspective*. Montreal and Kingston: McGill-Queen's University Press.
Coole, D., and S. Frost, eds. 2010. *New Materialisms*. Durham, NC: Duke University Press.
Coulthard, Dennis. 2014. *Red Skin, White Masks: Rejecting the Colonial Politics of Recognition*. Minneapolis, MN: University of Minnesota Press.
Depaepe, Marc, and Paul Smeyers 2008. "Educationalization as an Ongoing Modernization Process." *Educational Theory* 58 (4): 379–89. https://doi.org/10.1111/j.1741-5446.2008.00295.x.
Gadamer, Hans George. 2004. *Truth and Method*. 2nd ed. Translated by J. Weinsheimer and D.G. Marshall. New York: Crossroad.

Gannon, S. 2015. "Saving Squawk? Animal and Human Entanglement at the Edge of the Lagoon." *Environmental Education Research* 23 (1): 91–110. https://doi.org/10.1080/13504622.2015.1101752.

Gough, N. 2016. "Postparadigmatic Materialisms: A 'New Movement of Thought' for Outdoor Environmental Education Research?" *Journal of Outdoor and Environmental Education* 19 (2): 51–65. https://doi.org/10.1007/bf03400994.

Hampton, Eber. 1993. "Toward a Redefinition of American Indian/Alaskan Native Education." *Canadian Journal of Native Education* 20 (2): 261–310.

Heidegger, Martin. 2008. *Basics Writings: Martin Heidegger*. Edited by David Farrell. New York: Harper Perennial Modern Thought.

Ingold, Tim. 2000. *The Perception of the Environment: Essays on Livelihood, Dwelling, and Skill*. London: Routledge.

Labaree, David. 2008. "The Winning Ways of Losing Strategy: Educationalizing Social Problems in the United States." *Educational Theory* 58 (4): 447–60. https://doi.org/10.1111/j.1741-5446.2008.00299.x.

Mcphie, Jamie and David Andrew George Clarke. 2015. "A Walk in the Park: Considering Practice for Outdoor Environmental Education through an Immanent Take on the Material Turn." *Journal of Environmental Education* 46 (4): 230–50. https://doi.org/10.1080/00958964.2015.1069250.

Miller, J.R. 1996. *Shingwauk's Vision: A History of Native Residential Schools*. Toronto: University of Toronto Press.

Payne, P.G. 2016. "What Next? Post-Critical Materialisms in Environmental Education." *Journal of Environmental Education* 47 (2): 169–78. https://doi.org/10.1080/00958964.2015.1127201.

Rautio, P. 2013. "Mingling and Imitating in Producing Spaces for Knowing and Being: Insights from a Finnish Study of Child–Matter Intra-action." *Childhood* 21 (4): 461–74. https://doi.org/10.1177/0907568213496653.

Ross, Hamish, and Greg Mannion. 2012. "Curriculum Making as the Enactment of Dwelling in Places." *Studies in Philosophy and Education* 31 (3): 303–13. https://doi.org/10.1007/s11217-012-9295-6.

Spinoza, Baruch. 2006. *The Essential Spinoza: Ethics and Related Writings*. Edited by Michael L. Morgan. Translated by Samuel Shirley. Indianapolis: Hackett.

Truth and Reconciliation Commission of Canada. 2015. *Honouring the Truth, Reconciling for the Future: Summary of the Final Report of the Truth and Reconciliation Commission of Canada*. www.trc.ca.

Tuan, Yi-fu. 1977. *Space and Place: The Perspective of Experience*. Minneapolis: University of Minnesota Press.

15 Capuchin Missions in Mapuche Territory: The Education of an Original People in Chile from 1880 to 1930

SOL SERRANO AND MACARENA PONCE DE LEÓN

Educationalization, understood as the process of using schools to solve social problems, is one of the hallmarks of modernity and modernization (Depaepe and Smeyer 2008; Depaepe et al. 2008; Tröhler 2008; Labaree 2008; Bridges 2008). A concept that involves broader social considerations, educationalization is historically related to the massive expansion of schooling and the building of the modern state.

In colonial and post-colonial studies, religious missions that were established among Indigenous peoples have often been considered, along with colonialism and capitalism, as agents of acculturation of the Western civilizing project. The growth of Protestant and Catholic missionary activity in the nineteenth century went hand in hand with European colonial expansion, and this activity served as an acculturating agent that imposed a dominant cultural model. However, the civilizing project was not monolithic, and the thoroughness of the imposition of Western culture could have been relative. Indeed, in some cases, internal fissures within colonial efforts opened diverse paths of resistance for those subjected to the project (Depaepe 1995, 17). This chapter offers an examination of a historical situation that shows the complexity of processes of educationalization and confessionalization. It clearly documents the uniqueness of approaches among congregations, in this case the Capuchin Brothers from Bavaria working with the Mapuche people in Chile, and the people's dynamic use of schooling and forms of educationalization to empower themselves.

In the first section of this chapter, we examine the concept of Mapuche culture that was elaborated by the Bavarian Capuchins in the educationalization of redemption through Indigenous schools. We examine the missions and mission schools established by Bavarian Capuchin brothers from 1881, the time of the Chilean state's definitive military occupation of Mapuche territory, until the territory's consolidation in 1930. The brothers emphasized linguistic and ethnographic studies, elaborating a type of evangelization that would take as its starting point a conception of Mapuche culture as "organic." Thus, for the brothers, the Mapuche people's conversion to Christianity had to start from the richness of their own religiosity and values, as opposed to a forced assimilation through cultural extermination, which was the state's approach. This meant an unprecedented type of relationship between the missions and the Mapuche people. In practical terms, the brothers incorporated some elements of the Mapuche culture, like their language, into the Catholic liturgy and rituals, and praised and encouraged others. The missionaries became allies of the Mapuche in the efforts to defend Mapuche lands from expropriation.

In the second section, we analyse the mission schools and their approach to the process of educationalization. Although the Capuchin brothers partially succeeded in their goal to establish Indigenous schools to convert the non-believers, the schools functioned mainly to help consolidate the state's power and establish the diocesan church. Even so, the missional schools had an ethnic dimension that the state's public schools lacked. The missional school attended to a mixed population, Chilean, and Mapuche, which was part of the state's geopolitical strategy to make the annexed territory governable. Before the schools were in place, the autonomous Mapuche territory, which was the zone between the Cautín and Toltén rivers – what would eventually become the province of Cautín – had only been temporarily penetrated during military incursions, but never occupied by either missionaries or state officials (see figure 15.1). For that reason, establishing governability meant, in a first stage, organizing a civil government around the actors already settled in the region, with the purpose being to create institutionality and highlight the presence of the state. This is where the process of educationalization began, with the goal of installing a national state. The missions – and not the army or the state – penetrated the territory, effectively reaching the Mapuche population by establishing themselves in rural zones and setting their schools in motion.

Along with contributing to the consolidation of the national state, the missional school became a Catholic school, as the prefecture of La Araucanía became, for all practical purposes, a diocese. Conceptually, the mission schools were meant to educate the Indigenous children in their own language, but that did not happen. The mission schools sought to educate the Mapuche children and thus made schooling a central part of their communities; yet, in reality, there were no Mapuche schools, but simply Mapuche students in schools. These Catholic schools were assimilated into the national mixed education system, and, although they educated Mapuches, due to the establishment of the diocesan church, the missional sense of educating the unfaithful was no longer their main goal. The state then became secular in 1925 and adopted a laicized educational system, and, as Protestant and communist ideologies were increasing in popularity, missionary efforts were required to defend not the Mapuche, but the church itself.

Meanwhile, the Mapuche communities were demanding schools as an instrument of defence against the intrusion of the *winca* (white) world. These institutions, completely foreign to the Mapuche culture, played a significant role in the rise of a new social actor, the "literate" Mapuche, a figure organized through the defence of Mapuche lands and identity. Education, as the most influential factor in the strengthening of the Mapuche people, cut across all of the Indigenous elites and leaders, and also reached their vindictive alliances. The Mapuche used education to empower themselves politically as an ethnic group against the national state that had usurped their lands, backing up their new leaders and representatives in terms of their status as "literate" people. Thus, they used education to legitimate their historical demands in the forum of public opinion.

Evangelization, Civilization, and the Culture of the Other

Beginning with the Spanish conquest in the sixteenth century, Latin America became by definition a land of missions. Evangelization was the basis for the papal bulls that granted the territory to the Spanish and Portuguese Crowns. As administrative control over the continent was consolidated and Catholicism entrenched, the missions became less about converting pagans and more about providing religious services in rural regions or to the Indigenous communities. The missions among pagans were rather uncommon in nineteenth-century Latin America, and they were different from the mission of colonial expansion. After independence, these countries were no longer European colonies, and the continent was already mainly Catholic. The experience of the Mapuche people was unique, from a continental context, as, with the exception of a few Indigenous groups in Central America and the Amazon (Bengoa 1981, 3), they were the only ones who maintained their autonomy in part of their territories. After the Spanish defeat in the Battle of Curalaba (1598), a border was established that divided Mapuche and Spanish lands and included a "frontier space" set up as a zone of war and peace, of confrontation and exchange. It was in this zone that first Jesuit and then Franciscan missionaries settled, initially on an itinerant basis and then on a more stable one, but they never managed to fully establish themselves within Mapuche territory (Pinto 1988; Gaune 2016).

With Chilean independence in 1818, Mapuche autonomy became a problem for the territorial sovereignty of the young state. The southern national boundaries continued to shift under the pressure of agricultural expansion, and state bureaucracy was gradually consolidated. Once again, the state turned to the missions to "civilize" the frontier and managed to bring in Franciscan missionaries and Italian Capuchins (Pinto 1988; Serrano 1995; Donoso 2008; Milo 2002). Stable missions were settled in zones where significant numbers of Chileans and Mapuche peoples lived. Primary schools were set up to educate Mapuche children, although on a less stable basis than Chileans' schools and not inside Mapuche territory. By the time the Chilean state militarily occupied the autonomous territory in 1881, the missions were already in decline; then, following various petitions from the Chilean government and the Order in Rome, the Bavarian Capuchins arrived in 1896 to take control of the Apostolic Prefecture of the Araucanía under the Congregation for the Propagation of the Faith.

By the beginning of the twentieth century, the Capuchin missions constituted a unique experience, in that they were missions among infidels in an officially Catholic country. The missionaries were also singular, because they were not evangelizing in a colony of their home country but instead had a contract with a foreign state. These missions reflected the "enlightened paradigm" developed at the peak of Protestant and Catholic European missionary activity in the early nineteenth century, according to which Western education provided the means of "civilizing" pagan populations in order to convert them to Christianity (Bosch 2016, 217; Dufourcq 1993, 35; Delavignete 1962, 37). Religious supremacy went hand in hand with European colonial expansion, and to the civilizing ambitions were added the nationalist ones. The particularities of the Mapuche case and the Bavarian Capuchins, however, added new complexities to this paradigm, which we will uncover by taking a closer look at the missional concept of those who developed it (Depaepe 1995, 17).

Within the enlightened paradigm, the originality of the Bavarian missionaries lies in the convergence of critical and intellectual dimensions, specifically German Romanticism and the dialogue between theology and the so-called sciences of the spirit, especially linguistics, as a means to know the character and religiosity of a particular community. This configuration was the beginning of missiology. The first generation of Bavarian Capuchins that arrived in La Araucania were highly educated. They had a solid formation in Latin and Greek, characteristic of the neo-humanist curriculum of the gymnasium, which was supplemented by the study of German language and culture and a canon of scholarly readings that included, among others, the works of Herder, Goethe, Lessing, and Schiller (Albisetti and Lundgree 1991). Their religious formation coincided with the early rise of German missiology, which was institutionalized years later. Missiology's ties to the Romantic movement were acknowledged by contemporaries. Gustav Warbeck (1834–1910), the father of German Protestant missiology who greatly influenced the Catholic version, argued that it was important for missionaries not only to learn about the foreign cultures but also to show them respect and appreciation. Warbeck maintained that this charismatic capacity was typical of, if not unique to, Germans, because only those who were able to appreciate their own *Volkstrum* (popular customs and traditions) could appreciate those of foreign cultures (Bosch 2016, 306). Josef Schmidlin (1876–1944) was the theoretician behind the Münster or German school of Catholic missiology who provided its theological foundation and elaborated a methodology (Schmidlin 1917). Adopting the principle of adaptation for the sake of achieving efficient salvation of souls and the Christianization of pagan peoples, Schmidlin argued, required an understanding of these people's cultural and natural characteristics, with the priority being the study of the language, as it was the road that would lead to the heart of the culture (Santos 1991, 38). The universality of Christianity, Schmidlin said, had to be combined with the local religion, especially if that religion were primitive, with missionaries rejecting the aspects that ran contrary to Christian values and accommodating those that were compatible. This is why the study of the religious sciences was necessary for missionaries, as was their duty to contribute with their own studies (Santos 1991, 40). In effect, the missionaries provided Western science with studies of different cultures (Wall 1996, 197).

The Bavarian missionaries, who barely knew Spanish, undertook the study of the Mapuche language, Mapudungun, in order to learn about the Mapuche culture. An emblematic figure was Félix de Augusta (1860–1936), who was in born in Augsburg to a free-thinking Jewish father, who was a businessman, and a Catholic mother. He studied at the St Stephan Gymnasium, received a medical degree in Munich, and took theology courses in Dillingen, during which he paid special attention to the study of missions. Arriving in southern Chile with no understanding of Mapudungun, he concluded that "no one knows an Indian unless he knows his language," and so he spent two years on an island in a Mapuche community where no *winkas* (whites) lived (Mora Penroz 1993). He learned the language and then preached and taught in Mapudungun and also wrotebilingual devotional texts and a grammar book (Augusta 1903), the latter being one of his most important works. The grammar book was meant to help missionaries learn the Mapudungun language, while the texts were meant for the evangelization of the children who learned to read in their own language, a primarily oral language. Augusta transcribed Mapuche songs onto sheets of music and composed hymns in the language, put together a dictionary, translated some of the Gospels, and carried out an extensive compilation of narratives, which he edited in Spanish and Mapudungun.

The research of the Capuchins was quite extensive, but the missionaries were not ethnologists, anthropologists, philologists, or botanists. They were not missionaries *and* scientists. They were only missionaries, albeit modern ones. The two facets of their activity must be distinguished from each other, for the scientific aspirations were strictly auxiliary to the evangelical objectives. For the missionaries, science and religion were not on equal footing: science was subordinated to religion. This perspective reveals the fissures within the missions' civilizing paradigm and allows us to make important distinctions.

The Bavarian Capuchins constructed a narration and interpretation of the Mapuche culture that was unprecedented and utterly distinct from the predominant discourse of the Chilean elites (Casanueva 1998). Their study of the native culture, regardless of any anachronous judgments that might be made, established a bridge for understanding the Other that was distinct from that of strict scientific observation. This is because, while the missionaries recognized that the Other represented a source of information, they also had the intention to establish a line of communication through which, within the theological and ideological framework of the time, respect and appreciation could be conveyed, as pointed out by Warbeck. The major theme that runs throughout the intellectual production of the Capuchins is that the Mapuche people possessed a genuine culture – one that was primitive, yet not barbarian – that included the essential values that would enable it, as had been the case with many other ancient peoples, to become a civilized one. The Capuchins originality lies in their defence of the organic character of Mapuche culture and repudiation of the claim that they were an inferior race. They did not idealize the Mapuche, and indeed even criticized their customs on several occasions, but still insisted on the strength of their values.

The linguistic studies of Félix de Augusta were highly appreciated by the growing academic community of the University of Chile. Rodolfo Lenz, who held a doctorate in philosophy from the University of Bonn and was contracted as a professor of languages, had been the first to study the Mapuche language using a modern linguistic approach, and had published *Estudios Araucanos* around the same time Augusta arrived in Chile (Lenz 1895–7). He reacted to Augusta's book on grammar in this way: "Only a priest and a German could have studied the Mapuche language with as much precision and refinement" (Mora Penroz 1993, 56). The two men admired each other and communicated frequently, but their story also illustrates how linguistic study represented something very different for the scientist than for the missionary. When Lenz invited Augusta to research the history of the Mapuche language, offering him a class at the university, Augusta turned the invitation down because he was only interested in contemporary Mapuche. His efforts were meant to serve the mission. Nonetheless, he justified the compilation of Mapuche narratives (Augusta 1910) – that is, the "fixation" of Mapuche memory – for scientific purposes, because, as he prophesied, sooner or later the Mapuche culture was going to disappear. His prediction surely reflected his evangelical ambitions, but, it also contained a judgment about how this process would be accomplished: Would Mapuche culture disappear because it was barbarian, as the majority of Chileans believed, or because it was a transitory culture on the path to a higher level of civilization? The first vision involved extermination, the second, transformation. This excerpt from Augusta's work aptly synthesizes the critique of the enlightened vision within the civilizing paradigm of the Bavarian Capuchins:

> This nation [Mapuche], today so despised by a certain class of people who desire and propose the appropriation of their goods and even the extermination of their race, this nation lives, thinks, loves, they have their traditional laws, their religious ideas, their rituals, poetry, eloquence, songs, music, arts, their holidays and games, civic life, passions and virtues ... The Araucano is not the brutal man seen in the canteens of the Frontier, where from the breasts of a decanted civilization he's sucking the fatal venom that is destroying his race. (Augusta 1903, v)

The value attributed to the Mapuche culture was translated into liturgy through Mapuche sacrificial rites, with parts of the mass and sermon being delivered in Mapudungun. Further, although there is no evidence that Mapuche music was played, it is known that sacred hymns were translated from Spanish and German and sung in Mapudungun at a time when performing mass in anything other than Latin was still prohibited.

Augusta rejected Darwinism, of course, but also racism. Together with his colleague Gerónimo de Amberga, he criticized the racist theories that were becoming popular in Chilean circles (Crow 2013), and rejected phrenological measurement as a valid method of determining mental capacity, a practice that had been carried out in La Araucanía with the purpose of establishing the inferiority of certain races. For his part, Amberga was a controversial figure, going as far as justifying polygamy in anthropological terms, and chastising anyone in the academic coterie who suggested that the Mapuche culture was not capable of assuming the duties and rights of an educated nation, as well as those who wished for the disappearance of the culture in order to "no longer disturb the march of progress" (Amberga 1915, 6). He decried the imposition of the extermination approach, which had expelled the Mapuche from their lands, forcing them into ignominious poverty, writing, "What's left is the corpse of the civilization, the final act of a secular drama" (31). If, like the missionaries, Chile wanted to civilize the Mapuche people, their lands had to be returned and their children integrated through schooling.

The vision of the Capuchins regarding the Chilean occupation was extremely critical. Félix de Augusta explained the situation in all clarity to the Apostolic Nuncio: the soldiers took their livestock and the government had left the Mapuche with no more than three or four hectares per person. "Previously they were rich in cattle, sheep, and horses. The rustlers impoverished them and the judges were permanently biased against them, as were municipal authorities. Starting in 1881 they were transformed at a startling rate into subsistence farmers following Chilean traditions" (cited in Roettingen n.d., 31). In this context of violence and defeat, the missionaries were received with distrust by the Indigenous communities, for they suspected that after them would come the white usurpers, but the missions quickly became places of refuge, and the missionaries showed their willingness to confront Chilean farmers and businessmen in the field. They acted as interpreters and as advocates in their legal and bureaucratic actions, they pressured political authorities to change land policy, and they complained to the press about the injustices being committed on a daily basis. The Mapuche people "are not sad," said one missionary. "They are persecuted and abused" (Roettingen n.d., 34). To summarize, the relationship between missions, civilization, and colonialism was neither obvious nor mechanical and leaves room for distinctions.

The Capuchins' missionary project did not achieve its principal goal of establishing a genuine mission school, the core of which was to consist of both the Mapuche people who had not been converted to Christianity and those whose faith was still questionable or weak. This idea of school did not become a reality because, as will be discussed below, the settled population in the area was mixed and also because Mapuche parents did not want their children to be taught in Mapundungum. They preferred that their children be provided an education in which they would be taught to speak, read, and write in Spanish, so that they could defend their lands and avoid falling for ruses in the future. Thus, the mission school was in reality simply a rural school that the Mapuche preferred to the state schools, and it was soon converted into a regular Catholic school. The missionaries did not fail, however, to successfully carry out the phase of early evangelization that resulted in the implementation of the diocesan church.

The Geopolitics of Mapuche Scholarity: Missions and the State

The mission school of the Bavarian Capuchins was used as part of the national state's strategy to govern the recently occupied Araucanía. The historiography on the Mapuche people and the occupation of their lands has highlighted the role of education as a mechanism to civilize and acculturate the Indigenous, and to make of the Indian a citizen at the service of the Chilean nation (Bengoa 1981, 2008; Donoso 2008; Gundermann, Forester, and Vergara 2003). The church and the state coincided in this regard – with some discrepancies – and the cooperation between them was essential for mission deployment and state construction in the *Baja Frontera*, or Lower Borderlands, as the occupied region was called. There is thus a geopolitical dimension to the history of the Mapuche that cannot be disregarded. This was the educationalization of governance.

After the military phase of the occupation process was completed in 1881, the state had virtually no presence on this strip of "untwisted" land. Some forts and hamlets were separated by large distances, and there was no real knowledge about the territory's population. The few articles of news that circulated were related to the filing process, through which Mapuche lands, calculated around 500,000 hectares, were declared state property and were settled by Chilean immigrants. In their dispersal, each community of Indigenous families presided over by a *cacique*, or native chief, received a "grant" of land that was very small in comparison to their ancestral holdings, a measure that instantly turned them into small, poor landowners by disrupting their former communitarian production methods, cleaving not only the Mapuche economy but also their culture.

This context is important in understanding why the educationalization of the Indigenous children took on first-order geopolitical significance for both the state and the missions. Each believed in the need to conquer the territory: for the missionaries, it was necessary for the evangelization of pagans and the incoming colonists; for the state, it was necessary to establish its control over the population. The state took advantage of the exploratory and ethnographic strategy employed by the missionaries by using, in a first stage, the missional network of schools to civilly organize this rural territory without settlements. Municipalities had been the primary element of civil organization in the rest of the country, but, in this frontier zone, there were none, only missions and mission schools. In the province of Cautín, founded in 1887, state schools were introduced only later and in already urbanized areas. The first archival mention of one of these state schools dates back to 1889, in the city of Temuco, the administrative capital, together with eleven other schools located in municipalities that served as political centres (Memoria del Ministerio del Interior 1887, 552). The mission and the mission school became the initial mechanism through which the state established itself beyond the cities and into the "wilderness," as this isolated area was described. In fact, the first primary schools in the province were originally monitored by the Ministry of the Interior, and, when administrative control was transferred to the Ministry of Education, questions were raised regarding the schools' curriculum, as it was deemed unsuited to local needs (for example, its courses on arms and military command) (Briones 1892, 137). The educationalization perspective thus clarifies that the state's strategy was to delegate, to the Capuchin missionaries, the political problem of transforming the Indigenous people into colonists on their own land and thus "ensure the constitutional regime that has been established in the frontier" (Briones 1892, 321; González 2005).

When the Bavarian Capuchins took on the Araucanía mission in 1896, they didn't have a pre-established methodology or a defined missional scheme; instead they developed one based on their experiences. The challenge was to reach the pagan Mapuche communities, those that had had less contact with the *winca* world, although it wasn't entirely unknown to them. One method considered was the one employed by Augusta on Huapi Island: to spend an extended period of time living in an Indigenous community, long enough for Christianity to penetrate it through the mission school where the children received their religious education. The friars, however, concluded that, although this was the ideal method, it was not feasible because it required one missionary per community. For that reason, a system of "mission stations" was established – a "modern mission" as its prefect called it. The scheme comprised several largely autonomous units of operation that were built, maintained, and managed by the missionaries and were distributed in the rural zones with the highest concentrations of Indigenous inhabitants. Each station consisted of a large field for vegetable gardens and grazing, a house, a church, and a school. From the station, the missionaries would advance toward the most distant communities, founding chapels that were then visited twice a year and that could eventually become stations and schools. The Franciscan Congregation

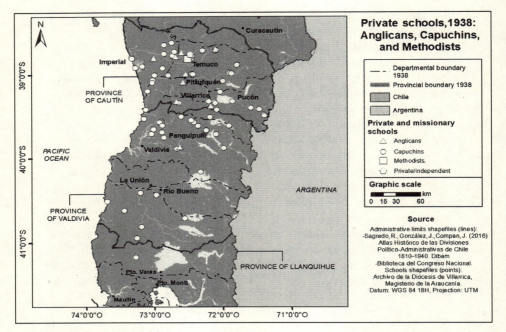

15.1 Private schools, 1938

of Nuns of Boroa, which the Bavarian Capuchins helped to found, was responsible for the catechism taught in these remote "poor man's huts" (*choza del pobre*) and "Indian shacks" (*ruca del indio*). The principle was that the mission stations were to be rural and not urban. According to the information displayed in figure 15.1, the stations of the occupied zone were all located in rural settlements. It was in these stations that Indigenous schools were installed, including some boarding schools.

Following the path traced by the missionaries, the state opened its own rural schools in the towns that grew up around the missions on the coast and in the valleys. Public schools thus followed the mission schools; others were opened near train stations, once railways were built in the region, and in former forts and at intersecting roads. The state did not, however, open schools in the so-called Andean fringe, choosing instead to leave the education of that zone completely in the missionaries' hands. Comparing the maps in figures 15.1 and 15.2, it can be deduced that only mission schools made it all the way to the stations at Villarrica and Panguipulli, a region that was still "nearly unknown" well into the twentieth century. The missionaries erected chapels and "rural schools" in this "wilderness" of dense forests linked by trails that disappeared in winter: these small centres were separated by as

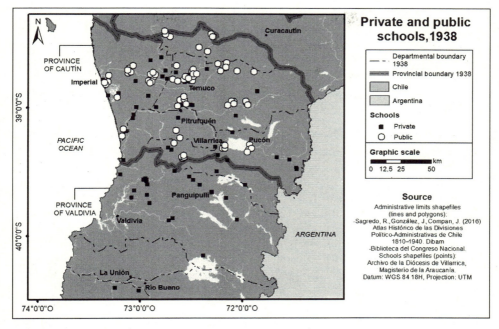

15.2 Private and public schools, 1938

many as eighty kilometres, a three-day trip on horseback (*El Austral*, 30 January 1930; Beck de Ramberga, 17 July 1930). The state lacked the capacity not only to establish itself in such geographical conditions but even to monitor changing population. In the missionary logic, moving a school from one location to another was part of the evangelizing method; but for the state, this type of "isolated rurality" posed a persistent problem, because state schools required, by law, the enrolment of a minimum of twenty-five students to open, a condition that demanded some sort of urban development that was practically impossible to achieve in this sparsely populated region. In 1900, the Prefectura de la Araucanía had established sixteen mission stations, and, according to the missionaries' calculations, there were 60,000 Indigenous inhabitants in the territory served by these stations, half of whom were Christians, and 45,000 Chilean inhabitants (Roettingen n.d., 73). In addition to the mission schools, there were twelve state-run schools in these territories (Memoria del Ministerio de la Justicia, Culto e Instrucción Pública 1901).

The mission stations served several purposes, which included defending the Indigenous community and providing health care and sometimes even material assistance, in addition to religious services and education. According to the Capuchin missiology, formal Western education facilitated an understanding of Christianity. That is why, at the beginning, the mission schools were conceived as schools for Mapuche children in which only Mapundungun would be used, and so the first textbooks and the first alphabet were in that language. After the children's parents demanded that the students be taught Spanish, the native language was never used in the schools, although sermons continued to be delivered in Mapundungun. In other words, while the missionaries devoted themselves to mastering the local language, the local population sought to learn the language of the state. The motive was political. As mentioned above, the parents wanted their children to master the language and writings of the colonists in order to defend their lands from the impact of widespread deceit, which arose from the brutal absence of the state in the settlement process. To put it in another way, the attempt to provide education in the native language – part of an evangelical strategy – failed very early on because of how the Indigenous groups made use of the schools. As a result, the children were "evange-literate" (Donoso 2008, 15).

The mission schools educated not only Mapuche children, but also, and mainly, the sons of Chileans and foreign immigrants, because the settlement pattern of the population was very quickly mixed. The Araucanian Census carried out in 1907 shows that 23 per cent (101,118 people) of the population inhabiting the region between the Bío Bío River in the north and the Gulf of Reloncaví to the south were Mapuche (*Memoria del Supremo Gobierno* 1908, xxii). According to the census, the Indigenous category included "those natives that still maintain their traditional way of life, costume, and language without attending to greater or lesser degrees of racial purity," while the so-called *mestizos* were excluded: because of their partial assimilation into Chilean culture, they were difficult to identify, even when they continued to display some Indigenous cultural traits (ibid., xxii).

The Chileans moved onto Mapuche lands very early on, which explains why the mission – and state – schools became mixed schools so soon. The Capuchins knew the area well and opted for educating the Indigenous children together with the children of poor Chileans, both as part of a civilizing project and as a strategy for populating the area. This aim was more successful at the mission boarding schools than at the mission day schools, where only 8 per cent of the student population was Indigenous. At the boarding schools, the proportion rose to 46 per cent. The strategy behind the boarding schools was to attract Mapuche students dispersed over a vast area, removing them from their familiar worlds and culture so that Western education could transform their communities through them. The Capuchins had no intention of removing students from their communities permanently; rather, they meant to send them back. That is why they struggled persistently and finally managed to achieve the establishment of boarding schools for girls, to be managed by the Sisters of Santa Cruz de Messingen and the Congregation of the Providence Sisters. Such schools provided a conscientious education that had little to do with missionary work: students were taught skills necessary to make a living through manual labour. These schools were an expensive propect for parents because the students were charged for their uniforms and food.

Around 1910, there were nine boarding schools, four of which were for girls. All of them had been transformed into urban schools for lower-middle-class children and incorporated into the national system as Catholic schools, just as the mission schools were. The proliferation of boarding schools and their transformation into technical schools, especially ones focusing on agriculture for boys and manual labour for girls, were key characteristics of this new phase in which labour was educationalized. The state delegated vocational education to the Capuchins in order to transform the Mapuche into colonists on the frontier. Financially, moreover, boarding schools were less expensive for the state because, even though they were subsidized by the Chilean government, they received significant funding from Bavaria and, to a lesser degree, from the Mapuche themselves, as well as from the archbishopric and civil society, notwithstanding the modest salary that the state paid the brothers. When a law regarding mandatory primary education was enacted in 1920, followed by the separation of church and state in 1925, the mission schools were declared "cooperators" of the educational function of the *Estado Docente* (teacher state) and subsidized just as any other cost-free private school. The 1920 law modified the rationale behind the allocation of resources, basing it on student attendance, which not only increased the subventions received but also introduced a market logic into the relationship between state and mission schools. The financing of the mission schools was critical from a political point of view because of the predominance of liberal governments that did not agree to support Catholic schools with public funds, as they felt those funds should support only state schools. Even so, and with the cooperation of Bavarian Catholics, the number of schools did increase. In 1930, the Capuchins operated twenty boarding and sixty day schools, while the number of state schools in the region had reached 221. That year, the missionaries testified to the Ministry of Education that they were educating around 6,000 Indigenous students.[1]

By the beginning of the 1930s, the original Capuchin initiative – focused on the mission itself – was no longer the same. The phase of settling the Mapuche people had concluded, and the Capuchins who were coming to Chile had experienced the First World War and the subsequent European conflicts that were more ideological than nationalist. The Prefecture of Araucanía had been declared the Apostolic Vicariate in 1928, and was given the task not to convert and educate the non-Christian Mapuche but rather to reinforce the role of the church and Catholic schools in defending Catholicism from the threats of Protestantism, free masonry, communism, the secularization of the state and society, and religious and political pluralism. The missionaries themselves began to concentrate on parish activities; lay professors, some of whom were former students and others who were Mapuche, replaced them at the schools.

To recapitulate, the schools founded by the Capuchins served the state-building objective and educated a segment of the Mapuche people who had asked for schooling. The acculturation process obviously produced results, although they were not completely successful because the Mapuche did not adopt Christianity the way the missionaries had planned, while the state, on the other hand, did not manage to exterminate their cultural identity. The Mapuche people demonstrated their strength and resistance over and over again. As had occurred so many times in the past, the exposure to new cultures did not imply an eradication of their identity, but rather gave it a new significance as they navigated the processes of urbanization, adopting and adapting education for social mobility, and organizing public and political spheres.

Empowering the Indigenous People

During the final stage of the occupation (1910–30), the education services provided to the Mapuche were also strategically used by the Mapuche themselves to defend their land and culture. As has already been shown, and in contradiction to theories that used to be predominant (Barman 2017, 3), the skills that could be attained in the Chilean schools – both those run by the state and by the missionaries – were perceived very early on by the Mapuche as instrumental for the preservation of their race. The new conditions imposed by the "Chileanization" effort to convert the Mapuche into "colonists" had a proportional effect on their way of life. Not only did the policies entail the loss of land, they also dismembered the political power of their communities and fragmented existing networks of solidarity, effectively making them peasants on small ranches, where alcoholism quickly spread (Cano 2012, 364). The last land grant was allocated in 1929. In that year, Chileans occupied one-fifth of Mapuche territory, and more than one-third of the dispossessions had taken place without state intervention – with over one thousand lawsuits seeking the restitution of communal lands waiting in court. The resistance, and especially the adaptability, of the Mapuche culture regarding the *winka* during this period can be seen very clearly. The Mapuche leaders used formal education for their own empowerment and to organize the political defence of their interests.

The leaders of Mapuche communities actively sought more schools and education in Spanish from the moment the Bavarians opened the first school. They themselves argued in the lawsuits they brought that their ignorance of Spanish had made them "deaf-mutes" and that, as such, they were unable to navigate the Chilean bureaucracy, much less defend their rights. Tomás Guevara, rector of Temuco's secondary school and one of the first leaders of the Indigenous association movement, declared in 1904 that Mapuche parents wanted, as fast as possible, for "their children to be Christians, to learn to read, write, and calculate so the *winkas* could not trick them" (Guevara 1904, 75).

The Mapuche children who actually attended school were a minority. During this entire period, the primary school enrolment rates in this region were the lowest in the country, especially with regard to Mapuche children. The 1920 census calculated that only 6.2 per cent of the Mapuche were literate, as compared to 40.2 per cent of Chileans (Censo de la población, 1925). In 1928, 1,683 of the 5,062 of the children in the region who were enrolled in primary school were Indigenous and their attendance at the external school was only 8 per cent of the total number of students. That same year, the national primary school coverage was close to 60 per cent of the school-age population, which, in comparison, made Indigenous education a scarce practice. These statistics demonstrate that only a minority of Indigenous children were brought up in the school system – an elite group that would take advantage of the opportunity and make of the "literate Mapuche" a new social actor whose leadership would be articulated through early Indigenous organizations.

The Sociedad Caupolicán Defensora de la Araucanía was organized in 1910 by mostly Indigenous primary school teachers, some of whom had attended the mission schools, inaugurating the contemporary Mapuche discourse of ethnic defence against the state. The emphasis on dignity in the group's arguments was a new element within demands for the return of Mapuche land, which of course remained central in their claims. The profile of the leaders of these organizations that emerges from the historiography portrays them as the children of *caciques* who had professed "loyalty" to the Chilean army during the occupation – the first generations of a new Indigenous culture that had received formal Chilean education, spoke Spanish, and shared kinship and political bonds that united them (Donoso 2008; Montesinos and Forester 1988).

The leader of the Sociedad Caupolicán Defensora de la Araucanía was Manuel Antonio Neculmán. He was the first primary school teacher educated in the state's training colleges and had worked as an interpreter first for the Chilean army and later for the Indigenous Settlement Committee created toward the end of the 1920s. He, together with some children of *caciques*, opened the first school founded and directed by a Mapuche professor in the occupied zone. One of his students, Manuel Manquilef, became known for his writings in Spanish and Mapundungun on psychology and folklore, and was one of the first Indigenous representatives elected to the lower house of Congress (Donoso 2008, 14). The pedagogical and academic background of the society's founders is important because it explains the value that the movement placed on education and civic and moral training for the progressive integration of Indigenous people into national life. Education represented the most immediate means for achieving this objective. Whereas self-defence had in the past meant picking up arms, it now meant seeking instruction.

The character of the Sociedad Mapuche de Protección Mutua de Loncoche was quite distinct. Founded in 1916 by Manuel Aburto Panguilef, it was the direct antecedent of the Gran Federación Araucana, formed in 1922 against the state, and it sought political autonomy through parliamentary representation to recuperate territorial autonomy. Panguilef led this transition. He had been educated in an Anglican mission and had become a pastor, a profession he left in order to devote himself to politics. He advocated the use of Mapudungun in schools, as well as Mapuche rituals and polygamy. He started schools and produced plays in theatres throughout the country, and in the process established relationships with workers' associations, moving closer to anarchism and socialism.

During the 1920s, this alliance between the Indigenous movement and political parties grew tighter, while the radicalization of Indigenous power and the ideological entrenchment of the conflict were related to the national political context, which was extremely convulsed. In 1924, a military coup overthrew President Arturo Alessandri Palma, producing a sudden rupture of the parliamentarian system. The 1925 Constitution resumed the presidential system, while the workers' associations and trade unions developed a solid corporative network, and the ideological pluralism in the party system became increasingly polarized with the entry of officially leftist parties into democratic politics (Meléndez 2012). That same year, the generals called for congressional elections, and Mapuche candidates, supported by the Gran Federación and the Democratic Party – a people's party for workers' rights – won seats. Their victory brought the Indigenous problem to Congress, tying the local dimension of defending the property rights of Indigenous individuals to the fleeting back and forth of national politics. These new ties between Mapuche associations and party leaders forced the association leaders to serve as intermediaries between their provincial constituencies and the state. These leaders brought the Mapuche problem to the national stage, and the legitimacy of their demands struck a chord in public opinion.

The response of the Catholic Church to the ideological turn in the quest for Mapuche empowerment was immediate. The missionaries had played an important part in promoting Catholic associations in their stations, which included devotional societies and charitable groups as well as mutual societies or co-ops, but in 1926, under the leadership of Bishop Guido Beck de Ramberga, the Union Araucana was reorganized under the slogan "God, Country, and Progress." De Ramberga felt that indoctrination was necessary to protect what he had accomplished among the Mapuche. In other words, he would fight ideology with ideology. The union was made up completely of Indigenous members who were organized on the basis of assemblies held at the mission stations, under the guidance of the missionaries who met annually in parliament. They produced a newspaper, *El Araucano*, and emphasized education, the defence of property rights, and racial solidarity, but the highest priority was on the moral indoctrination of the Mapuche. De Ramberga announced that no Catholic Mapuche could belong to the Gran Federación or the Caupolicán Society (*El Diario Austral*, 22 April 1927). He repeatedly denounced the proselytism of the leftist parties among the Mapuche, while the conservative sectors remained utterly indifferent to the plight of the Mapuche. The Gran Federación Acaucana and the Sociedad Caupolicán affiliated themselves with the Democratic Party and the World Anarchist Federation of Workers, expecting that these organizations would defend their interests. De Ramberga reacted with the comment that "our Catholic Party, its representatives, its lawyers, what have they done? Often, in the past, when the missionaries approached them about Mapuche interests, they did not even answer" (De Ramberga, San José de la Maquina, 14 May 1927).

The bishop's aim was to have the active official support of the Conservative Party for the Mapuche, taking into consideration that there were many Indigenous forces with the right to vote who belonged to the Catholic Party. Social Christian groups were organized with the support of conservative sectors and the ecclesiastic hierarchy through the Union Social Católica de Chile.

In 1927, the Division Law 4,169 was passed to protect Indigenous citizens from abuse and exploitation. The law set up the Tribunal Especial de Division (Special Tribunal Division), which acted as a genuine supreme court for complaints, devising a formula for the division of the communities and allocation of individual domain titles that did not satisfy many people. The Federación Araucana interpreted the law strictly and accused its authors of legalizing Indigenous misery by dividing the allotments and opening a path for them to be acquired by third parties. This was the end of the settlement period, and the long-standing conflict was quickly transformed into one of political pressure, prosecution, and concerted acts of violence. This "solution" triggered internal conflict among Mapuche constituencies, and the work of the Capuchins was directly blamed. The Federación Araucana asserted control over the "usurped" missions, along with their schools and colleges, declaring that the native-cum-colonist would no longer be satisfied with a couple of hectares of poor land. It called for the formation of a unified front, rejected the division of communities, and positioned itself as the defender of Mapuche culture against the church and state. In the 1930s, there were attempts to unify the leaders of Mapuche associations, as well as teachers, businessmen, and farmers, but without much success.

The church feared that the reframing of the conflict along such ideological lines among the defeated people would lead to missionaries being hunted down and killed. Bishop de Ramberga thus took it upon himself to establish a close collaboration with the government in order to maintain its economic support and convey a redeeming image of the Capuchins in the conflict zone. In speech after speech, he argued that the missionaries represented the Indians' only defence and resource. The missionaries, he held, had been their true advocates (*El problema indígena* 1928), and he compared their efforts to educate the Mapuche with the extermination approach that other frontier societies had adopted. While the North American maxim had been "the only good Indian is a dead Indian," here the Indigenous problem had been an "instruction problem," with the solution being led by "the priest, the missionary, and the Catholic bishop," with the support of the state (*El Diàrio Ilustrado*, 19 May 1928). De Ramberga intensified his efforts to open rural schools that were dedicated to teaching agricultural methods in areas that had been neglected, using civic education and improving the formation of Catholic Indigenous teachers organized by the Magister Society of Araucanía. In 1930, of the ninety-three teachers in the society, thirteen were Mapuche.

That same year, the Ministry of Education commissioned Arturo Huenchullén Medel, a former mission school student and well-known local politician, to carry out a study on Indigenous education. In his report, Huenchullén stated that there were 120,000 Indigenous individuals, many of whom were young, who were "adapted to civilization," and whose families were better off than Chilean families in the same circumstances. That year also saw the ordination of the first Mapuche priest at the High Seminary, and two Indigenous judges appointed in rural districts by the Intendent of Valdívia (Informe de la Gobernación del departamento de Arauco, 3rd quarter, 1931, Ministry of Public Education).

The conception of formal education as the most influential factor in the revitalization of the Mapuche people cut across all Mapuche leadership circles and advocacy groups. The Mapuche used education to gain political empowerment as an ethnic group working against the national state that had usurped and dispossessed them of their lands. They used it to legitimate their historic complaints in the court of public opinion. Schooling empowered these leaders to represent the voice of the Mapuche people in spite of the many contradictions and conflicting demands among the communities. At the conclusion of the settlement period, the results of their actions could not be seen as completely successful in terms of attaining their demands, but they were certainly a success in terms of maintaining and giving new meaning to the Mapuche people's identity.

This chapter has examined the educationalization of salvation of the Mapuche people through missionary work, and the place of education in the formation of the national state. In this process, the building of a "homogeneous nation" and having the Mapuche under control required the creation of governance for the territory where the Mapuche people were established. The missionary work and the diocesan school were strategic tools of the state used to accomplish those goals. Finally, this chapter examined how the Mapuche people developed political skills in defence of their own identity. It concludes that the educationalization process produced relative, complex, and unexpected results, and did not have a univocal and linear character.

NOTE

1 Beck de Ramberga, Valdidia, 30 July 1930, Archivo del Arzobispado de Villarrica, Material Crónica 1928–30.

REFERENCES

Albisetti, James, and Peter Lundgree. 1991. "Höhere Knabenschulen." In *Handbuch der deutschen Bildungsgeshichte. Band IV, 1870–1918. Von der Reichsgründung bis zum Ende des Ersten Weltkrieges*, edited by Christa de Berg. Munich: Verlag C.H. Beck.

Amberga, Geronimo de. 1915. *Estado intelectual, cultural y economico del Araucano*. Temuco, CL: Imprenta y Litografia Alemana.

Anderson, Benedict. 1993. *Comunidades imaginadas: Reflexiones sobre el origen y la difucion del nacionalismo*. Mexico: Fondo de Cultura Ecónomica.

Augusta, Félix. 1903. *Gramática Araucana*. Valdivia, CL: Imprenta Central J. Lambert.

– 1910. *Lecturas Araucanas*. Valdivia, CL: Imprenta de la Prefectura Apostolica.

Barman, Jean. 2017. "Introduction." *Historical Studies on Education* 29: 2–10.

Bengoa, Jose. 1981. *La Iglesia Catolica: El proceso colonial y la evangelizacion de los indigenas en Chile*. Santiago: Conferencia Episcopal de Chile.

– 2008. *Historia del pueblo mapuche, siglos XIX y XX*. Santiago: LOM Ediciones.

Bosch, D.J. 2016. *Transforming Mission: Paradigm Shifts in Theology of Mission*. New York: Orbis Books.

Bridges, David (2008). "Educationalization: On the Appropiateness of Asking Educational Institutions to Solve Social Problems and Economic Problems." *Educational Theory* 58 (4). https://doi.org/10.1111/j.1741-5446.2008.00295.x.

Briones, Plácido. 1892. *Memoria*.

Cano, Daniel. 2012. "Sin tierras ni letras ... Educación indígena en Chile, 1880–1930." In *Historia de la educación de Chile*. Vol. 2. *La escuela nacional*, edited by Macarena Ponce de León, Francisca Rengifo, Sol Serrano, 360–96. Santiago: Taurus.

Casanueva, Fernando. 1998. "Indios malos en tierras buenas: vision y concepcion del mapuche segun las elites chilenas del siglo XIX." In *Modernización, inmigración y mundo indígena: Chile y la Araucanía en el siglo XIX*, edited by Pinto de Jorge, 55–131. Temuco, CL: Universidad de la Frontera.

Censo de población de la República de Chile levantado el 15 de diciembre de 1920 (1925). Santiago: Sociedad Imprenta y Litografía Universo.

Crow, Joanna. 2013. *The Mapuche in Modern Chile*. Miami: University Press of Florida.

Delavignete, Robert. 1962. *Cristianismo y colonialismo*. Andorra: Casal i Va.

Depaepe, Marc. 1995. "An Agenda for the History of Colonial Education." In *The Colonial Experience in Education*, edited by de Antonio Nóvoa, Marc Depaepe, and Erwin V. Johanningmeier, 15–20. Gent, BE: CS.HP.

Depaepe, Marc, Frederik Herman, Melanie Surmont, Angelo van Gorp, and Frank Simon. 2008. "About Pedagogization: From the Perspective of the History of Education." In *Educational Research: The Educationalization of Social Problems*, edited by Paul Smeyers and Marc Depaepe, 13–30. Dordrecht, NL: Springer.

Depaepe, Marc, and Paul Smeyers. 2008. "Educationalization as an Ongoing Modernization Process." *Educational Theory* 58 (4): 379–89. https://doi.org/10.1111/j.1741-5446.2008.00295.x.

Donoso, Andres. 2008. *Educacion y nacion al sur de la Frontera*. Santiago: Pehuen.

Dufourcq, Elisabeth. 1993. *Les aventuriere de Dieu*. Paris: Editions Jean Claude Lattes.

Dussel, Enrique. 1986. *Los ultimos 50 años (1930–1985) en la historia de la Iglesia de America Latina*. Bogotá: Indo-American Press Service.

Espinoza, Enrique. 1897. *Geografía descriptiva de la República de Chile*. Santiago: Imprenta Encuadernación.

Gaunes, Rafel. 2016. *Escritura y salvacion: Cultura misionera jesuita en tiempos de Anganamon, siglo XVII*. Santiago: Ediciones Universidad Alberto Hurtado.

González, Jessika. 2005. "Elementos para el análisis del impacto de las políticas estatales en el proceso de construcción de identidad mapuche." *Pentukun* 5: 37–50.

Guevara, Tomás. 1904. *Costumbres judiciales*. Santiago: Imprenta Cervantes.

Gundermann, Hans, Rolf Forester, and Jorge Vergara. 2003. *Mapuches y aymaras: El debate en torno al reconocimiento y los derechos ciudadanos*. Santiago: Facultad de Ciencias Sociales de la Universidad de Chile.

Labaree, David. 2008. "The Winning Ways of a Losing Strategy: Educationalizing Social Problems in the United States." *Educational Theory*, 58 (4): 447–60. https://doi.org/10.1111/j.1741-5446.2008.00299.x.

Lenz, Rodolfo. 1895–7. *Estudios Araucanos*. Santiago: Imprenta Cervantes.

Luna, Laura. 2007. *Un mundo entre dos mundos: Las relaciones entre el Pueblo Mapuche y el Estado Chileno desde la perspectiva del desarrollo y de los cambios socioculturales*. Santiago: Ediciones Universidad Católica.

Meléndez, Felipe. 2012. "El rol de los partidos políticos en la determinación de la forma de gobierno bajo la Constitución de 1925." Seminario de Estudios de la República, Facultad de Derecho, Universidad de Chile, Santiago.

Memoria del Supremo Gobierno presentada a la Comisión del Censo de la República de Chile de 1907. (1908) Santiago: Imprenta Universo.

Memorias del Ministerio de Educación, 1927–32.

Memorias del Ministerio del Interior, 1881–1930.

Memorias del Ministerio de Justicia, Culto e Instrucción Pública, 1880–1927.

Milo, Diego. 2002. "Mision moral, Mision politica: Franciscanos en la Araucania 1843–1870." Master's thesis, Universidad de Chile.

Montesinos, Sonia, and Rolf Forester. 1988. *Organizaciones, líderes y contiendas mapuche (19001970)*. Santiago: Ediciones CEM.

Mora Penroz, Ziley. 1993. *P. Félix de Augusta o la pasion por el verbo Mapuche*. Temuco, CL: Editorial Kushe.

Pinto, Jorge. 1988. "Frontera, misiones y misioneros en Chile y Araucania (1600–1900)." In *Misioneros en la Araucania, 1600–1900*, edited by Jorge Pinto. Temuco, CL: Editorial Universidad de la Frontera.

– 2003. *La formación del Estado y la nación y el pueblo mapuche: De la inclusión a la exclusión*. Santiago: DIBAM, Centro de Investigaciones Diego Barros Arana.

El problema indígena y la constitución de la Propiedad Austral. La cuestión Araucanista y el socialismo. Obra de las misiones. 1928. Santiago: n.p.

Roettingen, Burcardo de. n.d. "25 años de actividad misional de los capuchinos bávaros en la Misión Araucana de Chile, 1896–1921." Unpublished manuscript, Archivo Diocesis de Villarrica, s.f.

Said, Edward W. 2016. *Orientalismo*. Barcelona: Penguin Random House.

Santos, Angel. 1991. *Teologia sistematica de la misión*. Navarre, ES: Editorial Verbo Divino.

Schmidlin, Josef. 1917. *Einführung in die Missionwissenachaft*. Münster: Verlag.

Serrano, Sol. 1995. "De escuelas indigenas sin pueblos y pueblos sin escuelas indigenas: La educacion en la Araucania en el siglo XIX." *Historia* 29: 423–74.

Taylor, Charles. 2009. *El multiculturalismo y "la política del reconocimiento"*. Mexico: Fondo de Cultura Económica.

Tröhler, Daniel. 2008. "The Educationalization of the Modern World: Progress, Passion, and the Protestant Promise of Education." In *Educational Research: The Educationalization of Social Problems*, edited by Paul Smeyers and Marc Depaepe, 31–46. Springer.

Walls, Andrew F. 1996. *The Missionary Movement in Christian History: Studies in the Transmission of Faith*. New York: Orbis Books.

Zenteno Julio. 1896. *Recopilación de leyes y decretos supremos sobre colonización, 1810–1896*. Santiago: Imprenta Nacional.

Concluding Analysis: Turning the Problem on Its Head – Looking to New Critical Directions

JOSH COLE AND IAN McKAY

Educationalization – "the trend in modernizing societies of transferring social responsibilities onto schools – with the function of schools thus evolving from the need to enforce moral behaviour, to solving social inequalities and to building a citizenry and improving productivity" (Bruno-Jofré, in the introduction to this volume, drawing on Depaepe (2012) and Depaepe and Smeyers (2008)) – is a broad and contested concept. That it arouses strong passions was very much in evidence in the arguments that took place the conference in Santiago, Chile, that gave rise to this collection. Implicit in many of the debates aroused by educationalization is the ideal – or the threat – of a pedagogical state bent on the imposition of a particular stance toward the social order. Educational programs and institutions are vested by the state with complex social and political obligations, some of which are today distilled in curricular programs combining a maximum of theoretical generality with a minimum of coherence. That education was fundamental to the state was a given in the thought of Plato and Aristotle; that it should enhance the capacity of each citizen to be self-governing within the context of a community was intrinsic to the thought of John Dewey, whose ideal of "progressive education" exerted a massive influence throughout the western hemisphere in the twentieth century. Educational/pedagogical innovations came to be associated with vast system-sustaining or system-challenging possibilities – perhaps ones that systematically conflated learning (individualistic and individualizing) with education (content-rich, purposive, and relational). In this conclusion, we suggest that contemporary neoliberalism has fundamentally transformed the terrain upon which all thought about education and educationalization must henceforth proceed. Both the classical tradition and twentieth-century progressivism, both of which suggested the possibility of a dialectical relationship between rulers and ruled, teachers and students, are challenged by the contemporary praxis of market-driven hypermodernity within which all such considerations are ruled out of order before they can even be discussed.

In short, what is missing from much discussion of educationalization is neoliberalism's drive to remould all social institutions and all individuals in accordance with market criteria, although William Pinar's contribution to this collection, particularly through his notion of "technologization" as late-capitalist "creative destruction," certainly points in this direction. As Eric Hobsbawm argues, no serious political entity – say a nation state, democratic or no – can afford to jettison a thorough-going educationalization of its citizens (2004, 295). It was certainly an insight familiar to John Dewey, who in *The School and Society*, first published in 1899, proclaimed:

> The [modern] change that first comes to mind, the one that overshadows and even controls all others, is the industrial one – the application of science resulting in the great inventions that have utilized the forces of nature on a vast and inexpensive scale: the growth of a world-wide market as the object of production, of vast manufacturing centres to supply this market, of cheap and rapid means of communication and distribution between all its parts ... One can hardly believe there has been a revolution in all history that is so rapid, so extensive, so complete. Through it the face of the earth is making over, even as to its physical forms; political boundaries are wiped out and moved about, as if they were indeed only lines on a paper map; population is hurriedly gathered into cities from the ends of the earth; habits of living are altered with startling abruptness and thoroughness ... Even our moral and religious ideas and interests, the most conservative because the deepest-lying things in our nature, are profoundly affected. That this revolution should not affect education in some other than a formal and superficial fashion is inconceivable. (1990, 9)

Dewey, to paraphrase Marshall Berman, had a considerable feel for modern change, and "for the suffering man on the rack." The altogether tougher analysis of modernity offered up by the Marxist tradition, however, gives us something more: a "grasp of what that rack is made of" (Berman 2002, 10). Without slighting Dewey and the vast tradition of progressive education he helped to shape, our point in this conclusion is to suggest that scholars of educationalization must pay close attention to "the rack" upon which vast contemporary educational systems, along with everyone in them, are pinned: the rack of a neoliberal order with totalizing ambition. And, more than this, they must attend closely, if they want to challenge that order, to the educational thinkers who grappled most intensively with it.

For decades, many educational theorists have been taken up with theoretical traditions, above all those associated with Michel Foucault, which, rather than illuminating the predicaments of educationists under conditions of neoliberalism, have deepened them. Post-humanist, post-historical and post-Marxist, such theory, often starkly simplified and even misconstrued, eliminates (as John Sanbonmatsu remarks) the five principles upon which any consistent alternative to a ruling order must depend: "1) the idea that leadership is necessary in [political] strategy; 2) that it is essential to study motives and interests and other objects of consciousness; 3) that having a view of the 'totality' or relations within the functional whole of society is required for effective political action; 4) that one cannot know 'doctrinally,' i.e., in advance of a given situation, what kinds of tactics or particular actions are appropriate; and 5) that the goal ... is *normative*, i.e., that it results in the transformation of a *situation* whereby one political or social order gives way to another" (Sanbonmatsu 2004 138). Without minimizing the extent to which particular Foucauldian concepts, especially governmentality, can be of service to critical scholars, we submit that the almost definitional resistance of most mid-to-late twentieth-century educational theorists to totality means that many of their theoretical approaches are now badly dated in an age of neoliberal revolution that is manifestly driven by capitalist imperatives and identifiable agents with ideological agendas. In short, the Age of Foucault has come to an end, and among democratic educational theorists, the search for an alternative framework of analysis must begin. We submit that educational theory should re-acquaint itself with the writings of a quite different intellectual, whose thought allows for a more systemic investigation of the new order in which we live: Antonio Gramsci.

The "first element" of Gramsci's radical democratic theory, Carlos Nelson Coutinho remarks, is the "primordial, irreducible" fact that "there really do exist rulers and ruled, leaders and led." This is not a "natural" or "eternal fact," and it was the mission of any genuinely revolutionary movement under conditions of modernity to challenge it (Coutinho 2012, 59; Gramsci 1995, 451; [*FSPN* Q11§66]).[1] In other words, educationalization is not a given; rather, it is constructed in concrete historical conditions. In contrast to Foucault (at least as commonly received among many theorists), Gramsci suggests that popular struggle can transform the "ruler/ruled" relationship, so that, at the very least, there is a dialectical relationship between them. Gramsci sought not the destruction of liberalism – he scorned as charlatans the supposed revolutionaries who made grand if empty gestures of their supposed "subversiveness"[2] – but the retrieval and transformation of its greatest achievements – that is, liberty of religious consciousness, juridical equality of all citizens without discrimination, and intellectual openness, all freedoms that were menaced, above all, by those who called themselves "liberals." He was particularly struck by the ease and rapidity with which liberals set aside such principles when they united in defence of a narrow property-based individualism. *Liberalismo* (liberalism as a full philosophy of human individuality and development) was in contradiction with *liberismo* (liberalism as a doctrine and practice of political economy). Liberalism in this second sense, the forerunner of today's neoliberalism, had become an obstacle to, not the instantiation of, liberty – if by "liberty" one meant the empowerment, flourishing, and freedom of the majority of the population. Herein lies the extraordinary contemporary resonance of Gramsci – he sought not the destruction of the liberal order nor the smashing of its cultural legacy, but its dialectical sublation in a new political and philosophical world in which its promise of liberty was finally realized, and in which educationalization along democratic lines could proceed.

Conventional liberals, from this Gramscian perspective, were confronted with a choice: either to persist in justifying (and, under fascism, violently defending) the capitalist economy with which they had traditionally been associated, or retrieving and developing what was authentically radical in their own tradition. If, to the conventional liberal, a largely uninformed public was but a minor problem, provided each individual within that public enjoyed the legal right to mobilize as he or she wishes, to the Gramscian democrat that widespread popular ignorance constitutes a dire dilemma. It could not be meaningfully rectified by "enlightenment from above" – that is, educationalization as Tröhler characterizes it – since this would merely work to confirm many oppressed people in their disabling sense of their own cultural inferiority. Gramsci was acutely aware of the social world in which schooling took place and, anticipating Pierre Bourdieu (whose theory of the "field/habitus" relationship is utilized interestingly by Jon Igelmo Zaldívar in his chapter in this volume), he analysed with great sensitivity the deeply implanted cultural suspicion with which the uneducated might well regard difficult subjects. He was also keenly alert to the attributes of formal education that induced timidity and alienation among students (Gramsci 1996, 230–1 [Q4§55]; Bourdieu 1977; Mayo 1999, 118). He was especially alert to the *physical* challenge those unused to intellectual labour confronted as they struggled to study for hours upon hours. For the majority of children, influenced "by social and cultural relations which are different from and antagonistic to those which are represented in the school curricula," there was simply no unity between school and life, instruction and education (Gramsci 1996, 35–6 [Q12§2]).

One could not change the existing culture by imposing a new system or understanding from above – and any such artificial imposition, no matter how "consistent," was doomed to failure. Moreover, such attempted impositions confirmed the "ruled" in their suspicion that they were unworthy to become "rulers": they entrenched the very "first cell" of political oppression a radical democrat was determined to change (Green and Ives 2010, 304). The revolutionary challenge to the "ruler/ruled" hierarchy required, rather, the more difficult path of engaging "both masses and intellectuals in a process of learning" (Morera 2002, 178). In this approach – one that could be applied in, but went well beyond, any strictly "educational" realm – "every teacher is always a pupil and every pupil a teacher" (Gramsci 1971, 350 [*SPN* Q10II§44]).

The Marxist tradition contains no firmer advocate of a thoroughly liberatory "educationalization" than Gramsci, no thinker or activist who so constantly turned his attention to the pedagogical mission of the workers' movement and, ultimately, of the state it would one day transform. In Gramsci's democratic theory, intellectuals played a key role. This was a "pedagogical politics," not only in the sense that a progressive workers' state would seek to educate its members in the values of the enlightenment, but also because each member of the movement would be intent on acquiring for himself or herself a more realistic and balanced understanding of the social order. They were called upon to become "educators of society" and were required to be resistant to crudely environmental arguments that made excuses for the passivity of individuals. As someone who began from the point of view not of the teacher but of a learner embarking upon a voyage of "self-knowledge, self-mastery and thus liberation" (Forgacs 1988, 54), Gramsci could even be considered a proponent of "liberal education" – meaning, as in the case of John Stuart Mill, the disciplined, focused acquisition of the skills of logical and empirical analysis.

Yet his was, in essence, a program of, to adopt Josh Cole's terminology in this collection, an "education that is not educationalization" – one that fundamentally transformed mechanical top-down models of "instructing the masses" into a much more dynamic democratic process. Education in the broad sense – one that extended far beyond strictly "scholastic" relationships – entailed a new generation engaging with the experiences of the old, absorbed "its experiences and its historically necessary values," and developed a personality of its own which is historically and culturally superior (Gramsci 1971, 350; [*SPN* Q10II§44]).

Gramsci's notion of education is one that is historically aware and reflexive. "Every relationship of 'hegemony' is necessarily an educational relationship and occurs not only within a nation, between the various forces of which the nation is composed, but in the international and world-wide field, between complexes of national and continental civilisations" (350; Q10II§48ii). Hegemony could not be reduced to a liberal notion of consensual politics, for what Gramsci wanted to explore was not the "apparent willingness of an individual to accept certain views and to engage in certain activities," but rather "the conditions for that willingness to be present" (Morera 2002, 178) Only an "inner discipline," and not one that was "external and mechanical," would suffice to create a coherent movement that was simultaneously united and individualistic. Collective thought in such a movement emerged as a result of concrete individual effort (Gramsci 2007, Q6§79).

When Gramsci pondered the contemporary "tendency against individualism" in the 1930s, he thought it correct to maintain a "necessarily contradictory attitude," because individualism itself had both positive and negative aspects, which could be evaluated only in concrete historical situations (Gramsci 1995, 269–70 [*FSPN* Q9§23]). In his twentieth-century conjuncture, the "historical development of organised capitalism" rendered anachronistic any "classical liberal scheme of an unmediated relationship between citizen and state, where the rational isolated individual makes choices between alternatives and elects representatives who determine policy in the interests of the whole" (Sassoon 2000, 23). Instead, the individual who sought to make a difference should join an organization reflective of his or her values and interests (ibid.). Thus, "liberal liberty" and "Gramscian liberty," although seemingly similar and committed to rationality, free expression, and so on, in fact constitute very different conceptions of the social world.

For Gramsci, one could contrast the "conformism" – or educationalization, for our purposes – that was imposed from above, "in an authoritarian manner," and the "conformism" that was "formed essentially from the bottom up," a pattern ultimately derived from one's position in the "world of production." The self-discipline acquired as a result of this ground-level "conformism" – the constitution of the individual by the surrounding community and society – was in fact the precondition of individual freedom, "including freedom of the individual" – or, an education that is not educationalization (Gramsci 1995, 277 [*FSPN* Q7§12]). To pretend that such moulding was superfluous or repressive was to ignore the social constitution of the very individual that liberalism claimed to revere – a position that combined determinism (because it held that in the tiny infant resided *in potentias* the future man or woman) and romanticism (because in leaving the young student without direction, it would essentially condemn him or her to the chaotic, disordered influences of the surrounding environment.) Educationalists who defend the "individual" without accounting for the social and economic structures within which that individual is placed are indulging in utopianism; and those many liberals who defended fascism as a necessary antidote to socialism in the 1920s and 1930s were, if nothing else, demonstrating how swiftly they were willing to jettison the political rights of the "individual" when it seemed that the property rights of the capitalist were in jeopardy.

Thus, Gramsci can be rightly seen as a critic of some of the interwar educational experiments, in both Italy and the Soviet Union, that were presented as the last word in "progressiveness." In Italy, he was the scourge of the "progressive" reforms introduced by Giovanni Gentile – ones that, among other things, subjected students to occupational streaming – which, to his eye, would simply keep oppressed subalterns in their cultural place. Central to Gentile's philosophy of education was the antithesis of "instruction" and "education," with the latter associated with the spontaneous development of a pupil's abilities and a more spiritual conception of life. Seemingly "liberal" measures – curricula designed for unambitious students, proliferating vocational schools offering a measure of mobility from unskilled to skilled labour, tolerance of non-official Italian in the formal school setting – all in fact furthered inequality through a vocational form of educationalization. The educational system was pleased largely to confirm the "common sense" of the subaltern students it received – bolstering, for example, their religious convictions and folkloric superstitions, not freighting them down with difficult philosophical abstractions (Gramsci 1996, 225–7 [Q4§55]).

Gramsci, who fought his way through an overwhelmed and underfunded school system to achieve a competence in linguistics, philosophy, and history, was having none of it. Such a system constituted "a process of continuing degeneration" for disadvantaged Italians. The vocational school, focused as it was on "immediate practical interests," was an affront to the fuller, more "traditional education" (what we might consider a "liberal arts education") represented by the "formative school," which, as he pointed out, "does not have an immediate interest." The vocational school both denied the innate intelligence of working-class children and young people while "perpetuating social differences." These differences were given concrete expression "by the fact that every social stratum has its own type of school designed to perpetuate a specific traditional function within that stratum." Further, schools generated these differences. As Gramsci argues, the "multiplication of types of vocational school ... perpetuate[s] traditional distinctions" while creating "new stratifications within these distinctions" out of whole cloth. The greatest affront of all was that this form of social control and reproduction through educationalization "appears and is proclaimed to be 'democratic,'" when it was (and is) anything but. Vocational schooling's pretensions to democracy and progressiveness are thus little more than an illusion (Gramsci 1996, 228–9 [Q4§55]).

In today's parlance, a "dumbed-down education" tailor-made for students destined for swift exit from the system, and sometimes presented in a Rousseauian language of respecting the child's individuality, actually resulted in preventing vast swaths of the population from effectively ruling themselves. Pinar's identification, in chapter 11 of this volume, of a "STEM state of mind," so beloved by contemporary neoliberal politicians and policymakers, is an important variant of this educational outlook. Blindness to the social logic underlying existing educational praxis guaranteed the perpetuation of the system's hierarchical effects. "To pretend that it is easy is to endorse that ease with which a minority succeed because they obtain from their social background those skills and values which most people must struggle to develop. It leads to collusion in the continuation of a rigid division of labour between a caste-like intellectual élite and those whose potential for understanding and knowledge remains unfulfilled, and a democratic relationship between specialist intellectuals and people – between rulers and ruled – continues to prove elusive" (Sassoon 2000, 32). It was important for children, even young children, to exit the school system with factual and conceptual baggage, with facts and dates and declensions. It was a cardinal error to insist upon a strict separation between "instruction" and "education," a doctrine of progressive education instantiated in the reforms of Gentile in the period of Mussolini (Gramsci 1971, 35–6 [*SPN* Q12§2]). As for the Soviet Union, where his two sons were being educated, Gramsci was critical of what he perceived as somewhat similar exercises in streaming children and inculcating in them firm notions of what their future careers should be. "What children needed above all, he thought," writes Frank Rosengarten, "was the chance to explore their potential abilities in a variety of modes and areas of expression. Children also needed early training in intellectual rigour, lest the subsequent advent of adolescent rebelliousness occur prior to the formation of character and self-discipline" (Rosengarten 1994, 20).

These views of Gramsci's could be, and were, taken to be advocacy of "conservative schooling" (Entwhistle 1979), but such an analysis was an oversimplification. For one thing, Gramsci was wholeheartedly in favour of the "active" school and intense collaboration between teacher and pupil. Anticipating Paulo Freire, he was fiercely critical of a "banking" approach to education that emphasized the fact-stuffing of passive students (Borg, Buttigieg, and Mayo 2002, 101), and he opposed attempts to indoctrinate them. He was intrigued and, to a point, impressed by free-school experiments (Gramsci 1995, 142). But he differed with much "progressive" practice in education that made a fetish of spontaneity. He disagreed with those who believed that children would discover truths by themselves: for here was a laissez-faire class-blind approach likely to result in subaltern students lacking "basic skills that would enable them to read, write, and struggle over complex problems, and, therefore, expand their capacities as critical intellectuals and citizens" (Giroux 2002, 58). More fundamentally, for Gramsci debates about education pertained to something much bigger than schooling. As Stanley Aronowitz puts it, "Gramsci's concept of education is ... only secondarily concerned with schooling" (2002, 115). The educational crises Gramsci analysed were not the cause "but rather a consequence and a reflection of a much broader moral, social, and cultural crisis" (Buttigieg 2002, 128). His assessment of schooling was, in short, an element in his general critical appraisal of capitalist modernity and liberal order as a complex totality. In this, he anticipated the important work of critical educational scholars such as Jean Anyon (2005), who insisted that educationalization without broader social reforms attacking poverty and inequality was bound to fail.

One can well understand why Gramsci was sidelined in so much postmodern educational theory in the late twentieth century. Not only did he stand for enlightenment values, including formal logic, classical culture, and disinterested inquiry which many late-twentieth-century platform revolutionaries took pleasure in denouncing, but he also expressly defended *elements* of traditional pedagogy (even, in certain contexts, learning classical languages, the bogeyman of many a progressive educationist). From his perspective, it was a sign of weakness on the part of radicals to devalue the work of those who had preceded them: "A generation that devalues the previous generation and is incapable of recognizing its great achievements and its essential significance is bound to be mean and lacking in self-confidence, even if it displays gladiatorial postures and a craving for greatness" (Gramsci 2007, 164 [Q8§17]).

Nietzsche's numerous twentieth-century "postmodern" progeny were quite right to find in Gramsci an unsympathetic figure whose critical realism and anti-utopianism stood in such vivid contrast to their supposed "subversiveness." Resignedly accepting that the most any radical can hope to achieve is the replacement of one repressive structure by another, and viscerally resistant to any notion of totality, they rightly saw in Gramsci a figure from a radical humanist tradition they sought to displace. Often, their hyper-functionalist portraits of a carceral archipelago in which schooling was always and everywhere simply about safeguarding an ideological state apparatus were paradoxically conjoined with the most extravagant "emancipatory" utopianism. As Gramsci himself discerned, those who volubly proclaimed their "rationalistic" hatred for the old order often were ineffective in linking their visions – often "utopias and crackpot schemes" – to a wider audience. They characteristically neglected the world of production – that is, labour – without which no new society could be established (Gramsci 2007, 165–6 [Q7§15]). They were, in that sense, myopically utopian.

From the 1960s and throughout the Americas, educationalization exploded in scale and scope with the arrival of the "baby boom," mass immigration, the development of "human capital" theory, and (as Daniel Tröhler argues) the perceived challenge of a Sputnik-launching Soviet Union. Schemes for the renovation of education abounded. Yet, as Gramsci had suggested years before, implicit in many of them was a tight integration of schooling with capitalist hegemony. As the American historian Michael Katz wrote in 1971:

> An official ideology that emphasis the importance of free enterprise and shuns [socialist] state interference has limited alternatives with which to [approach] poverty. Massive income redistribution or broad-scale intervention in the economy generally has not been acceptable. Education, on the other hand, has appeared to be an immediate and effective solution to social problems. There is a surface logic, which remains immensely appealing: Equipping children with appropriate skills and attitudes can cause the problems of unemployment and poverty to disappear. The illnesses of society become diagnosed as simply a lack of education, and the prescription for reform becomes more education. [This] unleashes a flurry of seemingly purposeful activity [that] requires no tampering with basic social structural or economic characteristics, only with the attitudes of poor people. (109)

In our own era, David Labaree alerts us to the deceptive quality of much of what seems to be "progressive" educational argumentation. Proponents of educationalization all too often adopt a language of "romantic" or "pedagogical progressivism" – entailing "a deep-seated aversion to formal schooling ... combined with a deep affection for a more spontaneous, natural, and self-directed form of education" – that often works to soften a more hard-edged program of business efficiency and narrowly defined vocational training. Progressive rhetoric served as ideological cover for the real work of reform: technocratic educationalization designed to sustain and reproduce an unequal social order (Labaree 2004, 146–7).

Indeed, it is in our own era that Gramsci's critique of the perils of capitalist educationalization resonates most powerfully. Education, once regarded (certainly by Gramsci) as a fundamental element of any modern state, is now "progressively" colonized by business. Neoliberalism's ascent has been mapped out by many scholars (see, for instance, Stedman Jones 2012). It had attained, according to many of them, a hegemonic position throughout the West by the 1980s. Preceded by a tightly controlled "Fordist" system of mass production, secure unions, high wages, welfare state institutions, expansive public bureaucracies, and states convinced of the merits of Keynesian economic planning, the neoliberal order entails the transformation of all these features: mass production is globalized and restructured, unions broken, wages repressed, the welfare state cut back, and bureaucracies pared down, and now inter-dependent states answer to agencies external to themselves. This totalizing transformation entails both a politico-economic and a philosophical rupture with the world of 1945–75. As David Harvey explains, neoliberalism "proposes that human well-being can best be advanced by liberating individual entrepreneurial freedoms and skills within an institutional framework characterized by strong private property rights, free markets, and free trade. The role of the state is to create and preserve an institutional framework appropriate to such practices ... Furthermore if markets do not exist (in areas such as land, water, education, health care, social security, or environmental pollution) then they must be created, by state action if necessary" (2007, 2). Yet, as Wendy Brown notes, neoliberalism is more than a "bundle of economic policies with inadvertent political and social consequences." There is a *political rationality* that "both organizes these policies and reaches beyond the market," one that entails "the powerful erosion of liberal democratic institutions and practices" (2005, 38). If indeed neoliberalism recuperates classical liberal assumptions about "the generation of wealth and its distribution," what truly makes it *"neo"* is its drive to reach "from the soul of the citizen-subject to education policy to practices of empire" (39). This is the hegemonic form of educationalization in our own time. Every action and every policy is submitted "to considerations of profitability," and, just as crucially, "all human and institutional action [is] conducted according to a calculus of utility, benefit, or satisfaction against a microeconomic grid of scarcity, supply and demand, and moral value-neutrality" (40).

In short, neoliberalism is not just an economic strategy. It is a new political totality. "The state openly responds to needs of the market, whether through monetary and fiscal policy, immigration policy, the treatment of criminals, or the structure of public education. In so doing, the state is no longer encumbered by the danger of incurring the legitimation deficits predicted by 1970s social theorists and political economists ... Rather, neoliberal rationality extended to the state itself indexes the state's success according to its ability to sustain and foster the market and ties state legitimacy to such success" (Brown 2005, 41). In short, *"the state must not simply concern itself with the market but think and behave like a market actor* across all of its functions, including law" (41; emphasis in original). And so it goes with *everyone* in a neoliberal order: "Neoliberalism normatively constructs and interpellates individuals as entrepreneurial actors in every sphere of life. It figures individuals as rational, calculating creatures whose moral autonomy is measured by their capacity for 'self-care' – the ability to provide for their own needs and service their own ambitions" (42). Every institution – education decidedly not excepted – is obliged to accept a market rationality. And every individual – students and teachers, again, not excepted – are to be judged according to whether they have performed as prudent subjects, as so many entrepreneurs and consumers. The state withdraws from some domains and privatizes some of its functions, but this by no means entails a dismantling of government; instead, it constitutes a "technique of ruling" in a political order in which "rational economic action suffused throughout society replaces express state rule or provision" (44).

This totalizing program is paradoxically one that entails the almost infinite fragmentation of society into a series of self-interested individuals (Rodgers 2010; Srnicek and Williams 2016), to the extent that one may wonder if a "public" even exists. And although the rhetoric of "liberal democracy" still persists, that works to disguise the extent to which we now live within a new order:

> We are not simply in the throes of a right-wing or conservative positioning within liberal democracy but rather at the threshold of a different political formation, one that conducts and legitimates itself on different grounds from liberal democracy even as it does not immediately divest itself of the name. It is a formation that is developing a domestic imperium correlative with a global one, achieved through a secretive and remarkably agentic state; through corporatized media, schools, and prisons; and through a

variety of technologies for intensified local administrative, regulatory, and police powers. (Brown 2005, 56–7)

Educationalization in a neoliberal order is central to this new hegemony. The growth of "charter" or "free" schools in the United States and the United Kingdom is a prime example. These schools are portrayed by neoliberal activists as the only reasonable alternative to public school systems, which are re-framed as "failed enterprise[s], filled by bad teachers, whose jobs are protected by powerful unions" (Ravitch 2010, n.p.). As the argument runs, such schools foster low-test scores and "dropouts" at alarming rates (i.e., according to the business logic at work, they have systematically diminishing "rates of return on investment"). If they were to be replaced by a "voucher system," or schooling "credits" that could be "spent" at privately run charter schools of the parent's choice, outside of the public system, all would be well. The curriculum could be made nakedly utilitarian, teachers could be fired for failing to deliver high scores on standardized tests, and seemingly intractable social problems like poverty and racism would simply wither away (ibid.).

Such an approach is the narrow vocationalism critiqued by Gramsci writ large. The neoliberals have not only had striking success with re-making schools but also with transforming universities, which have adopted, holus bolus, the apparatus of late capitalism. As the British critic Stephan Collini writes, this transformation is considered by its advocates to be a project of "modernization," in which universities are "acknowledged" to be "engines of economic growth ... closely aligned with the needs of industry, finance and commerce"; their funding being pegged to "the principles of a market economy"; their worth being judged in terms of "satisfaction" for students redefined as a "consumer[s]" of educational services; their administration overseen by "a senior management team at the apex of an executive structure [with] a proper business plan" (2017, 21). Further, any criticism of this transformation must be entirely shut down, "exposed, and disregarded, as the self-interested whingeing of a featherbedded elite who simply fail to understand, or want to deny, the nature and pace of social and economic change" (22). Just as it is reasonable to wonder whether anything like a "public" can survive the hyper-individualism entailed in a neoliberal order, so too we must ponder whether the commercialized, narrow, often content-free, and profoundly ahistorical character of so much contemporary schooling and higher education can allow us to continue to call it "education."

Educationalization historically meant a pervasive tendency to see schools as decisive forces in the world, responsible for creating citizens, maintaining democracy, creating social cohesion, and furthering capitalist productivity. Working from a radical humanist perspective, Gramsci hoped that schools might help young people acquire the disciplined and rigorous understanding of the world and thereby develop their capacity to understand and change it. For a generation of post-humanist and post-structuralist critics, he was deluding himself – schools were and always would be total institutions wherein discourses constructed subjects with, at most, a minimal capacity to determine the discourses by which they were to be interpellated. But for their twenty-first-century successors, this position may no longer be sufficient. It may suddenly seem to make a considerable difference, and not constitute merely a minor difference in styles of governmentality, if an institution is driven primarily by those aiming to make money and win cultural capital for their class. Gramsci's warnings about a narrow capitalist rationality masked as progressivism may, to them, seem uncannily prescient and productive, in ways unattainable by discourse theory alone. Nor, given the catastrophic social and educational results of destroying the public education system, can it seem as plain as it once was that educational systems can simply be written off as places of free inquiry, self-discovery, and, perhaps, the sites of future struggles, where the common sense of neoliberalism is analysed and contested.

There are, of course, important ways to escape the trap of contemporary educationalization. Now that we have confronted neoliberal educationalization as the "stony ground of the present conjuncture," to which we must "turn [our] face violently towards," we can consider alternatives to that stony ground (Stuart Hall, quoted in Eley 2002, 451). Such alternatives are proliferating in multiple educational sites, not least in the United States – one of the major founts of educationalization, past and present. Chicago, for example, has seen the rise of a radically anti-neoliberal re-imagining of the Chicago Teachers Union in the form of the Caucus of Rank-and-File Educators (CORE) built upon "organic teacher-community partnerships" as a means of opposing "school closures and turnarounds" made in the name of neoliberal educationalization (Uetricht 2014, 10). Similarly, Philadelphia's Caucus of Working Educators (WE) has built a grassroots movement against neoliberal education and other "closing of the commons," using the former as springboard for "collectively learning" about the latter, in order to overthrow it (Maton 2016). The massive teacher strikes in 2018 in Wisconsin also point in the direction of an "education that is not educationalization."

One can also find rich examples within the pages of this volume of resistance against modern (and neoliberal/postmodern) educationalization.

Rosa Bruno-Jofré demonstrates how Catholic education never really embraced the logic of educationalization, favouring instead a democratic vision that included education along the lines of liberation theology. Heidi MacDonald demonstrates how Canadian women religious immersed themselves in the culture and lifeways of those to whom they would proselytize, in the process giving these people the tools to create their own grassroots responses to the modern world. Sol Serrano and Macarena Ponce de León tell a similar tale regarding the peoples of the Mapuche Territory in Chile, as does Bonita Uzoruo in her analysis of the brutal colonial educationalization of Indigenous peoples in Canada giving way to teacher education programs attuned to Indigenous cultural and educational lifeways and the *Indian Control of Indian Education* initiatives. Pinar's critique of educationalization as technologization is countered by Ana Jofre's chronicle of how she and her colleagues are creating open-source tools to encourage radical andragogy in a revitalized digital public sphere. In our quest to understand educationalization and to create more democratic forms of education, we must never forget Gramsci's exhortation: to practise "pessimism of the intellect" while mining that stony ground for opportunities for new educational ideas and practices – ultimately based on the "optimism of the spirit" in schooling and society.

NOTES

1 Throughout this chapter, and following international convention, quotations from Gramsci are identified by their notebook (Quaderni or Q) and section (§), to allow for ease of consultation among the various available editions. SPN refers to *Selections from the Prison Notebooks*; FSPN to *Further Selections from the Prison Notebooks*.
2 "Many self-proclaimed destroyers are nothing other than 'procurers of unsuccessful abortions,' liable to the penal code of history" Gramsci (2007 25 [Q6§30]).

REFERENCES

Anyon, J. 2005. "What 'Counts' as Educational Policy? Notes Toward a New Paradigm." *Harvard Educational Review* 75 (1) (Spring): 65–88. https://doi.org/10.17763/haer.75.1.g1q5k721220ku176.

Aronowitz, S. 2002. "Gramsci's Theory of Education: Schooling and Beyond." In Borg, Buttigieg, and Mayo, 109–20.

Berman, M. 2002. *Adventures in Marxism*. London and New York: Verso.

Borg, C., J. Buttigieg, and P. Mayo, eds. 2002. *Gramsci and Education*. Lanham, MD: Rowman and Littlefield.

Bourdieu, P. 1997. *Outline of a Theory of Practice*. Cambridge: Cambridge University Press.

Brown, W. 2005. "Neoliberalism and the End of Liberal Democracy." *Edgework: Critical Essays on Knowledge and Politics*, 37–59. Princeton, NJ: Princeton University Press.

Buttigieg, J. 2002. "Education, the Role of Intellectuals, and Democracy: A Gramscian Reflection," In Borg, Buttigieg, and Mayo, 121–32.

Collini, S. 2017. *Speaking of Universities*. London: Verso.

Coutinho, C.N. 2012. *Gramsci's Political Thought*. Leiden, NL: Brill.

Depaepe, M. 2012. *Between Educationalization and Appropriation: Selected Writings on the History of Modern Educational Systems*. Leuven, BE: Leuven University Press.

Depaepe, M., and Paul S. 2008. "Educationalization as an Ongoing Modernization Process." *Educational Theory* 58 (4): 379–89. https://doi.org/10.1111/j.1741-5446.2008.00295.x.

Dewey, J. 1990. *The School and Society and the Child and the Curriculum*. Toronto: University of Toronto Press.

Eley, G. 2002. *Forging Democracy: The History of the Left in Europe, 1850–2000*. Oxford: Oxford University Press.

Entwhistle, H. 2002. "Antonio Gramsci and the School as Hegemonic." In *Antonio Gramsci: Critical Assessments of Leading Political Philosophers*, vol. 3, edited by J. Martin, 251–66. London and New York: Routledge, 2006.

– 1979. *Antonio Gramsci: Conservative Schooling for Radical Politics*. London: Routledge and Kegan Paul.

Forgacs, D., ed. 1988. *An Antonio Gramsci Reader*. New York: Shocken.

Giroux, H.A. 2002. "Rethinking Cultural Politics and Radical Pedagogy in the Work of Antonio Gramsci." In Borg, Buttigieg, and Mayo, 41–65.

Gramsci, A. 1971. *Selections from the Prison Notebooks of Antonio Gramsci*, translated and edited by Q. Hoare, Q and G.N. Smith. New York: International Publishers.

– 1995. *Further Selections from the Prison Notebooks*, translated and edited by D. Boothman. Minneapolis: University of Minnesota Press.

– 1996. *Prison Notebooks* Vol. 2, edited and translated by. J. Buttigieg. New York: Columbia University Press.

– 2007. *Prison Notebooks* Vol. 3, edited and translated by J. Buttigieg. New York: Columbia University Press.

Green, M., and Ives, P. 2010. "Subalternity and Language: Overcoming the Fragmentation of Common Sense." In *Gramsci, Language, and Translation*, edited by P. Ives and R. Lacorte, 289–312. Lanham, MD: Lexington Books.

Harvey, D. 2007. *A Brief History of Neoliberalism.* New York: Oxford University Press.
Hobsbawm, E. 2004. *Age of Extremes: The Short Twentieth Century, 1914–1991.* London: Abacus.
Katz, M.B. 1975. *Class, Bureaucracy, and Schools: The Illusion of Educational Change in America.* Expanded ed. New York: Praeger.
Labaree, D.F. 2004. *The Trouble with Ed Schools.* New Haven, CT: Yale University Press.
Maton, R. 2016. "We Learn Together: Philadelphia Educators Putting Social Justice Unionism Principles into Practice." *Workplace* 26: 5–19.
Mayo, P. 1999. *Gramsci, Freire, and Adult Education: Possibilities for Transformative Action.* London: Zed Books.
Morera, E. 2002. "Gramsci and Democracy." In *Antonio Gramsci: Critical Assessments of Leading Political Philosophers.* Vol. 4, edited by J. Martin, 177–90. London: Routledge.
Ravitch, D. 2010. "The Myth of Charter Schools." *New York Review of Books.* 11 November. http://www.nybooks.com/articles/2010/11/11/myth-charter-schools/.
Rodgers, D. 2011. *Age of Fracture.* Cambridge, MA: Harvard University Press.
Rosengarten, F. 1994. Introduction to *Letters from Prison,* by Antonio Gramsci. New York: Columbia University Press.
Sanbonmatsu, J. 2004. *The Postmodern Prince: Critical Theory, Left Strategy, and the Making of a New Political Subject.* New York: Monthly Review Press.
Sassoon, A. 2000. *Gramsci and Contemporary Politics,* 2nd ed. London: Routledge.
Srnicek, N., and A. Williams. 2016. *Inventing the Future: Postcapitalism and a World without Work.* London: Verso.
Stedman Jones, D. 2012. *Masters of the Universe: Hayek, Friedman, and the Birth of Neoliberal Politics.* New Haven, CT: Princeton University Press.
Uetricht, M. 2014. *Strike for America: Chicago Teachers against Austerity.* London: Verso.

Contributors

Felicitas Acosta is a full-time staff researcher and professor at Universidad Nacional de General Sarmiento, Argentina. She also holds a teaching position at Universidad Nacional de La Plata. She is vice president of the Argentine Society of Comparative Studies and former co-editor of *Latin American Comparative Education Journal*. For the past ten years she has specialized in research on the expansion of schooling from an international and historical perspective as well as issues regarding teacher education, policy transfer, and international assessment. She has been an international consultant for OEI/EUROsociAL, IIEP UNESCO, and UNICEF.

Chris Beeman, PhD, attends to the more-than-human world through travels in relatively wilder areas; attempts to enact a progressively more Autochthonous life; learns from places, Elders, knowledge keepers, and peers; and mentors students in the area of Indigenous ontologies as they relate to educative practice. He works with print, film, and paint to express ideas. His academic position is as an associate professor at Brandon University's Faculty of Education, where he teaches in both the undergraduate and graduate programs. He has received in various forms Social Sciences and Humanities Research Council funding for the past several years.

Rosa Bruno-Jofré is a professor and former dean of the Faculty of Education, cross-appointed to the Department of History, Faculty of Arts and Science, Queen's University, Canada. She is the founding coordinator of the Theory and History of Education International Research Group (http://educ.queensu.ca/their), and serves as senior founding co-editor of *Encounters in Theory and History of on Education* (http://library.queensu.ca/ojs/index.php/encounters). She has done extensive research on the history of education, the history of religious congregations, and educational theory from a historical perspective. She was awarded the George Edward Clerk Award by the Canadian Catholic Historical Association. Her authored and edited books have been published by University of Toronto Press and McGill-Queen's University Press, and she has published articles in *Educational Theory, Paedagogica Historica, Hispania Sacra*, the *Journal of Ecclesiastical History, Historia de la educación, Historical Studies in Education, Historical Studies* (CCHA), and the *Journal of the History of Ideas*, among others, as well as chapters in international collections.

Josh Cole holds a PhD from the Department of History at Queen's University, Canada. His research interests include the history of education, the history of liberalism, the history of modernity, and historical and contemporary cultural politics. He has contributed to scholarly collections published by the University of Toronto Press (Canada) and Klinhardt (Germany), as well as journals including *Paedagogica Historica: International Journal of the History of Education, Historical Studies in Education, Historia de la Educación, Teachers College Record, Encounters in Theory and History of Education*, and *Sembrando Ideas*. He is a core member of the Theory and History of Education International Research Group.

Ana Jofre obtained her PhD in physics from the University of Toronto, did postdoctoral work at NIST (National Institute of Standards and Technology) in Gaithersburg, Maryland, and taught and researched at the University of North Carolina in Charlotte for six years before transitioning her career toward the arts. She completed her MFA at OCAD University in Toronto, then worked first as a research fellow in the Visual Analytics Lab at OCAD University, and then later at the Institute for Pure and Applied Mathematics Culture Analytics program at UCLA in Los Angeles, California. Her publications and conference presentations cover a wide range of intellectual interests, from physics to critical theory, and she has exhibited her artwork internationally. Her creative and research interests include figurative sculpture, interactive new media, the aesthetics of camp and of the uncanny, public pedagogy, human-computer interaction, and data visualization. She is currently an assistant professor in Creative Arts and Technology at SUNY Polytechnic, in Utica, NY.

Heidi MacDonald is the Dean of Arts and professor of history and politics, University of New Brunswick Saint John. She is a historian of twentieth-century Canada with specializations in Atlantic Canada, the Great Depression, women religious (nuns), suffrage, and youth. Her SSHRC-funded project, Women Religious in Atlantic Canada since 1960, considers the intersection of women religious with feminism and the state in Atlantic Canada. Her publications include the co-authored monograph (with Rosa Bruno-Jofré and Elizabeth M. Smyth) *Vatican II and Beyond: The Changing Mission and Identity of Canadian Women Religious* (McGill-Queen's, 2017) and the forthcoming *We Shall Persist: Suffrage and Human Rights in Atlantic Canada* (UBC Press).

Carlos Martínez Valle is a professor at the Faculty of Education, Universidad Complutense, Madrid, and holds a PhD in political science and sociology. His doctoral thesis focused on the relations between religious and political conceptions of freedom in sixteenth- and seventeenth-century Europe and was published as *Anatomía de la Libertad* (2008). He worked as a research fellow and assistant professor at the Center for Comparative Education, Humboldt University, Berlin, and as a postdoctoral fellow at the Faculty of Education of Queen's University, Canada. His work combines intellectual history, comparative education, and the history of education. His research on the relations between religion, education, and politics has been published as "Jesuit Psychagogies" (*Paedagogica Historica*, 2013), "Conciencia libre y ley natural en el Calvinismo y Molinismo" (*Res Publica*, 2008), and "Early Modern Probabilism as a Secularizing Doctrine" (*Religion and Its Other*, 2008).

Ian McKay is the L.R. Wilson Chair in Canadian History at McMaster University, Canada. His books include *Warrior Nation: Rebranding Canada in an Age of Anxiety* (2012) and *The Vimy Trap: Or, How We Learned to Stop Worrying and Love the Great War* (2016), both co-authored with Jamie Swift; *The Quest of the Folk: Antimodernism and Cultural Selection in Twentieth-Century Nova Scotia* (2009; 1994); *In the Province of History: Tourism and the Romance of the Past in Twentieth-Century Nova Scotia* (2010), co-authored with Robin Bates; *For a Working-Class Culture in Canada: A Selection of Colin McKay's Writings in Political Economy and Sociology, 1897–1939* (1996); *Rebels, Reds, Radicals: Rethinking Canada's Left History* (2005); and *Reasoning Otherwise: Leftists and the People's Enlightenment in Canada, 1890–1920* (2008), which won the John A. Macdonald Prize from the Canadian Historical Association. His present project is a co-authored study of political theorist C.B. Macpherson, a renowned authority on liberal ideology and practice.

William F. Pinar took his BS in education at Ohio State University. He taught English at the Paul D. Schreiber High School in Port Washington, New York, in 1969–71, returning to Ohio State first to finish his MA and then to complete a PhD. He taught at the University of Rochester and Louisiana State University before accepting a Canada Research Chair at the University of British Columbia in Vancouver in 2005. He has authored or edited numerous books on teaching and curriculum in various countries.

Macarena Ponce de León Atria is the director of the Museo Histórico Nacional de Chile, and formerly an assistant professor at the Institute of History at the Pontifical Catholic University of Chile. She obtained a DEA (Diplôme d'études appliquées) at Paris I, Sorbonne-Pantheon in 1999, and her PhD at the Catholic University of Chile in 2007, where she was a postdoctoral fellow. Her main fields of research are the social and political history of Chile in the nineteenth and twentieth centuries, the relationship between society and the state through private charity and public welfare, and education. Her current research focuses on practices of political representation and the expansion of political citizenship in the twentieth century. She is author of *Gobernar la pobreza: Prácticas de caridad y beneficencia en la ciudad de Santiago, 1830–1890* (2011), and joint editor, with Sol Serrano, of the two-volume *Historia de la educación en Chile, 1810–2010* (2012).

Patricia Quiroga Uceda is a postdoctoral fellow at Universidad Nacional de Educación a Distancia (UNED) in Spain with a Juan de la Cierva scholarship from the Spanish Ministry of Economy and Competitiveness. She defended her thesis, entitled "The Reception of Waldorf Education in Spain," at Universidad Complutense de Madrid in 2015. She is a member of the Theory and History of Education International Research Group (THEIRG, Queen's University) and external member of Cultura Cívica y Políticas Educativas (Universidad Complutense de Madrid). Her research regarding Waldorf education has appeared in *Teoría de la Educación, Bordón, Encounters in Theory and History of Education*, and *Temps d'educació*. She has recently published the book *Rudolf Steiner: Conferencias sobre pedagogía Waldorf* (Biblioteca Nueva, 2018).

Sol Serrano is a professor in the Faculty of History, Pontificia Universidad Católica de Chile. She specializes in political and cultural history of nineteenth- and twentieth-century Latin America. She is the recipient of the History National Prize 2018. Her most recent book is *El Liceo, Relato, Memoria y Política*, published by Editorial Taurus in 2018.

Elizabeth M. Smyth is a professor of Curriculum Teaching and Learning (CTL) at the University of Toronto, where she has served in a variety of senior academic administrative positions. She holds degrees from McMaster University (Honours Bachelor of Arts and Master of Arts in History) and the University of Toronto (Bachelor of Education and Doctorate of Education). She is engaged in research on women religious as educators and the development of the professions. She is the recipient of the George Edward Clerk Award for outstanding contribution to Canadian religious history; the Lifetime Achievement Award from the History of Women Religious Network; and the Vivek Goel Award for citizenship and leadership from the University of Toronto. She is the editor and co-author of a number of books.

Joseph Stafford is a retired history teacher from the Algonquin and Lakeshore Catholic District School Board in Ontario. He has twenty-nine years of classroom experience and was a department head for seventeen years. In 2008, he received the Governor General's Award for Excellence in Teaching Canadian History. He recently completed his PhD in the history of education at Queen's University.

Daniel Tröhler is a professor of education at the University of Vienna, visiting professor of comparative education at the University of Granada, Spain, and visiting professor at the University of Oslo, Norway. His research interests are inter- and transnational developments and trajectories of education and curriculum between the late eighteenth century and today. In his studies he combines the history of ideas and institutional history in a broader cultural approach focusing on educational and political ideas and their materialization in school laws, curricula, and textbooks, as well as comparing different national/regional developments and their possible transnational influences. Several of his over 300 publications have been translated into different languages, including the AERA-award winning *Languages of Education: Protestant Legacies, National Identities, and Global Aspirations* (2011), which has been translated into Spanish, and *Pestalozzi and the Educationalization of the World* (2013), which has been translated into Spanish, French, and Japanese.

Bonita Uzoruo has excelled as an Indigenous educator within Ontario's public schools for over ten years. She is currently a graduate student in the World Indigenous Studies in Education MEd program at Queen's University, under the supervision of Dr Rosa Bruno-Jofré. Her research areas include decoloniality and the development of Aboriginal teacher education programs in Canada.

Jon Igelmo Zaldívar is an assistant professor at the Complutense University of Madrid (UCM, Spain), Department of Educational Studies. He defended his PhD thesis in 2011 at the UCM. He is a member of the research group Cultura Cívica y Políticas Educativas (UCM) and assistant to the coordinators of the Theory and History of Education International Research Group based at Queen's University. His recently authored and co-authored papers have appeared in journals such as *Educational Theory*, *Journal of Ecclesiastical History*, and *International Studies in Catholic Education*. He has also co-edited a book by University of Toronto Press (2017) along with Rosa Bruno-Jofré entitled *Catholic Education in the Wake of Vatican II*.

Index

Acosta, Felicitas, 16–17, 215–33
adult education, 12–13, 14, 42n2, 68, 85, 92, 94–7, 100–6, 130, 141–3, 145, 147–8, 254, 267, 349. *See also* Antigonish movement
agency, individual. *See* free will
Agrupación al Servico de la República, 178
Alcalá Synod, 56–7
Alcalá-Zamora, Niceto (pres., Spain), 180, 183
Alliance for Progress, 5, 140
Alphonse XII (king, Spain), 179
Alvarado, Gen. Juan Velasco, 138
Alward, Rev. David, 138
Amberga, Gerónimo de, 318–19
andragogy. *See* adult education
anthroposophy, 16, 195, 199, 203–10. *See also* Waldorf education/schools
   Anthroposophic Society of Spain, 207
   Biodynamic Agriculture Association for the Canary Islands, 207
   Rafael Workshop of Sociotherapy, 207
   Rudolf Steiner Publishers, 207

Antigonish movement, 12–13, 92–106, 106n2, 106n6, 106n8, 129–30, 132–3, 137, 146, 148, 254–5, 267. *See also* adult education
Antigonish, NS, 13, 92–106, 107n6. *See also* Antigonish movement; Nova Scotia
Anyon, Jean, 343
Aquinas, St Thomas, 59, 69, 79, 87n8, 139, 155, 158–61, 165. *See also* Thomism/neo-Thomism
Araucana mission (Chile), 20, 79, 313, 315–16, 318–19, 320–2, 324, 326–8, 330. *See also* Capuchin Order; missionary work
   Federación Araucana, 330
   Gran Federación Araucana, 20, 328–9
   Magister Society of Araucanía, 330
   Sociedad Caupolicán Defensora de la Araucanía, 20, 327–9
   Union Araucana, 330
Aristotelian theology, 69, 77, 103, 249n21
Aristotle, 58, 59, 69, 102, 249n21, 335
Arminian-Socinian, 61
Arminius/Arminians, 6n43, 61
Arndt, Ernst, 62

Aronowitz, Stanley, 343
Association of Adult Education (Canada)
   Citizen's Forum, 104
   Farm Radio Forum, 104
Augusta, Félix de, 316–19, 321
Augustine, St, 69, 71, 76, 154, 183
   Augustinian anthropology, 55
   Confessions, 76
Autochthony. *See* Indigeneity
Azaña, Manuel (pres., Spain), 187–8
Azeglio, Massimo d', 40

Bahrdt, Carl Friedrich, 33
Balaguer, Joaquin (pres., Dominican Republic), 143–4
Ball, Mother Frances, 116–18
Bani mission (Dominican Republic), 130, 143–7, 148. *See also* missionary work
Barad, K., 306, 307
Barbeyrac, Jean, 34, 44n7
Barbier, Euphrasie, 82
Barré, Nicholás, 71–5
   Institute of Charitable Teachers, 71–4
Basil the Great, 60
Basso, Keith: *Wisdom Sits in Places*, 300
Battiste, Marie, 289
Baum, Gregory, 130
Beeman, Chris, 18–19, 293–309
Benedict XVI (pope), 149
Benedictine Order, 79, 80, 185
Benioff, Marc, 240
Benjamin, Walter, 240
Bennett, John M., 166–7
Bergen, Abe, 286
Berger, Peter L., 16, 196–200, 204–6, 209–10. *See also* paradigm of pluralism
   The Many Altars of Modernity, 196
   structure of plausibility, 200, 204–5, 210

Berman, Marshall, 336
Bernstein, Basil, 5, 8
Beseke, Johann Melchior Gottlieb, 33
Bevin, Matt, 245
Beza, Theodore, 61
Bible History (school textbook), 165–6
Bieler, Heidi, 208
Biesta, Gert, 8
big data, 240
Bildung, 10, 29–30, 36–9, 40, 51, 57
Bosh, Juan (pres., Dominican Republic), 143
Bourbon monarchy, restoration of, 177, 187–8
Bourdieu, Pierre, 15, 178–9, 189, 338
   capital, 15, 178
   field, 15, 178
   habitus, 15, 178–9, 187, 189, 191, 338
Braudel, Fernand, 68–9, 84
Bridges, David, 5–6, 8, 129, 148, 208, 210, 302
British North America Act (1867), 118
British Workers' Education Associations, 95
Brown, Callum C., 196
Brown, Wendy, 345
Bruno-Jofré, Rosa, 3–21, 67–87, 132, 277, 335, 349
Bugenhagen, Johannes, 56
Bull, George, 163–4
Burlamaqui, Jean-Jacques, 34, 44n7
Bush, George W. (pres., US), 243
by faith alone, principle of, 32, 52–3, 70

Calasanz, José de, 74
   Pius Schools, 74
Calvin, John, 10, 43nn4–6, 50, 52–7, 60–3
   Institution de la religion chrétienne, 54–5
   penitential doctrine, 55

Calvinism, 10, 29, 30, 43nn6–7, 52–9, 61–3, 250n32
Calvinist Cévennes, 57
capitalism, 8, 13, 16, 76, 92–4, 96–101, 104, 106, 106n3, 106nn6–8, 132, 219, 242–3, 248n7, 248n15, 248nn17–18, 249n20, 254, 266, 312, 336–8, 340–1, 343–5, 347–8
Capuchin Order, 19–20, 183, 280, 312–31. *See also* Araucana mission (Chile)
Cardinal, Harold, 282
Carmelite Order, 80
Carnegie Corporation, 95–6
Carson, Rachel: *Silent Spring*, 28
Carter, Alex (bishop), 124
Carter, Gerald Emmett (cardinal), 124, 162
Carter, Sister Mary Lenore, 124
Cassidy, Dr J.J., 125
Catechetical Day, 164
Catholic Action, 15, 84, 87n8, 155–6, 161–2, 166–9, 171n7, 172nn19–20, 190
  Catholic Action Summer School, 167
  School of Catholic Action, 167
Catholic mind, 15, 67, 78–80, 155, 162, 166, 169, 172n20
Catholic National Action Party (Spain), 187–8
Catholic University of America, 97, 166
Caucus of Rank-and-File Educators (CORE), 348
Caucus of Working Educators (WE), 348
Centro de Educación para el Desarrollo Comunitario (CEDEC), 142, 148
Charbonnel, Armand de (bishop), 117–18

charism of congregations, 67, 79, 114, 129, 133
Chrétien, Jean (PM, Canada), 262
Christian Family Movement, 168
Chrysostom, John, 60
Cicero, 45n18, 58, 59, 60
  De Inventione, 59
Clarke, D.A.G., 306, 307
Clement XIV (pope), 76
Clérico, L., 218–19
Coady International Institute, 14, 136–8, 140–3, 147–8
Coady, M.M. (Moses), 92, 94, 96–106, 130, 137
  Masters of Their Own Destiny, 97
Code.org, 241
  Hour of Code, 241
coding, 241
Cole, Josh, 6, 12–13, 17–18, 20, 92–106, 129, 146, 254, 335–49
Collège de St Thérèse, 120
Collini, Stephan, 347
colonialism/colonization, 6, 10, 18–19, 72, 76, 79–80, 82, 85, 131, 246, 250n33, 277–90, 293–309, 312–31, 349
Comenius, John Amos, 62, 220–1, 233n6
  Didactica Magna, 221
Common Schools Act (1941), 115
Condorcet, Marquis de, 34
Conference of Latin American Bishops (1968), 131–2
confessionalism/confessionalization, 11, 13–15, 50–63, 67, 73, 75, 81–2, 154, 202, 204, 207, 312
conformity, 35, 58, 158, 197, 201, 203, 240, 242, 340
Congar, Yves, 80
Congregation for the Propagation of the Faith (Chile), 315
Congregation of the Providence Sisters, 325

conjonctures, 5, 84
Convention on the Rights of the Child, UN, 215–16
Conway, Jill Ker, 114
cooperative economics, 13, 99–101
Corpus Christi School, 79, 82–3
Cortázar, Fernando García de, 179
cosmology, 8, 79, 306
Costa, Joaquín, 189, 191
Coulthard, Dennis, 303
Council of Trent, 70, 72, 87n3, 130
counterpublic sphere. *See* Fraser, Nancy
Courtney Murray, John, 167
Cousin, Victor, 40
Coutinho, Carlos Nelson, 337
Cuban, Larry, 241
Cubequery, 264
Curtis, Bruce, 81, 170n3

Daly, Gabriel, 160
Danish folk schools, 95
Darwinism, 318
data visualization, 256–9, 265, 267
DataBlocks software, 263–6, 267
Daughters of Charity, 72
Dease, Anna (Mother Eucharia), 117
Dease, Bridget, 117
Dease, Ellen (Mother Teresa), 117–23, 126
Decade for Human Rights Education, UN, 216
Deinas, Jack, 286
Democratic Party (Chile), 329
democratization of data, 257, 265–6
Depaepe, Marc, 3, 4, 19, 75, 113, 190, 277, 294, 302, 304, 305, 309, 335
Department of Lay Organizations (US), 167
Der Synergistische Streit (Stefan), 61
Descartes, René, 75
    Cartesian dualism, 306

Development Program, UN (UNDP), 216
DeVos, Betsy, 243, 248nn18–19
Dewey, John, 45n16, 83, 84, 245, 335, 336
    The School and Society, 336
digital tools, 6, 21, 254–67
digitalization, 21, 246
Diocesan Catechetical Office, 164
Doane, Mary Ann, 240
Dogmatic Constitution on the Church, 84
Dominican Order, 61, 69–70, 80
    Dominican Sisters, 83
Dury, John, 62

"education that is not educationalization," 6, 13, 92, 94, 101–3, 105, 106n1, 106n2, 339–40, 348. *See also* Antigonish movement
El Araucano (newspaper), 329
Elders, 19, 297, 299, 304, 307, 310n4
Emberley, Peter C., 242
Enlightenment, Age of, 16, 29–30, 42, 50, 76, 157, 219–20, 224, 232n4. *See also* social contract
Erasmus, Desiderius, 43n4, 52, 61, 69
Errington, Jane, 115
Escartín, Eduardo Sanz y: *El Estado y la reforma social*, 189
Escola Tesófica Damón de Vallcarca, 196
Escolano, Agustín, 189
esotericism, 16, 195, 197, 203–7, 209–10
Eternal Commencement, The (school textbook), 165
Eudes, Jean, 72

Fathers of the Holy Cross, 80
Fenelon, 62

Ferdinand VII (king, Spain), 201
Fernández Soría, Juan, 188
Fichte, J.G., 37
First Nations, Metis, and Inuit (FNMI) peoples, 6–7, 18–19, 21, 22n3, 82, 135, 277–90, 293–309, 309n3. *See also* Indigenous peoples
First Vatican Council, 67, 77, 156
Fitzpatrick-Behrens, Susan, 140
Ford, Father George Barry, 83–4
Foucault, Michel, 337
Franciscan Order, 79, 314, 315, 321–2
    Franciscan Congregation of Nuns of Boroa, 321–2
Franco, Franciso (dictator, Spain), 16, 184, 191, 196, 199–200, 202–5, 207, 209–10, 210n2
    dictatorship, 191, 196, 199, 202–4, 207, 209
Fraser, Nancy, 13, 104
Fraternidad Internacional de la Educación, 196
Free Teaching Institute. *See* Institucion Libre de Enseñanza
free will, 10, 12, 44n9, 50, 52–9, 60–3, 68, 70–1, 86–7, 220, 277
Freire, Paulo, 8–9, 12–13, 85, 134, 255
    conscientization, 132, 134
    Pedagogy of the Oppressed, 132
French Revolution, 12, 30, 31, 44n7, 45n21, 68, 154, 218–19, 220, 232n1
Frente Civico Victoriano, 142
Froebel, Friedrich, 82
Fuchs, Estelle, 279–80

Gadamer, Hans George, 307
Gallicanism, 44n7, 71–2, 76
Gapminder, 257–8
    Gapminder World, 257
Gentile, Giovanni, 341–2
Gertrude, Mother Maria, 135–6, 138

Gibney, Frances (Mother Dosithea), 120–1
Gilson, Etienne, 163, 168, 170n2, 171n6, 171n8
Gleason, Philip, 163
Goethe, Johann Wolfgang von, 316
Gramsci, Antonio, 337–49
Grant, George, 17, 239–47, 247nn3–4, 248n7, 248nn10–11, 248nn14–15, 249n25, 249nn20–3, 250n30, 250n32, 250nn34–5
Grey Nuns, 140, 279
Grotius, Hugo, 61
Guevara, Tomás, 327
Gutiérrez, Gustavo, 131–2
Guyart, Marie (Ursuline Sister), 114

Habermas, Jürgen, 18, 29, 102, 255
    Erkenntnisinteresse, 29
Hall-Dennis Commission: *Living and Learning*, 125
Hampton, Eber, 302, 303
Hartlieb, Samuel, 62
Harvey, David, 345
Haslem, Sylvia, 286
Hastings, Reed, 240
Hawthorn Report, 281
Hayes, James (archbishop), 135–6, 138
hegemony, 99, 170n3, 225, 340, 344, 347
Heidegger, Martin, 79–80
Herder, Johann Gottfried, 316
High Commissioner for Refugees, UN, 216
Hobsbawm, Eric, 336
Hogg, Richey, 131
Huidobro, Father, 186
humanism, 11, 35, 36, 43n4, 56, 60–2, 69–70, 85, 87n8, 163, 246, 315, 337, 344, 348
Humboldt, Wilhelm von, 37

364   Index

Hume, David: *The History of England*, 76
Huss, Jan, 62
Husserl, Edmund, 79–80
Hutchinson, Mother Ignatia, 118

Ignatius of Loyola, St, 69–70, 116, 182
Imago Dei, concept of, 33
Indian Act (1876), 279, 281–2
Indian Association of Alberta: Red Paper, 282
Indigeneity, 19, 293–309, 309nn2–3
Indigenous education agenda, 6, 10, 18–21, 277–90, 293–309, 312–31. *See also* residential schools (Indigenous)
Indigenous peoples, 6, 7, 19–21, 82, 135–6, 225, 246, 280, 289, 312. *See also* First Nations, Metis, and Inuit (FNMI) peoples; Mapuche people (Chile)
Industrial Revolution, 76, 99, 220
Inglehard, Ronal: *Sacred and Secular*, 196
Ingold, Tim, 306
Institucion Libre de Enseñanza, 15, 178, 183
Institute of the Blessed Virgin Mary. *See* Loretto Sisters
Institute of the Christian Brothers, 71, 74, 233n6
Inter-American Episcopal Conference (1959), 131
International Covenant of Economic, Social, and Cultural Rights (ICESCR), 215, 223
internationalization, 84, 216–18, 222, 231
Inuit. *See* First Nations, Metis, and Inuit (FNMI) peoples
Irish Daughters of Mary Ward. *See* Loretto Sisters

Jansen, Cornelius, 71
Jansenism/anti-Jansenism, 61, 62, 71–2, 76
Jaspers, Carl, 79–80
Jesuits, 10, 11, 15, 50, 52, 57–62, 69–72, 75–80, 116, 126n2, 163, 177–92, 202, 314
  Estudios Eclesiásticos, 179
  Hechos y Dichos, 179
  Ibérica, 179
  Mensajero del Corazón de Jesús, 179
  Modern Schoolman, 163
  Ratio Studiorum, 70, 116, 126n2, 182
  Rázon y Fe, 179–80
  Sal Terrae, 179
Jofre, Ana, 6, 17–18, 132, 254–67, 349

Kant, Immanuel, 45n16, 75, 220, 232n4
Katz, Michael, 344
Kilpatrick, William, 83
King, Joyce E., 9
King, William Lyon Mackenzie (PM, Canada), 96
Kirkland, David E., 243
Kirkness, Verna, 286
Klaren, Peter, 139
Kmeic, Patricia, 115
Knowledge Keepers, 294, 298, 310n4
Komenski, Jon Amos, 62

La Salle, Jean Baptiste de, 71, 72, 74–5, 233n6
  The Conduct of Christian Schools, 74
Labaree, David, 4, 15, 18–19, 148, 177, 188–9, 222, 254, 293–7, 301–6, 308–9, 344
LaCapra, Dominick, 246
language(s) of education, 8, 51–2, 54, 77, 222

language(s) of schooling, 74, 222–4, 280, 283, 313, 317, 324
Latin America, 7, 16–17, 68, 85, 87n8, 130–49, 150n13, 150n15, 216, 221, 224–31, 255, 314. *See also* missionary work
　education rates, 226–30, 228f, 229f
　expansion of education, 226–30
　Movement of Basic Education, 255
Laughten, Jack, 286
Lenz, Rodolfo, 317–18
Lenz, T.S., 223
Leo XIII (pope), 45n21, 77–8, 139, 154–60, 165
　Aeterni Patris, 77–8, 155–6, 158–60, 162–3
　Rerum Novarum, 45n21, 78, 155, 159–60, 161, 189, 191
Lerena, Carlos, 200
Lernoux, Penny, 149
Lessing, Gotthold, 316
Levellers and Diggers, 62
liberal education, 78, 95, 339
liberalism, 76, 83, 106n3, 179, 337–8, 340
liberation theology, 14, 68, 85, 129–32, 137, 142–3, 146, 148–9, 349
Lipovetsky, Gilles, 205–6
Litch, Richard, 125
Locke, John, 61, 220, 232n4
Lonergan, Bernard, 155–6, 162
Loreto Sisters (Ireland), 117
Loretto Sisters (Canada), 14, 113–26
　Act to Incorporate the Sisters of Our Lady of Loretto, 120
　Mother Clement, 125
　Rules of the Institute of the Blessed Virgin Mary, 116
Louis XIV (king, France), 30, 247n1
Ludlow, Peter, 94

Luther, Martin, 10, 29, 34–6, 43nn4–5, 45n16, 50, 52–60, 61–3, 70, 220, 233n5
　The Bondage of the Will, 52
　two kingdoms doctrine, 35, 45n16
Lutheranism, 10, 29–30, 32–6, 38–40, 44n11, 53–9, 61–3
Lynch, J.J. (archbishop), 119–20

Mably, Gabriel Bonnet de: *Entretiens de Phocion*, 38
MacDonald, Heidi, 14, 129–49, 349
Macdonald, Sister Alice Marie, 124–5
MacKinnon, Father Art, 136
magisterium (Holy See), 12, 13, 14–15, 68–9, 76–7, 86, 155–6, 158, 160–1, 164, 169
Malagón, Antonio, 203–4
Manitoba Indian Brotherhood (MIB), 282, 283
　Wahbung: Our Tomorrows, 282
Mann, Horace, 40
Manovich, Lev, 259
Manquilef, Manuel, 328
Mapuche people (Chile), 20–1, 280, 312–31, 349. *See also* Indigenous peoples
　Mapudungun language, 20, 316–18, 328
　Sociedad Mapuche de Protección Mutua de Loncoche, 20, 328
Maria, Mother Stella, 135
Marianists, 80
Marists, 80
Maritain, Jacques, 87n8, 171n6, 190
Martínez, Enara García, 180
Martínez Valle, Carlos, 10–11, 50–63
Marwick, Arthur, 12, 68
Marxism, 100, 104–5, 336–7, 339
Mathias, Alex, 299, 307–8, 309n1
Maximum College of Granada, 177, 182–4, 188

Maximum College of Oña, 177, 182, 185–7, 188
Maximum College of San Ignacio, 177, 182, 184–5, 188, 191n1
McCool, Gerald A., 78–9, 163
McCrory, Gov. Patrick, 245
McGowan, Sister Catherine, 145–8, 151n23
McKay, Ian, 81, 106n2, 335–49
McLeod, Hugh: *Secularization in Western Europe, 1814–1914*, 196
Mcphie, Jamie, 306, 307
Mead, Margaret, 27
Medel, Arturo Huenchullén, 331
Medellín Conference. *See* Conference of Latin American Bishops (1968)
Melanchton, Philip, 56, 61
Die Notwehr Unterricht, 61
Methodism, 43n6, 279–80
Metis. *See* First Nations, Metis, and Inuit (FNMI) peoples
Mill, John Stuart, 339
millenarianism, 10, 50, 52, 60–3
Miller, J.R., 298, 300–1
Shingwauk's Vision, 298
Milton, John, 10–11, 50, 52, 57–60, 61
charity, 10–11, 59
Minim, Order of, 72, 87n4
Missionary Oblate Sisters of the Sacred Heart, 81–2
missionary work, 13, 18–20, 79–82, 85, 87, 116–18, 120, 130–48, 150n15, 279–80, 312–31. *See also* Araucana mission (Chile); Bani mission (Dominican Republic)
 enlightened paradigm, 315
 in Latin America, 135–49, 312–31
 missiology, 315–16, 322–3
 Peru, 130, 135–43
 training for, 130–9, 142–3, 145

modernity, 4, 8–15, 15–16, 21, 50–63, 67–72, 75–81, 86–7, 92–4, 99–101, 103, 106n6, 113, 119–24, 126, 157, 160–1, 196–9, 205–6, 239–40, 242, 244, 248n13, 254, 277, 312, 336–7, 343
Molina, Luis de, 10–11, 50, 52, 57, 59, 61, 70
Concordance of Free Will with the Gifts of Grace, 70
Concordia, 61
Molinism, 57–60, 61, 63
Moravian Church, 62
Morrison, James, 94–5, 97
Mounier, Emmanuel, 80
Mount, Graeme, 144
Movement of Grassroots Education (Brazil), 5
Moyano Law, 201–2
Mueller, D., 223
Murphy, Dr Alleyne, 146
Murray, Daniel (bishop), 116
mysticism, 57, 60, 61–2, 249n21
Müntzer, Thomas, 62

National Catholic Agrarian Confederation (Spain), 187
National Catholic Welfare Conference (US), 167
national Catholicism (Spain), 203, 207
National Commission on Excellence in Education (US), 28
National Defense Education Act (US), 27, 247n5
National Indian Brotherhood (NIB), 278, 282–3, 288–9
Indian Control of Indian Education, 278, 281–2, 288–90, 349
Native teacher education programs (NTEPs) (Canada), 18, 278, 282–90

Blue Quills School (AB), 285
Brandon University Northern Teacher Education Program (BUNTEP) (MB), 18, 278, 285–8, 290
　Indian and Métis Project for Action in Careers through Teacher Education (IMPACTE) (MB), 285–7
　Indian Cultural College (SK), 285
　Indian Teacher Education Program (ITEP) (SK), 285
　Maskwachees Cultural College (AB), 284
　Morningstar Project (AB), 284–5
　Native Indian Teacher Education Program (NITEP) (BC), 284
　Northern Teacher Education Program (NORTEP) (SK), 285
　Outreach Teacher Education Program (OREP) (AB), 284
　Program for the Education of Native Teachers (PENT) (MB), 285
Neculmán, Manuel Antonio, 328
neoliberalism, 8–9, 19, 68, 85–6, 226, 295, 303, 336–7, 348
neo-scholasticism, 14–15, 67, 69, 77–81, 84, 170n2
neo-Thomism. *See* Thomism/neo-Thomism
Newman, Cardinal, 78–9
Nietzsche, Friedrich, 343–4
Norris, Pippa: *Sacred and Secular*, 196
nouvelle théologie, 15, 80, 84
Nova Scotia, 13, 92–106, 107nn6–7, 107–8n9, 129, 136, 138, 142–3, 145, 149n3. *See also* Antigonish movement; Coady Institute

O'Donovan, Joan, 247, 250n32, 250n35
O'Malley, John, 12, 70

Oblate Fathers, 82, 279
Oblates of Mary Immaculate, 80
Oldenbarnevelt, Johan van, 61
Olier, Jean Jacques, 72
Ontario English Catholic Teachers' Association (OECTA), 124
Ontario Teachers' Federation, 124
ontological incommensurability, 19, 305–8
Ossenbach, G., 224

Palma, Arturo Alessandri (pres., Chile), 328
Palmés, Father Ferrán M., 184
Panguilef, Manuel Aburto, 328
paradigm of pluralism, 16, 196–200, 205, 209–10. *See also* Berger, Peter L.
paradigm of secularization, 16, 196–200, 204, 209–10. *See also* Taylor, Charles
Pastoral Constitution on the Church in the Modern World, 84
Paul VI (pope)
　Ad Gentes: Decree on the Mission Activity of the Church, 131, 133, 135, 138, 143, 147, 150n7
　Ecclesiae Sanctae II, 134
　Missions Schema, 131
　Perfectae Caritatis, 84, 133–4, 143, 147
　Populorum Progressio, 132–3, 135, 139, 141, 143
Pax Romana, 168
Peace Corps (US), 140
pedagogization, 3, 71, 82
Pelagianism, 58, 60–1
Pellicena, Mr, 185
Pérez-Agote, A., 200–1, 203
Pestalozzi, J.H., 38, 62, 82
Phelan, Gerald B., 162
phenomenology, 79

philanthropic gifts, 241
Phillip II (king, Spain), 182
Phillips, Paul, 82
Pietism, 62
Pinar, William, 5, 17, 239–47, 266, 336, 342, 349
Pius V (pope), 72
  Circa Pastoralis, 87n3
  Lubricum Vitae Genitus, 87n3
Pius VI (pope), 157
Pius VII (pope), 76
Pius IX (pope), 76–7, 154, 157, 165
  Dei Filius, 77, 154–5, 157–8
  Paster Aeternus, 154–5, 158
  Quanta Cura, 76
  Syllabus Errorum, 76–7
Pius X (pope), 77, 155, 160, 161–2, 171n7, 180
  Il Fermo Proposito, 161
  Non Abbiano Bisogno, 162
  Pascendi Dominici Gregis, 77, 160
Pius XI (pope), 79, 83, 155, 161, 167–8, 172n19
  Divini Illius Magistri, 79, 161, 170n1
  Divini Redemptoris, 172n19
  Ubi Arcano Dei Consilio, 161
Pius XII (pope), 12, 68, 131, 154, 162, 171nn6–7, 172n20
  Central Office of Catholic Action, 162
  Humani generis, 171n6
  Mystici Corporis Christi, 172n20
Plato, 102, 249n21, 335
Platonism, 61, 69, 243, 249n21, 249n23, 250n35
pluralism, 16, 149, 155, 161, 196–206, 210, 326, 328
Plutarch, 45n18, 59
Ponce de León, Macarena, 18, 19, 79, 280, 312–31, 349

Pontifical Commission for Latin America (1958), 131
Popkewitz, T.S., 219, 222
Popular Socialist Party (Spain), 187, 190
Portelli, John, 8–9
Power, Michael (bishop), 115–17
Presbyterian Kirk, 57
Presbyterianism, 43n6, 57, 58, 61, 279
Primo de Rivera, Miguel (PM, Spain), 180, 187–8, 190
privatization, 240–1, 346
probabilism, 10, 58–9, 72
progressive education, 335–6, 343–4
progressivism, 245, 335, 344, 348
Protestant Reformation, 11, 21, 32, 44n9, 52, 60, 62–3, 69–71, 73, 86, 182
Provincial Educational Association (NS), 97
Prynne, William, 61
psychagogies, 11, 50, 52, 55–6, 60, 62
  orthodox Protestant, 11
  public sphere, 18, 94, 255, 267, 349
Pufendorf, Samuel von, 32–3, 44n7
Puigróss, A., 224–5
Pultz, Father Louis, 168
Puritanism, 57, 61–3, 245, 250n32

Quest for Happiness series, 165–6, 172n15
Quiroga Uceda, Patricia, 16, 195–210

radio, 104, 134, 255, 267
Ramberga, Guido Beck de (bishop), 329–30
Randall, Stephen, 144
Ratzinger, Joseph (cardinal). *See* Benedict XVI (pope)
Redondo, E., 200–1
Reformist Party (Spain), 178

regenerationalism (Spain), 178, 188–91
Regiopolis College, 120, 126n1
Religieuses de Notre Dame des Missions (RNDM), 81, 82, 139–40
Religion: Doctrine and Practise (Cassilly), 165
religious indoctrination. *See* confessionalism/confessionalization
Remes, Jacob, 96
republicanism: classical, 11, 35–41, 43nn5–6, 45nn17–18, 51–2, 56–7, 60–2, 93; modern, 10, 15, 30, 40, 50–2, 59, 177, 185, 188, 190–1, 222, 254
Resewitz, Freidrich Gabriel: *Die Erziehung des Bürgers*, 39
residential schools (Indigenous), 6, 18–19, 82, 278–81, 297–8, 301–2, 305, 308. *See also* Indigenous education agenda
Revuelta González, Manuel, 180–2, 185
Ribadeneira, Pedro de, 182
Ribolits, Erich, 304
right to education, 16–17, 93, 207, 215–31
right to schooling, 17, 216–31
Ringer, F., 223
Ríos, Fernando de los, 183
Robertson, Don, 286
Robles, Gil, 187
Rosengarten, Frank, 342
Rossini, Gioachino: *William Tell* (opera), 36
Rousseau, Jean-Jacques, 34, 38, 45n15, 76, 220, 232n4, 247n3, 342
Considerations on the Government of Poland, 38, 232n4
Letter to d'Alembert, 38
Royal Commission on Fisheries, 96

Royal Commission on Maritime Claims, 96
Rubio, Marco, 245

Sacred Congregation of the Council, 164, 172n15
Salamanca School, 70–1
Sanbonmatsu, John, 337
Scarboro Missionary Fathers, 136–7, 140, 143–6, 148
Schiller, Freidrich, 36, 316
William Tell (drama), 36
Schiralli, Martin, 4
Schmidlin, Josef, 316
Schneider, Bertrand, 263
scholasticism, 11, 62, 70
Schriewer, Jürgen, 51, 217
Scott, Duncan Campbell, 298
Scott, Rick, 245
Second Spanish Republic, 15, 177–91, 202, 209
Slacker's Law, 187
Second Vatican Council, 45n21, 115, 129–32, 133–4, 161, 170n1, 204, 210n2
Dignitatis humanae, 150n5, 210n2
secularization, 16, 77, 80, 191, 196–204, 209–10, 239, 246, 247n3, 326
of education, 200–4, 209–10
segmentation, educational, 217, 218, 223–4, 226, 230, 233n7
Serrano, Sol, 18, 19, 79, 280, 312–31, 349
Seton, Elizabeth, 14, 129
Sharma, K., 263
Sheahan, John, 135
Sheehan, Antoinette, 124
Shneiderman, Ben, 259
Simon, B., 223
Sinclair, Murray, 303, 309n3
Singer, Natasha, 240–1

370 Index

Sistema Nacional de Apoyo a la Movilización (SINAMOS), 139
Sisters of Charity, 14, 129–30, 133–40, 143–8, 149n1
    Halifax, 14, 129, 140, 143–6, 149n4
    New York, 14, 129–30, 149n4
Sisters of Mercy, 139–40
Sisters of Our Lady of the Missions, 81–2, 139–40
Sisters of Santa Cruz de Messingen, 325
Sisters of St Joseph, 14, 115, 121–5, 139–40
    Constitution of the Sisters of St Joseph of Toronto, 115
Sisters of St Martha, 148
Sisters of the Holy Infant Jesus, 72, 74
Sisters of the Sacred Heart and Mary Immaculate, 81, 121–2
Skinner, James (archbishop), 135–6
Skinner, Q., 56
Smeyers, Paul, 3, 19, 75, 190, 277, 294, 302, 304, 309, 335
Smith, Adam: *The Wealth of Nations*, 76
Smith, Susan, 72
Smyth, Elizabeth M., 13–14, 113–26
social Catholicism, 77–8
social contract, 16, 219–20. See also Enlightenment, Age of
social justice, 14, 83–4, 100–1, 130, 133–4, 143, 147
Society of Jesus. See Jesuits
Socrates/Socratic method of learning, 103, 255, 266
sola fides, principle of, 53
sola gratia, principle of, 52–7
sola scriptura, principle of, 32, 34, 36, 52–3, 55
Solsola, Gov., 186

soul, 10, 27–42, 43n5, 44n9, 44n11, 44n14, 45n15, 50–5, 60, 62, 68, 70, 73–4, 82, 93, 113, 159, 167, 246, 250n35, 316, 345
Sozzini, Fausto, 61
Spanish Civil War, 191, 202–3
Spanish Confederation of Autonomous, 190
Spellman, Cardinal, 84
St Michael's College (University of Toronto), 14, 125
    Congregation of St Basil, 125
St Vincent de Paul, 14, 72, 129
Stackables, 264
Stafford, Elizabeth Ann (Mother Emerita), 121
Stafford, Elizabeth Margaret (Mother Irenea), 121
Stafford, Father Michael, 119–22, 126n5
Stafford, Joseph, 14–15, 154–70
Stafford, Mary Anne (Mother Alacoque), 121
Stanford school, 50–1
Statement of the Government of Canada on Indian Policy (White Paper), 281–2
Steiner, Rudolf, 16, 195, 204–5, 207. See also Waldorf education/schools
STEM (science, technology, engineering, and mathematics), 5, 239, 244
Sturm, J., 56
Suárez, Francisco, 10, 11, 50, 52, 57, 59, 63, 71
    Tractatus de Legibus ac Deo Legislatore, 71
Swedish Discussion Circles, 95
Synod of Dort, 61
systematization, educational, 217, 218, 222–4, 230

Tableau (data visualization tool), 265
Tamrat el Zeitoun (Israel), 195
tangible user interfaces (TUI), 262–7
Taylor, Charles, 16, 196–200, 204, 209–10. *See also* paradigm of secularization
A Secular Age, 196, 197–8
Theosophical Society, 195–6
THEIRG (Theory and History of Education International Research Group), 3, 92, 106n1
Thomism/neo-Thomism, 15, 69–70, 77, 79, 84, 87n8, 155–70, 170nn2–3, 171n6, 171nn9–10. *See also* Aquinas, St Thomas
Tompkins, Jimmy, 94–7, 102, 132, 137
Tompkins-Stange, Megan, 241
transition to democracy (Spain), 196–7, 207–8, 210
Trevor-Roper, Hugh, 62
Tribunal Especial de Division, 330
Tröhler, Daniel, 3, 4, 10–13, 16–17, 27–42, 51–2, 54, 59, 67–8, 92–4, 100–1, 105–6, 113, 129, 222, 223, 232n1, 239, 242, 247n1, 247n5, 248n6, 254, 277, 294, 305, 338, 344
Trujillo, Raphael (pres., Dominican Republic), 143
Trump, Donald J. (pres., US), 243, 295
Truth and Reconciliation Commission/Report (Canada), 6, 19, 280, 293, 297, 301–4, 309n3
Tuck, Eve, 288
Turgot, A.R.J., 34
tyrannicide, 11, 36, 45n18, 54, 59

ultramontane Catholicism, 67, 77, 86, 106n6
Union Social Católica de Chile, 329
United Nations Educational, Scientific and Cultural Organization (UNESCO), 216, 223, 226
United Nations Entity for Gender Equality and Empowerment of Women (UN-Women), 216
United Nations International Children's Emergency Fund (UNICEF), 216
United Nations Population Fund (UNFPA), 216
Upegui, Father Antonio, 184
Ursuline Sisters, 114–15, 121–2, 125–6
Brescia College, 125
Uzoruo, Bonita, 18, 277–90, 349

Valls Puig, Emilio, 185
Vatican I, 77–80
Vatican II, 14–15, 67, 80, 82–6, 124, 130–3, 134–6, 140, 143, 147–8, 150n8, 156–7, 159–61, 169–70, 170n1, 170n3, 170n9, 171n4, 204
Declaration on Christian Education, 84, 170n1
Law on Religious Freedom in Spain, 204
Pastoral Constitution on the Church in the Modern World, 84
Vergara, J., 200–1
Vienna Declaration and Programme of Action, 216
Villela, Sister Gabriela, 135–8, 140–2, 145, 148
Villepin, Dominique de (PM, France), 28
Viñao, Antonio, 200, 202–3, 209
Vincent de Paul, St, 14, 72, 129
Vives del Solar, Fernando, 78
vocational education. *See* vocational training

vocational training, 37, 74, 140, 207, 244, 325, 341–2, 345, 347
Vögelin, Hans Conrad, 38–9
Voltaire: *The Century of Louis XIV*, 76

Waldorf education/schools, 16, 195–210. *See also* anthroposophy; Steiner, Rudolf
El Jardín de Infancia Micael, 195, 207
Warbeck, Gustav, 316–17
Ward, Mary, 116
Watson, Peter, 69, 75–6
Welton, Michael, 94
white supremacy, 249n26
White, Dr J.F., 122
Williams, Raymond, 97, 170n3
Williamson, Ben, 239, 246, 247n2, 248n17, 250n29
Willmann, Otto, 41
Didaktik als Bildungslehehre, 41
winca (white) Chileans, 314, 321
Winckelmann, Johann Joachim: *Reflections on the Painting and Sculpture of the Greeks*, 37
Wisconsin, University of: adult extension activities, 95

Wolff, Christian, 33
Jus naturae methodo scientifica per tractatum, 33
World Anarchist Federation of Workers, 329
World Bank, 216, 223, 247n1
World Congress of the Lay Apostolate (1951), 167–8
World Declaration on Education for All, 215–16

Yang, Wayne K., 288
Young Christian Students, 142, 168
Young Christian Workers, 168

Zaldívar, Jon Igelmo, 15–16, 177–92, 338
Zinzendorf, Nicolaus, 62
Zuber, Johannes, 304
Zuckerberg, Mark, 240
Zwingli, H., 11, 33, 34–6, 38, 43nn4–6, 45n17, 54, 59
  civic humanism, 35–6
  republicanism, 35–8, 43n5
Zwinglianism, 10, 29, 34–6, 40, 43n6, 54